The Call to Care

Dimensions, Dilemmas, and Directions of Caring

Edited and with contributions by
- Arthur Olsen
- Jerome Freeman
- Mary Auterman
- Ron Robinson

EX MACHINA PUBLISHING COMPANY
Sioux Falls ● 1999

The Call to Care:
Dimensions, Dilemmas, and Directions of Caring

Copyright © 1999 by The Center for Ethics and Caring at Sioux Valley Hospital, Sioux Falls, S.D.

ISBN 0-944287-22-0

Library of Congress Catalog Card Number: 98-74834

Preface

The pages of the *Call to Care* arise out of our experiences in planning and team-teaching an interdisciplinary Capstone course for seniors at Augustana College entitled "An Invitation to Care: Issues of Life, Health, and Death."

The main purpose of a Capstone course in the Augustana Plan for general education is to encourage students to integrate their college experiences in relationship to fundamental questions and issues.

To bring Capstone courses about, Augustana College invited faculty from different disciplines to integrate their resources and approaches in developing and teaching such a course.

We responded from our different professions and backgrounds in literature, medicine, philosophy, theology, and nursing to develop a course in which the participants

> . . .will explore the meaning of life, health, and death in the light of human experience, recent developments in health and illness care, and the moral and public policy developments that have attended these developments. Selections from works of literature, philosophy, theology, and public policy will be used. The capacity of caring for the human life of self and others will be addressed. The fundamental question to be considered is, "How then shall we care for life in the face of death?"

This book of narrative and readings was developed for the students in the Capstone course that we have taught over ten years. We make them available now through the Center for Ethics and Caring at Sioux Valley Hospital as a companion for fellow students and individuals who find themselves called to care. It is our belief that the issues that face us in health and illness care are fundamentally human ones. The "Will to Be Healthy," as the theologian Karl Barth instructs us, is the will to carry out our life stories. Hence, caring for ourselves and others, as we go about living out our life stories in health and in the face of illness and death, reaches each of us as a call to care.

Part I collects materials that expand our understanding of the *dimensions* of caring; Part II focuses on the *dilemmas* of caring as we look at concrete cases that emerge at the beginning and at the end of life. Finally, Part III collects readings related to *directions* of caring. Consideration of the dimensions and dilemmas of caring engage us in the fundamental question — how then shall we live as we seek to make caring choices? Study questions are included to engage the reader in reflection on the issues of caring. The chapter introductions carry the narrative that has emerged for us as we have lived with these texts.

In the appendix we have included a sample syllabus that shows both how we have used the readings and the format we have developed for engaging students in group projects on topics related to the frontiers of caring. Diverse journals and other media regularly feature articles dealing with bioethics and health care. One of the goals of the course has been to encourage students to work collectively on an issue of community concern and to share their findings with the class in what we term "Project Rounds Presentations."

We have been enriched in our conversations with each other and with students and our guests from various health care fields whose interviews are included in this volume as we have pondered the materials that follow. We share them with you in the hope that you may find them stimulating and enriching as you respond to the call to care. As you do so we believe that you will become engaged as we have been in the practice of biomedical ethics.

Mary Auterman
Jerome Freeman
Arthur Olsen
Ron Robinson

Contents

Part I
Dimensions of Caring 19

CHAPTER ONE:
HEALTH AS THE WILL TO CARRY OUT
OUR LIFE STORY

CHAPTER TWO:
HEALTH, WHOLENESS, AND INTERVENTION

CHAPTER THREE:
HEALTH, LIFE, AND MORTALITY

CHAPTER FOUR:
CARING, MEANING, AND COURAGE

Part II
Dilemmas of Caring 153

Part III
Directions in Caring 303

Acknowledgement

This book is published under the auspices of the Center for Ethics and Caring at Sioux Valley Hospital.

The Center for Ethics and Caring is a cooperative effort of Sioux Valley Hospital, Augustana College, and the University of South Dakota School of Medicine. The Center provides a variety of resources for those interested in biomedical ethics and caring issues, including professionals in health care, educational institutions, and the community.

Financial support for the Center for Ethics and Caring at Sioux Valley Hospital and this publication is provided by the Abel and Norma DeGroot Endowment for Ethics and Caring at the Sioux Valley Hospital Foundation. Endowment funds help make possible unique health care related activities, and provide ongoing support for Center projects and programs.

The editors are deeply indebted to many who have contributed to this endeavor to put the Call to Care into the words of this volume: to the Capstone students who responded from the perspective of their majors and life experiences; to Sue Halbritter, Ann Wilson, Jon Soderholm, and Becky Nelson who shared insights from their activities on the frontiers of caring and whose interviews are included in this volume; to Mary Brendtro, Harriet Scott, and Knight Hoover for their participation in designing the course and selecting the materials; and to Margaret Robinson, Ellie Schellinger, Mary Freeman, and Ruth Olsen for proof reading.

The Call

The call to care comes concretely in the claim of another person upon us. We begin therefore with a case — the story of Susan who confides in you as a friend. She is anxious about what she has just learned about the status of her health.

Our narrative invites you, the reader, to respond with us to the call of Susan for our concern. We challenge you in this introduction to share with us the resources of the disciplines which we bring to this conversation: namely, literature, medicine, nursing, philosophy, and theology.

Susan's Case

The first thing you noticed about Susan was her smile. She had this grin that made you think she knew something funny about the world that other people didn't know.

You noticed her first in a freshman class in which she always seemed to know the right answers, even when you didn't. Sometimes, with that grin, she seemed to know the answers to questions that hadn't been asked, that hadn't been thought of yet. It irritated you a little at first until you realized that there was nothing the least arrogant about Susan's intelligence. When you had to miss class, you knew who to ask for notes. She was happy to fill you in over Cokes in the Huddle. She was generous with her knowledge and shared insights into things that sometimes amazed you. Like the time she said, "Really, when you think about it, everything is natural. A city is just as natural as a beehive or an anthill, isn't it? All this business about the conflict of man versus nature — well, if that's the case, it's just another civil war, the right hand wrestling with the left hand. Nature isn't something outside of us. It's what we are. The environment isn't like a backdrop in a play we're involved in. The environment is us." And so on. You didn't always agree with her, but you had to give her credit for making you think.

It wasn't long before you were her friend and felt privileged to be. You had the feeling when you were with Susan that other people were envious. And something strange happened when someone said, "Oh yes, you're Susan's friend." You were who you were, but somehow you didn't mind being known as "Susan's friend." You didn't mind at all. That made you part of a very select group.

You have a snapshot of you and Susan together. She's smiling. You're smiling. You can't see the photograph without smiling, even now. It's your favorite picture of her, taken in her dorm room. She's holding a teddy bear with one hand and hugging you with the other. Her blue eyes are bright, her cheeks are ruddy, and her brown hair looks windblown. It had been spring, you remember, and you had been out flying a kite. You are both mugging for the camera. On the back of the photo you have written in pencil the date and "Susan and me. Fun times."

A couple times she took you home to visit her family. She came from Brandon, just outside Sioux Falls. Her family had a big frame house looking over the Big Sioux River. Her father was a school teacher and her mother sold real estate. She had one older sister, Laurie, who was a nurse, and one younger brother, Jeff, who was a pest. After a while you caught on that Jeff was a nuisance because he was jealous of Susan. He wasn't yet ten, and he was used to getting all of her attention when she was around. He didn't want to share her. Seeing them together, you began to think what a great mother she would be sometime. She knew how to talk to him without babying him or seeming to patronize him. They were buddies. They had secrets together. You began to feel a little jealous yourself.

The family had dogs. Lots of dogs. They were all hunting dogs, golden retrievers. As you understood it, it had all started when Susan's father wanted to take up pheasant hunting. Before he bought a shotgun, he bought a dog. He never got around to buying a shotgun. Then they got another dog, a female, and then there were pups, and then they started to sell the pups for extra income. That was the excuse. The fact was that they all just loved dogs. They got so attached to them that they couldn't bear to sell them. Lots of time was spent at Susan's house brushing the dogs and petting them and shaking hands with them. They would bring you tennis balls for you to throw. There were tennis balls all over, even though as far as you could see none of the family played tennis. The balls were for the dogs.

Susan had a hard time deciding what her major was going to be. She took a lot of science at first, thinking she wanted to be a vet. But she loved literature, too. And she thought she'd like to work with people. She ended up as a history major. Her father taught history. She insisted that she wasn't going to be a teacher, however. Still, with a history major, she wasn't sure what else she could be. Easy, you always said: a politician. With that smile on a poster, she could run for president.

In the fall of her senior year, Susan got sick. No ordinary cold or flu, but something obviously more serious. Mono, somebody guessed. She was in the hospital by then. You went to visit her. She still looked good, as cheerful and smiley as ever. But thin and pale. You brought her flowers and a funny get-well card. You told her what was happening in school, filling her in as she once did for you. Then you asked her, "What is it? What have you got, anyway?"

And she smiled a funny smile and told you to sit down and stay a while. She had something to tell you.

—

Susan's doctor has laid it on the line: She has cancer, with a twenty percent chance of survival for one year. It seems quite certain that Susan is going to die.

—

That is the hard part for Susan; now the hard part for you. In each of the following instances, try to work out a solution that is both intelligent and humane. Justify your decisions. Give special thought to the way your college experience — what you have learned in courses in the general curriculum or in your specialized discipline — has prepared you (or has failed to prepare you) for these questions.

  1. Susan confides in you that she is afraid of dying. Naturally you want to bring her comfort. What can you do or say to ease her fears? Should you do anything, or leave it to the professionals, her doctor, her minister, her school counselor? One thing you are sure of, with Susan's intelligence the old platitudes won't work as they might with someone less astute or less complicated. You will have to pick your way carefully, if at all.

  2. You've never had trouble talking with Susan before, mostly because she more than kept up her end of conversation. Now, however, she lapses into strange silences during your visits to the hospital. Small talk doesn't seem to stretch as far as it once did, and reminiscences about the fun times seem somehow maudlin and, after all, rather limited. For

the first time you are starting to feel uncomfortable in Susan's presence. She seems to want you to visit her, but her silences are putting you off. You guess that she is sometimes as uncomfortable as you are. So, what do you do?

3. Susan has a problem with Jeff, who really doesn't understand what is going on. Right now he's angry, feeling that Susan has somehow betrayed him, is abandoning him. Their parents haven't been able to get through to him, but Susan thinks that you might be able to talk to him and explain. Do you accept this assignment? If you do accept, what do you plan to say?

4. There is some irony in the fact that Susan's birthday is just around the corner. You and some other friends had been planning a surprise party for her, but you aren't sure now that is either possible or appropriate. You get together with friends and try to decide what to do. What is your decision?

5. Whatever you decide about the party, you know that you are going to have to give her something for her birthday. You had in mind a ski outfit you'd seen in the mall, but that seems out, now. She will be 22 years old, and this is likely to be her last birthday. Knowing Susan as you do, what do you give her?

6. Doctors have given Susan a choice: she can have a series of operations and treatments that might prolong her life for six months or more. They are not offering a cure, and they say flatly that the procedures will not save her life. What has been suggested, however, is that, because of the rapid advances in technology lately, the extra time might bring hope for new treatments that might prove more beneficial. Susan is having a difficult time deciding. She asks you about it. Don't worry, she

says, she won't hold you responsible, but she's just wondering what you would do in her case? What do you advise?

7. Another choice: Whether to pursue her college studies during her illness. She is currently enrolled in a schedule of classes that would allow her to graduate with you in the spring, if she is still alive by that time. Her illness would make study difficult, of course, and she may have to miss many lectures. Her friends might tape the lectures, of course, and other special arrangements might be made, but she is not sure if she should go on. What would you advise?

8. During one hospital visit when you are lucky enough to catch Susan alone, she tells you something surprising and a little shocking. She has been having thoughts about suicide. It seems out of character at first, given Susan's vivacity, until you realize that during the later stages of her illness she is likely to be completely bedridden, heavily medicated, surrounded by apparatus designed by clever people to sustain her life as long as possible. It is not just life that is at question here, but, as they say, the "quality of life." Now, while she still has volition and means, Susan is thinking over her options. What do you say to her on this subject?

9. Susan shows you a will she has made out. She hasn't really all that much in the way of personal possessions, but it has obviously given her pleasure to apportion her belongings to family and to friends. In most cases her decisions are touching and appropriate, in some they are even funny, but there is a slight problem in your case. She has chosen to will you one of her golden retrievers. The problem is, you can't have pets where you live now, and after graduation you know that it will be difficult to find a reasonably-priced apartment that will accept a dog. With a house full of cats, you know

your parents would be reluctant to keep the animal for you. Still you don't want to seem ungrateful. What do you do?

10. Susan is not particularly religious, but she does go to a church, albeit not one of your faith. You think occasionally that some of the beliefs that you hold dear might offer some comfort to her. On the other hand, you wouldn't want to offend her or put her off with disagreements over dogma. At one time you wouldn't have thought twice about this question, but Susan has been going through changes, lately, and you are just not sure how she will respond. How do you proceed?

Ron Robinson

Philosophy, Theology, and the Call to Care

What is the basis of the call to care? Why care about Susan and her health or illness? Is it a matter of empathy and/or duty? Are there any guidelines for caring for one's own health or for caring about someone who is ill? What does it mean to be healthy? Why is Susan ill? Why not you or me?

Who, why, how, and *what-does-it-mean* questions are the stuff of philosophy and theology. Philosophers explain the call to care that comes in the claim of another person in various ways.

For Immanuel Kant the claim is an unconditional duty to respect the dignity of other persons. This means treating them as ends — worthy in themselves and not solely as means to my desires or ambitions.

For John Stuart Mill the claim of another person has to be understood individually and societally. I must understand that my obligation is not only to respect the liberty of my neighbor, as long as others are not harmed, but also to make decisions which better the situation of the greatest number.

The Jewish philosopher, Martin Buber, finds the claim of another person to be intrinsic and foundational to what it means to be a person. In his wise book called *I and Thou* (in German, *Ich und Du*),[1] Buber identifies two basic kinds of relationships: I-It and I-Thou. The first is one directional. It is the relationship that we have to objects and tools that we can easily pick up and manipulate. It is unfortunately the case that we sometimes treat people in this fashion, as well. When we do so, we respond to them as objects, as *its*, as means to our ends. The second type of relationship involves mutuality, which Buber describes as an I-Thou relationship. Although we no longer use the familiar form of *thou* in daily speech, we understand the intimacy that is implied by the word. You cannot fully know or care for another human being until there is an interaction which involves mutuality and respect. This I-Thou exchange, Buber explains, is possible not only between persons but also between persons and animals (as any pet-lover knows) and persons and nature (as poets and all those who love the out-of-doors know).

The claim of another person involves us in a kind of I-Thou encounter. Through this claim we learn to respect the thoughts and feelings of the Susans and Johns of this world. Their lives matter to us and we want to be of use as they and we come to terms with issues of life, health, and death that they may be facing. As we heed the call to care for Susan, we do so as beings who are addressed.

This response to other "thous" is foundational. We come into being in relationships. Ideally, we are conceived out of a loving relationship; nurtured in a womb; born into a family, a circle of those who address us and change our diapers. We are loved into being. In this sense the call to care is not merely an abstract duty spelled out in a utilitarian calculus. Rather, it is a claim in response to which we discover at the deepest level what it means to be a person.

Theologically speaking, the call to care is grounded in the divine initiative. God calls humankind into being in God's image. This means that we have the capacity and the responsibility to be in relationship not only with God, but with each other and with nature. The Biblical story is about the human condition — what happens when these relationships are broken — and the story of God's activity in the world to redeem people from slavery and to restore relationships. The word for health comes from the same root as the world for peace (*shalom*) in Hebrew. *Shalom* describes the way in which relationships ought to be. *Shalom* is a "state of wholeness possessed by persons or groups which may be health, prosperity, security, or the spiritual completeness of the covenant."[2]

Caring for Susan is rooted in God's caring for God's people. Just as God cared for the Israelites when they were strangers, we are called to care for others. It is a part of nurturing and restoring the wholeness of a community.

Caring for health in the Old Testament is, on one level, a prophylactic matter — a matter of duty and obedience. The focus is on the prevention of disease through proper rest (keeping the Sabbath), avoiding dangerous foods (i.e. pork or shell fish), avoiding incestuous relationships, developing appropriate sanitation measures and the like. In this perspective social justice is a health strategy — because poverty is dangerous to one's health.

If health is understood from the perspective of responsibility and prevention — why then illness? Why doctors? Can all illnesses be cured?

Why doctors? A Jew living about 180 B.C. counsels that the one who is ill should not only pray to the Lord and give up one's faults, but also give "the physician his place, for the Lord has created him."[3] The wisdom of doctors should be relied on, though not exclusively.

Why illness? This is a question that drives technological medicine. Are diseases such as the one faced by Susan preventable? Science keeps on searching for causes and for magic bullets. But illness can never be totally accounted for in that way. Individuals plagued with illness and disease claim our attention. They are the neighbors discovered by the Samaritan by the side of the road.

The line between what is preventable and curable and what is not is often fuzzy. Theology encourages respect both for the possibilities and the limitations of medicine. Theology encourages us to accept the limitations of treatment and to recognize that caring is more than curing. Caring means reaching out to the needs of Susan as a person who seeks to live out her life in the face of an illness that threatens death.

Arthur Olsen

[1]Buber, Martin. *I and Thou*, translated by Ronald Gregor Smith.
    New York: Charles Scribner's Sons, 1958.
[2]*Interpreter's Bible Dictionary. Vol. III*, p. 704. Abingdon Press, 1962.
[3]Sirach 38: 1-15. See this excerpt in Chapter Two.

Medicine and the Call to Care

One can learn much about the essence of caring from reflecting on medical practice. In recent decades, medicine has become a technical, highly scientific enterprise. There are many conditions that can be exquisitely treated by aggressive intervention. Examples include heart bypass surgery, organ transplantation, and even types of *in utero* surgery on the fetus. In the face of such wonders, it can be tempting to reduce medical art to the appropriate technological intervention. One can see this tendency not only in physicians and other caregivers, but also in the public. Often, in the face of illness, the plea is heard, "there must be something that can be done." After a stroke, in which a large part of the brain may be permanently injured, the family may be incredulous that some type of surgery or injection or medication cannot dramatically reverse the devastating process. All too often, such miraculous treatments simply do not exist. Equally troubling is the fact that many of our efforts at high tech intervention can easily lead to burdensome side effects, some anticipated and others not.

In the face of our stunning technological abilities and shortcomings, it is frequently evident to patients, families, and caregivers that there is more to illness care than mere science. There is as well a yearning for explanation, listening, compassion and a healing touch. Often in the corridors of a hospital, one can overhear patients and families remarking about how "the doctors don't know what's going on" or "the doctors don't explain anything" or "the doctor never comes around." Indeed, if one listens to patients and families in the hospital, or speaks to the public in general, it is evident that there exists in society much dissatisfaction with the way medicine is practiced. Anger and frustration abound at what is perceived to be the insensitivity and aloofness of some physicians. Moreover, if diagnosis and treatment are not going well, there is a natural instinct to assume that other (presumably smarter) doctors or a more prestigious institution may hold the key to a definitive cure. Difficulties can be compounded by the fact that in the face of serious or unexplained illness, patients and families are frequently "at their worst" in terms of their emotional state and coping abilities. There is much opportunity for misunderstanding, recrimination, and distrust.

As a response to the nature of medicine and the fallibilities of doctors, the following question is sometimes posed:

> If you were sick and needed delicate surgery (say heart bypass), would you rather have an understanding and compassionate surgeon with only average technical abilities, or would you choose a gruff, unapproachable surgeon who, while not particularly interested in understanding you as a person or explaining his reasons, was apt to get a surgically excellent result?

Whenever this question is proposed, respondents have usually chosen the technically more expert surgeon over a humanistic, mediocre one. The presumption exists that the practice of medicine is most essentially a scientific endeavor that will achieve good results if properly performed.

But often, indeed most of the time, it is not as easy as simply putting up with miscommunication and tolerating an aloof expert for the sake of "getting the job done." There are so many nuances and options in medicine that the issue "of what to do" often remains enigmatic. And as decisions are being sought, ethical and emotional quandaries can greatly complicate the issue of how to proceed. Life would be easier if medical care was essentially like calculus or elements of physics where given variables and manipulations predictably lead to an appropriate response. Often in medicine, we simply don't know which of several options is optimal for a given patient. For instance, if a 70-year-old man has a badly clogged carotid artery, he is at risk for a stroke. Nonetheless, it is not always clear whether he should be treated with medication (and if so, which of several should be chosen) or with a surgery that cleans out the artery. If the patient successfully undergoes surgery without complication, he no doubt is better off. Unfortunately, even in the best of hands, there is an inherent risk in such surgery for rare, but devastating, complications.

Most of the time in medicine it is not sufficient to summarily move from the fact of a blocked carotid artery to the need for surgery. In order to help decide what to do, the skilled physician seeks additional data through the patient's history, or "story." Such a narrative can give clues as to how to proceed. The patient may have a strong bias for a given treatment — perhaps for a definitive surgical intervention. Or perhaps the patient is intolerant of risk, and disinclined to have surgery. Or perhaps the patient has other health problems making the risk of anesthesia or surgery unacceptably high. The patient's story, properly developed, gives very important data in this regard.

In medical school, the student is taught to rely on objective, scientific data. Anecdote is spurned. Well-controlled scientific studies are touted as being critical to appropriate therapy. However, in addition to being trained as scientists, physicians are taught to deal with the patient's "story." Indeed, the initial component of the physician/patient relationship is traditionally a discussion of the patient's history. As the data of a patient's life is gleaned, the physician attempts to prioritize the patient's problems and offer therapy. In this setting, data from the revered scientific studies may or may not provide a definitive solution for the patient. Often, at this clinical level, anecdote and "story" can be critical elements in the determination of what to do. The physician not only relies on data from the patient and family, but also may well harken back to prior patients in similar situations. Thus, previous patient "stories," either personally experienced by the physician or described by mentors, play an important role as the physician develops a strategy for trying to help the patient. And knowledge of these stories help the physician understand the need to address the insecurities and questions that patients invariably have when facing major surgery. Through anecdote and experience, the physician can often skillfully find a path through the uncertainties and emotional turmoil that can threaten to overwhelm a patient.

In honing clinical skills, the student and physician come to realize that all types of "story" can prove helpful. Examples of insensitive and crass physician behavior can serve as cautionary tales, and instances of heroic caregiving can offer examples worthy of emulation. In this realm, "story" can help the physician move from the coldly theorctical to the plausible and meaningful.

In Susan's situation, an oncologist (cancer specialist) might well have a strong bias as to the best treatment for her type of malignancy. This oncologist might strongly favor a certain type of chemotherapy, and recommend aggressively forging ahead with the hope that Susan would be one of the 20 percent who survive for a year. And of course, the oncologist might stress that Susan could be an exception and live still longer than a year. But if the personal "story" of Susan, or of any patient, is indeed critical, then the oncologist's data on the relative merits of chemotherapy provide only part of the answer of how to proceed. What really needs to be addressed is what is, in fact, the best course of action for Susan, herself. When this type of query is considered, multiple issues need to be considered. To begin with, Susan probably wants to know what the "20 percent chance of survival for one year" really means. If she should be in the minority who survive a year, is there any realistic chance of living for an even longer term? Or is the overwhelming likelihood that her best hope, even with aggressive chemotherapy, is to extend her life for 8-12 months? And what are the real costs to her of chemotherapy? Certainly all types of chemotherapy have side effects, but individual responses to such drug therapy vary considerably. Susan needs to know the most likely complications she will experience, and then assess these from her personal perspective. For some patients, hair loss can be devastating. But for Susan, perhaps, baldness might evoke quirky comparisons to the pop singer Sinead O'Connor and be very tolerable. On the other hand, Susan might find intractable nausea and vomiting and pain unacceptable. If these prospects are the likely result of chemotherapy, she might not opt to accept such treatment.

In trying to decide what to do, or not to do, other important variables surface as well. Clearly Susan's family and friends loom important in her life. Her religious beliefs and personal instincts for confronting adversity are also important factors. Indeed, all of these elements, and more, make up Susan's "story." In reflecting upon them, it matters little whether Susan is a real patient or a fictionalized one. The issue for the caregiver is clear — what to do or not to do for Susan depends on a number of factors that must be carefully identified and reckoned with. Such assessment can make all the difference to the one being cared for and frequently to the caregiver as well. In Susan's case, the science of cancer treatment (*i.e.* chemotherapy and/or radiation) remains vitally important. But effective caring depends upon an intimate appreciation of her "story." In the end, optimal treatment choices may well be found in such narrative.

Jerome W. Freeman

Nursing and the Call to Care

The call to care from a nursing perspective is embodied in the Latin root word for nursing, *nutricia* — to nourish or to nurture. Nursing assists an individual's response to life situations and actual or potential health problems. Illness can precipitate a wide range of responses in individuals. Physically the person may experience pain or discomfort, loss of appetite, or fatigue. The psychological response may include the whole range of emotions, including fear, anxiety, anger, denial, and frustration regarding the illness, the prognosis, or the treatment.

In "Susan's Case" we are confronted with a young woman who is faced with the diagnosis of cancer and the prediction that she has a 20 percent chance of survival for one year. She confides that she is afraid of dying. A life-threatening illness such as Susan's often evokes fear and anxiety, as is true in Susan's case. Fear and anxiety can come from many sources: fear of the diagnosis itself, fear of dying as voiced by Susan, fear of pain and suffering, and fear of being abandoned by friends and family at the greatest time of need. Treatment options may pose another set of anxieties and fears — fatigue, nausea and vomiting, and other unpleasant adverse effects. For a young woman Susan's age, appearance may be very important. She may experience a significant amount of anxiety over the loss of her hair if chemotherapy is used. Caring includes helping Susan understand each option she may be given, so that she can make an informed choice.

How do we care for Susan as a friend or as a nurse or other health care professional? First and foremost, caring for Susan at this moment is being present — truly present to Susan. The word care comes from the Old English *caru* and Old High German *kara*, meaning to lament, to participate in another's suffering, to journey with another in suffering. Being present means listening empathetically while giving full attention to Susan. Rosemarie Parse refers to this silent presence as "silent emersion" with the other. Words are not always necessary. Two can journey together in silence. At times touch may be as important, or even more appropriate, than words. The "Ma Bell" adage, "reach out and touch someone" resonates for Susan. Touch conveys a sense of acceptance and connectedness. A life-threatening illness can give the sense of isolation, rejection, and aloneness. Touch and being present can fill the void where words seem inadequate. Presence also reaffirms the other's being and worth, resonating to emotional and spiritual needs.

Being present to Susan does not demand being comfortable in the situation. The very thought of cancer frequently leaves many people feeling uneasy. Even forms of cancer with high long-term survival rates stir up ideas of suffering, pain, and death. Caring for Susan means rising above one's own fears and discomfort to be present in some way to her. Caring for Susan may include visiting frequently, both in the hospital and after she is home. Being present may mean staying even when she does not feel like talking, and listening, really listening, to what Susan has to say. Susan may want to talk about the cancer, about her future or lack of it, about her lost dreams, or about the many questions that do not seem to have answers. Frequently persons in crisis are not seeking answers from others when they ask questions. They may be asking the questions because they need to hear them stated in order to grasp the reality of the situation. Listening and responding to the non-verbal expression and the feelings accompanying the words can be deeply appreciated. Being present conveys that Susan matters.

What are the theoretical underpinnings in nursing upon which to base caring? Florence Nightingale, in *Notes on Nursing: What it is and What it is Not*, states that the role of nursing is to "put the patient in the best condition to let nature act upon him." This was accomplished by creating a physical and emotional environment conducive to healing at the least expense of "vital power" to the patient. Nightingale viewed the nurse as an advocate for the patient (Nightingale, 1859/1946).

According to Jean Watson, nurse theorist and founder of the Center for Human Caring at the University of Colorado, love and caring are universal values. If our humanness is to survive, we need to nourish our humanity with love and caring. Based on this belief, Watson asserts that caring is a moral imperative in nursing. Caring in nursing emerges from a humanistic value system combined with a sound scientific knowledge base. Nursing integrates biophysical knowledge with knowledge of human behavior to promote wellness and to care for the sick.

Watson identifies three factors that underlie the philosophical basis for caring. These include humanistic-altruistic values and actions, the instillation of faith-hope, and the cultivation of sensitivity to oneself and to others (Watson, 1985). Providing encouragement and hope are important elements in caring for Susan or others. Developing an awareness of one's own feelings increases sensitivity regarding the other's feelings and fosters the empathetic *I-Thou* relationship. Thus, awareness of one's own fears and anxiety regarding life-threatening situations can work to promote an empathetic relationship and a supportive environment for Susan.

Mary Auterman

Nightingale, Florence. (1859/1946). *Notes on Nursing: What it is and What it is Not.* London: Hartison and Sons. Reproduced by offset in 1946, Philadelphia: Edward Stem & Co.
Parse, Rosemarie Rizzo. (1998). *The Human Becoming School of Thought.* Thousand Oaks, CA: Sage Publications.
Jean Watson. (1985). *Nursing: The Philosophy and Science of Caring.* Boulder, CO: Colorado Associated University Press.

The Call of Literature

While the call to care seems natural to the disciplines of medicine and nursing, and while it is a natural extension of the moral concerns of philosophy and religion, such an imperative issuing from literature may seem odd to the casual observer. Stories and poems, we are used to thinking, engage us in ways different from discursive prose. Only stodgy teachers insist on the "meaning" of literature. "A poem should not mean, but be," insisted the poet Marianne Moore. Shakespeare filled his plays with as much sex and violence as any popular movie, and took pride in keeping his audiences, who were mostly on foot, engaged in outrageous plot complications and delighted by the explosive music of his verse. Attending a performance of Shakespeare at the Globe Theatre was more like participation in an outdoor rock concert than attendance at a polite portrayal in the darkened playhouses of our own day. Nevertheless, the call was there because of the very nature of literature. Either you care or you stop reading or stop listening. It is in the storyteller's interest to keep the audience caring.

"Susan's Case" is a fiction which challenges us in a manner peculiar to fiction. We are asked to imagine ourselves into a situation and to respond to it intellectually and emotionally. More importantly, we are asked to imagine ourselves in Susan's place. The clearest call to care is on behalf of certain characters in a story or a poem. The purest lyric is a plea for understanding: "See what I see, feel what I feel." As lyric expression is extended to the dramatic, the plea is broadened to include the most unlikely persons, even those for whom we are not naturally inclined to care. In Shakespeare's *Tragedy of King Lear* we are from the beginning attracted to Cordelia, whose simple candor and unwavering principles seem no match for the hypocrisy and treachery of her selfish sisters. But surprisingly, she is banished, not to be seen again until the end of the play. Our attention is turned to Lear, whose foolish whim trapped him into a patently unfair act. Here is a person who is not easy to care for: he is willful, self-indulgent, petty, impulsive, the very image of what the habit of unchecked power might do to a man. We are tempted to believe that he deserves whatever he gets from Goneril and Regan, his ungrateful daughters. But as misery is heaped on misery, as he is stripped of every vestige of dignity and sanity, we are at first softened, then won over entirely. As he collapses over Cordelia's body in the final scene, we are hard pressed to withhold our tears. Similarly, Tolstoy's *The Death of Ivan Ilyich* presents us with a protagonist who hardly seems worthy of consideration, let alone our compassion. Ivan is a bureaucrat, a functionary who has been completely absorbed by comfortable middle-class standards which we can recognize as being a kind of living death. We recognize his world in our own, and as his incomprehensible suffering progresses, we care and care deeply, and for the most selfish of reasons: because we can see Ivan in what we are, or have been, or could become.

Moreover, literature furnishes models of caring, emotional instruction in the best ways to care. In *King Lear* we have Kent and the Fool and Cordelia as illustrations of people whose loyalty and compassion seems virtually unmotivated by selfish ends. In the parallel plot of the play, Edgar, who has been denounced by his father Gloucester, offers yet another example of what the Indian writer P. Lal calls "gratuitous compassion." Edgar nurses and saves from despair and suicide the parent who has been the cause of Edgar's own suffering. In *The Death of Ivan Ilyich* the servant Gerasim is the only person whom Ivan can trust at last to care for him wholeheartedly and honestly. Yet this apparent selflessness on the part of such ideal caregivers often has at its root a recognition of our common humanity. Gerasim's wish is that someone would do for him what he does for Ivan. And even in Lear's pre-Christian

England, such caring seems motivated by something akin to the Golden Rule.

What is perhaps most instructive about literature is the endless variety of situations presented for our study. Often we are struck by the universality of such situations. With Lear we have the ever-timely question of care for the elderly: "What to do with Daddy." Lear's infirmity, dementia, and decline toward death seem in many ways contemporary, as does the contention among his offspring about who should take care of him and what limitations should be placed on his behavior. And while Ivan Ilyich is clearly a creature of the 19th Century Russian bourgeoisie, Ivan's overpowering realization of mortality is universal, and his empty life is reflected in the self-absorption of 20th Century Yuppie and Boomer "lifestyles." When Kent, witnessing Lear's anguish, begs that the king's death be quick, he is expressing what so many feel in witnessing the final moments of a loved companion. When Edgar ministers to his father's suicidal despair, he is confronting a problem still with us. Each age brings its own complications to such dilemmas, conflicts of cultural notions, technological intensification of caring issues. William Carlos Williams, a physician who is hailed as one of the prime movers of modern poetry, can, in a story like "The Use of Force," demonstrate caring principles like autonomy and non-maleficence with greater economy and intensity than a discourse of many times the length.

That is not to say that discourse on these issues is not needed; what may be absorbed unconsciously in reading fiction and poetry often requires discourse to bring important matters to consciousness. Yet all of the disciplines involved in this venture have in common attention to story, whether it be a perplexing medical case history, Christ's parable of the Good Samaritan, or Victor Frankl's harrowing account of survival in a Nazi concentration camp. Discourse on principles are accompanied by these kinds of vivid tales and histories, which not only are compelling in themselves, but also offer opportunities for fascinating and instructive analysis.

Ronald Robinson

Lal, P., Introduction to *The Bhagavad-Gita*, Writer's Workshop Books, Calcutta, 1978.

The Editors

Mary Auterman, associate professor of nursing at Augustana College, teaches in the areas of adolescent health, maternity nursing, ethical and legal aspects of nursing, and is director of the Parish Nursing Center. She is a member of an Institutional Review Board for Protection of Human Subjects. She has a BSN from the University of Colorado, MA from the University of Iowa, and DNSc from Indiana University. She has contributed articles on adolescent pregnancy and on parish nursing to *South Dakota Nurse*, *Pacemaker*, and other publications. She has been active in the Association of Women's Health, Obstetrical and Neonatal Nursing, and the South Dakota Perinatal Association.

Jerome William Freeman is a practicing physician and educator. He is professor and chair of the Department of Neurosciences, University of South Dakota School of Medicine, and is also on the faculty of Augustana College. He has a particular interest in biomedical ethics and the use of literature in teaching about illness, the patient, and the caregiver. He serves as Director of the Center for Ethics and Caring at Sioux Valley Hospital. He has authored three volumes of poetry and a collections of essays.

Arthur L. Olsen, professor emeritus of philosophy and religion at Augustana College, continues to teach in the areas of ethics and biomedical ethics. As a member of four ethics committees at health care institutions, he is active in the practice of biomedical ethics. He is a member and current chair of the board for the Center for Ethics and Caring at Sioux Valley Hospital. As Provost and Academic Vice President of Augustana, he was instrumental in instituting Capstone courses and served as the first director of the Capstone project. A graduate of St. Olaf College, he has earned the MDiv from Luther Seminary and the ThD from Harvard University.

Ronald L. Robinson, professor emeritus of English and journalism at Augustana College, is a novelist and playwright whose books include *Thunder Dreamer* and *Kitchen Dance*. A graduate of Augustana, with an MA from the University of Minnesota, Robinson acts as editorial consultant for Ex Machina Publishing Company.

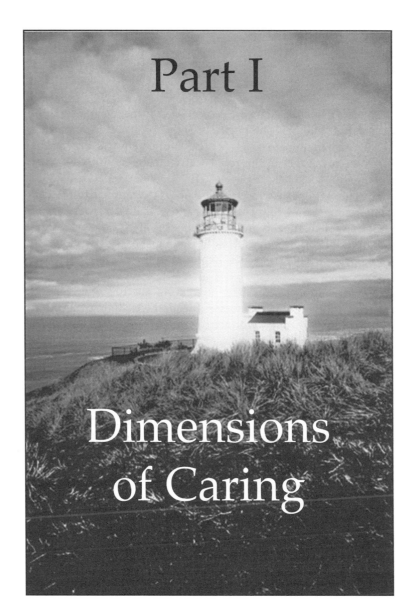

Part I

Dimensions
of Caring

W hat does it mean to care? To care means that something matters. The health of someone like Susan matters. It matters to us as friends, family members, or neighbors. For some it matters in the roles that we have as nurses or physicians.

How it matters — what is involved in responding to the call to care — is the theme of the readings and narrative in Part I.

Caring for the health and well-being of others engages us in the narratives of people's lives. Health is not just of the body but of the whole person. This concept is explored in the readings in Chapter One.

Which is the best strategy for caring for the whole person? Through cultivating wholeness — through wise living? Or through intervention — through wonder drugs and surgery? This debate is carried on in Chapter Two.

Caring for matters of health, life, and death engages us in reflection on our personal, concrete experiences of illness and mortality. This dimension is developed in Chapter Three.

Then finally, how do our experiences of life, illness, and death become a part of the stories of our lives? The call to care for our life stories is a call to courage. The readings in Chapter Four are stories of courage and the search for meaning.

Chapter One:
The Will to Carry Out
Our Life Story

Arthur Olsen

"The more accurately we understand the patient's life story and how its variables influence illness, the better job we are able to do in sorting out therapy/care options." — J. W. Freeman in "On Hearing the Story: A Parable."

"[The healthy person] ... lives the healthy or sick life of his body together with that of his soul, and again in both cases, and in their mutual relationship, it is a matter of life's history, his own history, and therefore himself. And the will for health as the strength to be as man is obviously quite simply, and without duplication in a psychical and physical sphere, the *will to continue* this history in its unity and totality." — From Karl Barth, *Church Dogmatics*, III/4, p. 357.

"Health is a dynamic life experience of a human being, which implies continuous adjustment to stressors in the internal and external environment through optimum use of one's resources to achieve maximum potential for daily living." — Imogene King, *A Theory for Nursing: Systems, Concepts, Process.* 1981, p. 5.

"The difficulty and the challenge of this subject is that in order to speak of health, one must speak of all dimensions of life which are united in man. And no one can be an expert in all of them. But confronting this challenge is the destiny of the philosopher and the theologian, insofar as they should envisage the whole of life." — Paul Tillich in "The Meaning of Health."

Caring for Susan isn't just about caring about her illness or about her health. Caring for Susan begins with respecting her life. This means respecting her will to be healthy, her ability to carry out her life story.

In order to respond to the claim of Susan for our care we need to know her story. This is the common insight from the disciplines of literature, medicine, nursing, philosophy, and theology considered in the introduction. The dynamics of caring through story is the theme of the readings in Chapter One. Patients and all those needing our care come wrapped in stories. Therefore, story needs to be respected as the way to knowing another person. Knowing the patient's story, Jerome Freeman reminds us, enhances the ability of the physician in "sorting out therapy/care options." And in a profound sense what we hear as we listen to Susan as she shares her concerns about her health, is her will to be healthy, her will to carry out her life story. She wants to know how the story she wished to live out may be compromised by her illness.

The definitions of health that come from theology and philosophy and nursing (quoted above) agree on this point. Health and disease have to do with the ability of persons to function as human beings, "to achieve maximum potential for daily living," in the words of the nurse Imogene King, or "to continue one's life story," in the words of the theologian Karl Barth.

From this perspective health is not a function of a person like metabolism, or hearing, or breathing, as Tillich points out. Health and disease are existentialist concepts that say something about the whole human being. Our concern for Susan begins with the threat that disease brings to her person, to her ability to carry forward her life story. As Arthur Frank has written about his experience with cancer in *The Will of the Body*,[1] the cancer is not just a thing, extraneous to the person, that can be attacked and destroyed by marshalling foreign legions of drugs. Illness has become a part of the person's experience.

In a word, caring for Susan means caring for her as person, body and soul. The caring question then is "How best can all of the resources of caring be used in responding to and supporting her as a human being?"

Caring begins with some sense of what it means to be human, and personally human. Tillich noted the difficulty and the challenge of doing so. In order to be caring about the health of a person, one must have in mind all of the dimensions of life that are united in a person.

At times, a holistic understanding of health seems to conflict with the scientific method and technological medicine. Following the dualistic view of the philosopher Descartes, society's approach has often been to compartmentalize the understanding of human enterprise into disciplinary parts. The result has been to separate the strategies of caring and curing. The focus of the practice of medicine shifted from the interpersonal relationship between the doctor and the patient to a focus on the biological nuts and bolts of the science of medicine. And an institution like the church, which in history pioneered caring for health in hospices, has focused on salvation rather than healing.

The irony is that Descartes' dualism was developed in part to defend the human and to empower the flourishing of technology. Thus he proposed the notion of two substances — material substance that stands under all of our measurements and judgments of size, shape, color, *etc.*, and mental substance that stands under our thinking and feeling. The advantage of this approach is, on the one hand, to prevent the reduction of the person to what is observable and measurable, and, on the other hand, to protect science from judgments that are not based on what is observable and measurable. Thus the psychologist and the priest assume the care of the soul, and technological medicine inherits the care of the body.

The unfortunate result of the dualistic approach is to divide Susan into component parts — Susan as a body machine that needs repair and Susan as a person. And all too easily caring for Susan as person becomes subordinate to technical questions about disease management and the search for a "magic cure" through surgical or medicinal intervention.

A holistic understanding of health draws attention to Susan as a person. We need to know Susan's medical prognosis, but we also need to know how this prognosis is to be interpreted and applied in the context of her life story.

On the one hand, professional health care workers (physicians and nurses) caring for Susan need to know whom they are diagnosing, touching, and treating. The former head of the nursing department at Augustana College was once asked why it was important for students going into nursing to take literature. Her answer: "In the course of their work nurses touch persons. Literature helps them understand the persons they touch."

And on the other hand, Susan needs to know at the deepest level that she is being treated as a whole person, not as an accumulation of data on a medical chart.

Consider the following experience of a Native American who did not feel that he/she was treated as a whole person.

> You go to a hospital and maybe once a day the doctor comes around and ... stays there, maybe five minutes [The doctor talks a little bit — and] asks you questions. Once in a while they give you a little medicine, just a little bit of it. About the only thing they do is to put something in your mouth to see how hot you are. The rest of the time you just lie there, but the medicine men help you all the time— they give you lots of medicine and they sing all night. They do lots of things all over your body. Every bit of your body is treated. (John Noble Willard, "Navajo healers successful where medicine falls short." *New York Times* 7 July 1972, p 27. Quoted by James B. Nelson and JoAnne Rohricht in *Human Medicine*, p. 15)[2]

When the whole person is cared for it is clear that caring is a more embracing concept than curing. Caring certainly includes and benefits from the discoveries of MRI scans and all the other resources of technological medicine. As Nelson and Rohricht put it,

> If I am ill, I certainly need the therapeutic skills and techniques, but I need more than that. I also hunger for those who give themselves to me not just technologically, because of my physical defects, but also personally and for my own sake. (p. 28)[3]

And human needs persist even after medical intervention is futile. It is our deepest hope that Susan can be cured. But we do not abandon her if this turns out not to be the case. Susan's life story doesn't cease because she has a disease. Her claim upon us as a family member, friend, physician, or nurse is to support her will to be healthy. We are called to support her will to carry forward her life story in these new and difficult circumstances.

The readings in Chapter One are intended to engage the reader in the role of story in caring.

The first two pieces are by physicians who explore the importance of story in responding to the needs of patients. For Jerome Freeman story is a way of knowing, a way of understanding and communicating with patients. Richard Weinberg needed to have another physician hear his story before he found healing.

The pieces by Karl Barth and Paul Tillich provide challenging reading — but they are pivotal in several respects for understanding the call to care as it is developed in this book.

They are pivotal in the first place as contributions of individuals from the first half of the twentieth century who anticipated the need to think of health and human beings holistically. They resist the dualistic legacy of the French philosopher, Rene Descartes, which divided the knowledge of the human being into disciplinary parts, body and soul. They are pivotal in the second place for the models they suggest for thinking holistically about human beings and their health.

From a theological perspective, Karl Barth invites us to think of the unity of the person in his or her story, and to think of health as the will to carry out one's life story. Note carefully how story and narrative are suggested as a way to integrate knowledge of the body and knowledge of the self. Underscored is the importance of story in understanding the needs of another, such as Susan, as a whole person. This perspective opens up a way of understanding the important but limited role of the physician who even at best can know only a part of the patient's story. An additional insight is his suggestion that the will for individual health is not separable from the will for community health. The call to care for the health of individual persons carries with it a call to care for the health of the communities in which individuals live.

From a philosophical perspective, Paul Tillich (1886-1965) proposes the metaphor of "dimensions of life" for understanding the role of health, disease, and healing in human beings. He speaks of dimension "in order to indicate that the different qualities of life in man are present within each other and do not lie alongside or above each other." From this perspective all aspects of the human being — mechanical, biological, psychological, spiritual, and historical — must be understood as dimensions of the whole person, not separate parts.

A final insight of Tillich's which pertains to the call to care has to do with the risks inherent in growth — in carrying out one's life story. In order to grow, each self must move out of itself and interact with other selves and the environment. There are twin dangers. One is losing oneself through the risks that come from those interactions. Disease is one of these risks. The opposite danger is not growing because the self does not venture out. Thus, carrying out one's life story involves the risks of vulnerability and disease as well as the possibilities of health and meaningful life.

Henri Nouwen, a counselor and a priest, explores the role of listening and story in caring for the elderly. "The elderly remind us," he observes, "that care is distinctly different from cure." Cure focuses attention on the one giving care, be it doctor, psychologist, or minister, and hence on the achievement and success of the caregiver. In caring we enter into the life story of the one being cared for.

[1]Frank, Arthur W. *The Will of the Body: Reflections on Illness.* New York: Houghton Mifflin Co., 1991.

[2]Nelson, James B., and Rohricht, JoAnne. *Human Medicine,* revised edition. Minneapolis: Augsburg, 1984.

[3]*Ibid.*

On Hearing the Story:
A Parable

Jerome W. Freeman

Recently, my wife and I were visiting at the College of St. Benedict in Minnesota. Joseph, an artist there, is completing a large, three-panel sculpture out of limestone. His work is exquisite in detail and vision.

Joseph indicated that some days earlier he had been working on a panel, chipping flakes from one of his images with a hammer and chisel. He suddenly became aware of someone standing behind him, watching. When he stopped and turned to talk to his visitor, he found only a very stern and seemingly angry middle-aged man. "Where is your model," the visitor asked. Joseph explained that he doesn't use a model, but chisels out the images in his sculptures freehand. While making this explanation, Joseph suddenly surmised that this disgruntled gentleman might be a stonecutter from a local granite works. Following up on this instinct, Joseph added, "I don't think I have the talent to sculpt from a model — that must require considerable skill." With this, the visitor's expression immediately changed from anger and reserve to one of friendliness. "I'm one of the stonecutters and we always work from models," he proclaimed. Then the visitor proceeded in an animated fashion to explain how stonecutting was done and how it is becoming a lost art. He even produced a series of photographs of some of the projects he had worked on, and noted that stonecutters labor in anonymity as opposed to celebrated artists like Joseph.

In describing this encounter, Joseph was particularly struck by the way the visitor's demeanor changed from one of anger and almost hostility, to friendliness. Joseph suspected that the cutter had read a recent newspaper article about his work and had come to the studio very dubious of the whole project. In the cutter's mind, true craftsmanship and skill lay in the ability to carefully copy an image from a model onto granite. The visitor was skeptical of any sculpture done freehand and, apparently, was actually angry at an artist such as Joseph for having the temerity to attempt it.

In this story, Joseph reveals himself to have considerable skill in terms of quickly perceiving the nature of another's concern, and then breaking down the barriers to communication and mutual understanding. He clearly felt privileged to have stumbled upon the cutter's vision of life and art. In medicine, we are frequently called upon to make similar leaps of discernment, and to work to bridge the divisions which can separate us from our patients. A major key to the physician's success, in my judgment, resides in the ability to be genuinely interested in our patients as persons. We need to remind ourselves and each other of the importance of learning what our patients do for a living and who their families are, as well as what the patient's fears, expectations, and aspirations may be.

When we record patient histories either by dictating or writing longhand, we are in fact giving implicit testimony to the importance of focusing on particulars when making treatment decisions. Indeed, we are creating a form of literature as we weave the patient's life story into a clinical narrative. Oftentimes, the decisions we ultimately make are best generated when we are able to carefully sift the technical possibilities and value judgment options through the specific intimacies of such precise patient data. The more accurately we understand the patient's life story and how its variables influence illness, the better job we can do in sorting out therapy/care options.

When our professional lives are viewed in this way, it is evident that what we do as physicians has a critical relationship to narrative and storytelling, and to seeing individuals in the complex context of their lives. In this realm of interpersonal communication reside many potential treacheries and triumphs for our efforts as physicians. When it comes to listening, I suspect that we can always improve our effectiveness and that we are never quite as good as we would like to be.

The Laying On of Hands
Richard B. Weinberg, MD

I had been dreading the call all day. I was in the library when my pager sounded and, as I walked to the wall phone, I had an ominous premonition. It was my brother. "They found abnormal lymph tissue on the chest x-ray," he said. "What does it mean?" Struck with an upwelling of nausea, I sagged against the wall. Healthy, active, he had gone for the x-ray at my urging, after complaining of fevers and strange chest pains for over a month. "Well, it could be lots of different things . . . ," I began, reassuring him; but I knew. Like my grandparents and sister before him, my brother had lymphoma.

There was much to do. I made phone calls, contacted friends, arranged for a referral to a specialist in his city. I flew down to be with him before his diagnostic thoracotomy. It was lymphoma. A particularly aggressive variety. Together we called home to deliver the bleak news, and the next day I picked up my bewildered and frightened parents at the airport and drove them to the hospital. Together we sat as the oncologists explained the treatment options. When I was not at my brother's bedside, I spent my time in the medical library reviewing the literature and on the phone seeking opinions from prominent experts. In the end my brother chose a new, but promising, chemotherapy protocol at a nearby university hospital and, after the first uneventful cycle, I returned home to work. But every week we would talk on the telephone about his progress, the side effects, his law school classes, life. He achieved a remission that lasted for the summer, and happiness returned to his voice. We made plans for a trip. But then the fevers returned, and he began an inexorable decline, sickened even more by repeated cycles of "salvage therapy." His phone calls came more often and more urgent, and it became progressively harder for me to encourage him and give him hope.

That was when the pain began. I first noticed it as an empty, hollow sensation in my chest at the end of the day. I dealt with it by ignoring it. But as the days passed, the pain became more insistent. It was gnawing and pressing, like a balloon expanding inside my chest. Heartburn, I told myself, and stopped off at the GI clinic to grab some H2 blockers; but they provided no relief. Stress, I told

From *Annals of Internal Medicine.* 1992; 117:83-84. Used by permission.

myself; but neither exercise, nor alcohol, nor attempts to relax made any difference. The pain became constant and kept me awake at night. There had to be an explanation.

Was it angina? A cardiology fellow sneaked me into the heart station one evening and after hours of EKGs, treadmills, and echos pronounced my heart remarkably normal. The pain grew more intense. Maybe atypical pleurisy? I got a chest x-ray in the emergency room and brought it to Radiology. "Lung fields are normal. . . no effusions. . . mediastinum's a bit generous, but its probably a normal variant," the radiologist on call rattled off before he turned back to his board. The mediastinum is *generous*?! No! It couldn't be lymphoma! That night I palpated the lymph nodes in my neck, axilla, and groin. They did feel a bit prominent. Soon they became tender, and as the days passed I was certain that they were growing larger. Meanwhile the pain became unbearable. I became obsessed with finding a diagnosis. I prepared a blood smear on myself, and peering down the microscope I saw my death: smudge cells! Leukemia! I grew faint. What will I do? I can't die now! How will I tell my parents? As I panicked, my eye latched onto the tube of blood. A grey top. Fluoride. Metabolic poison. Kills white cells. Pseudo-smudge cells!

In the cold sweat of temporary redemption, I finally accepted the limits of self-diagnosis. I needed a doctor. But who? I knew as well as any informed layperson the names of the experts at our university hospital. But credentials could be deceptive. I had seen them at the bedside, listened to them at conferences, read their clinic notes, and weighed their advice on the wards. So who was the best doctor for my problem? The society cardiologist who couldn't read a cardiogram? The hotshot oncologist whose housestaff nickname was "mad dog"? The famous pulmonologist who was never in town? If I made the wrong choice, I knew that my symptoms would be zealously pursued with painful tests which, if they didn't disclose a diagnosis, would leave me more miserable than ever. Who? Then suddenly it was clear. Of course! Dr. Davidson!

Dr. Davidson was not a rising star in the Department of Medicine. "I admit he's a very good teacher," the Chief of Medicine was often heard to say, "but he just isn't publishing." "Of course he isn't," one wanted to scream back, "He's out there on the wards every day, like you should be!" And Dr. Davidson certainly tried to be "academic." He was always talking excitedly about his review on gonococcal infections in the inner city. "It's just about finished," he'd cheerfully tell us on rounds, "and it's certainly going to raise some eyebrows." But it never seemed to appear in print. The house-staff didn't care; we loved him.

He was an internist, and at the bedside he shined. It was Dr. Davidson who discovered that an elderly lady admitted three times in one month with near fatal status asthmaticus, had recently pur-chased a new parakeet — and was deathly allergic to it. It was Dr. Davidson who saved a man with tearing chest pain from emergency angiography by pointing out that he had ruptured his pectoralis from an over-enthusiastic weight-lifting session. When the Dean came down with a serious viral pneumonia, it was Dr. Davidson who sat outside his door and fended off the well-meaning Department Chiefs who descended in multitudes to give conflicting orders to the housestaff. "The Dean just needs to be left alone, and he will get better," he insisted. And he did. And mysteriously, whenever it all became overwhelming and you started to think about quitting medicine, it was Dr. Davidson's arm that came down over your shoulder. "Hey. Let's go down to the doctor's dining room for a cup of coffee," he'd say. You went, and he'd listen, and then it didn't seem so bad.

Surely, I thought, if something's wrong, Dr. Davidson will know. I found him on the wards, told him that I hadn't been feeling well, and asked if he would look me over. He suggested that we go to his office. It was disorienting to be sitting on the other side of the exam-ining table, but Dr. Davidson quickly put me at ease, and soon I was pouring out the whole sorry tale of my chest pain and my brother's illness. It took quite a while. During his physical examination he poured over every inch of my body, felt for lymph nodes, and lis-tened intently to my heart. When he finished, he looked at my chest x-ray and then scribbled a note in my chart. I dressed and, with my heart pounding, turned to face him.

"Do we need any tests?"

"No, I'd say you've done a pretty good job of that," he said with a smile.

"Then you know what's wrong?"

"Yes, I think I do."

"Is it lymphoma?" I choked out, fearing the worst.

"No, your lymph nodes feel normal to me and given the way you've been poking at them, it's no wonder they're a bit tender."

"My heart . . ."

"Your heart is fine."

"Ulcer. . . ?"

"No."

"Are you telling me that I'm imagining all of this?"

"No. The pain is real."

"Then what's wrong with me? What's causing the pain?" I demanded.

"You have heartache."

"Heartache?" The word struck me like a slap to the face.

"Yes. Your brother is seriously ill. You are his best friend, and you've served as his personal physician as well. You've helped guide him to the best treatment, comforted him during the tough times, and given him the strength to go on. You've had to be strong for him and for your family. Now things don't look so good, you know the prognosis of his condition, and you fear what is to come. But no one really understands how much it all hurts you. You love your brother very much, and so you feel his pain in your heart."

Tears streamed down my cheeks. I could not speak. "It's okay to have heartache," Dr. Davidson continued. "It's the price you pay for loving someone. And not many of us do as good a job of it as you're doing now, you know." The famous arm came gently down across my shoulder. "Now you keep right on being a good brother and a good doctor," he said, offering me a handkerchief. He sat with me, and after some time I composed myself.

"Thank you," was all I could say.

"You're certainly welcome. We'll talk about things again soon, right? Now, how about a cup of coffee in the doctor's dining room?"

My chest pain eased throughout the afternoon and by evening was gone. Like in the tale of Rumpelstiltskin, once Dr. Davidson had called the name of the demon, its power was vanquished. And although afterwards the heartache returned now and then, I no longer feared it. My brother died three months later after a valiant struggle, and I gave the eulogy at his funeral. I finished my fellowship and found a faculty position in another city. I later heard that Dr. Davidson — his magnum opus never completed — was denied tenure and had left the university for another job. I also heard that he was still teaching housestaff and was happy.

In The Oath we swear ". . . to consider dear to me as my parents, him who taught me this art. . ." — and to assist our fellow physicians with every kindness should misfortune befall them. And so it should be. For we carry a special burden: We have learned of the pain that disease brings to mankind and know that often we are powerless to stop it. And when the thin veneer we erect to protect ourselves from this knowledge is shattered, demons that lurk in our minds are unleashed to terrify our souls. In such times we cannot heal ourselves. Rather, in such times, as the Good Doctor Davidson knew, we must heal one another.

Richard B. Weinberg, MD
The Bowman Gray School of Medicine
Winston-Salem, NC 27157

The Will to Be Healthy

Karl Barth

Karl Barth (b. 1886, d. 1968) was a Swiss Reformed theologian who perhaps more than any other theological thinker set the tone and the questions for theology in the twentieth century. His "Commentary on the Romans" spoke to a generation whose optimism for the human prospect had been destroyed by two world wars. Like Tillich he found himself in opposition to Hitler. His activity in drafting the Barmen Declaration, which critiqued National Socialism, forced him to leave a teaching post in Bonn, Germany. He then carried on his theological work in Basel, in his native Switzerland. For Barth, ethics is about understanding the human story as grounded in God's story. In the Biblical narrative we meet the commanding God, knowable to us in Jesus Christ as Creator, Redeemer, and Liberator. God, the commander of humankind, wills human freedom, the freedom to relate to God and fellow human beings, and thus the freedom to act out the stories of their lives as the unity of body and soul.

The excerpt below spells out the implications of the freedom that humans have been granted for living out their life stories for understanding health. Health is to be understood as being of the whole person, body and soul. Health is not an end in itself. It is the will to live out one's life story, body and soul. How is this will best supported? What is the role of the physician? Why must my will for health involve concern for the health of my neighbor? (English spelling has been kept in the following text.)

Health as Strength to Live Out One's Story

Let us now raise the question of respect for life in the human sphere. In its form as the will to live, it will also include the will to be healthy. The satisfaction of the needs of the impulses corresponding to man's vegetative and animal nature is one thing, but health, although connected with it, is quite another. Health means capability, vigour and freedom. It is strength for human life. It is the integration of the organs for the exercise of psycho-physical functions...

If man may and should will to live, then obviously he may and should also will to be healthy and therefore to be in possession of this strength too. But the concept of this volition is problematical for many reasons and requires elucidation. For somehow it seems to be part of the nature of health that he who possesses it is not conscious

From Karl Barth, *Church Dogmatics*, III/4, trans. A. T. Mackay *et al.* (Edinburgh: T&T Clark, 1961), pp. 357-63. Used by permission.

of it nor preoccupied with it, but hardly ever thinks about it and cannot therefore be in any position to will it...

If this is so, we must ask whether a special will for health is not a symptom of deficient health which can only magnify the deficiency by confirming it. And a further question which might be raised with reference to this will is whether we can reasonably affirm and seek health independently, or otherwise than in connexion with specific material aims and purposes...

Yet included in the will to live there is a will to be healthy which is not affected by these legitimate questions but which, like the will to live, is demanded by God and is to be seriously achieved in obedience to this demand. By health we are not to think merely of a particular physical or psychical something of great value that can be considered and possessed by itself and therefore can and must be the object of special attention, search and effort. Health is the strength to be as man. It serves human existence in the form of the capacity, vitality and freedom to exercise the psychical and physical functions, just as these themselves are only functions of human existence. We can and should will it as this strength when we will not merely to be healthy in body and soul but to be man at all: man and not animal or plant, man and not wood or stone, man and not a thing or the exponent of an idea, man in the satisfaction of his instinctive needs, man in the use of his reason, in loyalty to his individuality, in the knowledge of its limitations, man in his determination for work and knowledge, and above all in his relation to God and his fellowmen in the proffered act of freedom. We can and should will this, and therefore we can and should will to be healthy. For how can we will, understand or desire the strength for all this unless in willing it we put it into operation in the smaller or greater measure in which we have it? And in willing to be man, how can we put it into operation unless we also will and seek and desire it? We gain it as we practise it. We should therefore will to practise it. This is what is demanded of man in this respect.

Though we cannot deny the antithesis between health and sickness when we view the problem in this way, we must understand it in its relativity. Sickness is obviously negative in relation to health. It is partial impotence to exercise those functions. It hinders man in his exercise of them by burdening, hindering, troubling and threatening him, and causing him pain. But sickness as such is not necessarily impotence to be as man. The strength to be this, so long as one is still alive, can also be the strength and therefore the health of the sick person. And if health is the strength for human existence, even those who are seriously ill can will to be healthy without any optimism or illusions regarding their condition. They, too, are commanded, and it is not too much to ask, that so long as they are alive they should will this, *i.e.*, exercise the power which remains to them, in spite of every obstacle. Hence it seems to be a fundamental demand of the ethics of the sick bed that the sick person should not cease to let himself be addressed, and to address himself, in terms of health and the will which it requires rather than sickness, and above all to see to it that he is in an environment of health. From the same standpoint we cannot count on conditions of absolute and total health, and therefore on the existence of men who are already healthy and do not need the command to will to be so. Even healthy people have great need of the will for health, though perhaps not of the doctor. Conditions of relative and subjectively total ease in relation to the psycho-physical functions of life may well exist. But whether the man who can enjoy such ease is healthy, *i.e.*, a man who lives in the power to be as man, is quite another question which we need only ask, and we must immediately answer that in reality he may be severely handicapped in the exercise of this power, and therefore sick, long before this makes itself felt in the deterioration of his organs or their functional disturbance, so that he perhaps stands in greater need of the summons that he should be healthy than someone who already suffers from such deterioration and disturbance and is therefore regarded as sick in soul or body or perhaps both. And who of us has not constantly to win and possess this strength? A fundamental demand of ethics, even for the man who seems to be and to a large extent really is "healthy in body and soul," is thus that he should not try to evade the summons to be healthy in the true sense of the term.

The Story of Body and Soul

On the same presupposition it will also be understood that in the question of health we must differentiate between soul and body but not on any account separate the two. The healthy man, and also the sick, is both. He is the soul of his body, the rational soul of his vegetative and animal body, the ruling soul of his serving body. But he is one and the same man in both, and not two. Health and sickness in the two do not constitute two divided realms, but are always a single whole. It is always a matter of the man himself, of his greater or lesser strength, and the more or less serious threat of ever increasing impotence. It is he who has been predominantly ill and he who may be predominantly well. Or it is he who must perhaps go the opposite way from predominant health to predominant sickness. It is he who is on the way from the one or the other. Hence he does not have a specific healthy or sick life of the soul with particular dominating or subjugated, unresolved or resolved inclinations, complexes, ties, prohibitions and impulses, and then quite apart from this, in health or sickness, in the antithesis, conflict and balance of the two, an organic vegetative and animal life of the body. On the contrary, he lives the healthy or sick life of his soul in his body and with the life of his body, so that in both, and in their mutual relationship, it is a matter of his life's history, his own history. Again, he does not have a specific physical life in the sound or disordered functions of his somatic organs, his nervous system, his blood circulation, digestion, urination and so on, and then in an upper storey a separate life of the soul. But he lives the healthy or sick life of his body together with that of his soul, and again in both cases, and in their mutual relationship, it is a matter of his life's history, his own history, and therefore himself. And the will for health as the strength to be as man is obviously quite simply, and without duplication in a psychical and physical sphere, the will to continue this history in its unity and totality. A man can, of course, orientate himself seriously, but only secondarily, on this or that psychical or physical element of health in contrast to sickness. But primarily he will always orient himself in this contrast on his own being as man, on his assertion, preservation and renewal (and all this in the form of activity) as a subject. In all his particular decisions and measures, if they are to be meaningful, he must have a primary concern to confirm his power to be as man and to deny the lack of power to be this. In all stages of that history the question to be answered is: "Wilt thou be made whole?" (Jn. 5⁶), and not: "Wilt thou have healthy limbs or be free of their sickness?" The command which we must always obey is the command to stand upright and not to fall.

From exactly the same standpoint again there can be no indifference to the concrete problems of getting and remaining well. If in the question of health we were concerned with a specific psychical or physical quantity, we might be interested at a distance in the one or the other, and seek health and satisfaction first in psychology and then in a somatic form of healing, only to tire no less arbitrarily of one or the other or perhaps both, and to let things take their course.

But if on both sides it is a matter of the strength to be as man, on both sides we are free from the anxious or fanatical expectation that real decisions can and must be made, but also free to give to the psychical and physical spheres the attention due to them in this respect because they are the field on which the true decisions of the will for health must be worked out. It is precisely in the continuation of his life of soul and body that the history of man must continue in the strength to be as man. What he can do for the continuation and therefore against every restriction of his life of soul and body, he ought to will to do if he is to be healthy, if he is to live in this strength, and if his history is to proceed in the strength of his being as man. In order that this strength may not degenerate into a process in which he is only driven as an object and is therefore no longer man, in order that he may remain its subject and therefore man, he must be on the watch and active for the continuation and against the constriction of his psychical and physical life. The fact that he wills to rise up and stand in this power, and not to fall into weakness, is not in the least decided by the various measures which he might adopt to maintain and protect his psychical and physical powers. He could adopt a thousand measures of this kind with full zeal and skill, and yet not possess the will to maintain this strength, thus lacking the will for health and falling in spite of all his efforts. But if he possesses the will to win and maintain this strength, it is natural that he should be incidentally concerned to take the necessary precautions to preserve and protect his psychical and physical powers, and this in a responsible and energetic way in which the smallest thing is not too small for him nor the greatest too great.

How Best Support the Story of Body and Soul?

At this point, therefore, we may legitimately ask, and must do so in all seriousness, what is good, or not good, or more or less good, for the soul and body. There is a general and above all a particular hygiene of the psychical and physical life concerning the possibilities and limitations of which we must all seek individual clarity by investigation and experience and also by instruction from a third party, and to which we must all keep in questions of what we may or may not do. In such a hygiene God's gifts of sun, air and water will be applied as the most important factors, effective positively in the psychical no less than the physical sphere. Hygiene is the foundation of every prophylactic against possible illness, as it is also the main basis of therapy where illness has already commenced. We have to realise, however, that in all the negative or positive measures which may be taken it is a matter of maintaining, protecting and restoring not merely a strength which is necessary and may be enjoyed in isolation, but the strength even to be at all as man. It is because so much is at stake, because being as man is a history enacted in space and developing in, with and by the exercise of the psychical and physical functions of life, that attention is demanded at this point and definite measures must be incidentally taken by all of us. Sport may also be mentioned in this connexion. But sport has, legitimately, other dimensions, namely, those of play, of the development of physical strength and of competition, so that it may even constitute a threat to health in the true sense of the term as it now concerns us. We shall thus content ourselves with the statement that sport may form a part of hygiene, and therefore ought to do so in specific instances.

The Role of the Doctor

The question has often been raised, and will never find a wholly satisfactory answer, whether the measures to be adopted in this whole sphere really demand the consultation of a doctor. The doctor is a man who is distinguished from others by his general knowledge of psychical or physical health or sickness on the basis of tradition, investigation and daily renewed and corrected experience. He is thus in a position to pass an objective verdict on the psychical or physical health or sickness of others. He is capable of assisting them in their necessary efforts to maintain or regain health by his advice or orders or even, if necessary, direct intervention. What objections can there be to consulting a doctor? If we acknowledge the basic fact that we are required to will the strength to be as man, that we are thus required to will psycho-physical forces, and that we are thus commanded to take all possible measures to maintain or preserve this basic power, there seems to be no reason why consultation of a doctor should not find a place among these measures. This is the wise and prudent verdict of Ecclesiasticus in a famous passage (c. 38): "For of the Most High cometh healing... the Lord has created medicines out of the earth, and he that is wise will not abhor them.... And he has given men skill that he might be honoured in his marvellous works. With such doth the physician heal men, and taketh away their pains. Of such doth the apothecary make a confection; and of his works there is no end, and from him is peace over all the earth" (vv. 2 ff.).[1] Therefore, "give place to the physician, for the Lord has created him; let him not go from thee, for thou hast need of him. There is a time when in their hands there is good success. For they shall also pray unto the Lord, that he would prosper that which they give for ease and remedy to prolong life" (vv. 12 ff.).

What do we have against the medical man? Apart from a general and illegitimate passivity in matters of health and sickness, the main point seems to be that there are reasons to suspect the objectivity of the knowledge, diagnosis and therapy of a stranger to whom we are required to give place and confidence at the very heart of our own history, handing over to him far-reaching powers of authority and instruction. The more a man understands the question of health and sickness correctly, i.e., the question of his own strength to be as man and therefore of the continuation of his own life history, the more he will entertain this kind of suspicion in relation to the doctor, not in spite of but just because of his science as general knowledge, and the objectiveness of his verdict, orders and interventions. Is not health or sickness, particularly when it is understood as strength or weakness to be as man, the most subjective thing that there is? What can the stranger with his general science know of this strength or weakness of mine? How can he really help me? How can I surrender myself into his hands?

Yet this form of argument, and the suspicion based upon it, is quite mistaken, and Ecclesiasticus is in the right against it. For it rests on a misunderstanding in which the doctor himself may share through a presumptuous conception of his position, but which may well exist only on the part of the suspicious patient. Health in the true sense of the term as strength to be as man is not to be expected from any of the measures which can be adopted in the sphere of psychical and physical functions as a defence against sickness or for the preservation or restoration of health. There exists, more perhaps in the imagination of others than on the part of experts, or at any rate of genuine and serious experts, a medical and especially in our own day a psychological totalitarianism and imperialism which would have it that the doctor is the one who really heals. In this form, he must truly be warded off as an unpleasant stranger. There is, in fact, an ancient and in itself interesting connexion between medical and priestly craft. But both doctors and others are urgently asked not to think of the medical man as occupying the position and role of a priest. In all these or similar presumptuous forms, he will probably not be able to help even in the sphere and sense in which he might actually do so. It was probably in some such form that he confronted the woman of whom it is written in Mk. 5[26]: "She had suffered many things of many physicians, and had spent all that she had, and was nothing bettered, but rather grew worse." But in his true form, why should not the doctor be the man who is really able to assist others in his own sphere? And why should he not be looked upon in this way even when he perhaps appears in that perverted form?

In what way can he help? Can he promote the strength to be as man? No, this is something which each can only will, desire and strive for, but not procure nor attain of himself. This is something which even the best doctor can only desire for him. And he will be a better doctor the more consciously he realises his limitations in this respect. For in this way he can draw the attention of others to the fact that the main thing in getting well is something in which neither he nor any human measure can help. If he is a Christian doctor, in certain cases he will explicitly draw attention to this fact. He will then be free to help where he can and should do so, namely, in the sphere of the psychical and physical functions. In relation to these, to their organic, chemical and mechanical presuppositions, to their normal progress and its laws, to their difficulties and degeneracies, to their immediate causes, and to that which can be done in certain circumstances to promote their normal progress and prevent their disturbance, in short, to human life and its health and sickness, there exists more than individual knowledge and opinion. Within the limits of all human knowledge and ability, there are general insights the knowledge of which is based on a history, rich in errors but also in genuine discoveries, of innumerable observations, experiences and experiments, and there are also the general rules to apply this history in the diagnosis and therapy of the individual case. For in this sphere every man, irrespective of his uniqueness before God and among men, is also a specimen, a case among many cases to be classified in the categories of this science, an object to which its rules may be applied. To be sure, each is a new and individual case in which the science and its rules take on a new and specific form. It is the task and business of the doctor to find and apply the new and specific form of the science and its application to the individual case. Hence he is not for any of us an absolute stranger in this sphere. He is a relative newcomer to the extent that each case is necessarily new. But from the standpoint of his science and its

practice he is a competent newcomer, and as such he deserves trust
rather than suspicion, not an absolute confidence, but a solid relative confidence that in this matter he has better general information
than we have, and that for the present we can hopefully submit to
his judgment, advice, direction and even intervention in our own
particular case. Those who cannot show this confidence ought not
to trouble the doctor, nor to be troubled by him. But why should we
not show this modest confidence when dealing with a modest doctor?

Ecclesiasticus is quite right to say: "The Lord has created him
too." Medical art and science rest like others on a legitimate use of
the possibilities given to man. If the history of medicine has been as
little free from error, negligence, one-sidedness and exaggeration as
any other science, in its main development it has been and still is,
to lay eyes at least, as impressive, honourable and promising as, for
instance, theology. There is no real reason to ignore its existence or
refuse its offer. How can the doctor help? Obviously by giving free
play, and removing the obstacles, to the will for real health, i.e., the
will to exist forcefully as man, which he cannot give to any of us but
to which he may supremely exhort us. Psychical and physical illness is naturally a hindrance to this will. It restricts its development.
It constitutes an external damaging of it. The doctor's task is to
investigate the particular type and form of illness in any given case,
to trace its causes in the heredity, constitution, life history and mode
of life of the patient, and to study its secondary conditions and consequences, its course thus far, its present position and threatened
progress. If humanly speaking everything depends on that will, is
it not a great help to be able to learn with some degree of reliability
what is really wrong, or more positively what possibilities of movement and action still remain in spite of the present injury, and within what limits one may still will to be healthy? And these limits
might, of course, be extended. The doctor goes on to treat the
patient with a view to arresting at least the damage, to weakening
its power and effect, perhaps even to tackling its causes and thus
removing it altogether, so that the patient is well again at least in the
medical sphere. And even if the doctor cannot extend the limits of
life available, he can at least make the restrictive ailment tolerable,
or at worst, if there is no remedy and the limits become progressively narrower, he can do everything possible to make them relatively bearable. All this may be done by the doctor within the limits of his subjective mastery of his medical science and skill. He can-

not do more, but at least he cannot do less. And in this way he can assist the will to live in its form as the will to be healthy. In this respect he can encourage man in the strongest sense of the word, and by removing, arresting or palliating the hampering illness he can give him both the incentive to do what he may still do, i.e., to will to be healthy, and also joy and pleasure in doing it. Having done this to the best of his ability, he should withdraw. He has no power in the crucial issue of the strength or weakness of the patient to be as man. He has no control over the will of the patient in this antithesis. Indeed, he has only a very limited power even over the health or sickness of his organs, of the psychical and physical functions in which that strength and the will for it must express themselves in conflict against the weakness. But if he does his best where he can, we must be grateful to him.

Social Responsibility and the Will to be Healthy

Finally, we have to remember that, when seriously posed, the whole question of measures to be adapted for the protection or recovery of the freedom of vital functions necessarily goes beyond the answers given by each of us individually. The basic question of the power to be as man, and therefore of the will for this power and therefore for real health, and the associated question of its expression and exercise, are questions which are not merely to be raised and answered individually but in concert. They are social questions. Hygiene, sport and medicine arrive too late, and cannot be more than rather feeble palliatives, if such general conditions as wages, standards of living, working hours, necessary breaks, and above all housing are so ordered, or rather disordered, that instead of counteracting they promote and perhaps even cause illness, and therefore the external impairing of the will for life and health. Respect for life in the form in which we now particularly envisage it necessarily includes responsibility for the standard of living conditions generally, and particularly so for those to whom they do not constitute a personal problem because they personally need not suffer or fear any threat from this angle, being able to enjoy at least the possibility of health, and to take measures for its protection or recovery, in view of their income, food, working hours, rest and wider interests. The principle *mens sana in corpora sano* can be a highly short-sighted and brutal one if it is only understood individually and not in the wider sense of *in sociatate sana*. And this extension cannot only mean that we must see to it that the benefits of hygiene, sport and medicine are made available for all, or at least as many as possible. It must mean that the general living conditions of all, or at least of as many as possible, are to be shaped in such a way that they make not just a negative but a positive preventative contribution to their health, as is the case already in varying degrees with the privileged. The will for health of the individual must therefore take also the form of the will to improve, raise and perhaps radically transform the general living conditions of all men. If there is no other way, it must assume the form of the will for a new and quite different order of society, guaranteeing better living conditions for all. Where some are necessarily ill the others cannot with good conscience will to be well. Nor can they really do it at all if they are not concerned about neighbours who are inevitably sick because of their social position. For sooner or later the fact of this illness will in some way threaten them in spite of the measures which they take to isolate themselves and which may be temporarily and partially successful. When one person is ill, the whole of society is really ill in all its members. In the battle against sickness the final human word cannot be isolation but only fellowship. In this present context the bald assertion must suffice.

---

[1]For text of Ecclesiasticus (Sirach) see p. 71.

On Nursing

Jerome Freeman

Things are different now.
The season of illness has come
And life's blameless mirror
No longer reflects
Your health and confidence
Of yesterday and before.
All is cracked and splintered.
The painful shards of truth
Pierce you from all sides.

Diagnosis is made,
Then treatment begun.
The doctor has prodded
And nodded and left
For the night.

Only the nurse is at hand
To help engage the darkness.
A gentle touch is balm
To your fear and pain.
There is need for sitting
And listening and caring,
Before helping you turn
And covering you with drowsiness.

The memory of your fissured image
In a troubled glass
Becomes opaque for a time
With darkness and sleep.
The nurse will be there.
The night watch is secure.

From *Easing the Edges*, Copyright © 1994 by Jerome Freeman. Used by permission.

The Meaning of Health
Paul Tillich

Paul Tillich (b. 1886, d. 1965), a German theologian, was compelled to leave Germany in 1933 because of participation with Religious Socialists who opposed Hitler. He lived out a career as a philosopher and theologian at Union Seminary in New York, then at Harvard University and finally at the University of Chicago. Tillich was a thinker who liked to explore the connections between disciplines, between philosophy and theology, theology and science, and religion and health. Tillich proposes that life be understood holistically, that is, made up of different dimensions, not separate parts. Thus, health, disease, and healing are best understood in relationship to the person.

T he difficulty and the challenge of the meaning of health is that in order to speak of health, one must speak of all dimensions of life which are united in man. And no one can be an expert in all of them. But confronting this challenge is the destiny of the philosopher and the theologian, insofar as they should envisage the whole of life. In any case, only a limited part of the immense problem can be covered.

A Logical Consideration

The title is not "the concept of health," but "the meaning of health." Concepts are defined by subsumption to a more embracing concept; meanings are defined by being brought into configuration with other meanings. This method is in many cases more adequate and not less scientific than the method of subsumption. In our case, it is definitely adequate for a very fundamental reason. Health is not an element in the description of man's essential nature — his *eidos* or *ide*, as Plato would say; his created nature, as theology would express it. Health is not a part of man or a function of man, as are blood circulation, metabolism, hearing, breathing. Health is a meaningful term only in confrontation with its opposite — disease. And disease contains a partial negation of the essential nature of man. Conversely, in order to understand disease, one must know the essential nature of man as well as the possible distortions of it. In contemporary language one would say that health and disease are existentialist concepts. They do not grasp something of man's essen-

From *Perspectives in Biology and Medicine* 5 (Autumn 1961). Used by permission of the estate of Paul Tillich.

tial nature; certainly they presuppose this nature and the knowledge of it; but they add a new element, the possibility and reality of its distortion. Health and disease are very good examples of existentialist concepts. Like theology, medicine always did unite essentialist and existentialist elements in its thought. Therefore, psychotherapy, especially in its psychoanalytic form, and existentialism have influenced each other profoundly in the last 50 years; and the idea of an existentialist psychotherapy is only a confirmation and systematization of an actual situation. Life processes include two basic elements: self-identity and self-alteration. A centered and balanced living whole goes beyond itself, separates itself partly from its unity, but in doing so it tries to preserve its identity and to return in its separated parts to itself. Going out from one's self and returning to one's self characterizes life under all dimensions, from the structure of the atom to the growth of the plant, to the movement of the animal, to the creativity of the mind, to the dynamics of historical groups. One can call this dialectics of life processes because it implies contrasting movements, a yes and a no, as in a searching conversation. And all dialectical thought is nothing but a mirror of such life processes.

The contrast between self-identity and self-alteration produces two dangers for every living being. The first is to lose one's self in going beyond one's self and not being able to return to one's self. This happens if special processes separate themselves from the whole and produce dispersion into too many directions, a wrong kind of growth, a loss of the uniting center. In all these cases (which are represented by particular bodily and mental diseases and personal disintegrations) the self-identity is threatened and often completely lost (change of personality and memory).

In reaction to the awareness of this danger, the opposite danger appears. Afraid to lose one's identity, one is unable to go out from one's self into self-alteration. Perhaps one has attempted it, but after having been frustrated, one retreats to a limited form of existence in which the self-identity on a reduced basis is preserved; and it is not only preserved, it is compulsively defended as in most cases of psychoneurosis.

If we ask how it can be explained that the dialectics of life processes are interrupted and how its flux is stopped, we may name three main causes: accidents, intrusions, imbalances. A consideration of these would lead deeply into the philosophy of life, and especially of medicine; we can only point to some characteristics of

these causes of disease, as well as to their common cause. They are
rooted in what I call the ambiguity of life and of all its processes.
Ambiguity means that in every creative process of life, a destructive
trend is implied; in every integrating process of life, a disintegrat-
ing trend; in every process toward the sublime, a profanizing trend.
These ambiguities of life produce the concrete causes of disease.
The ambiguities of encounter of being with being make destructive
accidents unavoidable, be it bodily injuries or psychological trau-
mata.

The ambiguities of assimilation of elements of the surrounding
world — in food, breathing, communication — make unavoidable
the destructive intrusions of strange bodies, as in bodily or mental
infections; the ambiguities of growth, that is, bodily growth or the
development of one's spiritual potentialities, make unavoidable the
appearance of imbalances. Generally speaking, disease is a symptom of the universal ambiguity of life. Life must risk itself in order
to win itself, but in the risking it may lose itself. A life which does
not risk disease — even in the highest forms of the life of the spirit
— is a poor life, as is shown, for instance, by the hypochondriac or
the conformist.

Health, Disease, and Healing
Under the Different Dimensions of Life

When I spoke of dimensions of life, there was implied a rejection
of the phrase "levels of life." This must now be made explicit. Man
should not be considered as a composite of several levels, such as
body, soul, spirit, but as a multidimensional unity. I use the
metaphor "dimension" in order to indicate that the different qualities of life in man are present within each other and do not lie alongside or above each other. One can expediently, but not necessarily,
distinguish the physical, the chemical, the biological, the psychological, the mental, and the historical dimensions. Different distinctions as well as more particular ones are quite possible. What is
important, however, is to see that they do not lie alongside, but
within each other, as in the metaphor "dimension" the dimensional lines cross each other in one point.

This point, in our consideration, is man. He is multidimensional
unity; all dimensions, distinguishable in experienced life, cross in
him. In every dimension of life, all dimensions are potentially or
actually present. In the atom only one of them is actual. In man all

of them are actually present; he does not consist of levels of being, but he is a unity which unites all dimensions. This doctrine stands against the dualistic theory which sees man as composed of soul and body; or body and mind; or body, soul, and spirit, etc. Man is one, uniting within himself all dimensions of life-an insight which we partly owe to the recent developments of medicine, especially psychiatry.

As confirmation of this idea, one may refer to "psychosomatic" medicine. But although this is not incorrect, one should not forget that a hyphen between "psycho" and "somatic" represents the statement of a problem and not a solution.

The multidimensional unity of life in man calls for a multidimensional concept of health, of disease, and of healing, but in such a way that it becomes obvious that in each dimension all the others are present.

I shall follow the series of dimensions as indicated before and in each case show the meaning of health and disease and the function of healing as determined by the ideas of health and disease in what one could call a philosophy of life in medical terms.

Mechanical Dimension

Under the predominance of the physical dimension, health is the adequate functioning of all the particular parts of man. Disease is the non-functioning of these parts because of incidents, infections and imbalances. Healing, then, is the removal of the diseased parts or their mechanical replacement surgery. The prevalence of surgery since the Renaissance is based on an image of man (classically formulated by Descartes) which views him as a well-functioning body-machine, the disabled parts of which are removed or replaced so that after successful surgery, health means the functioning of the machine with reduced or artificially strengthened force. Analogies to bodily surgery in the other dimensions can be found, for instance in the removal of elements in the psychological makeup of a person by psychotherapeutic methods. The patient is healed but reduced in power of being. A conspicuous case in which bodily surgery and psychological reduction are united is lobotomy, the total being reduced to a rather low functioning, but in some respect being healed. And under the dimension of the spirit there can also be found an analogy in the moral and educational repressing of vital trends which have become infected or imbalanced, and dangerous for the whole. But such healing of the person is surgery; its healing is reduction of the power of being.

Chemical Dimension

There is no bodily surgery which does not consider the chemical processes in the body that is operated on. Health in this dimension is the balance of chemical substances and processes in a living organism. Here, reduction by sedatives and increase by adding stimulating substances to the organism are equally important. But it is not full healing in either case. The present drug-medicine fashion puts before us a profound problem. If it is possible to determine the self-altering as well as the self-preserving life processes in a living being from the dimension of chemism, what does this mean for the dimensions of the psychological, the spiritual, and the historical? In answering this, one must realize that even if we imagined the total determination of individuals on this basis as possible, the question would remain: What about the chemism of those who determine the chemical composition of others? Who decides? Here the dimension of health in the social-historical structure — with its presuppositions of spirit, morality, culture, and religion — appears in the health idea of the "brave new world."In this idea of human health, self-alteration is reduced to a minimum and life dries up.

Biological Dimension

Disregarding these extremes, which are threats on the horizon of our life, we must consider the biological dimension in which the balance is achieved between self-alteration and self-preservation. This is done by acts in which the total organism in its relation to environment and world is the object of healing, as for instance through rest, awakening of interest, increased movement, change of food and climate, etc. This is well expressed in the word "recreation," which indicates that the created vitality was stopped either in its power of going out beyond itself or in its power of returning to itself. Either the life processes had been reduced to routine existence or they were excited by the innumerable stimuli of daily life. Here a new dimension appears. The attempt to recreate life in the biological dimension demands the inclusion of the problem of health in the dimension of self-awareness — the psychological.

Psychological Dimension

Health in the dimension of self-awareness shows the dialectical structure of life processes most clearly. The processes of psychological growth demand self-alteration in every moment — in receiving reality, in mastering it, in being united with parts of it, in changing it, etc. But in all this a risk is involved, and this accounts for the reluctance to take all these encountered pieces of reality into one's centered self; thus the desire to withdraw into a limited reality becomes effective. One is afraid of going out and one defends compulsively the limited place to which one has retired. Something went wrong in the process of pushing ahead. And now a reduced health is unconsciously produced. The reduced health of the neurotic is the limited health he is able to reach — but reality makes him aware of the dangers of his limitation and so he wants to overcome the limits with the help of the analyst. If in reaching some degree of liberation, reality shows itself to him irrefutably, the question arises whether the neurotic can face reality. Often he can, sometimes he cannot; and it is left to the judgment of the healer whether he shall even try to heal if the result is so ambiguous.

We can compare the causes of psychological diseases with the causes of bodily diseases. Traumatic experiences stand in analogy to accidents (and are sometimes caused by accidents) and are the intrusion of forces which remain alongside the centered self as strange elements which are not taken into the center. Healing means helping to make somebody aware of these inhibitions of the outgoing processes and accepting the fact of limited health, because if it is accepted, its compulsory form is undercut and openness for pushing ahead becomes possible. Then, of course, the danger arises that the outgoing process may become so uninhibited that the return is stopped and self-identity is destroyed.

Spiritual Dimension

Again we are in the situation that we have separated the dimension of self-awareness from the dimension of spirit ("spirit," with a small s designating the life in meanings and values inherent in morality, culture, and religion). In these three functions of the spirit, the problem of health receives another depth and breadth, which then, conversely, is decisive for all the preceding dimensions. Morality is the self-actualization of the person in his centered encounter with the other person. This act is the basis of life in the dimension of the spirit. It is not the subjection to a law from God or man, but it is the actualization of what we potentially are, of our created nature. Its distortion in the line of outgoing is legalistic repression of parts of our being. Its distortion in the line of self-identity as a person is the lawless explosion of all possibilities.

Here the psychotherapeutic problem becomes the moral problem of the person and his self-actualization. And healing is the power of overcoming both distortions. But the healing of the spirit is not possible by good will, because the good will is just that which needs healing. In order to be healed, the spirit must be grasped by something which transcends it, which is not strange to it, but within which is the fulfillment of its potentialities. It is called "Spirit" (with a capital S). Spirit is the presence of what concerns us ultimately, the ground of our being and meaning. This is the intention of religion but it is not identical with religion. For as a function of the human spirit and as a realm of human activities, religion also stands under the dialectics of all life and under its ambiguities and, because its claims are higher, is even more profound than the others. Religious health is the state of being grasped by the Spirit, namely the Divine Presence, enabling us to transcend our religion and to return to it in the same experience. Unhealthy religion is the state of being enslaved — socially or personally — by a concrete religious system, producing bigotry, fanaticism, inordinate self-destructive ecstasy, dogmatism, ritualism. But neither is it healthy if in the break-through out of all this one loses the identity of a personal and communal religious center.

It must be added here that the healing power of the Spiritual Presence is far removed from the magic practice of "faith-healing." There is such a thing, a magic force from man to man. And without doubt the magic influence of the healer on the patient or of the patient upon himself is an element in most forms of healing. (Magic: the impact of one unconscious power upon another one.) But this is not the healing power of being centered in the universal, the divine center.

Here again the question arises how the healing helper, in most cases the minister or priest, can judge (like the psychoanalyst) whether the self-restriction to a religion of limited health (accepting authority, relying on a conversion experience) should be accepted or revealed in its limitation; and the same question arises in a well-established remoteness from a concrete religion. When is conversion required for Spiritual health?

Historical Dimension

When dealing with the cultural function in the light of the idea of health, we are driven to the last of the dimensions of life, the historical. The decisive question here is: To what degree is personal health possible in a society which is not a "sane society" (Erich Fromm)? "By creating a sane society" is an inadequate answer: first, because it disregards the ambiguities of historical existence which can be conquered only fragmentarily; second, because it overlooks the fact that without personal health in the leading groups, no social health is possible (the communist society). The cultural situation of a society has the same dialectics — the inhibition against pushing forward or the impossibility of returning to a guiding set of symbols. The unsolved situation in this respect is partly the result, partly the cause of the lack of health in all the other dimensions. But this goes beyond our limited subject.

Healing, Separated and United

The road through the many dimensions, and the meaning of health within them, has shown (1) that the dialectics of life processes are the same under each dimension; (2) that in each of them the others are presupposed; (3) that there is always a fulfilling and a reducing idea of health; (4) that complete healing includes healing under all dimensions.

This raises the question of the justification of limited healing. Human finitude makes particular healing necessary. The hurt finger requires surgical or chemical help, the physically healthy neurotic requires psychotherapeutic help. There are special helpers and healing methods called for under every dimension. But this independence of particular ideas of health and healing is limited by the mutual within-each-otherness of the dimensions. This is partly untrue to the human situation and leads to a phenomenon I would call "unhealthy health." It comes about if healing under one dimension is successful but does not take into consideration the other dimensions in which health is lacking or even imperilled by the particular healing. Successful surgery may produce a psychological trauma; effective drugs may calm down an uneasy conscience and preserve a moral deficiency; the well-trained, athletic body may contain a neurotic personality; the healed patient of the analyst may be sick through a lack of an ultimate meaning of his life; the conformist's average life may be sick through inhibited self-alteration; the converted Christian may suffer under repressions which produce fanaticism and may explode in lawless forms; the sane society may be the place where the pressure of the principles of its sanity may produce psychological and biological disruptions by the desire for creative insanity.

Particular healing is unavoidable, but it has the tendency to provoke diseases in another realm.

Thus, it is important for healers always to cooperate in every healing situation. This requirement was embodied in the ideal of the *soter*, the saviour (precisely, "the healer") who makes healthy and whole. The word has been applied to medical men, to gods of healing, to great rulers, to divine-human mediators. They all were considered to be healers. But the ideal was the one healer, the saviour, whose healing powers indicate the coming of the new eon. This is the background of the New Testament accounts of healing which should not be taken as miracle stories, but as stories pointing to the universal healer.

This mythological symbol, which was applied to the man Jesus, shows the unity of the religious and the medical most clearly. And if salvation is understood in the sense of healing, there is no conflict between the religious and the medical, but the most intimate relation. Only a theology which has forgotten this relation, and sees salvation as the elevation of the individual to a heavenly place, can come into conflict with medicine. And only a medicine which denies the non-biological dimensions of life in their significance for the biological dimension (including its physical and chemical conditions) can come into conflict with theology. But an understanding of the differences as well as the mutual within-each-otherness of the dimensions can remove the conflict and create an intensive collaboration of helpers in all dimensions of health and healing.

The concept of health cannot be defined without relation to its opposite — disease. But this is not only a matter of definition. In reality, health is not health without the essential possibility and the existential reality of disease. In this sense, health is disease conquered, as eternally the positive is positive by conquering the negative. This is the deepest theological significance of medicine.

Care and the Elderly
Rev. Henri J. M. Nouwen

Introduction

A minister is called to care, to care for his people, to care for his people in the name of the Lord. This sounds rather obvious, quite acceptable and clearly biblical. But still . . . every time we try to give care its central place in our lives as ministers, the obvious proves less acceptable, the acceptable less biblical and the biblical less obvious than we had thought.

I am very glad for the opportunity to speak about care and the elderly because of my conviction that it is exactly in our care for the elderly that the real nature of care reveals itself to us. For, although care for the elderly is in no way different from care of children, adolescents, young adults and middle-aged people, it has the unique potential to unmask the illusion of the obvious and acceptable and to criticize our often unconscious misconceptions about ministry.

Thus, ministry to the elderly starts by allowing the elderly to minister to us and care for the elderly starts by creating in us the space where care can be recognized in its real nature. The millions of elderly, not only those whose physical and mental vitality allows them to articulate their needs, but also, and even more, those who have become silent by loneliness and isolation, carry with them a great treasure of collective wisdom, which needs to be continually discovered and held in esteem.

It is about the wisdom that I would like to speak. I will do this by asking your attention to two questions: (1) What do the elderly teach us about care? and (2) How do we offer care to the elderly? After having responded to these two questions. I hope to conclude with a remark about care and the Gospel.

I. What do the elderly teach us about care?

A. Care versus cure.

The elderly remind us, in many ways, that care is distinctly different from cure. In our contemporary society this is far from obvious and certainly not very acceptable. We live in a world in which people are more concerned with cure than with care. What we want is to bring about changes, to make a visible difference. To be a pro-

From "Care and the Elderly," in Carol Lefevre and Peggy Lefevre (eds.), *Aging and the Human Spirit: A Reader in Religion and Gerontology, (2nd Ed.).* Exploration Press, Chicago, 1985. Used by permission of Nouwen estate.

fessional means to master the skills with which we can repair what
is broken, put together what has fallen apart, reunite what is dis-
joined, restore what has decayed, and heal what is ill. In short, to be
a professional is to be someone who cures. Doctors are considered
to be good doctors when their patients who entered a hospital on
stretchers can leave it on their own feet. Psychologists are called
competent when their clients feel less confused after treatment than
before. Social workers are seen as capable when their interventions
make a difference for the life of the community. Also ministers are
praised according to successes of their programs and projects. In all
this the main question is: How much cure can we bring about? It is
our accomplishments, our achievements, which count. They make
us feel at home in this world and they give us a sense of being "with
it."

But slowly, imperceptibly, maybe, we have made our sense of
"self" dependent not on who we are, but on what we do, not on our
inner strength, but on the results of our work, not on our personal
integrity, but on the praise or blame of our milieu. Thus, without
even realizing it, our altruistic concern to cure the ills of others has
made us so much oriented toward success that we have become
what others make us; in other words, we have sold our soul to the
world. I am not suggesting that cure, as skillful professional work,
is unimportant. I am only saying that, when the ability to bring
about changes in the lives of others becomes the criterion of our
sense of self and therefore of our vocation, we pervert the basis of
our ministry and endanger our own spiritual health. This is the
great message of the elderly, not so much by what they say as by
who they are. The elderly do not offer to the professional who is primarily concerned with cure much chance of satisfaction. They confront the doctor with the limitations of his healing powers, the psychologist with the relativity of self-fulfillment, the social worker
with the lasting ambiguities in human relations, and the minister
with the undeniable reality of death. In short, they confront all who
live with the illusion of any final cure. But it is exactly this confrontation that opens the way for a constant reawakening of our primary call which is not to cure but to care.

B. *The nature of care.*
What then is care? The word care finds its origin in the word
"kara" which means: to lament, to mourn, to participate in suffering, to share in pain. To care is to cry out with those who are ill, con-

fused, lonely, isolated and forgotten, and to recognize their pains in our own heart. To care is to enter into the world of those who are broken and powerless and to establish there a fellowship of the weak. To care is to embrace affectionately those who are only touched by hostile hands, to listen attentively to those whose words are only heard by greedy ears and to speak gently with those who are used to harsh orders and impatient requests. To care is to be present to those who suffer and to stay present even when nothing can be done to change their situation. To care is to be compassionate and so to form a community of people honestly facing the painful reality of our finite existence. To care is the most human of all human gestures, in which the courageous confession of our common brokenness does not lead to paralysis but to community.

The elderly with their unique place in their own and in our histories can show us the irreplaceable value of this ministry of care. Because in their midst lies hidden the great wisdom of old age.

This wisdom says not only that all human healers have to face death, the great mocker of all cures, but also that through the love of a caring friend we can come in touch with the deeper cravings of life. This wisdom makes us aware not only of the illusion of immortality, but also shows us new life whenever someone says with a word or gesture: "I see your pain, I cannot take it away, but I won't leave you alone." This wisdom not only makes us remember that there are many doctors, counselors, ministers, priests, who offered help, but also makes us grateful for those who by their kindness, personal interest and authentic concern offered care far beyond the limitations of their curing expertise. It is this great wisdom of old age, sadly enough hidden for many elderly themselves, which needs to be discovered over and over again in the midst of our blinding world so that the elderly can be our teachers, revealing to us the great human vocation of care.

When cure is not undergirded by care, then doctor and patient, psychologist and client, minister and parishioner, are tempted to relate to each other as the powerful to the powerless, the knower to the ignorant, the have to the have-not. The false silence of a doctor, the pretentious distance of a psychologist, and the self-righteous snobbery of a minister often inflict pains which hurt more than heal the wounds they want to cure. Many people have returned from a clinic cured but depersonalized and not a few felt offended by the spiritual manipulations of those who preached them the good news. But when the humble confession of our basic human brokenness forms the ground from which all skillful healing comes forth, then cure can be welcomed not as a property to be claimed, but as a gift to be shared in gratitude. Thus, the great wisdom of old age is that cure without care is more harmful than helpful, but that for those who make care their primary concern, cure is no longer a property to be claimed, but a gift to be shared.

C. Resistance against care.

Are we willing and ready to hear this message of the elderly? It certainly is not an easy message. Who wants to hear that more important than to change the world is to become a real part of it? Who wants to confess that our good intentioned attempts to influence the life of others can make us violent and even destructive? And who wants to give up his or her claims on life, health, and happiness as properties to be conquered and is willing to receive them as gifts to be shared? To say it a little more traditionally: "Who wants to be converted?" And especially: "Who wants to be converted by the elderly?"

Let us at least realize that we carry in us a deep-seated resistance against care. This is not so strange. Because to cry out with those who suffer, to be present to their pains and to show compassion with their anxieties asks us to come in touch with our own sufferings, pains and anxieties. Is it not true that those who confront us with their many unanswered and unanswerable questions often raise deep apprehensions in us since they challenge us to raise the same questions in our own lives? When someone says: "I do not know if it is worth staying alive," the person may confront us with a question that we have not yet dealt with ourselves: and when someone else shows fear for death, he or she may ask us to become aware of our own hidden denial of mortality. I am not saying that we help people by confessing that we have the same problems and pains as they have. That is not caring, that simply is commiserating. But I definitely believe that we can only care to the degree that we are in touch with our own doubts and fears and can only listen to the story of others with our own story in heart and mind.

Those who ask for care invite us to listen to our own pains, to know our own wounds and face our own brokenness. And when those who ask for care are the elderly we are also invited to realize that all pains are acolytes of our unavoidable death. It is therefore not so surprising, certainly not in our pain and death-avoiding world, that we have a deep-seated resistance against care, a resistance against the recognition of our own wounds and our own need of healing. But it is exactly by breaking through this resistance that true liberation can take place, liberating the giver as well as the receiver of care. The great mystery of care is that it always involves the healing liberation, redemption and conversion, not only of the one who is cared for but also of the one who cares. When both come together in common vulnerability, then both experience a new community, both open themselves to conversion, and both experience new life as grace.

Thus, the elderly not only teach us what real care means, but they also show that care only becomes real in a mutuality in which those who care and those who are cared for are both aware of their wounds and open for the healing gifts to each other.

II. How do we offer care to the elderly?

We now can ask how concretely can we offer care to the elderly. I'd like to discuss in some detail three concrete ways of caring: Listening with care, playing with care, and working with care.

A. Listening with care.

To listen remains one of our most precious and rewarding forms of ministry. To listen is to become a student of your parishioner. Just as teachers learn their material best by preparing it for presentation to their students, so too troubled parishioners start understanding best their own story when they have to tell it to a receptive listener. If ministers were to think of themselves as eager students who want to learn the story of others, they probably would worry less about their techniques. Let us reflect for a moment on our own experience. Isn't the interested listener who really wants to know our story one of the greatest gifts of life? When we have a chance to tell our story to someone who cares, we are blessed. Because it is in the listener that we discover that we have a story to tell in the first place. When someone says. "Tell me more. I really want to know," then we begin to realize the uniqueness of our life and the "never-heard" quality of our story. Then we become aware of the connections between events and of the trends and patterns that have led us to this place and this time. Then we start to take ourselves seriously enough to believe that our story constitutes a unique part in the mosaic of human existence (a contribution to which we are responsible). In the eyes of the listening-receiver, we discover that we have a gift to be grateful for, even when that gift is a life full of distortions and conflicts.

Listening, however, is not a sympathetic nodding or a friendly repetition of hmm, hmm, hmm. No, it is a very active awareness of the coming together of two lives. When I listen, I listen not only to a story, but also with a story. It is exactly against the background of my own limited story that I discover the uniqueness of the story which I am privileged to hear. It is precisely with my own articulate awareness of the piece of living which I represent that I can be surprised, sadly or gladly, and can respond from the center of my own life. Thus, listening is a very active and extremely alert form of care. It might even be a listening with words, gestures, laughs, smiles, tears and touch. It all depends on who is telling the story and who is receiving it. The important thing is that two lives are coming together in a healing way. It is like weaving a new pattern with two different life stories stretched out on the same loom. After a story is told and received with care, the lives of two people have become different. Two people have discovered their own unique stories and two people have become an integral part of a new fellowship.

It will be clear that careful listening to the elderly has a special quality because the elderly have such a full story to give. Careful listening to the elderly is revealing to them the uniqueness of their contribution to the experiment of living and to receive their story as a lasting gift which transcends the boundaries of birth and death. It has nothing to do with a patient hearing of the same old tales. Instead, it is a freeing of the human experience from the chains of the individual memory and a way of integrating this experience in the common human memory which remains available as a source of learning to all generations.

B. Playing with care.

To play is one of the most precious ways of being together and creating human fellowship. To play is the affirmation of the goodness of the here and now and the celebration of the moment. We play not because we want to accomplish something, but simply because we are alive. When we play we are most ourselves, because in play we realize that all we are and all we have is a free gift. When you watch children running behind a ball up and down the street, climbing in trees, jumping over fences, trying to catch each other, hiding in self-made huts and self-dug holes, clowning with Indian feathers, cowboy hats, fire helmets and Zorro suits, getting wet, dirty and bruised . . . when you watch all that, then you might suddenly sense, with a certain melancholy, that life is a playful dance in the presence of God.

It is no secret that in becoming adult we necessarily become more human. In fact, it seems that the wisdom of childhood is easily forgotten. Play is soon replaced by competition and celebration by rivalry. Even the games which often fill our weekends ask more attention for the records of a few super-athletes than for the creative interaction of many loving people.

Is it possible for the elderly to refind the wisdom of the child in a second playfulness? To care for the elderly means to play with the elderly in the hope that by playing together we will remind each other that dancing is more human than rushing, singing more human than shouting orders, poetry more human than *The Wall Street Journal*, and prayers more human than tactful conversations. To play with the elderly is to recapture the truth that what we are is more important than what we achieve. It is not a regression to a childish state, but a progression to a second innocence in which the acquired skills and insights of adulthood are fully integrated. This second innocence can lead us to the mature and critical realization that celebration is the most human response to life. This is of utmost importance in our worship. When worship is no longer play and when all gestures and words have become deadly serious, then we have made God into another demanding boss and have forgotten that he is a loving father who calls us children and not rivals, friends and not slaves.

To play with the elderly, therefore, does not require us to become part of a card or poker game — although that might be part of it — but it means to help in the development of a lifestyle in which life can be enjoyed and celebrated. This can include walks to rediscover nature, poetry to rediscover words, music to rediscover sounds, and prayer to rediscover God. It can include all that may bring us together in a common reverence for creation and open our hearts in gratitude.

C. Working with care.

The third form of care for the elderly is to assist in the development of a new sense of work. One of the great tragedies of our time is that in human creativity usefulness has been divorced from beauty. The dominant question in work has become: "How practical is it and what does it cost?" Whole cities have been built so exclusively useful that their sheer ugliness did visible harm to the physical and mental health of those who live there. The irony of usefulness, is that, when beauty is no longer part of it, it quickly becomes useless. In the days when the houses, churches and cities were built which now attract tourists from all over the world, beauty was not perceived as an added decoration of useful things, but as the quality to which all work was directed.

To work with care means to work for beauty as the context in which people can affirm each other's humanity. I am more and more convinced of the great damage which ugliness does to our inner sense of wholeness. Impersonal buildings evoke impersonal behavior, cold and gray housing complexes create cold and gray responses of those who live in them. Are we enough aware that the feelings of loneliness, isolation, rejection and despair are not only related to interpersonal situations but also to the simple absence of beauty? Many elderly starve from lack of beauty. They often live in rooms or houses so void of nature or art that there is nothing to talk with or about. You cannot talk to bare walls, but you can converse with a painting, a wallhanging, a flower, and even with a well made piece of pottery.

Our society makes the elderly think that after retirement, work is no longer important. Our society says to the elderly: "You have become useless since you can no longer perform useful work." To care for the elderly means to dispel this illusion and to work with them for beauty. Making something, not because someone needs it, nor because it can be sold, but simply because it is beautiful might, paradoxically, give birth to the most useful creations. The life and work of many artists prove the point.

A divinity school student who enjoyed "useless" needlepoint work once said: "God created the world with all the plants, trees and animals, with all the mountains, valleys, seas and rivers . . . but God did not do needlepoint work." That seems to express very well the great value of work with care. It indeed would be an invaluable service to our society when the elderly would ask new attention for the deep human desire to participate in God's creative work and would work together with those who care to make a more beautiful world.

Conclusion

We saw how the elderly teach us that care and not cure is the basis of ministry, that all changes in our concrete life situation can only be fruitful when they are gratefully received in the context of a mutual vulnerability. We also saw how listening, playing and working are three ways of careful presence to the elderly in which the basic values of life can be reclaimed and reaffirmed.

What does this mean for the Gospel of Jesus Christ? Everything, since to care is indeed to have the mind of Jesus Christ, who "did not cling to his equality with God, but emptied himself . . . and became as we are" (Philippians 2. 6-7). The great mystery of our salvation is that God came to us in Jesus Christ, not first of all to take our pains away but to share them. He did not cling to his power to cure but cared. He cried out with us by entering so deeply in our human situation that nothing human is alien to him. To care, therefore, is not only the most human of all human acts, but also divine in nature since by caring we participate intimately in God's redemptive work. When in careful listening we lift up the story of one person into the larger story of mankind, we also connect the human story with God's story. When by careful play we say that being is more important than achieving, we also reaffirm the divine revelation that we all are children of one God. And when by work with care we create beauty in which people can live joyfully, we also realize the common human vocation to give visibility to the Glory of God in the midst of our world.

Thus in caring for the elderly we are not just fulfilling one of our many human obligations, but we are witnesses to the love of God, Whose divine care became present to us in His Son Jesus Christ, our Brother and Lord.

Questions to Consider for Preface and Chapter One

1. What similarities and differences in the response to Susan's case do you find in the perspectives of philosophy, medicine, nursing, and literature? What is the importance of story in each of these perspectives?

2. In what way is caring for Susan hindered when knowledge of Susan is compartmentalized into knowledge about her physical well-being and knowledge about her as a person? Is there an opposite danger in not distinguishing between these types of knowledge?

3. In "On Hearing the Story: A Parable," by J.W. Freeman, why did the artist, Joseph, need to know something of the stonecutter's story in order to interpret his criticism? How is this parable applied to the work of a physician?

4. "The Laying On of Hands," by Richard Weinberg:
   a. What symptoms made him anxious about his health? Why did he stop trying to diagnose himself?
   b. Why did he choose Dr. Davidson? What was there about Dr. Davidson's manner that put him at ease?
   c. In what way was the patient's story important for Dr. Davidson in arriving at a diagnosis?

5. "The Will to be Healthy" by Karl Barth:
   a. How is health defined?
   b. What all is included in the will to be human?
   c. How do body and soul come together in willing to be human?
   d. How can doctors help? What are the limits of doctors?
   e. How is concern for individual health connected with concern for public health?

6. "The Meaning of Health" by Paul Tillich:
   a. Why "meaning of health" rather than "concept of health?"
   b. Identify the role of the two basic elements in life processes.
   c. Why does he prefer to speak of the different dimensions of life rather than of the levels of life?
   d. In summary, what is the meaning of health?

7. "Care and the Elderly," by Henri J. M. Nouwen:
   a. What does he mean by the claim that the primary call is not to cure but to care? How do the elderly help us learn this?
   b. What concrete ways of caring for the elderly does he propose? Have you had any experiences of caring for the elderly to share in discussion?

Chapter Two:
Health, Wholeness, and Intervention

Arthur Olsen

"My son, when you are sick do not be negligent, but pray to the Lord, and he will heal you. Give up your faults and direct your hands aright, and cleanse your heart from sin... And give the physician his place, for the Lord created him: let him not leave you, for there is need of him." [Sirach 38:9,10,12]

"The myths of Hygeia and Asclepius symbolize the never-ending oscillation between two different points of view in medicine. For the worshippers of Hygeia, health is the natural order of things, a positive attribute to which men are entitled if they govern their lives wisely... More skeptical or wiser in the ways of the world, the followers of Asclepius believe that the chief role of the physician is to treat disease, to restore health by correcting any imperfection caused by the accidents of birth or of life."
— Rene Dubos, *The Mirage of Health*, Anchor Books, NYC, 1959.

Heeding the call to care for the health of another person, such as Susan, must engage us in her life story. This is because "the will to be healthy," as noted in Chapter One, is in its deepest sense the will to carry out one's life story. Every person, as the theologian Karl Barth observes, "lives the healthy or sick life of his body together with that of his soul and again in both cases, and in their mutual relationship."

Attention to story thus involves sensitivity to the whole person, to body and soul, to both the psychical and physical spheres of the person. As noted in the preface, the perspectives of philosophy, medicine, nursing, and literature converge on this point.

Philosophy grounds the call to care in the claim of other persons, such as Susan, upon us. Persons come wrapped in stories, not just statistical data.

Medicine needs to know about Susan as a person, not just the clinical facts, in order to recommend the right treatment.

Nursing, in order to assist Susan by responding to her needs, must draw on both biophysical knowledge and knowledge of human behavior.

Literature is the medium of the story. The role of the storyteller is to keep the audience caring about Susan.

Granting the importance of caring for the whole person, body and soul, what strategy of caring should be followed? Through cultivating wholeness, as through wise living? Or through science, as with wonder drugs and surgery? We will look at the tension between these two approaches (1) in Biblical literature (excerpt from Sirach) and (2) in Western medicine's oscillation between the ways of Hygeia and Asclepius.

The Biblical Perspective (Sirach)

As noted in the introduction, caring for health in the Old Testament is on one level a matter of duty and obedience. Human beings, created in God's image, have the capacity and the responsibility to be in relationship not only with God but with each other and with nature. The Hebrew word shalom describes the way in which relationships ought to be. Shalom is a state of wholeness which includes the health, prosperity, and spiritual completeness of individuals and groups. The health codes that regulate such matters as diet, sexual relationships, and sanitation are obviously intended to direct the community in living healthy lives. Even the prophetic calls to care for the poor and the widows can be understood as a call to care for community health.

If healthy lives are a result of right living, it would appear that disease comes as a result of not living wisely. Taken to its logical conclusion there would be no need for the physician and her bag of remedies if people would live wisely. In the passage from Sirach quoted at the beginning of this chapter, a Jew living in Hellenistic culture put into writing the question and the answer that was usually transmitted orally: Why should someone who lives wisely need a physician? The answer: Both strategies are necessary. When illness comes, the son is admonished to pray to the Lord for healing and to give up his faults. Caring for health is a matter of duty and personal responsibility. But in addition he is admonished to give the physician his place, for the Lord created him. There is a time when success lies in the hands of physicians, for they too will pray to the Lord for success in diagnosis and healing for the sake of preserving life.

The Myths of Hygeia and Asclepius

The debate over strategy, according to the distinguished biologist, Rene Dubos is embodied in Western medicine in the myths of Hygeia and Asclepius.[1]

On the one hand there is "Hygeia, the lovely goddess who once watched over the health of Athens... probably an emanation, a personification of Athena, the goddess of reason... the guardian of health." She "symbolized the belief that men could remain well if they lived according to reason."

But Dubos notes that Hygeia was remembered from myths of the past rather than an actual person. And her beliefs never truly touched the hearts of people. Her cult progressively gave way to the healing god, Asclepius.

"Asclepius, the first physician according to the Greek legend, achieved fame not by teaching wisdom but by mastering the use of the knife and the curative plants. In contrast to Hygeia, the name Asclepius is of very ancient origin. Apparently Asclepius lived as a physician around the twelfth century B.C. "He was already known as a hero during Homeric times and was created a god in Epidaurus around the fifth or sixth century B.C."

What is the best strategy for caring for the health of the whole person? For the worshippers of Hygeia, health is the natural order of things, a positive attribute to which people are entitled if they govern their lives wisely. According to these beliefs, the most important function of medicine is to discover and teach the natural laws that will ensure a healthy mind in a healthy body. These notions contrast with those of the followers of Asclepius who are more skeptical or wiser in the ways of the world. The followers of Asclepius believe that the chief role of the physician is to treat disease, to restore health by correcting any imperfection caused by the accident of birth.

Dubos' chapter on "Hygeia and Asclepius" proposes to show that these strategies are indeed complementary and that the tendency to romanticize the role of Asclepius (whether in ancient or modern medicine) is mistaken.

To those who think that practice of real medicine is essentially a modern discovery — the result of the emergence of scientific medicine — Dubos poses the provocative question, "How do we explain the success of the healing arts going way back to Hippocrates, long before so-called modern medicine?"

The following words, carved on the tombstone of Hippocrates in Cos testify to his reputation in ancient times:

HERE LIES HIPPOCRATES
WHO WON INNUMERABLE VICTORIES
OVER DISEASE
WITH THE WEAPONS OF HYGEIA

Why was this reputation deserved? Does the validity of this heritage continue? Dubos answers in the affirmative for the following reasons:

First, Dubos notes examples of the importance of and the success of Hippocrates' teaching that "man would have a good chance of escaping disease if he lived reasonably."

Hippocrates was aware that the health of a person is related both to the life of the patient as a whole and to his environment, not just to the diseased part of the body. Thus if Silenius eats cheese before bedtime and gets sick and Proclops, his friend, who also eats cheese before bedtime does not, Hippocrates reasoned that "Silenius, the man was sick, and not Silenius' stomach. As it happened, Silenius had spent a strenuous day at the gymnasium. He was tired and overheated when he ate the cheese. Thus, a surplus of 'fire' had upset his humoral balance. To correct this, Hippocrates advised Silenius to avoid strenuous exercises or to cool off before eating."

The task of the physician (the root meaning of which is nature) was "to be skilled in Nature," and thus "strive to know what man is in relation to food, drink, occupation, and which effect each of these has on the other." This meant not only understanding the person, but also the relationship of the person to the environment.

Physicians practicing medicine in the heritage of Hippocrates have carried on this understanding. It is easy for the contemporary practitioner of medicine to smile at the tradition of the practice of medicine by the fashionable English physician of the seventeenth century who "went on sick calls dressed in a silk coat, breeches, and stockings, with buckled shoes, lace ruffles, full-bottomed wig, and carrying a gold-headed cane." Yet they practiced successfully the healing arts drawing on "great powers of observation, medical acumen, and knowledge of mankind."

Secondly, Dubos observes that major developments in health improvement in the last several centuries have come about through the Hygeia approach, that is, through the practice of right living, individually and socially. In England, for example, large scale improvements in health were achieved through the recognition that the negative social effects of the Industrial Revolution had to be overcome in order to improve health. Thus public health measures, such as improvement in sanitation and water supply, were necessary to overcome disease. Modern medicine has rightly called attention to the etiology of disease. It has been an important breakthrough to look for the cause of disease, and then to seek the magic bullet to eliminate it. However, this approach fails to take into account the environmental factors that have encouraged the development of disease.

And finally Dubos contends that the development of modern drugs is not so much the beginning of a new era, as further advancement along a road that medicine has been traveling for centuries. Aspirin, for example, goes back to the work of Rev. Edward Stone who observed that people who most often suffered rheumatic pains frequently lived in wet areas. He "postulated that God in His mercy had certainly placed in these same areas some antidote for the pain. Inspired by this faith, he discovered in 1763 that an extract of the willow bark was indeed highly effective in relieving the pains of rheumatism." Over a half a century later, chemists established that the therapeutic effectiveness of this willow bark was due to the presence of a substance called salicyclic acid. This substance was finally marketed under the name aspirin.

Dubos draws on the stories of the discovery of penicillin and quinine to make the same point. The development of anti-microbial medicines is not a substitute for, but a companion to wise living.

Dubos reminds us that the discovery of antimicrobial drugs, the so-called magic bullets, do not conquer disease. His book is appropriately titled *The Mirage of Health*. The struggle to stop germs and disease is vastly misunderstood if it is assumed that health will triumph because a wonder drug has been discovered. Nor did justice triumph on the western frontier where the hero single-handedly "blasts out the desperadoes who were running rampant through the settlement." The larger context needs to be considered or the work of the hero will have been in vain. Similarly the larger context of disease treatment, represented by Hygeia and the call for wise living in the tradition of Hippocrates, is an important corrective to the hubris of modern scientific medicine.

Dubos believes that the debate between the Hygeia and the Asclepius perspectives is ongoing, and that it is present in every civilization. He intimates that the Hygeia perspective has been significantly overlooked in the past. What about today? Please reflect on a contemporary debate over strategy between Asclepius (represented by Ron Robinson) and Hygeia (represented by Mary Auterman).

---

[1]Dubos, Rene. *Mirage of Health: Utopias, Progress, and Biological Change*, Ch. 5. New Brunswick: Rutgers University Press, 1987. The argument of chapter 5, "Hygeia and Asclepius," is summarized here. The book was originally published in 1959. Rene Dubos (1901-1982), a distinguished microbiologist, was an early critic of the exaggerated claims of technological medicine. He did research in the area of infectious diseases and antibiotics. He was very interested in the social implications of technology.

Why Should the Physician be Honored?

Sirach 38: 1-15

Sirach, the author of this piece that has been referred to as Ecclesiaticus (or the church book), was a Jew living in a Hellenistic culture who in about 180 B.C. put in writing the wisdom that was usually transmitted orally. Included in this work are these verses which deal with the question — why should someone who believes in God also honor a physician?

¹Honor the physician with the honor due him
 according to your need of him, for the Lord created him:
² for healing comes from the Most High,
  and he will receive a gift from the king.
³The skill of the physician lifts up his head,
  and in the presence of great men he is
   admired.
⁴The Lord created medicines from the earth,
  and a sensible man will not despise them.

⁵Was not water made sweet with a tree
  in order that his power might be known?
⁶And he gave skill to men
  that he might be glorified in his glorious
   works.
⁷By them he heals and takes away pain;
⁸ the pharmacist makes of them a compound.
 His works will never be finished;
  and from him health is upon the face of the
   earth.

⁹My son, when you are sick do not be negligent,
  but pray to the Lord, and he will heal you.
¹⁰Give up your faults and direct your hands
   aright,
  and cleanse your heart from all sin.
¹¹Offer a sweet-smelling sacrifice, and a memor-
   ial portion of fine flour,
  and pour oil on your offering, as much as you
   can afford.

[12]And give the physician his place, for the Lord
        created him;
    let him not leave you, for there is need of him.
[13]There is a time when success lies in the hands
        of physicians,
[14]   for they too will pray to the Lord
    that he should grant them success in diagnosis
    and in healing, for the sake of preserving life.
[15]He who sins before his Maker,
    may he fall into the care of a physician.

From *The Holy Bible*, NRSV.

Asclepius v. Hygeia

The following debate was staged before an audience of students to dramatize the philosophical differences between Asclepius, the Greek god of healing, and Hygeia, the goddess of health. Mary Auterman represented Hygeia, Ron Robinson, Asclepius.

Mary: Hygeia and Asclepius symbolize the never ending oscillation between two different points of view of medicine and health in general. Hygeia was a Greek goddess who watched over the health of Athens. And she probably was a personification of the goddess Athena, who was the goddess of reason. Hygeia symbolized the belief that humans could remain well if they lived according to reason, meaning a balanced and reasonable life. Asclepius has his roots apparently in a human form. Asclepius was a physician in very ancient Greece who was elevated to the realm of a god. He represented the healing arts of curing, as opposed to hygiene or balanced living. Ron, would you like to introduce Asclepius?

Ron: First of all, I have to point out that a lot of what you've heard about Asclepius so far is wrong. And some of what has been implied is wrong.

Asclepius is not the arrogant doctor figure — the swaggering figure with the gold-capped cane; instead, he is the most caring of physicians. He is unable to refuse his healing arts even to those whom the gods have doomed to death. And that was his tragedy according to the ancient stories. When he revived men whom the gods had destined for death, the gods grew jealous and destroyed him. He was punished, in other words, for exactly the same reason that Prometheus was.

Prometheus was one of the great heroes of humankind; he stole fire from the gods, not for himself, but to give to humans, who had been left in this world with so little. The story of Prometheus, whose name means forethought, is that he had created man and that his brother Epimetheus, whose name signified afterthought, had forgotten to provide for any kind of special trait for man. Epimetheus had given all these wonderful traits to other creatures, like fur for warmth or speed to protect from enemies. Prometheus became upset with the vulnerability of humans and decided that one thing that could help humans in their struggle with the other animals would be fire. And so Prometheus went up to Mt. Olympus, stole fire from the gods, and presented it to humankind. Thus

Prometheus was established as a great champion of humankind. But what did the gods think of this? The gods perceived somebody who was setting himself up above the gods. He was full of hubris, overweening pride. And you know what they do with people who have such pride? They destroy them. Prometheus was punished by being given, as a wife, Pandora, who as you know is the one who opened that box and let all the bad things out in the world. The other punishment was that Prometheus was chained to a rock, and every day an eagle came down and tore out his liver and every night it grew back again. Suffering, real suffering, he went through. Why? Because he had the *chutzpa*, the guts, to take on the gods.

And the same thing applies to Asclepius. He acted out of caring. He had the healing arts at his disposal and he knew that he could save people and felt that he must; he couldn't do otherwise, even if the gods said people must die. Asclepius said, "I can save humans." And so he did. And he incurred the wrath of the gods, was sent to Hades, but of course he became a great hero among men. He became a god among men, a man-god. That sacrifice is not just mythological either. Physicians in the Asclepian mode in early times literally sacrificed their own lives in fighting diseases and suffering. The early historians record how physicians died more often than any other class of citizens from exposure to disease. And this kept on until really fairly recently.

Throughout Western history, moreover, Asclepius was especially caring of the suffering poor. He didn't care and his followers didn't care if the poor had no money to pay. They got by with that because there were people who had money to pay and so they just asked a little bit more from them. Take a little bit from the rich and then apply that to treating the poor. He invented this idea of cost-shifting for the common good. This is a part of the Asclepian tradition, and so I'm proud to be an Asclepian. And I will defend him to the death.

Mary: But you know, Asclepius didn't have near the power Hygeia did. If they'd have listened to Hygeia... A little more background on Hygeia: If you look at the ancient Greek and the ancient Roman mythology, healing and health was the goddess' domain until about the 8th or 6th century B.C. And from then on it vacillated, as epidemics came along. Various gods and goddesses were seen as protecting health, and if a goddess or god could not protect the people, the deity was replaced by one who could. Hygeia was the goddess of health in Athens from the eighth until the fifth century B.C.

During the 5th century Asclepius came into power. Hygeia was not forgotten, but she was relegated to one of his retinue. Usually he was accompanied by two goddesses: Hygeia and Panakeia. Hygeia really is our portrayal now of community health and preventative health care. The word *Hygeia* comes from the word meaning health. When we focus on prevention of disease rather than just treatment of disease, we're looking at the rule of sanitation, rightful living. My partner doesn't like the term, but this perspective champions a good lifestyle. Hygeia focused on prevention, the natural order of things. And if one looks at history, it is not the curing and the healing mechanisms of Asclepius that really have controlled disease. The incidence of tuberculosis declined long before there were ways of curing it or even treating it, simply by improving sanitation: pure water, pure air, restful lifestyle. Particularly the pure water and pure air paid dividends. Yellow fever was conquered by cleaning up the environment and the water. Up until World War I more fighting soldiers, worldwide, died of disease than died in the battles. This was related to sanitation and the living conditions soldiers endured during these times.

Florence Nightingale focused all her work in the Crimean War on providing a healthy environment in which the soldiers could heal. She provided them with fresh air, pure water, good food, and a comfortable place to rest, thus increasing the survival rate of soldiers. Caregivers don't need to look only to the curing aspect or healing aspect when attempting to control disease and improve longevity. Nutrition, exercise, and sanitation can promote healthy longevity.

Ron: Florence Nightingale, incidentally, is a pretty good example of the Hygeian way of thinking of things. She scorned doctors to a large extent, did she not?

Mary: She scorned doctors interfering in the nursing care. Also on nursing she says, "Doctors are to pay attention to medical care, nurses are to pay attention to nursing." In Nightingale's time doctors were trying to tell nurses how to work.

Ron: Did she really believe in microbes and germs and so forth?

Mary: No, she did not. She scorned the microbe theory. Most physicians did not believe it either. Florence did believe in cleanliness.

Ron: And yet, germs exist?

Mary: They do.

Ron: I just wanted to get that clear. I want to back up here to straighten one thing out. And that is the implication that Asclepius is a physician-god who relies upon only one strategy—healing. Let's go to this myth again, because myths have meaning. And the myth portrays Asclepius as the physician-god. He has his two daughters, Panakeia, on the one hand, and Hygeia on the other. Now, you think about what that means...he is the father. He has Hygeia representing health and prevention and all that sort of thing. And he has Panakeia who represents curing through symbols and various drugs and so forth. What does the myth mean? It means that one aspect of the healing art was represented by Hygeia. And he had two sons as well, Macaen and Polidarius, one representing surgery and the other representing internal medicine. You get the point? Myths have meanings, myths are emblematic. Epimetheus and Prometheus, forethought and afterthought, they are different aspects of knowing. And Asclepius and his sons and daughters represent aspects of medicine. Asclepius is the one who pulls everything together. When followers of Hygeia suggest that she represents a holistic approach, they've got it upside down. It's Asclepius who represents the whole of the medical art and Hygeia is the specialist.

Now, let me just talk about "lifestyle." I love to talk about that term because I hate it. You see it in the newspaper all the time. It's used because people can't think of a better phrase like "a way of life" or "the way we live" or something closer to the truth. I think the term "lifestyle" is demeaning in many ways. And it is not really representative of the way things are. Let me first tell you a little story that Mark Twain used to tell about an elderly woman who was on the verge of death. She was perplexed because she had lived an exemplary life. Have you ever smoked? "No." Ever had anything to drink? "Never touched a drop." How about food... you eat lots of sweets? "No, no. I'm very moderate and temperate in the

way I eat." And Mark Twain said, "Well, there you are. She was a
sinking ship with no ballast to throw overboard."

What does this woman represent? The healthy lifestyle. And
death creeps up on her anyway. And who do you call on in that situation? Too late for Hygeia, right? Time to call in Asclepius, because
he might be able to do something.

Mary: It's true that Asclepius may have a place. But, he's gotten
too much attention in terms of just the healing and curing... they are
so imbalanced partly because cures are always so much more dramatic then prevention. And so, society focuses all its energy, publicity, and money on cures. Some 95% of the American health care
dollars go to treatments and cures, 5% to prevention. So this lady
lived a pretty good lifestyle, although she didn't say what her childhood was like. But maybe she inherited some bad genes. Asclepius
couldn't do a whole lot with those yet either.

Ron: DNA, right?

Mary: We have not perfected gene therapy yet. We're working on
it, but it hasn't been very successful and it probably won't improve
the length of life much. It might improve the quality of life for some
people.

Ron: Well, your alternative then is to get people to change, right?

Mary: To get people to change.

Ron: And that's so easy, right?

Mary: No, it's not easy.

Ron: Look at these other people here... look at Art Olsen. I can tell
you because I have eaten with him that he really digs in and he
loves food. And look how slender he is. I mean, life isn't fair. I have
been overweight all my life... I have been on one long diet all my
life... and let me tell you, it's not just hard, it's *terribly hard* to diet.

Mary: But the rewards are worth it.

Ron: Well that may very well be...

Student: I don't like the word "diet." I think there's a difference because a diet to me is "I'm going to quit eating or cut way back" and watching what you eat maybe means cutting out so many good things.

Another student: Everybody's on a diet. When you're checked into a hospital, everybody's put on a diet.

Mary: I agree.

Ron: Well, I'm watching what I eat...I watch it very carefully. My doctor says I'd better, you know.

Mary: He does. I'll vouch for that.

Ron: It's been hard folks. This is my point. And some of you "watching your diet" are doing it out of the corner of your eye, and have no conception of what I'm talking about. My wife smokes, and she's tried many times to stop. She hates to go to the doctor to be told, "You really should quit smoking." These things are difficult. And, people will scare you to death. They'll tell you all kinds of horrible stories about what will happen if I go on eating the way I'm eating or if my wife goes on smoking the way she's smoking. There are all kinds of horror stories. The point is that you don't change your lifestyle the way you put on a new coat or a new dress. "Hey, I'm changing my style." No, it's not that easy. Because a person's life, the fabric of one's life, is woven of millions of threads, and you can't change one thing without changing others. There aren't little separate compartments: eating, drinking, and smoking. The whole thing has to change. That's the   reason I don't like the word "lifestyles."

Mary: Hygeia never said it was going to be easy. Panakeia thought things could be easier. But Hygeia never said it was going to be easy, she just said it was going to be worthwhile. Society has found it makes a difference if we watch how we live and what we do to maintain our health. We controlled many communicable diseases even before vaccines came along by what we did in terms of the environment and sanitation. During the Industrial Revolution we had what was called "Crowd Diseases," diseases that broke out in the crowded work and living spaces of people who flocked to the city during the Industrial Revolution. Human crowding also gives way to social problems. Medication and healing don't prevent that, and so we need to work on preventative aspects. Physicians need to get socially and politically involved as well as just trying to heal. The poverty and unhealthy living conditions must be combatted.

Today air pollution still exists in a different form: smog, radon, and secondhand smoke. We still have water pollution, but now it's due to insecticides and pesticides and things that we put on the crops, or it's due to big feed lots that contaminate the ground water underneath the aquifers. We still need to focus on the prevention, the environmental aspects of it, and not just on the curing.

One place where the Asclepian Model has fallen down is our overuse of certain drugs, particularly the antibiotics. They seemed to be the magic bullet. Well, that magic bullet has misfired in some diseases. We have antibiotic-resistant organisms. Penicillin was the miracle drug that was going to cure all infections. Now many infections are resistant to penicillin. Then we moved to the streptomycins and teramycins...all the mycins on the end. Vancomycin was up there at the top of the list and that was the one that was going to take care of everything that all the rest of them didn't take care of. Now we've got organisms, including some staphlococcus aureus, resistant to vancomycin. The HIV infection we've never gotten on top of. Many bacteria are becoming resistant, so now we get problems in soft tissue wounds, surgical incisions, bones. So, the Asclepian model hasn't always bailed us out.

Ron: Let me talk about that magic bullet thing for a while. Because this is the rap that comes up on Asclepius all the time. "Doctors rely on the magic bullet and they're going to have miracle drugs and everything. Well, you know, those things worked. They worked. In the last century, for example, women often died following childbirth.

Mary: Postpartum fever. After delivery.

Ron: One of the great causes of death during that century, was it not? Could it be prevented today, could it be treated today?

Mary: It could be treated, but it is even more effective if we prevent it. The greatest drop in incidence followed the introduction of handwashing before and after caring for the women in labor or after delivery.

Ron: But, suppose you can't prevent it? We keep coming back to this. What this reminds me of is the Titanic. It was to be an unsinkable ship with all these *preventions* like air compartments that would hold up the ship forever. What happened? They hit an iceberg. Now what do you need? A crew that knows what to do. Where to put the lifeboats down, how to direct people into them, how to *save people* on that ship. That's what you want. You want the Asclepian at that point.

My grandmother who died of postpartum fever would have lived probably in this age of antibiotics. My great grandfather died from a knee wound that he had suffered 17 years earlier at the Battle of Monocacy in the Civil War. His years of suffering could have been stopped with antibiotics. And so let's not knock the magic bullets. They're worth something. They are valuable.

One other thing, what about the article on the front page of today's paper?

Student: An HIV patient's health is being improved because of medication that's helping him increase his T cells.

Ron: That's right. Protease inhibitors. The summer of 1996 this all came about. Across the country there were thousands of people expecting to die. Along come the protease inhibitors and patients of HIV suddenly were saying, "Hey, we're going to live." It's a marvelous thing. Now, they may not live forever, but then, who does? Their life is prolonged. That's worth something, is it not? Is that not a contribution of the Asclepian way of thinking? I think it is.

Mary: In the Hygeian way, they would not have been involved in some of the activities that may have given them the HIV infection. HIV/AIDS infections are related to risk behavior. Sometimes the links between the risks and the person is less direct than others. Decreasing the risk behavior would in turn decrease the risk for the infection at all levels, including in the newborn infant and the health care worker. Some health care workers and physicians have died of HIV acquired in the course of their work. The very first health care worker who died from HIV contracted from a non-needle stick, happened to be a friend of my family. And yes, there are babies who develop HIV infection from their mothers.

Going back to the drugs... my great grandfather died of complications of a ruptured appendix back in 1863. My dad's younger sister died of ruptured appendix in 1926. My dad always said, if we had had antibiotics, Josephine would never have died. But my dad died of complications of ruptured appendix *because* of a reaction to the antibiotics. We didn't know it at the time, but it was a new antibiotic, it was to be one of those miracle drugs. It killed all the natural organisms in his body, infection took over, he couldn't fight it.

Ron: But would you want to give up antibiotics because you're risking that happening? I keep thinking about how many lives are saved by people who are aware that there are treatments now so that cancer is not necessarily a death sentence, which is the way it was thought about not many years ago. Simply because people can say, "I'd better go to the doctor; he may deal with this." I know of people who hid their illness, who did not go to the doctor. They were aware that they had something and they didn't want to tell the doctor about it because they thought they must have cancer and that meant they were going to die. And because they postponed treatment, they did die. I think that was a terrible consequence of our earlier helplessness in treating cancer. The very idea that there are treatments out there for some of these things is a good thing. For heart disease, strokes, diabetes, and other major killers, advances have been made, and these advances have fostered a healthier attitude, because patients don't give up as easily. They don't fall back immediately to self-hatred and regret: "Oh, if only I'd lived right when I was younger, I wouldn't be going through this." Facing up to the disease, realistically weighing the possibilities of cure, seeking help immediately, all of these attitudes promoted by the knowledge that help may be available, constitute a healthier way of looking at things. "Oh, yes, I did wrong, but now, with the grace of God and improvements in medical technology, I may get through."

Mary: But we can decrease the incidence of heart disease and cancer. It's estimated that probably 90% of lung cancer is related to cigarette smoking. So, if we eliminated cigarette smoking, including secondhand smoke, we could significantly decrease lung cancer.

What we need to do in this country is put more emphasis on the prevention without losing the treatment and the cures, because we need both of those. It is of interest that the Surgeon General has estimated that the current youth, 15-25-year-olds, will be the first generation in American history not to experience an anticipated increase in longevity over the previous generation. It is estimated the lives of that age group will be shorter.

Ron: Let me conclude by saying that I will have served my duty here if I have impressed upon you the idea that Asclepius acknowledges the complexity of health. That he is not simplistic about it. There are no simple answers either in prevention or cure. And if the healers seem on the quest of the magic bullet, all right. Not all diseases are subject to vaccines, that's true. But I can remember when in the summer time particularly in the 30s and the 40s you didn't go anywhere, you didn't dare do anything. Parents would say, "No you can't go swimming." Why? One word, "polio." And it struck fear into the hearts of children. It hung like a cloud over people in those days. And I want to tell you, for the people who lived in that time, the name Jonas Salk means a great deal. Well, we may say, not all diseases are subject to vaccines, but if that's a magic bullet, so be it. The Hygeians have an equivalent in "just saying no" to unhealthy behavior. Both approaches are equally simplistic. What we need is some kind of melding of curative treatment and prevention/right living. Finally, the reality of amazing treatments and vaccines may have allowed people to trust too much in these health strategies to the detriment of prevention, but I'm not satisfied with that and you'd have to go some to convince me that that really happens.

Mary: We need the cures. Vaccines have changed the nature of how we live with communicable diseases. Polio was devastating, and so were others: small pox, diphtheria, and tetanus. But, we need to put a greater emphasis on a pattern of living that creates a more healthy body and a more healthy life so that we don't need to rely as much on antibiotics and cures. If we can decrease the incidence of cancer and other very costly illnesses, we wouldn't need to do quite so much cost-shifting. Treatments for illnesses are very expensive. So, we need a balance.

Questions to Consider for Chapter Two:

1. Sirach 38:1-15: Why should the physician be honored? Any indications that individuals are responsible for their own health?
2. According to Rene Dubos:
    a. What do the myths of Hygeia and Asclepius represent in health care?
    b. From the point of view of Hippocrates, what is disease and how is cure to be achieved?
    c. What has contributed most to the conquest of epidemic diseases? Wonder drugs? Public health measures? Explain.
    d. What is meant by the concept of magic bullets in medicine? Why is Dubos critical of this approach?
3. The debate between Hygeia and Asclepius:
    a. Which are the strongest arguments of each? The weakest?
    b. If you were asked to participate in such a debate, which side would you choose to represent? Give reasons.

After

Jerome Freeman

After the rain, we emerged
onto front porches and sidewalks.
Some went barefoot savoring
cool grass between toes, as the air
smelled of celebration, of grievances
forgotten, of debt deferred.

Your shortness of breath seemed
less pressing as you stood lean
under glistening leaves. You looked
ready for a new project, as if
the burden of your heart attack
washed away in the storm.

Spirals of steam arose from the street
like our impulses to perceive what we
most ardently yearned for.

Chapter Three:
Health, Life, and Mortality
Arthur Olsen

"Perhaps a writer must live long enough to experience the resonance of life, the way certain events echo and reverberate down a long hallway. What time teaches is that almost everything that happens can be found to have some significance when set next to other experiences. The meaning is in the sympathetic vibrations, the resonance itself, whether the echoes sound in a single life or in the lives of many people." — Ron Robinson, "Joining the Majority."

"The Irish speak sometimes, I understand, of 'joining the majority,' by which they mean dying. As I grow older, I see more and more clearly that the phrase is not a euphemism, but rather a truism. The dead are a majority, all right: Cousin Roger, Dr. Latson, Belle Latson, the kid who wanted to watch the house move down Main Street, the family friend who chose to eat rat poison, most of my best teachers, many of my friends, people who have been important in my life, some of them the kindest, gentlest, and most honorable people I have known, my grandparents, my mother. We will join them, sooner or later. That we know in our bones. What we don't know, really, is how to live." — Ron Robinson, "Joining the Majority."

What is the most effective way to support the will to be healthy? Which voice speaks most directly to your assessment of the call to care? Is it Hygeia urging us to live wisely and prudently? Or is it the bold word of Asclepius who moves in to solve our health problems with new vaccines or drugs or the latest new techniques of surgery? Which strategy should win our support? Which voice should be heard by those who wish to improve the caring potential of our health care system?

We ourselves do not agree what the emphasis should be, as is evident from the passion of the new dialogue between Hygeia and Asclepius that we have presented for you.

Perhaps the oscillation between these two voices is ongoing because both perspectives are necessary. The question will be which to emphasize at a particular time — how to strike a balance. Each voice taken by itself is eminently reasonable. Each voice taken alone is inadequate. Of course wise living is important. More should be spent on prevention and public health. And of course Asclepius is right. We cannot just tell the child born with the AIDS virus that her parents should have lived more wisely. We need both voices.

Why is this so? Perhaps it is because the answers, as Dubos seems to suggest, are complementary, not contradictory. Each voice has an authentic ring. We do need Hygeia's persistent, if preachy, wisdom. Lifestyle is important. Modern medicine may have lulled us into the complacent view that problems of health are in principle solvable by the diligent efforts of Asclepius. Yet Hygeia alone can lead to the judgment that all illness is a result of irresponsible behavior and can be eliminated by a simple change in behavior.

In his essay on "The Meaning of Health," Paul Tillich rightly observes that the risk of illness is a dimension of the human condition. There are two dangers for every living being. One is to lose one's self in the process of self-alteration. There are risks involved in growth. A wrong kind of growth can result in various types of bodily and/or mental diseases. The opposite risk comes from self-limiting growth in order to avoid the risks that come from growth. Staying home so as to avoid contact with the diseases of another is, in the long run, a self-defeating strategy.

As we respond to the call to care, our task is both to accept responsibility as human beings for our own health and the health of our neighbors and to do so without assuming that the presence of illness is deserved, and thus blameworthy.

In the New Testament, Jesus refuses to draw a simple connection between illness and personal responsibility and to focus instead on God's concern for compassionate healing. Thus he turns back the question put to him by his disciples when they came across a man blind from birth. "Rabbi, who sinned, this man or his parents, that he was born blind?" Jesus responds: "Neither this man nor his parents sinned: he was born blind so that God's works might be revealed in him." (John 9: 2-3)

As we weigh the strategies for caring — through wise living and/or through medical intervention — it is important to learn to listen to our everyday experiences with illness and suffering. To answer the call to care for ourselves and our neighbors in illness and health requires the ability to enter into our own and the stories of others with empathy.

The essay that follows grew out of one of the planning sessions for this course. We realized that thinking about caring had to be done concretely, not abstractly. Each of us began recounting personal experiences. What it felt like when a favorite pet died. Or how our parents dealt with illness and aging.

Ron Robinson's reflections began during preparation for the course with the provocative observation, "When I was fifty I thought that God was calling in the chits." We asked him to write about his experiences. The result: "Joining the Majority: A Reflection on the Mysteries of Mortality." We invite you to read it as a catalyst for gathering and reflecting on your own experiences with the mysteries of mortality.

Joining the Majority:
A Reflection
on the Mysteries of Mortality
Ron Robinson

I.

I had not yet turned ten when I had my first taste of mortality. A cousin, Roger Hansen, who was just a little older than I, died of a ruptured appendix. Even in the early 1940s such a death was shocking. An operation for the removal of an infected appendix was fairly routine by then. But Cousin Roger's pain had not been seen for what it was by his mother and father. They had delayed in taking him to the hospital, and, worse, had treated his stomachache by giving him a laxative.

During the two weeks after Roger died, I became suddenly aware of aches and pains in my own body. I remember lying awake at night in agony over an elusive hurt that gathered in my lower right side, exactly where, as I was given to understand, my appendix was located. I remember, in my childish panic, praying. I remember asking God not to let me die.

It struck me as some kind of cruel joke that the human body had been put together with this strange thing inside, a thing about the size and shape of your little finger, the only function of which seemed to be to collect grape seeds and cherry pits, fester, swell, burst, and kill. I was used to the idea of danger lurking somewhere out there. My mother had warned me of cars; I had been raised on the streets of a little Iowa town. My mother worked as a waitress in a cafe run by my grandparents. She had taught me about the fatal results that may come from running barefoot over rusty nails, trying to pet dogs that had lather dripping from their jowls, and accepting candy from dark-complexioned strangers.

One summer my father farmed a place owned by his father, and besides discovering the delights of riding a pony and splashing in my choice of two creeks that ran through the property, I found out that country life had its perils as well. A boy could drown in a wagonload of flax, be sucked down as though by quicksand. The great white horses that my father drove for planting could kill with one kick. That summer taught me, as well, of the death that came down from the skies. A dozen times at least my mother herded my father and me into the little earthen cellar under the gray house, where we huddled until storm clouds blew over.

That was the same summer my rat terrier was hit by a truck on Main Street. We had just piled out of the Ford sedan and were starting across the street to the East End Cafe for Sunday dinner. My mother screamed and cried when the dog was crushed, and I followed her example. I remember pounding on the side door of the cafe and calling for my grandparents to let us in so we could somehow escape the horror of what we had seen. That was the first time I had ever seen death with my own eyes, and the experience drove home all the lessons my mother had given me about the threats that hung about the heads of little boys. But that there was this thing inside me, ticking like a bomb, was a new and even more frightening knowledge.

Up to then the one person I knew who had died had been very old: my great grandmother Belle Latson, 93, doddering, white haired, wrinkled as a leathery apple left unpicked into the winter, a frail, ancient doll whose death came as a kind of blessing. She had been married to a doctor, Joel Latson, who practiced in Iowa Falls, making house calls by horse and buggy in the 1870s. Sometimes, I was told, coming back home late at night, he would fall asleep, giving the horse its head to find its way back to the livery. I could imagine the buggy rattling along over wet, midnight cobblestones, in and out of the yellow glow of the gaslights at the corners of the streets. I could imagine someone peeking out a window, roused out of sleep by the hoof-claps and wheel-squeaks, and recognizing the buggy and smiling and perhaps saying aloud: "Dr. Latson again." He was, it seemed, something of a miracle-worker. In an old leather album there was a sepia photograph of a hand misshapen by a tumor the size of a plum. Mounted beside it was another photograph of the same hand, the tumor gone, the skin smooth. Dr. Latson's surgery, I was told—which was not so amazing as that it was also Dr. Latson's hand. I never ceased to wonder how that could be: Had he done it with only something to numb his ailing hand, or with no pain-killer whatever? How could he endure the pangs enough to operate? But alongside this mystery lay a larger one: Why had he, having healed himself once, not saved himself a second time. He had perished, I understood, in the midst of a cholera epidemic, struck down by the very disease he was fighting. He had been still young. My grandfather had been a baby when his father died and remembered nothing of him. My great-grandmother raised her child alone, never remarried, outlived Dr. Latson by all those decades, mostly in the same house where she had lived so short a time with her husband, and died finally, quietly, "in her sleep" as they said, like a candle burnt low, guttering, its flame grown tiny, drowned finally by the last few drops of wax in the cup of the holder.

Now inside me was the awareness that death was not only for the very old. Death had come like a prankster and had taken Cousin Roger, with whom I had splashed in those creeks on that farm that seemed even then to be receding into myth. Death had planted this thing in me that might explode at any time. I was told that dead people went to heaven, and I supposed that Roger was there, along with my rat terrier and "little Grandma" Latson. I could imagine it, but not very clearly. I was a little shaky on where heaven was and what the dead did there. It might indeed be a pleasant place, as it was rumored to be, but I was made suspicious by my mother's warnings and by the plain truth that nobody really seemed willing to die. I could believe in heaven, if only as a place where the dead cavorted as the elves did with Santa at the north pole. But I thought that there must be something I was not being told; adults were full of secrets about such things, exchanging knowing looks over my head. And sometimes adults seemed to know something they would not admit even to each other. That private knowledge, which they seemed so full of, frightened me most of all. If there was a heaven, why was my mother, of all the people I knew the most likely to get there, so afraid of dying? I, for one, would like to take no chances. Let me live, I prayed. Let me live until I am old, and then die in my sleep. Yet let me not be so old and feeble as my great grandmother, for whom age had been such a burden. Let me live then to be old, but not very old—old enough to know what it is adults know, all the secrets, and old enough to have married and to have children and grandchildren and to find what it is I want to do when I grow up, and to do it, and to be happy doing it. And, thinking that God would appreciate a little more exactness in this prayer, that He would be better able to fulfill it if it were as clear as an order for bacon and eggs at my grandparents' cafe, I set an age beyond which I was sure I would no longer care if I died.

Let me live, I prayed, to be 50.

II.

In the fall of 1985 my wife and I were invited to a friend's house for the evening along with another couple, also old friends. Over dessert the talk turned to the unpleasant choices that we all must face soon, the hard tasks before us. Although nobody said so outright, the subject was death.

Both of the other families had been forced within the previous year to deal with the deaths of their family dogs. The dogs were old, poodles, born of the same dam, in fact. Both dogs had grown feeble and incontinent at last, and had to be put to sleep. The husbands, two of my closest friends, both said that it had been one of the most difficult things that they had ever had to do, to make the decision and to see the decision through. One of them vowed that he would never have another dog. His argument was moving but, it seemed to me, ultimately unconvincing: having a pet, he asserted, put an enormous emotional strain on the pet-keepers and amounted to something like cruelty to the animal. He recited his own childhood experience of having seen his dog struck by a car but not killed outright. In picking it up to carry it out of harm's way, he had been bitten savagely all up and down one arm by the animal in its blind rage at the pain it was suffering. He allowed that the beast would have suffered in any case but declared he needn't have been a part of it. My friend is a most sensitive and considerate person, and I suspect that even today he must feel a sharp stab of pain in his arm when he thinks of that incident. He is an outdoorsman and delights in seeing animals in the wild. He was obviously distressed at having collaborated in the confinement and suffering of pets all those years. And most recently, having been forced to witness the killing of a dog beloved by him and by his wife and by his two sons, he had decided to end his complicity.

My other friend was not so extreme in his pronouncements, but he did acknowledge that we do not really anticipate such painful moments when we casually choose a pet. We do not think of what all we are buying when we make this purchase. His theme was that we tend to live without foresight and therefore take things too lightly until we are brought face-to-face with suffering and death. It was not only the death of pets he was thinking of, but the aging and death of relatives and of friends. His mother had recently died. She had been in a nursing home during those last months. It had been a difficult time for him, obviously, even though he was accustomed to managing his affairs in a very thoroughgoing and organized manner. We take things for granted, he suggested, live as though things will remain the same forever, and are shocked when things change so drastically. We find ourselves growing older, he said, and entering middle-age, which has less to do with an arbitrary number of years lived than with a situation: standing between the coming-of-age of our children and the coming-of-death of our parents. We are overwhelmed with the impression of our own fragile mortality.

As the only husband there who had not gone through what the others had so recently suffered, who still had a family dog and whose parents were both still living, I was well-warned. "You will have to deal with these things," said the friend who had just buried his dog and his mother.

True enough, I said, but I didn't want to think about it. There were many things I didn't want to think about just then. I was 49 years old. I would be 50 in just six months.

III.
The morning after that night out was a Saturday. I woke to an awful stink of feces and urine. Our dog had had "an accident" on the bedroom rug. I was about to launch into a tirade against the animal when I noticed that she was crouching oddly and seemed unable to move. She had apparently lost control of her hindquarters. I called to my wife: "Something's wrong with Indy."

Indy was short for Independence. She had been born on the Fourth of July, Independence Day, some sixteen years before on a farm near my wife's home place outside Howard, South Dakota. She was a mongrel, a mixture of Norwegian elkhound, collie, and German shepherd. As a pup she had been too cute to resist, with the coloration of a collie, muted genetically to white and tan, with some black woven in, the contribution of the shepherd, and the elkhound tail curving up over her haunches. My daughter had grown up with the dog, and the family photograph albums were full of snapshots of the two of them, apart and together, getting older. Now my daughter was 18, a freshman in college, and the dog was about as old as dogs are allowed to get. As we cleaned up, wrapped Indy in a blanket, and headed for the veterinarian, the conversation of the night before was clear in my mind. One of those hard decisions was being forced upon me all too soon.

Indy had lived with us first in a little house across from the college where I taught. When we moved into the assistant resident quarters in one of the college dorms, dogs were not allowed, so

Indy was sent back to my wife's home place, where she spent two glorious years off the leash, chasing rabbits and pheasants and occasionally a neighbor's chicken. When we finally accumulated enough money for a down payment on a house and a small piece of land of our own, we reclaimed the dog. She spent the last ten years on our little acreage on the east side of Sioux Falls. I had hoped she would be able to roam there with some freedom, but she often ran away when she was off the chain.

Twice she had to be picked up from the humane society. Once she had clawed down the screen door of a house several blocks away, desperate to get in, to escape some real or imagined threat. Twice she had attacked and killed some of our neighbor's caged rabbits, causing damage in the hundreds of dollars and stopping just short of decimating a cage containing a special breed valued at over a hundred dollars each. Even when chained, she was sometimes a nuisance. She had an unreasoning fear of fireworks, thunderstorms, and other explosive noises. Her birthday was almost without exception an agonizing time for her. We had either to sedate her or to send her to a kennel in the country during the Fourth of July holiday. Once we left her chained in the garage on the fifth of July to go to a movie, forgetting that firecrackers were likely to be heard then as well as earlier. We returned to find that she had wrapped herself around the brand new garden tractor and had completely shredded the foam-rubber cushion on the seat of the machine. She spent most of her day alone, chained or caged in a small runway beside the garage, while my wife and I taught and my daughter went to school. She didn't even act like other dogs. The idea of fetching was completely alien to her. She could watch balls or sticks thrown all day and not have it occur to her that she might go after them and bring them back. Nevertheless, she was affectionate and tolerant of our failings, and she afforded us much pleasure and comfort.

In 1980 we spent several months in Mexico on leave. Rather than take Indy with us, we boarded her at a kennel. At the house we rented in Villa Corona, in the state of Jalisco, we were adopted by a little black dog which we were tempted to bring back with us. The red-tape and paperwork were too much for us, however, and we had to consider that we might not be doing the dog much of a favor in bringing her back to share boredom and confinement with Indy. On our return to the United States, we found Indy much changed by the months she had spent in the kennel. She seemed somehow shrunken, her legs bowed out, toadlike. Perhaps she really had aged greatly in that short time, or perhaps we had just been remembering her as younger and more erect.

On that cool fall Saturday the veterinarian offered us the choice I had been dreading. Indy had a problem with the spine which denied her control of her back legs. The condition often proved incurable and fatal, but treatment which might prolong her life a while longer was possible. She might, in fact, recover completely from the condition. But then, again, she might just have her agony extended.

I elected to have her put to sleep.

I was given another choice: did I want to be with her when she received the injection, or did I want to wait in the anteroom? Here I felt I had no real choice at all. Having decided that she would die, I could not do less than to see it through, to try to bring some little comfort to her at last. The vet explained how the injection would work. It was quick, he said, and painless. It would be over instantly. She would simply fall immediately and deeply into the final sleep. Yes, I said, that is what I wanted for her.

But that is not quite what happened. I gathered the dog up and put her on the metal table. She was apprehensive: she had been to the veterinarian often before and knew that the metal table meant that she was to suffer some indignity or pain. She was shaking. She wanted out of there. I tried to calm her, speaking her name over and over in what I hoped would be a soothing tone. I held her paws. She looked at me with those brown eyes, clouded now with age, pleading with me for assurance. The vet prepared the hypodermic with cool professionalism, found a place to make the injection in her shoulder, pressed the plunger slowly and firmly. I saw immediately that something had gone wrong. Indy's eyes grew larger, until the whites showed at the corner, she yelped a few times, then she emitted a long, grating whine, something like a wolf howl, that had in it the overtones of a primitive death cry, a plaintive complaint and a warning. The howl seemed to last for minutes. Then it stopped. Indy's eyes were no longer on me but on something beyond me. It was a death stare. She was gone.

I looked away and sobbed. The vet apologized. He had not counted on the dog's poor circulation. Her veins were apparently heavily obstructed. Instead of killing her instantly, the poison had worked slowly. She had, he admitted, felt some pain, perhaps. Perhaps, I thought, she knew what was happening to her. Animals are supposed to be unlike humans in not really knowing they are going to die. I had never really trusted that supposition, however. Animals had some understanding of death, I guessed, enough to fear it above all else. The panic that I had heard in Indy's last howl had seemed to confirm that.

We took Indy's body back to the acreage wrapped in that same old blanket we had tucked about her to bring her to the vet. I dug a grave just north of the cherry tree in the orchard. I lay her in the trench with the blanket still about her, and covered her over and replaced the sod. In her later years, she had dreamed sometimes, her legs jerking in abbreviated running motions as she made little yelps. We imagined she was dreaming of chasing rabbits as she had in those brief years of freedom on the farm. Now I hoped that, if there was no heaven for dogs, there might be at least one long, lasting dream of rabbits ever pursued, of endless open fields where a dog could run free.

Her death was more horrible for me than I had ever imagined it would be. I felt guilty for having decreed her death when in fact she might have been sustained a good while longer. I heard over and over that awful death howl, saw vividly that last look of panic and betrayal in her eyes. And I wondered what other terrifying decisions lay ahead for me, and how soon.

IV.

I wrote many poems that fall and winter. I was teaching creative writing, and talking to those young, enthusiastic students always seemed to get my own juices flowing faster. Some of the poems were printed in the Mankato Poetry Review, including a long poem about that summer spent on an Iowa farm, "Cornstalk Fiddle." In it I remembered my mother herding us into the cellar to escape tornadoes and thunderstorms, and I remembered as well that she had once tried to show me how my pony should be ridden and had got thrown off for her trouble. I remembered that my mother had warned me to stay away from the rat terrier during thunderstorms, thinking animals somehow draw lightning. I remembered the dog's death and the passing of the season and the sense of losing something that could be found again only in memory.

Someone has said that writing is the act of discovering the legend of one's childhood. My own childhood seemed to open before me that fall like a vast, inexhaustible storehouse of literary subjects. I remarked to my students that they were foolish to think that they had not lived long enough to have experiences worth writing about.

They had likely had enough experience in 18 to 22 years to mine for the rest of their lives. They could, I suggested, retire to a darkened room, as Proust had, and scribble lyrics and novels for decades without further reference to the outside world.

I see now that I overstated the case. Perhaps a writer must live long enough to experience the resonance of life, the way certain events echo and reverberate down the long hallway. What time teaches is that almost everything that happens can be found to have some significance when set next to other experiences. The meaning is in the sympathetic vibrations, the resonance itself, whether the echoes sound in a single life or in the lives of many people. Ultimately the echoes touch readers and resound in them, the way undampened strings of a harp will vibrate unplucked in response to a solo horn or to a whole orchestra.

No human experience is too particular, if it is true, to lack universality. There is no folly, no madness, no bizarre act of cruelty, no noble act of heroism by any one person of which any other member of the species is not capable. Indeed, what is most remarkable about humankind is both the breadth of its emotion and activity and the compression of this infinity into so narrow a compass. When we think that the depths of depravity have been reached, someone sinks farther yet, and when we think we have seen humanity at its best at last, it is bettered. The landmarks of good and evil stand like athletic records, and will fall tomorrow or next year or in a decade or a century. And at the same time there is in each of us really not so great a distance between these extremes. A thread separates hope and despair, happiness and grief, and there is no more than a handspan between heaven and hell.

I remember attending a wake when I was ten or eleven. It was for a friend of the family, a woman who had been very kind to me, in particular, and had given me gifts including, most memorably, a red toy wheelbarrow. Her children, one daughter and three sons, were about my parents' age or a bit younger. The boys always hung around the East End Cafe and treated me like a nephew, although we were unrelated. I remember one of the sons returning in an Army uniform during the war, hardened by boot camp, and inviting me to punch him in the stomach. I remember his laughing at my attempts, and I remember scraping my knuckles on his brass buckle. Another son, also unmarried at the time, I always suspected of being in love with my mother. My father, I think, suspected the same thing. One wild Saturday night my father got into a brawl with this other son in the vacant lot outside the cafe and nearly killed him by beating his head against the brick wall of the grocery store. I have no doubt that my father would have killed this rival, if he had not been pulled off.

This family owned an implement shop in our town, and I often loitered there, playing with nuts and bolts and odd pieces of machinery, fancying that I was constructing something unique and useful. Then one night the implement shop burned down. I remember watching the orange glow of the flames from my bedroom window. There was some speculation that the fire might have been deliberately set. It was not long after the fire that the mother died.

That this woman had been a drinker was discussed openly in our family. She drank whiskey in prodigious quantities, I was led to understand, which accounted for her thinness and a kind of shrunken quality about her, as though her essential juices had been sucked out of her. One sees such drinkers on the streets of a small town, those who regard whiskey as a substitute for food, their cheeks hollow, sinewy cords showing on their necks. Why this woman should drink so was a mystery to me. And another mystery was why she had died in the way she did. I always felt like a radio detective who had all the clues, but didn't know how to make sense of them. Was her death a clue to her drinking or her drinking a clue to her death? And what was her generosity and her kindness to me a clue to?

At her wake I was seated by a large potted fern whose fronds uncurled from tight spirals and reached out to entangle me. Coffee was served, I recall, and I had some, along with a large quantity of cream and sugar, and cookies and sweet bars brought in by neighbors and served on plates which circulated endlessly and were endlessly refilled. And I listened to the talk. Most of the talk was about the dead woman. She had been a Catholic at some time, but her funeral was conducted in the Methodist church since she had committed the sin of suicide. A young blond man, a friend of the family, had been a house guest and had heard her die. He seemed particularly affected by her passing, which I thought no wonder. He wept openly and shamelessly. He had heard the death rattle, it was said, but had not known what to make of it, had not known it for what it was until later.

I had heard men weeping before in that house, during the war, when the youngest son enlisted, the last of the three to go into the service. My father had taken me along on an afternoon farewell party. There had been drinking and laughing and sobbing, most of all on the part of the youngest son, who was convinced that he would die in the war. As it happened, he saw no combat and returned unmarked.

The wake reminded me of that farewell party somehow. There was, I guessed, some drinking going on, a bottle being circulated somewhere out of my sight, and a good deal of weeping. But as the night went on, there was a good deal of laughing, as well. It was as if the mourners could endure only so much sorrow and sought relief in merriment. The wake, I saw, was a kind of farewell party, and a party was a party, regardless of the occasion. The point became less and less that this woman had died, that at some time during a black night of despair she had eaten rat poison and had thrashed about in the nets of her own casting and had at last blown her last breath in a cackle that had been heard and misunderstood by the young house guest; the point became more and more that we lived, though she had died, and that life goes on, will go on, in all of its marvelous absurdity, like an endless play in which members of the cast have exits and entrances, bid tearful farewells to go to their deaths and come back without a scratch.

That fall and winter before my 50th birthday, I was overflowing with poetry. I seemed to want to record everything that had ever happened to me and to find the meaning in all of it. I suppose, really, that I was throwing myself a farewell party, and that I was scared to death.

V.

There were more bizarre ways to die than my mother had ever warned me of. I remember reading with a kind of horrified fascination the long accounts of the bombing of Hiroshima and Nagasaki by *New York Times* correspondent William Laurence, reprinted in Iowa as they were in papers all over the country. It seems strange now to think of this nine-year-old child poring over the *Des Moines Register*, absorbing every word, in awe at the power cached in an atom, thunder-struck at the immensity of the destruction that had been set loose in the world. And yet the war had been brought to an end by those cataclysmic eruptions.

The end of the war was the end of life as I knew it. I could remember no time when there was not a war, when Franklin Roosevelt had not been president of the United States, when my mother had not worked at my grandparents' cafe. Now everything seemed to be changing at once. The war was over, Roosevelt was dead; my grandfather Latson was dead, following his mother within years; my grandmother had sold the cafe and had moved in with us, sharing my bedroom and my bed; and my father was talking of buying an acreage so that we would have more room. Once we moved onto the acreage, my mother became pregnant. I had the eerie feeling of having been plucked out of one life and plunked down in another in which innocence was lost. I suppose many people felt something like that after the war. The shops and gas stations that had been "closed for the duration" were reopened. Veterans returned with, it seemed to me, a gray, haunted look in their faces, a strange mixture of fear, cruelty and resentment. Some soldiers did not return.

At a Labor Day celebration after the war I recall seeing a strange entertainment among the carnival rides and attractions set up on Main Street. For the price of a dime or some other pittance, one could circulate around a display of black and white photographs taken in the German concentration camps: thousands of skeletal bodies, mass graves, spectral faces, gaunt and hollow-eyed, staring directly at you through barbed wire. The ghastly gallery was popular with boys my age, I remember, who were too young to be admitted to the girly shows. The only naked bodies we were allowed to see were dead ones. Morbidity was acceptable; eroticism was not.

One summer someone bought a house and moved it onto another lot across town. The route took the house down Main Street. A classmate of mine, the son of the town harness-maker, was engaged in the boyish pastime of watching the building as it lumbered along the pavement. It must have been an irresistibly grotesque sight to see a two-story house creaking past the false-front stores. My schoolmate was walking abreast of the wheeling structure, marking its progress, when a gable of the house caught on a wire strung across the street and pulled a corner of the drug store—literally a ton of bricks—down on the boy's head. If my mother had still been working in the cafe, I might very well have been watching the procession along with my friend. There had been little on the streets and alleys of the town that escaped my notice when I was an urchin among them. Now, I had graduated to the acreage, where I shot my Red Ryder carbine beebee-gun and imagined myself somewhere out on the open range.

The acreage was not without its own horrors, of course. In the kitchen of the new house my father and I sat facing each other, he with his back to the rear door, I with my back to the cellar door. My mother sat facing the window, where she could look out toward the orchard to see the plum, pear and apple blossoms in the spring and the ripening fruit during the summer and fall. One chill winter morning, with the orchard made transparent by frost, my mother watched a neighbor burn to death. The old woman had been tossing kerosene on a cob fire, we learned later, when her apron caught the flame. What my mother saw was the woman running out the door ablaze, screaming, before collapsing into the snow. After that, my mother made me change places with her at the table.

The "new" house was actually quite old, having been built around the turn of the century. My grandmother took the whole second story for herself, having helped to pay for the place. She rented rooms to school teachers for a time. She had a kitchen, bathroom, two bedrooms and a living room. She kept more and more to herself, particularly because my father resented her living with us. I sometimes felt like a rope in the tug of war between them, and I'm sure that my mother and later my little sister felt much the same way. The animosity lasted throughout my high-school years, during junior college and college, and was still there when I was at last out on my own, first as a reporter and news director and then as a college teacher. The hatred even survived the long and tortuous demise of my grandmother. She suffered a "stroke" and never fully recovered. For four years she lasted, then three nursing homes and finally back into a bed set up in the living room of her upstairs apartment. For the last two years, my mother nursed her daily. I was at Mesa Verde, Colorado, working on a research project, when she died. I'd been out of touch for several weeks when I called to find that the funeral was in progress. It was senseless for me to return then. A few days later I received, at the Mesa Verde post office, a letter which contained a program of the funeral. The photo in the program showed her heavy-set, smiling. When I was very young, I called her "big Grandma" to distinguish her from my great-grandmother. She had been grossly overweight most of her life and developed diabetes in her later years, no doubt a factor in her circulation problems. During those last few years in bed, however, she became a living skeleton whose rare flickering recognition manifested itself in a grinning death's head. One was reminded of those photographs of concentration camp victims. Among the ghosts of Anasazi on the cedar-covered mesa, I remembered and mourned.

My mother's grief at my grandmother's death was likely augmented by a great relief. She never spoke of exactly how death finally came, but she never seemed quite the same after that. One is perhaps never the same after passing such a landmark in one's life.

Even now, however, my father will curse my grandmother for having circumscribed his life and my mother's. He will return again and again to the same stories: of her having used my mother shamelessly for cheap labor in the cafe, of her having been tight with the money she got from the cafe, of her having "stolen" many of his tools, of her having had the trees about the house trimmed so severely that they never recovered, of her "predicting" her own final illness, of her leaving nasty notes of warning among her belongings to be found after her passing. To hear him, one would believe that every thing she did, even her dying, was done in spite. The dead stay with us for so long, whether out of love or out of hate.

VI.

My 50th birthday arrived right at the beginning of the spring semester. For once I was rather glad that the frenetic activity of the school year distracted me from the occasion. We had a special meal, I opened gifts and cards and smiled a good deal and thanked everyone. I had the sense of wanting to minimize the event, to shrug it off.

My parents called that evening to greet me. Neither could believe that I was really 50, that they really had a child that old. My father said he must be old, although he didn't feel that old. My mother sounded just a little worn. I asked her what was wrong. She said she hadn't been feeling well. Had she been to the doctor? Oh, yes, but he hadn't helped her much. He told her she had shingles. She asked if I knew what shingles were. I did. I knew of a man in Sioux Falls who had been debilitated for years with shingles, a very painful disease without a real cure. The symptoms went away in time, but the affected person suffered greatly while waiting for the disease to end. My mother said her doctor thought it might be a matter of weeks, perhaps months. The good thing, I thought, was that it wasn't really dangerous. I'd never heard of anyone dying of shingles.

I called my parents back a week or so later. My mother sounded more hesitant in her speech now. It hurt, she said, and nobody seemed to know what to do about the pain. There were salves and pills, but nothing seemed to help. She got no more than one or two hours of sleep a night. She wondered if I'd be down again soon. I told her I'd get down as soon as I could find a weekend free.

My wife and I had resolved to do more entertaining that year. Our house is small and packed with many belongings and is difficult to keep tidy, so we had been tending in recent years not to have many people in during the school year, when we both taught. But we felt compelled to have in a new member of the department and her husband. We planned a meal, cleaned up the house, and rented a movie to watch: *Kiss of the Spider Woman*. Halfway through the film, the phone rang. It was my sister, who was living in Sioux Falls at the time. She had just been on the phone to our parents and was distraught. Mother was in a bad way, she said. And she was worried about our father, who was not good at coping with things. Call them, she said, to see what I thought. My mother answered my ring. She, too, sounded upset, but mostly with my sister, who was talking about marrying someone she had never met, a sailor with whom she had corresponded. As for herself, my mother said, the shingles were no better, she was getting no sleep, and there were other things bothering her. She catalogued a long list of complaints. I asked to talk to my father. He sounded weary. They had been trying everything they could think of, he said, to get some relief for my mother. He was angry with my sister for introducing yet another complication into an already messy situation. I understood. He was a simple man and a man of habit, and any departure from his routine was both tiring and frightening. I offered to come down to try to help. He accepted. I said I'd be down the next morning.

That Sunday I saw my mother's shingles for the first time. The ugly rash began under her left breast and ran in a band halfway around her body. It looked truly painful, like a poison ivy scald, but still it was just a rash. However, having become something of an expert by now, she explained that the disease affected the nerves directly. My father bathed her and applied ointment daily, but she seemed little comforted by these attentions. Besides, she had all these other ailments. She was constipated, perhaps because of the pain-killers she had been taking, and there were other pains that seemed unrelated to the shingles, and she could not sleep. She wandered around the house at night alone, because my father needed his sleep and could not stay up with her. While I was there she sat in her chair and closed her eyes and seemed to doze, but after a short time she opened her eyes again and looked at me and said, "I wasn't sleeping. I was just trying to rest." I could see she was feel-

ing very sorry for herself, and I tried to buck her up, but she would-
n't be cheered. She looked at me often with a strange smile, full of
attempted bravado, but really plaintive, as though she mourned for
herself, for me, and for all humanity. Before I left I promised to come
down as often as I could. I didn't see much that I could do, but at
least I could sit up with her through the lonely nights.

The next Saturday I drove my father's car to a larger community near my home town so that my mother could be examined again
by the doctor she had been seeing. I wanted him to pay attention
particularly to one of her major complaints. She suspected that her
constipation was being brought about by some kind of intestinal
blockage. She spoke to him and was examined, and I spoke to him
afterwards. He did not see that she had anything major wrong with
her outside the shingles. We both knew what she was afraid of: cancer. But he had absolutely no evidence of that. He would not object
particularly if we wanted to take her to another doctor. Before I left
that weekend, I said I would make arrangements for her to see a
doctor at the clinic in Sioux Falls where my wife and I had been
going for years. The doctor at the clinic asked my mother to bring
in all the medication she had been taking regularly. The bottles and
brown plastic vials she gathered together filled a paper sack about
half the size of a regular grocery bag. The medication included vit-
amins that had been prescribed by a chiropractor, various prescription drugs that she had been taking for years for chronic conditions
such as heartburn and high blood pressure, medicine that had been
prescribed for her shingles, non-prescription drugs that she had
tried out of desperation because she or my father had heard from
friends or relatives that they might help. I went with her to see the
doctor. I had taken the precaution of listing carefully all of her ailments on a three-by-five note card, because one of my mother's
complaints about other doctors was that they never seemed to want
to take the time to hear her through. The doctor listened patiently,
examined her completely, and asked again and again if there were
anything else that gave her discomfort. I was impressed with his
thoroughness and his apparent compassion. He arranged to have
her admitted to Sioux Valley Hospital for more tests.

The tests were negative. My mother did not have any cancer that
anyone could detect, or any blockage of the intestinal track at all. I
thought my mother would be relieved, but she wasn't. She was
angry, in fact. She listened to the doctor's diagnosis with obvious
disdain, although she nodded on cue and seemed to be accepting

his verdict unemotionally. She had been disgusted with the tests she had undergone and confided in me later that the doctor was too young to know what he was talking about. It was at this time that she developed a mannerism that I saw often over the next several weeks. She would clench her mouth tight, grimace, and shake her head with a kind of shudder of denial, as though what she felt was beyond words, beyond any expression other than this opaque sign.

Spring was late in coming that year. Winter held on, cold and wet, through April. I travelled the 240 miles to and from my home town almost every weekend and called frequently during the week. One of my father's sisters had been helping to care for my mother and was alarmed with the change she saw in my mother's personality and thinking. My aunt suggested that my mother see a psychiatrist in Spirit Lake, a town about twenty miles away. My mother agreed to take the trip with my father and my aunt. I called the psychiatrist after he had talked to my mother. He said she was hearing voices and exhibiting other signs of mental distress. He suggested we urge her to get further help with her problems. He recounted some of the things my mother had said. She had told him about my great-grandfather Latson, the doctor. He seemed impressed. His voice was filled with sympathy and caring.

The next few weeks are a jumble in my mind. The most hectic time of the school year was upon me, and I was struggling to get through courses, get papers read, keep up with daily assignments, and at the same time fulfill obligations to my parents. In the midst of all this my sister had decided to go ahead and get married in spite of my parents' objections. In a surrealistic episode that would seem more appropriate in a Fellini movie, I witnessed the wedding in the county court house. The bride wore an elaborate wedding dress that seemed to me better suited for a church wedding. The groom wore his blue uniform; he had left his dress whites at the base in Virginia and had not guessed that the wedding would take place so precipitously. The judge delivered a little homily on the seriousness of the occasion before going through with the brief civil ceremony. The bridesmaid giggled a lot with the bride. The bridesmaid was worried that the judge would recognize her as a defendant in a drunken driving case he had ruled on a few weeks earlier. The judge spoke with the groom afterwards; he was interested in what aircraft carrier the groom was serving on. I can't remember saying more than a sentence or two, but I remember thinking how much stranger than fiction life is; if I had tried to put the scene into a novel, I would have been accused of straining the reader's credulity. Speaking to me privately later, my sister remarked that she thought her new husband "seemed like a nice guy."

Saturday, late in April. Quite early in the morning I call my father to see how things are going. I desperately need this weekend to catch up on my school work, but I feel obliged to check on my mother's health. My father is sounding exhausted, desperate. He has not slept. My mother has been on a rampage all night, he says. She seems bent on running away. In a hushed undertone, he adds: "She has matches." I'm not sure that I have heard correctly, and I ask him to repeat. "She has matches. I got some away from her, but she got some more. She wants to burn something up." He is almost crying. I tell him I'll be right down.

When I arrive, I see that my mother has changed into a person different from any I've known before. She is restless and won't remain seated for more than a minute or two at a time. She has packed some of her clothing into a plastic bag, but it is unclear whether she wants to run away or to take the bag of clothing out and burn it. The clothes are dirty, she says, and makes one of those faces grotesque with loathing, like a gargoyle. But while she babbles about leaving, it is clear that she is afraid to go outside. Something or someone is waiting for her out there, she says, and the way she peeks out through the curtains leaves no doubt in my mind that she believes it. I ask her to give me the matches. She shows me the packet of safety matches curled up in her palm, but won't relinquish it. A refrain has entered her speech: she is going to die. She has said as much before, but there seems a new certainty in the pronouncement now. I try to reason with her: she has had a thorough physical examination and nothing fatal was discovered. She tells me that I don't know anything, that the doctors don't know anything. I mention the psychiatrist. She looses a stream of obscenities that shocks me. The psychiatrist, she says, is worse than a fool. He is a bastard. He tried to tell her things that weren't true. Her eyes are filled with strange, meaningful shifts and stares, as though she hears or sees things I do not. I try to calm her down. I talk about the shoots of the flowers now showing themselves. There will be tulips, soon, and after them the irises, and later the peonies. "Not for me," she says. "I won't be here."

While my father distracts her, I call the psychiatrist again, then my sister, then a hospital in Spencer, Iowa, that has a mental ward, then the sheriff's office in Emmetsburg, the county seat.

Arrangements are made to commit my mother to the mental ward for care.

Out of the confusing scenes that followed I remember a handful most vividly. My father has gone off perhaps to get the car ready. My mother has noticed that a hem has come loose in the cuff of my father's pants. She has made him change pants and has got out her sewing kit to mend the cuff. I watch her trying to thread the needle. She can't get the thread through the eye. She wets the end of the thread in her mouth, sharpens it into a point, stabs it at the eye of the needle, misses, tries again. I offer to help her, but she refuses. She tries, over and over, with a demonic intensity. She has always been, before this illness, a patient woman, but her present patience is beyond human endurance. I watch her, fascinated, relieved that at least for the moment she is not ranting irrationally or pacing restlessly about. But as time goes on, as she fails again and again to thread the needle, I am overcome with a feeling for which I have no adequate name. In part it is resignation, in part a kind of grief, in part a recognition of an essential state of being. My poor mother, poor me, poor mankind.

VII.

If your sanity is ever called into question, you can take some comfort in the knowledge that there is a structure in place in many states to help protect your rights. Either you may commit yourself to a mental facility for treatment, or relatives may commit you, but only with sufficient evidence that you are exhibiting behavior harmful to yourself or to others. In Iowa, an advocate decides whether committal is necessary or wise.

On that Saturday afternoon, after my sister had arrived, we persuaded my mother that we were going to get her some help and got her into the car, and my father drove all of us to Emmetsburg, to the sheriff's office. My sister waited with my mother in the car while my father and I went in and signed the papers necessary to put my mother in the Spencer hospital. After a while, the advocate arrived and asked us some pointed questions about my mother's behavior. We told him in essence what I have written above. He signed his approval.

The drive to Spencer was an additional fifteen miles. My mother now began to understand what was going on. We gave our reassurances, but she showed signs of being difficult. She didn't want to go to any hospital, she said. We told her it was to help her. At the hospital, she did not want to get out of the car. Some assistants came to help her out. The nurses knew her first name and used it over and over as they talked to her, as though they were old friends. The hospital staff did not waste much time with persuasion, however. They opened the car door and pulled her out. She shouted and screamed and cried and held onto the car as though her life depended on it. But the nurses were practiced. They pried loose her fingers and got her out and into a wheelchair. As soon as she was in the wheelchair, my mother fell silent and seemed to cave in upon herself. It was as though, having suffered this gross indignity, she was resigned to whatever befell her. I had heard the term "unconditional surrender" before, but I had never before seen a person so totally relinquish control, become so completely submissive, so entirely defeated. Seeing that made me feel both regret and shame and not a little foreboding. We had all participated that day in something that could never be erased from our memories, or ignored, or completely excused. I could not bear to think how this event would affect how we in this family looked at each other, and if I could not bear the thought, I wondered how my mother ever could. We might argue, I thought, that we had all done what we thought we must. But doing-what-one-must seemed less an argument than a rationalization just then. I doubted that I would want to be judged on that basis. In short, I thought we had all made an enormous mistake.

Later, when I saw my mother in her room, I started to feel a bit better. It was, after all, just a hospital room. It was painted in soothing lavenders and pastels and seemed quite comfortable, even cozy. We had to wait a while for the psychiatrist appointed to my mother's case to come in from his Saturday golf game. He asked us many questions about her medication. We told him all we could think of to help. When we were alone with her, however, my mother's state of mind became evident. "I've done something bad," she said, with absolute conviction. The thought of her doing something consciously bad seemed ludicrous to me, and I told her as much. But she insisted: "I've done a bad thing." The phrase reminded me of the way children talk about minor peccadilloes, but she was quite solemn and serious about it. I asked her about it. I tried to guess what she thought she might have done that was so terrible. As I questioned her, she started hint that sex was at the root of her guilt: she had slept with the devil, she had a venereal disease. I was aghast. My mother had always been the gentlest, the kindest of women, sustained by a quiet but firm faith. She regularly attended the Methodist church, took part in Bible studies and circles, read the bible, believed. But her faith had been little comfort to her in this illness. The new young minister had visited her often, but he had been unable to soothe her anguish. What had gone wrong? It occurred to me that, beset by unrelieved pain, she had come to think that she was being punished. And because the punishment was so agonizing, she was forced to imagine a sin that would be equal to it. In the twisted logic imposed by her illness, she had come upon the most horrible sins as the source of her torment. That, at least, explained her present low self-esteem, her fevered wish to scorch her world with cleansing flame. But looking at her, I saw that she was full of other secrets, crimes too terrible even to suggest, for which she felt a crushing weight of guilt.

Bad things do happen to good people, to repeat the pronouncement the young Methodist minister often used in an attempt to ease my mother's self-torture. But surely it takes an extremely sophisticated mind to understand how that can be. While I can pierce the paradox, I still can't help decrying the injustice that my mother, who most needed to understand, could not.

During the next several days, my mother seemed to respond to the treatment she was getting at the hospital. During my visits, however, I noticed that her tranquility was accompanied by an ever more profound silence. She was becoming less and less responsive. On a Sunday visit, I found myself feeding her, spooning soup into her mouth, speaking to her in those casual, oh-so-normal tones about trivial matters, as though to create the illusion that nothing was wrong, that life was going along pretty much as it always did. Her eyes were on my face as I brought the soup-spoon to her lips and caught the trickles at the corners. Her regard was, I thought, benign, trusting. I was reminded of the way a pet looks at its master, full of wonder and native knowledge and a deep lack of comprehension.

I took my leave. I think she managed to say goodbye. Within a week she was dead.

VIII.

I suppose I knew as soon as I heard the page for me on the Commons P.A., calling me to the phone while I was having coffee with colleagues. The caller was a nurse at my mother's hospital, and her reluctance to give me detailed information increased my suspicions. She would tell me only that my mother had suffered an "incident" and that the doctors thought I should come immediately. I drove home at once to grab a few clothes and to leave a note for my wife, then set off on the familiar highway to Iowa.

As I drove, I tried to prepare myself for the worst. I tried to think what to do if my mother were really dead, what needed to be done. I found that I couldn't concentrate. An oppressive gloom settled on me, and I kept replaying in my mind the events of the past several weeks. The day was warm. The long winter had at last receded for good. I was reminded of a day much like this one decades before when I had hitch-hiked down this same road, a junior in college, to celebrate the coincidental occasions of Mother's Day and my sister's birthday. Those occasions were again just a few days off.

When at last I was told directly that my mother was dead, I discovered I was not prepared at all, in spite of all the foreshadowing. I heard a great howl escape from me and felt my legs give way and felt immersed in a sickening numbness. That numbness, I think, saved me. My brain went on working on the problem of what must be done. I called back to Sioux Falls, to my family, and told them. Somebody asked if we wanted to see my mother. My father said no, he couldn't. I went in to see her with my aunt, the one who had cared for her some toward the end. I'm not sure whether it was a recovery room that we were ushered into. A plastic curtain was pulled back, and there was my mother. Apparently no one had touched her since her death. She was lying in a hospital bed, with the head section cranked about halfway up. Her mouth was partially agape and her eyes were open and glaring. My aunt said in an offended tone that someone should have closed her eyes. I reached up and with forefinger and thumb touched the upper lids and drew them down, but she had been dead for a while and the lids would not close completely. She had the look of someone who pretended to sleep.

The doctors were not sure precisely why she had died. Sometime around noon she had become obviously distressed. The nurses thought that she was having a heart attack. Emergency procedures were undertaken. The medical staff, I was assured, had done everything it could to save her.

My father was unconsolable. He had been taken completely off-guard. He could only repeat over and over that he couldn't believe it. Finally my sister came. We went home, the three of us.

For the next few days, my brain went on automatic pilot. We cleaned the house, got ready for the funeral. We were told the autopsy results: my mother had died of a thrombosis lodged in a lung. A blood clot, perhaps from her legs, which had been ruined by years of waiting tables, had broken loose and had driven like an arrow to her chest and had killed her. My father's sisters were curious about the cause of death; you could tell they had their own theories. They were disappointed by the autopsy ruling and suspicious of it. Perhaps they were right to be: can a physical examination ever really tell what kills a person? "Thrombosis," my aunts repeated, as though they'd never heard of such a thing. Might as well say "disappointment" or "pain" or "fear." There is no end of things that kill but that cannot be found in an autopsy.

We got through the funeral and the days and weeks afterward. We had our usual Fourth of July celebration at our place in Sioux Falls. Both my sister and my father came. As I barbecued chicken on the outdoor grill, my father talked to me. "I know now why I worked so hard all those years," he told me. "Why was that?" I asked him. "Why," he said, "for your mother."

Five months had passed since my 50th birthday. At least, I thought, the worst had happened.

IX.

I approached that fall with special dread. I had been recruited into the position of department chair and was faced with numerous duties I hadn't encountered before. I was teaching freshman composition again for the first time in several years, as well, and felt nervous about how teaching methods and subject matter in that course had changed. The hectic pattern of my life kept me from dwelling too long on my mother's death or my father's profound mourning.

Then, in late September, just as the leaves were starting to turn, I became ill. Friday night, after a long week, I sat in the chair watching television, clicking idly around the channels, when I was pierced with a sharp pain in my side, the lower right side of my abdomen, where my appendix was. I remember feeling no panic. I calmly told my wife what was happening, and she drove me to the hospital emergency room.

The pain had become excruciating, but the E.R. staff refused to give me anything to ease the torture until someone determined what was causing it. I had tests, x-rays, was prodded and poked. One hour passed, then another. I was more miserable than ever. Two or three doctors had by now seen me and had tried to determine what was wrong. For various reasons they were not supremely confident in my own self-diagnosis: appendicitis. Finally, after three and a half hours, I was given a pain killer, put on an I.V. and admitted to the hospital to stay overnight, for observation.

The drug dulled the pain immediately, but I still felt uncomfortable. Then, sometime in the early morning, the pain vanished entirely and I slept.

On Saturday, the doctors were still not sure what had happened. One told me she thought it might have been a kidney stone. But surely, I said, if the stone had passed I would have known it. There were a few more tests and everything seemed normal. They let me go home.

Now it's Sunday. I am feeling relieved, normal. I read, listen to the radio, eat well, drink well. But when I go to the bathroom to relieve myself, I realize I am not at all well. I cannot urinate. Suddenly, I see clearly what has happened: it is a kidney stone all right, and it has shaken loose and is now rattling around in my bladder, plugging up the outlet like a ball-valve when I try to urinate. I call the doctor, the one who had suspected a kidney stone. She is strangely cautious about accepting my conclusion. But can I blame her? After all, yesterday I was just as strongly convinced I had appendicitis. She suggests finding relief in a tub of hot water. It works. I call her back, and she says she will set up a meeting Monday with a urologist.

The problem seems to be, the urologist informs me, that the stone is too large to pass normally. There is a procedure, however, that will give me relief. It is essentially a matter of going in and getting the stone. He assures me that it should be a relatively painless matter. But he is worried about something else. I appear to have a hernia. Perhaps I should contact a surgeon to look into the possibility of having a hernia operation at the same time. Fine. I go to see the surgeon immediately. He has a bit of a problem, however. He can't find any hernia. He does a lot of poking and I do a lot of coughing, but it is no go. As far as he is concerned, I don't need a hernia operation. That is just fine with me. I don't like the sound of "operation." "Procedure" I can put up with, but an "operation" I'd just as soon forego.

When I was a kid, I had absolute faith in doctors. I remember feeling better just seeing our old family doctor. I remember him working miracles: curing my nausea, for example, with the simple expedient of propping my feet up on the examination table. But my belief in doctors seems to have gone the way of my belief in the tooth fairy, Santa Claus and the Easter Bunny. I no longer can give them my complete trust. I will put myself in their hands, but only with the understanding that I have no other choice. I remember the doctor who put off our call about our daughter's rash by saying "all kids have rashes," and the E.R. doctor who said it was measles, although she had been vaccinated, and the doctor who, when it turned out to be a reaction to sulfa that kept her hospitalized over two weeks, refused to blame anybody because "it could just as well be a reaction to aspirin." Doctors are only human, it will be said. Granted. But it makes me nervous, all the same, when they say nobody dies of a kidney stone. Nobody dies of shingles, either.

The "procedure" was set up for the end of the week. I was prepped, was wheeled into a room bristling with stainless steel equipment, had my feet put into stirrups, was given a shot, and was told to count backward from 100. I got to 99.

I woke up feeling as though I had been used as a wishbone. A nurse hovered over me. "What went wrong?" I asked her. Because it was obvious that something had gone wrong. The procedure, after all, was not supposed to hurt. She told me I had had an operation. That explained it. Yes, I understood: somebody had impaled my lower abdomen on a rusty railroad spike.

I had, in fact, been out for several hours. At last my doctor arrived to say that the "procedure" had failed, that he had been forced to operate to remove the stone. I would be out of commission for some time.

The next day I was visited by two colleagues, the same friends who a year before had warned me of all the hard decisions I would have to make. They took one look at me and said that they would make arrangements to take over my duties at school. They reckoned I would be out for at least a month, by the looks of me.

During my hospital stay, I was impressed with the care shown by the nurses. I couldn't have been a pleasant patient to deal with. Only when they insisted on my walking the morning after the operation was I annoyed with them. They must take a course in that at nursing school: "How to force the patient to do something that will cause him misery and agony because IT'S FOR HIS OWN GOOD." This sort of treatment, of course, leads to fantasies by the patient about what the nurses might be forced to do FOR THEIR OWN GOOD.

But did I die? Of course not. Did I recover? Within reason. I went home after about a week, wore a catheter for about a month after that. Finally I went back to school and picked up teaching again. My evaluations suffered.

For Christmas, my daughter got me another dog, a golden retriever. The dog loved to shake hands. I named her Lady, after a dog I had had as a kid. I took a half-year leave. I wrote a lot. When my 51st birthday came around, I felt an immense sense of relief. I was alive.

I am alive in quite a different way from what I was before. My life is that of a person who has had a reprieve. Every year over 50 I count as a year given to me that I don't deserve. It is perhaps silly or even superstitious to think that way, but that is nevertheless the way I feel. I got to be 50, and I didn't die. My mother did, though, and I was as sick as I've ever been. It was, I have reason to believe, a tragic year, a dangerous year. I learned many things, I suppose, but I remain most struck by what I do not know.

There is a mystery in things that quite defies our rational intelligence. The mystery is in what we do and why we do it. The source of the mystery is our ability to hold a conviction based on nothing more than "a funny feeling," or to hold two contradictory convictions simultaneously with absolutely no sense of paradox. And convictions, as we all know, are what we act upon. We state our views, but we act out our convictions. That is why we surprise each other more by what we do than by what we say. How can we understand each other when we cannot even understand ourselves? All we have are these echoes that reverberate down the marble halls, our past lives speaking to us, the dead speaking to us.

The Irish speak sometimes, I understand, of "joining the majority," by which they mean dying. As I grow older, I see more and more clearly that the phrase is not a euphemism, but rather a truism. The dead are a majority, all right: Cousin Roger, Dr. Latson, Belle Latson, the kid who wanted to watch the house move down Main Street, the family friend who chose to eat rat poison, most of my best teachers, many of my friends, people who have been important in my life, some of them the kindest, gentlest and most honorable people I have known, my grandparents, my mother. We will join them, sooner or later. That we know in our bones. What we don't know, really, is how to live.

I have been at a loss to know how to end this treatise on mortality. The meaning, as I have said before, lies in the resonance. But this past Saturday we had a picnic with friends at Newton Hills, south of Canton. It was a beautiful still fall day, and the isolated cottonwoods shone like yellow jewels in the sunlight among the rolling hills of duller oak. As the sun sank, we gathered around the picnic table for apple pie, these friends whom we have known so long, among them those two who had warned me one fall night years ago of what I must prepare for. We had seen a vee of geese go over, heading south, so low we could hear the whirr of their wing feathers. We had seen a red-tailed hawk scouting the sky far up. We were moved by the beauty and the serenity to sing, to recite poetry. We were old friends, and were easy with one another, not awkward or embarrassed. We had nothing to prove and nothing to lose. And as the sun vanished down the west, the full moon rose in the east. We hadn't realized it, but they were in direct opposition just then. We were fewer than we had been on such picnics before. Others of our number had joined the majority. But there was no sadness in us, no cheap sentimentality. We were beyond that, too. And for the moment we were beyond hope and regret. We were simply there—poised between sunset and moonrise—and, each of us, beatified. What can one call such grace but a gift?

October 1989

Questions to Consider for Chapter Three:

1. What experiences of your own did you find yourself thinking about as a result of reading this article?

2. What does Robinson mean by resonance? See section IV. Identify 3-4 of the key experiences that resonate in Robinson's life.

3. Do any of his experiences resonate with yours? For example?

4. How does Robinson bring the essay to conclusion?

On Depression
Jerome Freeman

You could see tragedy coming
from a distance slowly,
like the wagon train inching
in and out of view over
undulating prairie.

Warning calls were muted
by your remove and distraction.
And by the time depression
settled in, it seemed too late
to act or care.

Important things were lost,
as when the perfect phrase
comes to the writer just
before sleep and is forgotten
by dawn.

In the ample night you awaken
still to strains of uncertainty.
Your compass is awry
and much can go wrong.
If something matters now

it's the practical. Where
to draw the line. How
to learn the nuances
of things. Whether to
start over.

Chapter Four:
Caring, Meaning, and Courage
Arthur Olsen

"The rezin I wanted to write a book about having cansur is because every book I read about kids with cansur they always die, I want to tell you kids dont always die. If you get cansur dont be scared cause lots of people get over having cansur and grow up without dying. Like Mike Nelson and Doug Cerny and Vince Barpness and President Reagan and me." — Jason Gaes, *My Book for Kids with Cansur*, p. 13.

"When a man finds that it is his destiny to suffer, he will have to accept his suffering as his task; his single and unique task. He will have to acknowledge the fact that even in suffering his is unique and alone in the universe. No one can relieve him of his suffering or suffer in his place. His unique opportunity lies in the way in which he bears his burden." — Victor Frankl, *Man's Search for Meaning*, p. 99 (Washington Press).

How is it possible to live boldly and well when we become fully aware of our limits? When we have tasted our own mortality? How shall we care for those facing these questions? How is it possible to care when we face these questions?

Thinking about health, life, and mortality becomes real as we deal with our everyday experiences with illness and death. Each of us has private galleries of memory vignettes that resonate with Ron's — how we felt when a favorite pet died, or how families dealt with the illness of a brother, or cousin, or grandmother. Ron Robinson's essay illustrates how these experiences can resonate, that is, echo and reverberate down the long hallway of one's life. Shaken by the death of his cousin when he is only 10 years old, Ron prays to live to the age of 50. But at age 50 after witnessing his mother's death and wondering why the doctors could do so little for her and then suddenly dealing with his own illness, the taste of mortality develops more fully into personal realization. The Irish

way of speaking of death as "joining the majority" is not a
euphemism, but a truism.

The questions linger. How is it possible to live boldly and well
when we are fully aware of our limits? Isn't it morbid to dwell all
the time upon matters of death, and not life?

Ron's essay suggests that it is not possible to avoid reflection on
limits and mortality. These were issues and experiences that he carried with him from childhood into adulthood. We suggest that to
avoid reflection is illusory, unhealthy, and in the end uncaring.

Youth cannot be shielded from reflection. For a tragic few of the
young, an awareness of the fragility of life can lead to suicide. The
persistence of teenage suicide is a disturbing phenomenon.

For some the question is buried in busyness only to emerge now
and again as it did for Robinson at age 50 as he had suddenly to deal
with his own illness and that of his mother's.

For others a "so-what" attitude, a kind of secular fatalism, may
develop. Why not live boldly and ignore the warnings? All the fun
activities and tasty foods are off limits. Live boldly, despite the perils. Smoke, despite the warnings from the surgeon general on the
package. Drive without seat belts. It is, after all, my life isn't it?

Or complacency may develop from an opposite direction. To be
sure, issues at the end of life are problems, but for my grandparents
who may need to be thinking about nursing home arrangements,
not for me. The quandaries of aging may sometime affect me — but
not now. I will deal with it when the time comes.

In the end, Robinson's reflections affirm that living with an
awareness of mortality can lead not to morbid reflection but to the
discovery of the gift of life. This is in line with existentialist thinkers
who urge that knowledge of the certainty of death is a call to choose
life — now. The needed response, in the language of theologian Karl
Barth, is the "will to be healthy." The will to carry out our life stories in the words of the philosopher/theologian Paul Tillich is "the
courage to be," a call to affirm meaning in spite of suffering.[1]

How can mortality, illness, and death be included in one's life
story? The question is not whether, but how?

A story has a plot line, a meaning. Discouragement comes when
things don't fit or add up, as with physical infirmities. Is it possible
to will a life story in the face of illness (the onset of which one has
no control over) or imprisonment (in which all apparent freedoms
have been eliminated). The "will to be healthy" includes the will to
meaning.

According to James Nelson in the book *Human Medicine: Ethical Perspectives on Today's Medical Issues,* the will to meaning is one of three essential dimensions of being human. "In the first place, to be personally human is to be social . . . A second dimension of human personhood is the capacity to experience both limitation and freedom . . . A third major dimension . . . is the self's religiosity," which Nelson, drawing on Frankl's work, describes as the will to meaning.[2]

How is it possible to find meaning and affirm life with courage in the face of illness, imprisonment and death? We invite you to carry these questions with you as you read the selections by Jason Gaes, *My book for kids with cansur* and Victor Frankl, *Man's Search for Meaning.*

---

[1]Tillich, Paul. *The Courage To Be.* New Haven: Yale University Press, 1952.

[2]*Human Medicine, op. cit.,* ch. 1.

Ten-Year-Old with Rheumatoid Arthritis

Jerome Freeman

Morning begins the battle again
as she lies quietly thinking
of movement. Tentative stretching
immediately laces coils of pain
around each joint, fiercely
locking them into immobility.

It seems better for a time
to let her mind arise effortlessly
from bed and roam about,
making lithe preparation
for the day. She sees herself
twirling across the room
in a dressing ballet, before
descending stairs two
at a time to startle the family
at breakfast routine.

Her musings propel her
to gingerly work elbows and
fingers just enough to sense
the painful ratchet. Catching
her breath, she tries again.

My book for kids with cansur
A Child's Autobiography of Hope
Jason Gaes

Jason Gaes, of Worthington, Minn., had just completed kindergarten when he was diagnosed with Burkitt's lymphoma. He was given a 20 percent chance of survival and was not expected to live to reach his seventh birthday. After six months of treatment, he told his mother he wanted to stop. "Jason got sick and tired of being sick and tired," said his mother, Geralyn Gaes. But she promised him if he went on, she'd give him "the biggest party in the world, where all the ladies wear new dresses and all the men drink beer." He got the party two years later. In 1985, he started writing the book from which the following pages are excerpted.

The rezin I wanted to write a book about having cansur is because every book I read about kids with cansur they always die. I want to tell you kids dont always die. If you get cansur dont be scared cause lots of people get over having cansur and grow up without dying. Like Mike Nelson and Doug Cerny and Vince Varpness and President Reagan and me.

Having cansur isnt fun. In fact its the pits but its not all bad either. You get lots of cards and presents when your in the hospital. You have to have cansur to get in vited to go to Camp Courage.

When your bald you dont have to worry about getting shampoo in your eyes when your sick from a treet-ment you get to stay home from school and when your done having cansur you get to have a big party. The best party in your whole life.

My Party

There are a couple bad parts of
having cansur too. There's blood
tests. I got used to those so I could
go in by myself but if your scared
of blood tests have your mom or Dad
cover your eyes. If you cant see
the needle it doesn't hurt as much
as if your sister pinches you. And you
dont cry everytime you get pinched
do you?

Then there's putting an iv in
your hand and spinals and bone
mairos. Ivs arent so bad.
The nurses say done before
you get to 3. The spinals and
bone mairos are bad no matter
how far you count but they go
faster if you curl up tight and try
to relacks. That's hard to do
but try thinking about your party
till the bad part is over.

Being scared is a bad part of cansur too. It makes you feel bad and makes your stumick hurt. But Dr Karen will tell you what is going to hurt so you dont need to be afraid of everything. And it doesnt help to be afraid anyway. If you get cansur you might as well not even be afraid cause your probly not even going to die anyway.

If you can find it get a poster that says Help me to remember Lord that nothing is gonna happen today that you and me cant handle together. Then hang it in your room and redd it at night when your scared. If you get scared and cant quit go and talk to your Mom and she can rock you or rub your hair.

And the rest of the days
when you don't have a treetment
try to forget you have cansyr
and think about something
else. Shoot baskets or go
swimming.

Sometimes   even if you do everything
just like everybody else a pees of your
cansur can break off and go to
your lungs and grow there. If the
drs can't get it out then your probly
gonna die when your a kid. My
Mom said when me and Tim was
babys in her stumick we liked it in
there so good the dr had to give my
Mom a shot to make us come out.
But now that I'm outside I wouldnt
never want to go back.

She says going to heaven is probly like that. Once we get there we won't want to come back here. We'r just scared about going to heaven because we never been there. You can see your Grandpa again and pretty soon your Mom will be there too. Then Adam or Tim cause every bodys godda die sometime.

Sometimes when your sick from a treetment you miss school but try to make up your work cause colij makes you have all your work done before you can be a doctor. And I'm going to be a doctor who takes care of kids with cansur so I can tell them what its like.

Jason Gaes, *My book for kids with cansur*, illustrated by Tim and Adam Gaes, Melius Publishing, Inc., Pierre, S.D. Copyright © 1987 by Jason Gaes. Reprinted by permission.

THE BURDEN
Jerome Freeman

for Ben

Having one more blood test
Is not so bad
Unless you are 10 years old
And sick to death
Of diets and sugar and insulin
And having reactions
And being different
And seeing no light at the end
Of your tunnel or promise
Of being done with it all.

From *Man's Search for Meaning*
Viktor E. Frankl

The excerpts below are from the book Man's Search for Meaning *written in 1946 by Viktor E. Frankl "to convey by way of a concrete example that life holds potential meaning under any circumstances, even the most miserable ones."*

The concrete example, of course, is from the tragic experiences of Viktor Frankl himself, who survived three years (from 1942-1945) in Auschwitz and Dachau. His mother, father, brother, and pregnant wife were not so fortunate. The were killed in concentration camps.

The focus of Frankl's narrative is not on the great horrors which are described elsewhere, but on the "everyday life in a concentration camp." He writes, not to draw attention to the "suffering of the mighty," but to the lives of the unrecorded victims." This is obviously the narrative of an insider. We meet the author, not as the celebrated psychiatrist he would later become, but as one more prisoner — number 119,104 — whose life work is snuffed out when the precious manuscript of his book is taken from him and destroyed. Though he lost everything, family and career, he retained the freedom to choose how he would respond to these experiences of suffering.

Frankl tells his story with the detachment of a trained psychological observer, who lets us into the drama of prisoners who find that search for meaning is possible in even the most deprived of circumstances. The excerpts are taken from his description of the three phases of the "inmates' mental reaction to camp life," following admission, after entrenchment in the routine of the camp, and after release. Is meaningful life, is freedom to choose possible under these most miserable circumstances? The book is written to explain why Frankl believes that the answer to the question is yes.

Though modest in size, Frankl's book has ben enormously influential. At the time of his death on September 2, 1997, it had been translated into 24 languages. Over ten million copies have been sold.

When one examines the vast amount of material which has been amassed as the result of many prisoners' observations and experiences, three phases of the inmate's mental reactions to camp life become apparent: the period following his admission; the period when he is well entrenched in camp routine; and the period following his release and liberation.

The symptom that characterizes the first phase is shock. Under certain conditions shock may even precede the prisoner's formal admission to the camp. I shall give as an example the circumstances of my own admission.

Fifteen hundred persons had been traveling by train for several days and nights: there were eighty people in each coach. All had to lie on top of their luggage, the few remnants of their personal possessions. The carriages were so full that only the top parts of the windows were free to let in the grey of dawn. Everyone expected the train to head for some munitions factory, in which we would be employed as forced labor. We did not know whether we were still in Silesia or already in Poland. The engine's whistle had an uncanny sound, like a cry for help sent out in commiseration for the unhappy load which it was destined to lead into perdition. Then the train shunted, obviously nearing a main station. Suddenly a cry broke from the ranks of the anxious passengers, "There is a sign, Auschwitz!" Everyone's heart missed a beat at that moment. Auschwitz — the very name stood for all that was horrible: gas chambers, crematoriums, massacres. Slowly, almost hesitatingly, the train moved on as if it wanted to spare its passengers the dreadful realization as long as possible: Auschwitz!

With the progressive dawn, the outlines of an immense camp became visible: long stretches of several rows of barbed-wire fences; watch towers; search lights; and long columns of ragged human figures, grey in the greyness of dawn, trekking along the straight desolate roads, to what destination we did not know. There were isolated shouts and whistles of command. We did not know their meaning. My imagination led me to see gallows with people dangling on them. I was horrified, but this was just as well, because step by step we had to become accustomed to a terrible and immense horror.

Eventually we moved into the station. The initial silence was interrupted by shouted commands. We were to hear those rough, shrill tones from then on, over and over again in all the camps. Their sound was almost like the last cry of a victim, and yet there was a difference. It had a rasping hoarseness, as if it came from the throat of a man who had to keep shouting like that, a man who was being murdered again and again. The carriage doors were flung open and a small detachment of prisoners stormed inside. They wore striped uniforms, their heads were shaved, but they looked well fed. They spoke in every possible European tongue, and all with a certain amount of humor, which sounded grotesque under the circumstances. Like a drowning man clutching a straw, my inborn optimism (which has often controlled my feelings even in the most desperate situations) clung to this thought: These prisoners look quite well, they seem to be in good spirits and even laugh. Who knows? I might manage to share their favorable position.

In psychiatry there is a certain condition known as "delusion of reprieve." The condemned man, immediately before his execution, gets the illusion that he might be reprieved at the very last minute. We, too, clung to shreds of hope and believed to the last moment that it would not be so bad. Just the sight of the red cheeks and round faces of those prisoners was a great encouragement. Little did we know then that they formed a specially chosen elite, who for years had been the receiving squad for new transports as they rolled into the station day after day. They took charge of the new arrivals and their luggage, including scarce items and smuggled jewelry. Auschwitz must have been a strange spot in this Europe of the last years of the war. There must have been unique treasures of gold and silver, platinum and diamonds, not only in the huge storehouses but also in the hands of the SS.

Fifteen hundred captives were cooped up in a shed built to accommodate probably two hundred at the most. We were cold and hungry and there was not enough room for everyone to squat on the bare ground, let alone to lie down. One five-ounce piece of bread was our only food in four days. Yet I heard the senior prisoners in charge of the shed bargain with one member of the receiving party about a tie-pin made of platinum and diamonds. Most of the profits would eventually be traded for liquor — schnapps. I do not remember any more just how many thousands of marks were needed to purchase the quantity of schnapps required for a "gay evening," but I do know that those long-term prisoners needed schnapps. Under such conditions, who could blame them for trying to dope themselves? There was another group of prisoners who got liquor supplied in almost unlimited quantities by the SS: these were the men who were employed in the gas chambers and crematoriums, and who knew very well that one day they would be relieved by a new shift of men, and that they would have to leave their enforced role of executioner and become victims themselves.

Nearly everyone in our transport lived under the illusion that he would be reprieved, that everything would yet be well. We did not realize the meaning behind the scene that was to follow presently. We were told to leave our luggage in the train and to fall into two lines — women on one side, men on the other — in order to file past a senior SS officer. Surprisingly enough, I had the courage to hide my haversack under my coat. My line filed past the officer, man by man. I realized that it would be dangerous if the officer spotted my bag. He would at least knock me down; I knew that from previous experience. Instinctively, I straightened on approaching the officer, so that he would not notice my heavy load. Then I was face to face with him. He was a tall man who looked slim and fit in his spotless uniform. What a contrast to us, who were untidy and grimy after our long journey! He had assumed an attitude of careless ease, supporting his right elbow with his left hand. His right hand was lifted, and with the forefinger of that hand he pointed very leisurely to the right or to the left. None of us had the slightest idea of the sinister meaning behind that little movement of a man's finger, pointing now to the right and now to the left, but far more frequently to the left.

It was my turn. Somebody whispered to me that to be sent to the right side would mean work, the way to the left being for the sick and those incapable of work, who would be sent to a special camp. I just waited for things to take their course, the first of many such times to come. My haversack weighed me down a bit to the left, but I made an effort to walk upright. The SS man looked me over, appeared to hesitate, then put both his hands on my shoulders. I tried very hard to look smart, and he turned my shoulders very slowly until I faced right, and I moved over to that side.

The significance of the finger game was explained to us in the evening. It was the first selection, the first verdict made on our existence or non-existence. For the great majority of our transport, about 90 per cent, it meant death. Their sentence was carried out within the next few hours. Those who were sent to the left were marched from the station straight to the crematorium. This building, as I was told by someone who worked there, had the word "bath" written over its doors in several European languages. On entering, each prisoner was handed a piece of soap, and then — but mercifully I do not need to describe the events which followed. Many accounts have been written about this horror.

We who were saved, the minority of our transport, found out the truth in the evening. I inquired from prisoners who had been there for some time where my colleague and friend P__ had been sent.

"Was he sent to the left side?"

"Yes," I replied.

"Then you can see him there," I was told.

"Where?" A hand pointed to the chimney a few hundred yards off, which was sending a column of flame up into the grey sky of Poland. It dissolved into a sinister cloud of smoke.

"That's where your friend is, floating up to Heaven," was the answer. But I still did not understand until the truth was explained to me in plain words.

But I am telling things out of their turn. From a psychological point of view, we had a long, long way in front of us from the break of that dawn at the station until our first night's rest at the camp.

Escorted by SS guards with loaded guns, we were made to run from the station, past electrically charged barbed wire, through the camp, to the cleansing station; for those of us who had passed the first selection, this was a real bath. Again our illusion of reprieve found confirmation. The SS men seemed almost charming. Soon we found out their reason. They were nice to us as long as they saw watches on our wrists and could persuade us in well-meaning tones to hand them over. Would we not have to hand over all our possessions anyway, and why should not that relatively nice person have the watch? Maybe one day he would do one a good turn.

We waited in a shed which seemed to be the anteroom to the disinfecting chamber. SS men appeared and spread out blankets into which we had to throw all our possessions, all our watches and jewelry. There were still naive prisoners among us who asked, to the amusement of the more seasoned ones who were there as helpers, if they could not keep a wedding ring, a medal or a good-luck piece. No one could yet grasp the fact that everything would be taken away.

I tried to take one of the old prisoners into my confidence. Approaching him furtively, I pointed to the roll of paper in the inner pocket of my coat and said, "Look, this is the manuscript of a scientific book. I know what you will say; that I should be grateful to escape with my life, that that should be all I can expect of fate. But I cannot help myself. I must keep this manuscript at all costs; it contains my life's work. Do you understand that?"

Yes, he was beginning to understand. A grin spread slowly over his face, first piteous, then more amused, mocking, insulting, until he bellowed one word at me in answer to my question, a word that was ever present in the vocabulary of the camp inmates: "Shit!" At that moment I saw the plain truth and did what marked the culminating point of the first phase of my psychological reaction: I struck out my whole former life.

*　*　*

I think it was Lessing who once said, "There are things which must cause you to lose your reason or you have none to lose." An abnormal reaction to an abnormal situation is normal behavior. Even we psychiatrists expect the reactions of a man to an abnormal situation, such as being committed to an asylum, to be abnormal in proportion to the degree of his normality. The reaction of a man to his admission to a concentration camp also represents an abnormal state of mind, but judged objectively it is a normal and, as will be shown later, typical reaction to the given circumstances. These reactions, as I have described them, began to change in a few days. The prisoner passed from the first to the second phase; the phase of relative apathy in which he achieved a kind of emotional death.

Apart from the already described reactions, the newly arrived prisoner experienced the tortures of other most painful emotions, all of which he tried to deaden. First of all, there was his boundless longing for his home and his family. This often could become so acute that he felt himself consumed by longing. Then there was disgust; disgust with all the ugliness which surrounded him, even in its mere external forms.

Most of the prisoners were given a uniform of rags which would have made a scarecrow elegant by comparison. Between the huts in the camp lay pure filth, and the more one worked to clear it away, the more one had to come in contact with it. It was a favorite practice to detail a new arrival to a work group whose job was to clean the latrines and remove the sewage. If, as usually happened, some of the excrement splashed into his face during its transport over bumpy fields, any sign of disgust by the prisoner or any attempt to wipe off the filth would only be punished with a blow from a Capo. And thus the mortification of normal reactions was hastened.

At first the prisoner looked away if he saw the punishment parades of another group; he could not bear to see fellow prisoners march up and down for hours in the mire, their movements directed by blows. Days or weeks later things changed. Early in the morn-

ing, when it was still dark, the prisoner stood in front of the gate
with his detachment, ready to march. He heard a scream and saw
how a comrade was knocked down, pulled to his feet again, and
knocked down once more — and why? He was feverish but had
reported to sick-bay at an improper time. He was being punished
for this irregular attempt to be relieved of his duties.

But the prisoner who had passed into the second stage of his psychological reactions did not avert his eyes any more. By then his
feelings were blunted, and he watched unmoved. Another example:
he found himself waiting at sick-bay, hoping to be granted two days
of light work inside the camp because of injuries or perhaps edema
or fever. He stood unmoved while a twelve-year-old boy was carried in who had been forced to stand at attention for hours in the
snow or to work outside with bare feet because there were no shoes
for him in the camp. His toes had become frostbitten, and the doctor on duty picked off the black gangrenous stumps with tweezers,
one by one. Disgust, horror and pity are emotions that our spectator could not really feel any more. The sufferers, the dying and the
dead, became such commonplace sights to him after a few weeks of
camp life that they could not move him any more.

I spent some time in a hut for typhus patients who ran very high
temperatures and were often delirious, many of them moribund.
After one of them had just died, I watched without any emotional
upset the scene that followed, which was repeated over and over
again with each death. One by one the prisoners approached the
still warm body. One grabbed the remains of a messy meal of pota-
toes; another decided that the corpse's wooden shoes were an
improvement on his own, and exchanged them. A third man did the
same with the dead man's coat, and another was glad to be able to
secure some — just imagine! — genuine string.

All this I watched with unconcern. Eventually I asked the
"nurse" to remove the body. When he decided to do so, he took the
corpse by its legs, allowing it to drop into the small corridor
between the two rows of boards which were the beds for the fifty
typhus patients, and dragged it across the bumpy earthen floor
toward the door. The two steps which led up into the open air
always constituted a problem for us, since we were exhausted from
a chronic lack of food. After a few months' stay in the camp we
could not walk up those steps, which were each about six inches

high, without putting our hands on the door jambs to pull ourselves up.

The man with the corpse approached the steps. Wearily he dragged himself up. Then the body: first the feet, then the trunk, and finally — with an uncanny rattling noise — the head of the corpse bumped up the two steps.

My place was on the opposite side of the hut, next to the small, sole window, which was built near the floor. While my cold hands clasped a bowl of hot soup from which I sipped greedily, I happened to look out the window. The corpse which had just been removed stared in at me with glazed eyes. Two hours before I had spoken to that man. Now I continued sipping my soup.

If my lack of emotion had not surprised me from the standpoint of professional interest, I would not remember this incident now, because there was so little feeling involved in it.

* * *

Apathy, the main symptom of the second phase, was a necessary mechanism of self-defense. Reality dimmed, and all efforts and all emotions were centered on one task: preserving one's own life and that of the other fellow. It was typical to hear the prisoners, while they were being herded back to camp from their work sites in the evening, sigh with relief and say, "Well, another day is over."

It can be readily understood that such a state of strain, coupled with the constant necessity of concentrating on the task of staying alive, forced the prisoner's inner life down to a primitive level. Several of my colleagues in camp who were trained in psychoanalysis often spoke of a "regression" in the camp inmates retreat to a more primitive form of mental life. His wishes and desires became obvious in his dreams.

What did the prisoner dream about most frequently? Of bread, cake, cigarettes, and nice warm baths. The lack of having these simple desires satisfied led him to seek wish-fulfillment in dreams. Whether these dreams did any good is another matter; the dreamer had to wake from them to the reality of camp life, and to the terrible contrast between that and his dream illusions.

I shall never forget how I was roused one night by the groans of a fellow prisoner, who threw himself about in his sleep, obviously having a horrible nightmare. Since I had always been especially sorry for people who suffered from fearful dreams or deliria, I wanted to wake the poor man. Suddenly I drew back the hand which was ready to shake him, frightened at the thing I was about to do. At that moment I became intensely conscious of the fact that no dream, no matter how horrible, could be as bad as the reality of the camp which surrounded us, and to which I was about to recall him.

Because of the high degree of undernourishment which the prisoners suffered, it was natural that the desire for food was the major primitive instinct around which mental life centered. Let us observe the majority of prisoners when they happened to work near each other and were, for once, not closely watched. They would immediately start discussing food. One fellow would ask another working next to him in the ditch what his favorite dishes were. Then they would exchange recipes and plan the menu for the day when they would have a reunion — the day in a distant future when they would be liberated and returned home. They would go on and on, picturing it all in detail, until suddenly a warning was passed down the trench, usually in the form of a special password or number: "The guard is coming."

I always regarded the discussions about food as dangerous. Is it not wrong to provoke the organism with such detailed and affective pictures of delicacies when it has somehow managed to adapt itself to extremely small rations and low calories? Though it may afford momentary psychological relief, it is an illusion which physiologically, surely, must not be without danger.

During the later part of our imprisonment, the daily ration consisted of very watery soup given out once daily, and the usual small bread ration. In addition to that, there was the so-called "extra allowance," consisting of three-fourths of an ounce of margarine, or of a slice of poor quality sausage, or of a little piece of cheese, or a bit of synthetic honey, or a spoonful of watery jam, varying daily. In calories, this diet was absolutely inadequate, especially taking into consideration our heavy manual work and our constant exposure to the cold in inadequate clothing. The sick who were "under special care" — that is, those who were allowed to lie in the huts instead of leaving the camp for work — were even worse off.

When the last layers of subcutaneous fat had vanished, and we looked like skeletons disguised with skin and rags, we could watch our bodies beginning to devour themselves. The organism digested its own protein, and the muscles disappeared. Then the body had no powers of resistance left. One after another the members of the little community in our hut died. Each of us could calculate with fair accuracy whose turn would be next, and when his own would come. After many observations we knew the symptoms well, which made the correctness of our prognoses quite certain. "He won't last long," or, "This is the next one," we whispered to each other, and when, during our daily search for lice, we saw our own naked bodies in the evening, we thought alike: This body here, my body, is really a corpse already. What has become of me? I am but a small portion of a great mass of human flesh... of a mass behind barbed wire, crowded into a few earthen huts; a mass of which daily a certain portion begins to rot because it has become lifeless.

*   *   *

In spite of all the enforced physical and mental primitiveness of the life in a concentration camp, it was possible for spiritual life to deepen. Sensitive people who were used to a rich intellectual life may have suffered much pain (they were often of a delicate constitution), but the damage to their inner selves was less. They were able to retreat from their terrible surroundings to a life of inner riches and spiritual freedom. Only in this way can one explain the apparent paradox that some prisoners of a less hardy make-up often seemed to survive camp life better than did those of a robust nature. In order to make myself clear, I am forced to fall back on personal experience. Let me tell what happened on those early mornings when we had to march to our work site.

There were shouted commands: "Detachment, forward march! Left-2-3-4! Left-2-3-4! Left-2-3-4! Left-2-3-4! First man about, left and left and left and left! Caps off!" These words sound in my ears even now. At the order "Caps off!" we passed the gate of the camp, and searchlights were trained upon us. Whoever did not march smartly got a kick. And worse off was the man who, because of the cold, had pulled his cap back over his ears before permission was given.

We stumbled on in the darkness, over big stones and through large puddles, along the one road leading from the camp. The accompanying guards kept shouting at us and driving us with the butts of their rifles. Anyone with very sore feet supported himself on his neighbor's arm. Hardly a word was spoken; the icy wind did not encourage talk. Hiding his mouth behind his upturned collar, the man marching next to me whispered suddenly: "If our wives could see us now! I do hope they are better off in their camps and don't know what is happening to us."

That brought thoughts of my own wife to mind. And as we stumbled on for miles, slipping on icy spots, supporting each other time and again, dragging one another up and onward, nothing was said, but we both knew: each of us was thinking of his wife. Occasionally I looked at the sky, where the stars were fading and the pink light of the morning was beginning to spread behind a dark bank of clouds. But my mind clung to my wife's image, imagining it with an uncanny acuteness. I heard her answering me, saw her smile, her frank and encouraging look. Real or not, her look was then more luminous than the sun which was beginning to rise.

A thought transfixed me: for the first time in my life I saw the truth as it is set into song by so many poets, proclaimed as the final wisdom by so many thinkers. The truth — that love is the ultimate and the highest goal to which man can aspire. Then I grasped the meaning of the greatest secret that human poetry and human thought and belief have to impart: The salvation of man is through love and in love. I understood how a man who has nothing left in this world still may know bliss, be it only for a brief moment, in the contemplation of his beloved. In a position of utter desolation, when man cannot express himself in positive action, when his only achievement may consist in enduring his sufferings in the right way — an honorable way — in such a position man can, through loving contemplation of the image he carries of his beloved, achieve fulfillment. For the first time in my life I was able to understand the meaning of the words, "The angels are lost in perpetual contemplation of an infinite glory."

In front of me a man stumbled and those following him fell on top of him. The guard rushed over and used his whip on them all. Thus my thoughts were interrupted for a few minutes. But soon my soul found its way back from the prisoner's existence to another world, and I resumed talk with my loved one: I asked her questions, and she answered; she questioned me in return, and I answered.

"Stop!" We had arrived at our work site. Everybody rushed into the dark hut in the hope of getting a fairly decent tool. Each prisoner got a spade or a pickaxe.

"Can't you hurry up, you pigs?" Soon we had resumed the previous day's positions in the ditch. The frozen ground cracked under the point of the pickaxes, and sparks flew. The men were silent, their brains numb.

My mind still clung to the image of my wife. A thought crossed my mind: I didn't even know if she were still alive. I knew only one thing — which I have learned well by now: Love goes very far beyond the physical person of the beloved. It finds its deepest meaning in his spiritual being, his inner self. Whether or not he is actually present, whether or not he is still alive at all, ceases somehow to be of importance.

I did not know whether my wife was alive, and I had no means of finding out (during all my prison life there was no outgoing or incoming mail); but at that moment it ceased to matter. There was no need for me to know; nothing could touch the strength of my love, my thoughts, and the image of my beloved. Had I known then that my wife was dead, I think that I would still have given myself, undisturbed by that knowledge, to the contemplation of her image, and that my mental conversation with her would have been just as vivid and just as satisfying. "Set me like a seal upon thy heart, love is as strong as death."

This intensification of inner life helped the prisoner find a refuge from the emptiness, desolation and spiritual poverty of his existence, by letting him escape into the past. When given free rein, his imagination played with past events, often not important ones, but minor happenings and trifling things. His nostalgic memory glorified them and they assumed a strange character. Their world and their existence seemed very distant and the spirit reached out for them longingly: In my mind I took bus rides, unlocked the front door of my apartment, answered my telephone, switched on the electric lights. Our thoughts often centered on such details, and these memories could move one to tears.

As the inner life of the prisoner tended to become more intense, he also experienced the beauty of art and nature as never before. Under their influence he sometimes even forgot his own frightful circumstances. If someone had seen our faces on the journey from Auschwitz to a Bavarian camp as we beheld the mountains of Salzburg with their summits glowing in the sunset, through the little barred windows of the prison carriage, he would never have believed that those were the faces of men who had given up all hope of life and liberty. Despite that factor — or maybe because of it — we were carried away by nature's beauty, which we had missed for so long.

In camp, too, a man might draw the attention of a comrade working next to him to a nice view of the setting sun shining through the
tall trees of the Bavarian woods (as in the famous water color by
Dürer), the same woods in which we had built an enormous, hidden munitions plant. One evening, when we were already resting
on the floor of our hut, dead tired, soup bowls in hand, a fellow
prisoner rushed in and asked us to run out to the assembly grounds
and see the wonderful sunset. Standing outside we saw sinister
clouds glowing in the west and the whole sky alive with clouds of
ever-changing shapes and colors, from steel blue to blood red. The
desolate grey mud huts provided a sharp contrast, while the puddles on the muddy ground reflected the glowing sky. Then, after
minutes of moving silence, one prisoner said to another, "How
beautiful the world could be!"

Another time we were at work in a trench. The dawn was grey
around us; grey was the sky above; grey the snow in the pale light
of dawn; grey the rags in which my fellow prisoners were clad, and
grey their faces. I was again conversing silently with my wife, or
perhaps I was struggling to find the reason for my sufferings, my
slow dying. In a last violent protest against the hopelessness of
imminent death, I sensed my spirit piercing through the enveloping
gloom. I felt it transcend that hopeless, meaningless world, and
from somewhere I heard a victorious "Yes" in answer to my question of the existence of an ultimate purpose. At that moment a light
was lit in a distant farmhouse, which stood on the horizon as if
painted there, in the midst of the miserable grey of a dawning
morning in Bavaria. "*Et lux in tenebris lucet*" — and the light shineth
in the darkness. For hours I stood hacking at the icy ground. The
guard passed by, insulting me, and once again I communed with
my beloved. More and more I felt that she was present, that she was
with me; I had the feeling that I was able to touch her, able to stretch
out my hand and grasp hers. The feeling was very strong: she was
there. Then, at that very moment, a bird flew down silently and
perched just in front of me, on the heap of soil which I had dug up
from the ditch, and looked steadily at me.

* * *

We have stated that that which was ultimately responsible for
the state of the prisoner's inner self was not so much the enumerat-
ed psychophysical causes as it was the result of a free decision.

Psychological observations of the prisoners have shown that only the men who allowed their inner hold on their moral and spiritual selves to subside eventually fell victim to the camp's degenerating influences. The question now arises, what could, or should, have constituted this "inner hold"?

Former prisoners, when writing or relating their experiences, agree that the most depressing influence of all was that a prisoner could not know how long his term of imprisonment would be. He had been given no date for his release. (In our camp it was pointless even to talk about it.) Actually a prison term was not only uncertain but unlimited. A well-known research psychologist has pointed out that life in a concentration camp could be called a "provisional existence." We can add to this by defining it as a "provisional existence of unknown limit."

New arrivals usually knew nothing about the conditions at a camp. Those who had come back from other camps were obliged to keep silent, and from some camps no one had returned. On entering camp a change took place in the minds of the men. With the end of uncertainty there came the uncertainty of the end. It was impossible to foresee whether or when, if at all, this form of existence would end.

The latin word *finis* has two meanings: the end or the finish, and a goal to reach. A man who could not see the end of his "provisional existence" was not able to aim at an ultimate goal in life. He ceased living for the future, in contrast to a man in normal life. Therefore the whole structure of his inner life changed; signs of decay set in which we know from other areas of life. The unemployed worker, for example, is in a similar position. His existence has become provisional and in a certain sense he cannot live for the future or aim at a goal. Research work done on unemployed miners has shown that they suffer from a peculiar sort of deformed time — inner time — which is a result of their unemployed state. Prisoners, too, suffered from this strange "time-experience." In camp, a small time unit, a day, for example, filled with hourly tortures and fatigue, appeared endless. A larger time unit, perhaps a week, seemed to pass very quickly. My comrades agreed when I said that in camp a day lasted longer than a week. How paradoxical was our time-experience! In this connection we are reminded of Thomas Mann's *The Magic Mountain*, which contains some very pointed psychological remarks. Mann studies the spiritual development of people who are in an analogous psychological position, i.e., tuberculosis patients in a sanatorium who also know no date for their release. They experience a similar existence — without a future and without a goal.

One of the prisoners, who on his arrival marched with a long column of new inmates from the station to the camp, told me later that he had felt as though he were marching at his own funeral. His life had seemed to him absolutely without future. He regarded it as over and done, as if he had already died. This feeling of lifelessness was intensified by other causes: in time, it was the limitlessness of the term of imprisonment which was most acutely felt; in space, the narrow limits of the prison. Anything outside the barbed wire became remote, out of reach and, in a way, unreal. The events and the people outside, all the normal life there, had a ghostly aspect for the prisoner. The outside life, that is, as much as he could see of it, appeared to him almost as it might have to a dead man who looked at it from another world.

A man who let himself decline because he could not see any future goal found himself occupied with retrospective thoughts. In a different connection, we have already spoken of the tendency there was to look into the past, to help make the present, with all its horrors, less real. But in robbing the present of its reality there lay a certain danger. It became easy to overlook the opportunities to make something positive of camp life, opportunities which really did exist. Regarding our "provisional existence" as unreal was in itself an important factor in causing the prisoners to lose their hold on life; everything in a way became pointless. Such people forget that often it is just such an exceptionally difficult external situation which gives man the opportunity to grow spiritually beyond himself. Instead of taking the camp's difficulties as a test of their inner strength, they did not take their life seriously and despised it as something of no consequence. They preferred to close their eyes and to live in the past. Life for such people became meaningless.

Naturally only a few people were capable of reaching great spiritual heights. But a few were given the chance to attain human greatness even through their apparent worldly failure and death, an accomplishment which in ordinary circumstances they would never have achieved. To the others of us, the mediocre and the half-hearted, the words of Bismarck could be applied: "Life is like being at the dentist. You always think that the worst is still to come, and yet it is over already." Varying this, we could say that most men in a concentration camp believed that the real opportunities of life had passed. Yet, in reality, there was an opportunity and a challenge.

One could make a victory of those experiences turning life into an inner triumph, or one could ignore the challenge and simply vegetate, as did a majority of the prisoners.

Any attempt at fighting the camp's psychopathological influence on the prisoner by psychotherapeutic or psychohygienic methods had to aim at giving him inner strength by pointing out to him a future goal to which he could look forward. Instinctively some of the prisoners attempted to find one on their own. It is a peculiarity of man that he can only live by looking to the future — sub specie aeternitatis. And this is his salvation in the most difficult moments of his existence, although he sometimes has to force his mind to the task.

I remember a personal experience. Almost in tears from pain (I had terrible sores on my feet from wearing torn shoes), I limped a few kilometers with our long column of men from the camp to our work site. Very cold, bitter winds struck us. I kept thinking of the endless little problems of our miserable life. What would there be to eat tonight? If a piece of sausage came as extra ration, should I exchange it for a piece of bread? Should I trade my last cigarette, which was left from a bonus I received a fortnight ago, for a bowl of soup? How could I get a piece of wire to replace the fragment which served as one of my shoelaces? Would I get to our work site in time to join my usual working party or would I have to join another, which might have a brutal foreman? What could I do to get on good terms with the Capo, who could help me to obtain work in camp instead of undertaking this horribly long daily march?

I became disgusted with the state of affairs which compelled me, daily and hourly, to think of only such trivial things. I forced my thoughts to turn to another subject. Suddenly I saw myself standing on the platform of a well-lit, warm and pleasant lecture room. In front of me sat an attentive audience on comfortable upholstered seats. I was giving a lecture on the psychology of the concentration camp! All that oppressed me at that moment became objective, seen and described from the remote viewpoint of science. By this method I succeeded somehow in rising above the situation, above the sufferings of the moment, and I observed them as if they were already of the past. Both I and my troubles became the object of an interesting psychoscientific study undertaken by myself. What does Spinoza say in his Ethics? — "Affectus, qui passio est, desinit esse passio simulatque eius claram et distinctam formamus ideam." Emotion, which is suffering, ceases to be suffering as soon as we form a clear and precise picture of it.

The prisoner who had lost faith in the future — his future — was doomed. With his loss of belief in the future, he also lost his spiritual hold; he let himself decline and became subject to mental and physical decay. Usually this happened quite suddenly, in the form of a crisis, the symptoms of which were familiar to the experienced camp inmate. We all feared this moment — not for ourselves, which would have been pointless, but for our friends. Usually it began with the prisoner refusing one morning to get dressed and wash or to go out on the parade grounds. No entreaties, no blows, no threats had any effect. He just lay there, hardly moving. If this crisis was brought about by an illness, he refused to be taken to the sick-bay or to do anything to help himself. He simply gave up. There he remained, lying in his own excreta, and nothing bothered him any more.

I once had a dramatic demonstration of the close link between the loss of faith in the future and this dangerous giving up. F__ , my senior block warden, a fairly well-known composer and librettist, confided in me one day: "I would like to tell you something, Doctor. I have had a strange dream. A voice told me that I could wish for something, that I should only say what I wanted to know, and all my questions would be answered. What do you think I asked? That I would like to know when the war would be over for me. You know what I mean, Doctor — for me! I wanted to know when we, when our camp, would be liberated and our sufferings come to an end."

"And when did you have this dream?" I asked.

"In February, 1945," he answered. It was then the beginning of March.

"What did your dream voice answer?"

Furtively he whispered to me, "March thirtieth."

When F__ told me about his dream, he was still full of hope and convinced that the voice of his dream would be right. But as the promised day drew nearer, the war news which reached our camp made it appear very unlikely that we would be free on the promised date. On March twenty-ninth, F__ suddenly became ill and ran a high temperature. On March thirtieth, the day his prophecy had told him that the war and suffering would be over for him, he became delirious and lost consciousness. On March thirty-first, he was dead. To all outward appearances, he had died of typhus.

Those who know how close the connection is between the state of mind of a man — his courage and hope, or lack of them — and the state of immunity of his body will understand that the sudden loss of hope and courage can have a deadly effect. The ultimate cause of my friend's death was that the expected liberation did not come and he was severely disappointed. This suddenly lowered his body's resistance against the latent typhus infection. His faith in the future and his will to live had become paralyzed and his body fell victim to illness — and thus the voice of his dream was right after all.

The observations of this one case and the conclusion drawn from them are in accordance with something that was drawn to my attention by the chief doctor of our concentration camp. The death rate in the week between Christmas, 1944, and New Year's, 1945, increased in camp beyond all previous experience. In his opinion, the explanation for this increase did not lie in the harder working conditions or the deterioration of our food supplies or a change of weather or new epidemics. It was simply that the majority of the prisoners had lived in the naive hope that they would be home again by Christmas. As the time drew near and there was no encouraging news, the prisoners lost courage and disappointment overcame them. This had a dangerous influence on their powers of resistance and a great number of them died.

As we said before, any attempt to restore a man's inner strength in the camp had first to succeed in showing him some future goal. Nietzsche's words. "He who has a *why* to live for can bear with almost any *how*," could be the guiding motto for all psychotherapeutic and psychohygienic efforts regarding prisoners. Whenever there was an opportunity for it, one had to give them a why — an aim — for their lives, in order to strengthen them to bear the terrible how of their existence. Woe to him who saw no more sense in his life, no aim, no purpose, and therefore no point in carrying on. He was soon lost. The typical reply with which such a man rejected all encouraging arguments was, "I have nothing to expect from life any more." What sort of answer can one give to that?

What was really needed was a fundamental change in our attitude toward life. We had to learn ourselves and, furthermore, we had to teach the despairing men, that it did not really matter what we expected from life, but rather what life expected from us. We needed to stop asking about the meaning of life, and instead to think of ourselves as those who were being questioned by life— daily and hourly. Our answer must consist, not in talk and medita- tion, but in right action and in right conduct. Life ultimately means taking the responsibility to find the right answer to its problems and to fulfill the tasks which it constantly sets for each individual.

These tasks, and therefore the meaning of life, differ from man to man, and from moment to moment. Thus it is impossible to define the meaning of life in a general way. Questions about the meaning of life can never be answered by sweeping statements. "Life" does not mean something vague, but something very real and concrete, just as life's tasks are also very real and concrete. They form man's destiny, which is different and unique for each individual. No man and no destiny can be compared with any other man or any other destiny. No situation repeats itself, and each situation calls for a dif- ferent response. Sometimes the situation in which a man finds him- self may require him to shape his own fate by action. At other times it is more advantageous for him to make use of an opportunity for contemplation and to realize assets in this way. Sometimes man may be required simply to accept fate, to bear his cross. Every situ- ation is distinguished by its uniqueness, and there is always only one right answer to the problem posed by the situation at hand.

When a man finds that it is his destiny to suffer, he will have to accept his suffering as his task; his single and unique task. He will have to acknowledge the fact that even in suffering he is unique and alone in the universe. No one can relieve him of his suffering or suf- fer in his place. His unique opportunity lies in the way in which he bears his burden.

For us, as prisoners, these thoughts were not speculations far removed from reality. They were the only thoughts that could be of help to us. They kept us from despair, even when there seemed to be no chance of coming out of it alive. Long ago we had passed the stage of asking what was the meaning of life, a naive query which understands life as the attaining of some aim through the active cre- ation of something of value. For us, the meaning of life embraced the wider cycles of life and death, of suffering and of dying.

Once the meaning of suffering had been revealed to us, we refused to minimize or alleviate the camp's tortures by ignoring them or harboring false illusions and entertaining artificial opti- mism. Suffering had become a task on which we did not want to turn our backs. We had realized its hidden opportunities for achievement, the opportunities which caused the poet Rilke to write, "*Wie viel ist aufzuleiden!*" (How much suffering there is to get through!) Rilke spoke of "getting through suffering" as others would talk of "getting through work." There was plenty of suffering for us to get through. Therefore, it was necessary to face up to the full amount of suffering, trying to keep moments of weakness and furtive tears to a minimum. But there was no need to be ashamed of tears, for tears bore witness that a man had the greatest of courage, the courage to suffer. Only very few realized that. Shamefacedly some confessed occasionally that they had wept, like the comrade who answered my question of how he had gotten over his edema, by confessing, "I have wept it out of my system."

*   *   *

And now to the last chapter in the psychology of a concentration camp — the psychology of the prisoner who has been released. In describing the experiences of liberation, which naturally must be personal, we shall pick up the threads of that part of our narrative which told of the morning when the white flag was hoisted above the camp gates after days of high tension. This state of inner suspense was followed by total relaxation. But it would be quite wrong to think that we went mad with joy. What, then, did happen?

With tired steps we prisoners dragged ourselves to the camp gates. Timidly we looked around and glanced at each other questioningly. Then we ventured a few steps out of camp. This time no orders were shouted at us, nor was there any need to duck quickly to avoid a blow or kick. Oh no! This time the guards offered us cigarettes! We hardly recognized them at first; they had hurriedly changed into civilian clothes. We walked slowly along the road leading from the camp. Soon our legs hurt and threatened to buckle. But we limped on; we wanted to see the camp's surroundings for the first time with the eyes of free men. "Freedom" — we repeated to ourselves, and yet we could not grasp it. We had said this word so often during all the years we dreamed about it, that it had lost its meaning. Its reality did not penetrate into our consciousness; we could not grasp the fact that freedom was ours.

We came to meadows full of flowers. We saw and realized that they were there, but we had no feelings about them. The first spark of joy came when we saw a rooster with a tail of multicolored feathers. But it remained only a spark; we did not yet belong to this world.

In the evening when we all met again in our hut, one said secretly to the other, "Tell me, were you pleased today?"

And the other replied, feeling ashamed as he did not know that we all felt similarly, "Truthfully, no!" We had literally lost the ability to feel pleased and had to relearn it slowly.

Psychologically, what was happening to the liberated prisoners could be called "depersonalization." Everything appeared unreal, unlikely, as in a dream. We could not believe it was true. How often in the past years had we been deceived by dreams! We dreamt that the day of liberation had come, that we had been set free, had returned home, greeted our friends, embraced our wives, sat down at the table and started to tell of all the things we had gone through — even of how we had often seen the day of liberation in our dreams. And then — a whistle shrilled in our ears, the signal to get up, and our dreams of freedom came to an end. And now the dream had come true. But could we truly believe in it?

The body has fewer inhibitions than the mind. It made good use of the new freedom from the first moment on. It began to eat ravenously, for hours and days, even half the night. It is amazing what quantities one can eat. And when one of the prisoners was invited out by a friendly farmer in the neighborhood, he ate and ate and then drank coffee, which loosened his tongue, and he then began to talk, often for hours. The pressure which had been on his mind for years was released at last. Hearing him talk, one got the impression that he had to talk, that his desire to speak was irresistible. I have known people who have been under heavy pressure only for a short time (for example, through a cross-examination by the Gestapo) to have similar reactions. Many days passed, until not only the tongue was loosened, but something within oneself as well; then feeling suddenly broke through the strange fetters which had restrained it.

One day, a few days after the liberation, I walked through the country past flowering meadows, for miles and miles, toward the market town near the camp. Larks rose to the sky and I could hear their joyous song. There was no one to be seen for miles around; there was nothing but the wide earth and sky and the larks' jubilation and the freedom of space. I stopped, looked around, and up to the sky — and then I went down on my knees. At that moment there was very little I knew of myself or of the world — I had but one sentence in mind — always the same: "I called to the Lord from my narrow prison and He answered me in the freedom of space."

How long I knelt there and repeated this sentence memory can no longer recall. But I know that on that day, in that hour, my new life started. Step for step I progressed, until I again became a human being.

The way that led from the acute mental tension of the last days in camp (from that war of nerves to mental peace) was certainly not free from obstacles. It would be an error to think that a liberated prisoner was not in need of spiritual care any more. We have to consider that a man who has been under such enormous mental pressure for such a long time is naturally in some danger after his liberation, especially since the pressure was released quite suddenly. This danger (in the sense of psychological hygiene) is the psychological counterpart of the bends. Just as the physical health of the caisson worker would be endangered if he left his diver's chamber suddenly (where he is under enormous atmospheric pressure), so the man who has suddenly been liberated from mental pressure can suffer damage to his moral and spiritual health.

During this psychological phase one observed that people with natures of a more primitive kind could not escape the influences of the brutality which had surrounded them in camp life. Now, being free, they thought they could use their freedom licentiously and ruthlessly. The only thing that had changed for them was that they were now the oppressors instead of the oppressed. They became instigators, not objects, of willful force and injustice. They justified their behavior by their own terrible experiences. This was often revealed in apparently insignificant events. A friend was walking across a field with me toward the camp when suddenly we came to a field of green crops. Automatically, I avoided it but he drew his arm through mine and dragged me through it. I stammered something about not treading down the young crops. He became annoyed, gave me an angry look and shouted, "You don't say! And hasn't enough been taken from us? My wife and child have been gassed — not to mention everything else — and you would forbid me to tread on a few stalks of oats!"

Only slowly could these men be guided back to the common-place truth that no one has the right to do wrong, not even if wrong has been done to them. We had to strive to lead them back to this truth, or the consequences would have been much worse than the loss of a few thousand stalks of oats. I can still see the prisoner who rolled up his shirt sleeves, thrust his right hand under my nose and shouted, "May this hand be cut off if I don't stain it with blood on the day when I get home!" I want to emphasize that the man who said these words was not a bad fellow. He had been the best of com-rades in camp and afterwards.

Apart from the moral deformity resulting from the sudden release of mental pressure, there were two other fundamental expe-riences which threatened to damage the character of the liberated prisoner: bitterness and disillusionment when he returned to his former life.

Bitterness was caused by a number of things he came up against in his former home town. When, on his return, a man found that in many places he was met only with a shrug of the shoulders and with hackneyed phrases, he tended to become bitter and to ask himself why he had gone through all that he had. When he heard the same phrases nearly everywhere — "We did not know about it," and "We, too, have suffered," then he asked himself, have they really nothing better to say to me?

The experience of disillusionment is different. Here it was not one's fellow man (whose superficiality and lack of feeling was so disgusting that one finally felt like creeping into a hole and neither hearing nor seeing human beings any more) but fate itself which seemed so cruel. A man who for years had thought he had reached the absolute limit of all possible suffering now found that suffering has no limits, and that he could suffer still more, and still more intensely.

When we spoke about attempts to give a man in camp mental courage, we said that he had to be shown something to look for-ward to in the future. He had to be reminded that life still waited for him, that a human being waited for his return. But after libera-tion? There were some men who found that no one awaited them. Woe to him who found that the person whose memory alone had given him courage in camp did not exist any more! Woe to him who, when the day of his dreams finally came, found it so different from all he had longed for! Perhaps he boarded a trolley, traveled out to the home which he had seen for years in his mind, and only in his mind, and pressed the bell, just as he has longed to do in thousands of dreams, only to find that the person who should open the door was not there, and would never be there again.

We all said to each other in camp that there could be no earthly happiness which could compensate for all we had suffered. We were not hoping for happiness — it was not that which gave us courage and gave meaning to our suffering, our sacrifices and our dying. And yet we were not prepared for unhappiness. This disillusionment, which awaited not a small number of prisoners, was an experience which these men have found very hard to get over and which, for a psychiatrist, is also very difficult to help them overcome. But this must not be a discouragement to him; on the contrary, it should provide an added stimulus.

But for every one of the liberated prisoners, the day comes when, looking back on his camp experiences, he can no longer understand how he endured it all. As the day of his liberation eventually came, when everything seemed to him like a beautiful dream, so also the day comes when all his camp experiences seem to him nothing but a nightmare.

The crowning experience of all, for the homecoming man, is the wonderful feeling that, after all he has suffered, there is nothing he need fear any more except his God

---

Questions to Consider for Chapter Four:

1. What reactions do you have? What impression do you get of Frankl? Why is he interested in narrating these experiences?

2. Describe the three phases of the psychology of the prisoner that Frankl observes.

3. Is it possible for someone to retain freedom and humanity in this kind of desperate situation? Explain?

4. Frankl, an internationally known psychiatrist and founder of an approach to psychiatry known as logo-therapy, first published this book anonymously. Why do you suppose this was the case?

5. Other comments or reactions?

Holocaust Exhibit and the Dance

Jerome Freeman

Footsteps roll echoes along marble floors
of the Landmark Center. I crawl with
fascination and dread through the exhibit,
drawn like the elder Pliny to his volcano.

Photos of somber faces and discarded
bodies and loss of innocence stir up
silent clamor around me. An inscription
on a dull wall asks how these images
can exist. There are no answers here.
A custodian at the exit seems a grim
Charon, measuring my passage
as though hallway was hallowed Styx.

Hearing music, I blankly cross
to the railing. In the lobby below
an assembled crowd concentrates
on eight Polish dancers, swirling joyful
ribbons and tradition before them.

Eerie juxtaposition gives witness
to darkness and second chances.

Part II

Dilemmas
of Caring

W hat is the right thing to do? This is the persistent and disturbing question that faces us as we seek to make concrete decisions with respect to the call to care. Who gets care? Who decides? Are there limits to care? The dilemmas facing caregivers are the theme of the readings in Part II.

Are there any guidelines or principles to assist us as we face the dilemmas of caring? And in particular, who is the primary decision maker? Who is the caregiver or the recipient of care? What about in the case of the child who refuses treatment? Is force ever justified? These dilemmas of autonomy are addressed in the readings in Chapter Five.

Are there limits to who gets care? This is the question of justice that arises out of the case of Rose Brech in Chapter Six. A Sioux Falls resident, she asked the county commissioners of Minnehaha County, S.D., to pay for a heart and lung transplant operation in 1985.

Dilemmas in care decisions at the end of life are the topic of the cases and readings in Chapter Seven. In seeking to do good (beneficence) and to avoid harm (non-maleficence), when does the effort to do good sometimes result in harm? Are there limits to the good that can be done at the end of life?

Dilemmas arising in care decisions at the beginning of life are the topic of readings in Chapter Eight. All of the principles (autonomy, justice, non-maleficence, and beneficence) are involved here. How shall communities work to prevent the birth of fetal alcohol syndrome babies? Is there a conflict between women's rights and the well-being of the unborn child? Are there limits to the use of technology in saving premature babies?

Chapter Five:
Respecting the Person
Arthur Olsen

"Ethical and value issues are inextricably interwoven throughout the fabric of patient care.
Inevitably, they contribute to the complexities of
caring and to the ongoing challenges encountered
by caregivers. I believe that true caring is best
accomplished when specific expertise and attention
are devoted to resolving these unavoidable bioethical conflicts." — J. W. Freeman in "Reflections on
the Teaching of Bioethics."

"In the mutuality of the patient-physician relationship, each one is to be respected as a person
and supported in her or his autonomous decisions,
insofar as those decisions are not, in particular circumstances, overridden by other ethical obligations." — "Ethical Dimensions of Informed
Consent," from the Committee on Ethics of the
American College of Obstetricians and
Gynecologists.

What is the right thing to do in caring for persons who face
issues of life, health, and death? Are there any guidelines
or principles to assist us in facing the perplexing ethical
dilemmas that may arise in making decisions about care? Should
restraints be imposed on an elderly patient in a nursing home for
his own good, even if it is against his will? Should the county pay
for an expensive heart-lung transplant operation for a mother who
can't afford it? Is it right to withhold tube feedings from Nancy
Cruzan who is comatose and cannot answer for herself? Should the
knowledge of genetic predisposition to disease be available to
insurance companies?

These are questions that require reflection and ultimately decisions to act. This means thinking through reasons for the rightness
or wrongness of actions. There is a need for ethics and in particular
biomedical ethics. As you wrestle with the cases and essays in Part
II you are invited to enter into the practice of biomedical ethics.

The Need for Ethics

Simple, clear-cut answers are not available for questions like these. Deliberation and reflection are required. Often there are grave possibilities to consider as alternatives are weighed, each of which has something to be said for or against it.

Much depends upon the particulars of the situation and the patient's story. What are the patient's wishes? What are the resources in the nursing home for additional supervision of someone at risk of falling? Are there alternative strategies? Is the need for restraint temporary? In a moral dilemma there are often thoughtful rationales for different and opposing choices.

A sound approach to the dilemmas of caring is arguably grounded in the call to care. This call, as developed in the readings and discussion of Part I, Dimensions of Caring, is rooted in the claim of other persons upon us. Responding to the needs of other persons, like Susan, engages us in the stories of their lives. This is because "health" pertains to the whole person, whose story includes not only the facts of bodily limitations and disease, but also the influences of family and friends. To care for another person, therefore, requires attention both to the medical facts and to the story of the one being cared for.

From this point of view it becomes clear that regardless of the guidelines or principles drawn upon to make difficult decisions in concrete cases, respect for personal humanness is at the heart of the matter. Dilemmas arise because we are not certain how best to respect the personhood of those who claim our care. Should restraints be imposed? Should tube feeding be stopped? These are difficult and unavoidable questions that you and I must face. Medical analysis and ethical reflection are required and decisions must be made. It has been aptly observed that not to decide is to render a decision.

The claim of another person for care is fundamentally an ethical, moral one. Thus, the obligation to respect the right of a patient to choose whether or not to accept surgery or medication may be understood as a moral obligation. Society may also choose to express it legally. Congress passed the Patient Self-Determination Act in 1990 requiring that all patients entering a hospital or a nursing home be asked whether or not they have an advance care directive.

We now ask if there are moral principles or guidelines to guide us in considering the dilemmas of health care decisions. Consider, for example, the question of whether or not to impose restraints on a resident of a nursing home. Is it ever right to override the wish of the resident not to have restraints? This is the moral question. Should there be rules or laws governing the practice? This is the legal question. Determining whether ethical principles should be upheld by the passage of laws is a separate though important issue.

The search for principles and guidelines is the task of ethics. Ethics is that discipline of philosophy and theology that seeks to answer questions of the rightness or wrongness, goodness or badness of actions. Theoretical ethics (meta-ethics) asks these questions foundationally. What is the nature of "good"? Applied ethics relates the deliberation to specific situations.

Biomedical ethics (or bioethics) is the application of the discipline of ethics to the concrete issues arising in health care, medical practice, and research related to life (such as drug and genetic testing). Reflection on these issues has spawned new journals (such as *The Hastings Center Report* and the *Kennedy Institute of Ethics Journal*), and a new discipline, biomedical ethics. The interest in this discipline is broadly based, involving not only professional theologians and philosophers, but also practitioners of health care (physicians, nurses, administrators), legislators, recipients of health care, and concerned citizens. For example, in 1961 an ethics committee of citizens was established at Swedish Hospital in Seattle to help decide who should receive the benefit of the new dialysis machine. At that time there were not enough machines to respond to the demand. Today many health care institutions have their own ethics committees.

In the practice of biomedical ethics an interest in articulating principles has emerged. This development was in part stimulated by an act of Congress. In 1974 Congress passed the National Research Act that suggested a National Commission for the Protection of Human Subjects be established to "identify basic ethical principles which should underlie the conduct of biomedical and behavioral research involving human subjects" and "to develop guidelines which should be followed in research to assure that it is conducted in accord with such principles." The final report was called the Belmont Report. In this report, the twelve commissioners (including two professional ethicists) advanced three principles: respect for persons, beneficence, and justice. No persons should be experimented on without their informed consent (respect for persons). Only those experiments should be conducted that have reasonable chances of benefiting persons (beneficence). And the fruits of research should be fairly available to those needing the benefit (justice).[1]

Various articulations of these principles have become an essential part of the vocabulary of biomedical ethics. For example, in 1979 Tom Beauchamp and James Childress, scholars associated with the Kennedy Institute of Ethics at Georgetown University, expanded the list to four principles in the first edition of *The Principles of Biomedical Ethics*.[2] They stressed autonomy, non-maleficence, beneficence, and justice. This text and subsequent editions (now in its fourth edition) have been a basic part of the workshops in biomedical ethics sponsored several times a year by the Kennedy Institute of Ethics at Georgetown University.

The Story of Biomedical Ethics

The story of biomedical ethics is the story of a practice that has deep roots in Western civilization. In this sense it is not a new ethic. Rather, it is a tradition of reflection that has enjoyed a phenomenal growth since 1960 in response to the inhumane practices of the holocaust and new developments in health and medicine.

Roots of the Practice

The title of a series of lectures to the Harvard Medical School by Albert Jonsen, ethicist at the medical school at the University of Washington, is appealing: "The New Medicine and the Old Ethics." The old ethics, that is, the tradition of ethical reflection drawn from Greek and Hebrew roots, has new questions to consider. The task is not to start ethics anew but to carry forward the practice of ethical reflection to respond to the perplexing questions raised by the new medicine. [3]

It is significant that the National Commission for the Protection of Human Subjects, referred to above, declared that the principles presented in the Belmont Report were "both profoundly rooted in the moral traditions of Western civilization" and implied in many previously published codes. Thus, in recommending that the conduct and application of behavioral and biomedical research be done in accordance with the principles of respect for personhood, beneficence, and justice, the commission was carrying forward the Western heritage of ethical practice to the new frontiers. Consider briefly the roots of this practice of ethics. It is a story of theory and practice.

In the Greek tradition Aristotle reminds us that ethical reflection is not just theoretical like geometry, but practical, arising from specific situations and cases. The work of a pilot or a physician is evaluated in practice. A pilot is one who steers the ship so that it does not crash on unforeseen rocks. The physician cares for the health of the patient. A pilot who allows the ship to wreck on the shoals is not really a pilot. And a physician who does not care for the health of the patient is not really a physician. Virtues such as prudence or courage serve to guide the person in specific situations. The courageous person is neither timid nor foolhardy. What this means for the sailor or physician must be understood in *practice*. Thus, the Hippocratic oath is a guide to the *practice* of physicians, admonishing them to treat according to their ability and judgment but never to act in such a way as to injure or wrong the patient.

Attention to application is also a distinguishing feature of the Hebrew Old Testament. Broad prohibitions are outlined in a commandment like "Thou shalt not kill," but what this means is developed in relationship to specific situations. If a man has an ox that is known to be dangerous and it gores and kills a neighbor, the owner cannot say, "It wasn't me but my ox." The owner is responsible. (Exodus 21:28 f.f.) The spirit of the commandments is summed up as loving God with one's whole heart (Deut. 6:4-5) and one's neighbor as one's self (Lev. 19:18). What this means is frequently illustrated in specifics. Love strangers, remembering that the Hebrews themselves had been strangers in Egypt. Care for widows and orphans. And, as we have suggested earlier, care for matters of health and neighborhood (*c.f.* chp. 2).

The practical specificity of the Hebrew Old Testament is affirmed in the New Testament in Jesus' teaching in parables. Does God care about those who have gone astray? Indeed! The prodigal son is invited back by the loving father. The story of the Good Samaritan comes in response to the questions of the lawyer who, after agreeing that he should love God with heart and soul and his neighbor as himself, asks "And who is my neighbor?" In the specifics of the parable, the neighbor is the person who has been beaten and robbed and left at the side of the road.

As Albert Jonsen has pointed out, the themes from these traditions provide the substance for ethical reflection in Western medicine. They are integrated by pivotal thinkers such as Thomas Aquinas. Aquinas (b. 1225, d.1275), philosopher-theologian, argues that persons seeking to do the right thing should be guided not only by the virtues learned from Aristotle (including courage, prudence, temperance, and justice), but also by the virtues of faith, hope, and love in the Christian tradition. The theme of compassion embodied in the Good Samaritan story finds expression in hospitals (places of hospitality for strangers) and in orders of knighthood: Knights Hospitaller of St. John (of Jerusalem). And the practical wisdom espoused in Aristotle's philosophy develops into a casuistry — that is, a method to bring moral judgment to bear on specific situations or cases. The distinction between ordinary and extraordinary treatment comes from this tradition of casuistry. When is it best to treat and when not to treat? Life is a gift from God that should be cared for. Employing ordinary treatment measures is obligatory, mandated by a respect for life. But treatment at any cost is not required. Some treatment may ask too much of the person's resources or strength and is therefore not obligatory.

In more recent centuries the story of Western ethics is carried on by philosophers such as Immanuel Kant and John Stuart Mill who seek to ground practical judgments on rational principles established by reason. They represent two fundamentally different ways of grounding the obligation to care for life but are agreed on the fact that the task of ethics is to relate moral approaches to specific situations or cases. For Kant, the central principle is *duty*, grounded in the categorical imperative. Succinctly put, in all situations persons must be treated as ends and not means. For Mill the foundation is *utility*. The outcome for all people will be best if each person is treated with respect.

The Recent Story of Biomedical Ethics

Ethical reflections from ancient times to the present have championed respect for personhood. Unfortunately, human history includes horrific examples of behavior gone awry. The terrible experiences of holocaust survivors, such as Victor Frankl, are both striking and shocking. And they help us understand the phenomenal growth of recent developments in biomedical ethics.

In *Man's Search for Meaning* Victor Frankl describes the almost total disregard for the humanness of the prisoners. Frankl also eloquently portrays persistence of a will to meaning, a will to humanness, in some persons. He observes in himself and others that those who survive are those who don't give up the will to meaning. Such prisoners discover that even when all freedoms are taken away externally — when prisoners are deprived of all previous signs of identity (clothing, jewelry, manuscripts) and given only the identity of a number — the freedom to choose their interior thoughts cannot be taken away. Frankl set himself the task of rewriting a manuscript that had been taken away from him and destroyed.

In important respects biomedical ethics has flourished in the shadow of World War II atrocities and the attempts of the Nuremberg trials and the Nuremberg Code to prevent their repetition. Principles were sought to prevent the disrespect for human life that developed so blatantly during the Nazi regime. The most obvious feature of this disrespect was the total disregard of the consent of those imprisoned or experimented on. Individuals like Frankl were forced into concentration camps. Many were executed, while a few were saved for work under inhuman conditions. Disrespect was only slightly less visibly present in the attitudes towards experimentation and eugenics of the Nazi doctors. Experimentation on prisoners without their consent was justified on the grounds that the larger good would be served by the knowledge gained. The policies of genocide had their small beginnings, according to Leo Alexander, in the attitude that "there is such a thing as life not worthy to be lived."[4] This attitude justified the maltreatment and even the elimination of the handicapped.

Somewhat to the chagrin of contemporary ethicists in the United States, the practice of eugenics had spokespersons in the United States in the 1930s. This sometimes resulted in the sterilization of the mentally handicapped without their consent. And certain classes of people were experimented on without their consent, as in the Tuskegee project, designed to study the effects of syphilis on black males. The research project was continued into the '60s, long after drugs had been developed to ameliorate the disease. Congress commissioned the Belmont Report to ensure that experimentation would be carried out with the consent of those involved and for their benefit.

A second reason for the recent flourishing of biomedical ethics is the need to respond to the new dilemmas posed by the awesome developments in 20th century medicine. The ability to sustain life with machines and to transplant organs like hearts and lungs has led thoughtful people to conclude that technology has outrun our

ethics. As we consider what can be done in reproductive technology or in developing machines that can keep people alive indefinite-
ly, we hear an array of urgent and disturbing questions. Does the
end justify the means? Because we can do something, should we? Is
turning off Karen Ann Quinlan's respirator causing death or cooperating with death? If there is a shortage of treatments like dialysis
machines, who gets them?

The flourishing of the literature of biomedical ethics has come in
response to these questions. The need existed to provide people
struggling with these issues (the researchers, the caregivers, and the
recipients of care) with principles to guide reflection. Albert Jonsen,
one of the commissioners who produced the Belmont Report, put it
this way, "The philosophical ethics of that era had very little to say
about the substantial content of moral decision and action.
Theological ethics used terms that were incomprehensible to many
who were not believers or who were believers of a different sort. We
had to find an idiom that at one and the same time, expressed substantive content and was comprehensible to many listeners."

The attempt to identify principles, such as we will be using to
consider the dilemmas of caring, helps provide policy makers,
health care professionals, and care recipients with a language that
clarifies issues and encourages reflection and discussion. This effort
encourages an interdisciplinary approach to these issues.

The emergence of ethics committees is a kind of paradigm of
what is at stake. They include lay people as well as professionals.
We need the voice of the professional for expertise in scientific and
medical diagnosis. But we also need other perspectives to evaluate
the issues of human flourishing that affect us all. Together we question whether to treat or not to treat; how to experiment humanely
for human benefit; how to make caring decisions that respect persons, avoid harm, and are just.

The Principles

Before proceeding to the readings for this section, further reflections on the benefits and limitations of principles is warranted. First
a warning: principles need to be understood in relation to specific
cases. Hence each chapter presents study questions which invite the
reader to be engaged in the discussion. Frequently easy answers are
not evident. Decisions are based on careful analysis of cases and
application of the perspectives embodied in the principles. How

can we best care for human flourishing as we weigh the alternatives?

Principle one: *Respect for autonomy.* Autonomy means literally self (*autos*) law (*nomos*). Rational human beings have a right to be involved in decisions made about their care. It is their life, their story. They are the ones called upon to will to be healthy, to carry out their lives with courage. What does a person want? What would other reasonable persons in similar situations want if they could express themselves? To respect the person, consent must be informed. Engaging in the practice of respecting autonomy is the theme of the readings in Chapter Five. Respecting autonomy is not the same as saying that the wishes of the patient always rule.

Principle two: *Non-maleficence.* Literally this means to do no harm. In a certain sense this idea is self-evident. To respect persons, certain kinds of behavior are out of bounds. This is because human beings are intrinsically valuable. This principle invites consideration of and evaluation of risk. In a way, all medication involves risk. What is an acceptable level? The patient should be involved in this determination. When does the effort to do good result in unacceptable harm? In the Roman Catholic tradition the principle of double effect is emphasized. Although good is intended, harm may occur. An action to save the mother may put the fetus at an unintended risk of harm. As a second example, medications have warning labels noting that unintended side effects can occur. In the clinical realm, the hoped-for benefits and risks must be carefully assessed.

Principle three: *Beneficence.* This means to do good. What is the best for the patient? This is certainly related to "do not harm." But there is a difference. The obligation to do good has a different moral edge. "Do not kill" is a kind of absolute admonition. But when do I risk my own life to save another person? How much is required of the caregiver? What if there is a conflict between what the patient wants and what seems best medically for that patient?

Principle four: *Justice.* Who gets the goods of caring? This is the question of distribution. On a macro-level, it is the question of budget. How much funding goes to which type of research? How can we be sure that everyone gets what is needed, especially those who can't afford it? On a micro-level, who gets an organ for transplant if there aren't enough to go around? The other principles can be thought of on a one-on-one, individual basis. The principle of justice requires us to think of the community of those needing care.

We invite you now to become engaged in the practice of bio-medical ethics beginning with cases and readings relating to autonomy and informed consent.

[1]Albert R. Jonsen in the forward to *A Matter of Principles: Ferment in U.S. Bioethics,* edited by Edwin R. DuBose, Ron Hamel, and Lawrence J. O'Connell, p. xiv. Valley Forge, Pa., Trinity Press International, 1994.

[2]Tom L. Beauchamp and James F. Childress. *Principles of Biomedical Ethics.* New York: Oxford University Press, 1994.

[3]Albert R. Jonsen. *The New Medicine and the Old Ethics.* Cambridge Mass., Harvard University Press, 1990.

[4]Quoted by Tom L. Beauchamp and James F. Childress in the fourth edition, p. 231.

Reflections on the Teaching
of Bioethics
Jerome W. Freeman, M.D.

The health care arena is paying increasing attention today to the importance of bioethics. Most medical schools offer their students some degree of formal exposure to medical ethics.[1] Many nursing schools include some education in ethics/values, although there is no general agreement thus far about how these topics should be incorporated into the curriculum.[2] And I think it is clear that a consensus has developed over the last 20 years that certain dilemmas in medical care can be analyzed and resolved successfully through the application of widely accepted ethical principles — particularly the principles of autonomy, non-maleficence, beneficence, and justice.

While I have no doubt that the use of these basic ethical principles is a helpful and prudent way to deal with ethical dilemmas, I contend that the "principle approach" needs to be broadened in order for the principles to be optimally utilized. Specifically, I submit that emphasis should now be given to three elements: the innate *disposition* of the caregiver, the role that *emotions* play in ethical quandaries, and the matter of *collegiality* among various caregivers. I am convinced that failure to pay attention to these three elements can compromise the usefulness of the traditional ethical principles.

The *disposition* (character) of the caregiver is a critical attribute, but I concede that it is difficult to define precisely. When Pellegrino issued his critique[3] of the "principle approach" to ethical decision making, he suggested the possibility of returning to what was formerly called "virtue ethics." The difficulty with this approach, in my view, is that the term "virtue" carries religious connotations, thereby making it inadequate for universal application in our diverse, secular society. My preference is to use the word "disposition," in the sense it was used by Aristotle, connoting an acquired propensity for working for "the good." While this is still an abstract notion, it does conform to current societal usage, as in the familiar concept of "a good person." I believe that in the health care arena, goodness carries the notion of self-sacrifice and "doing for others."

From *The Journal of Continuing Education in the Health Professions*, Volume 14, pp. 56-60. Copyright © 1994 The Alliance of Continuing Medical Education and the Society of Medical College Directors of Continuing Medical Education. Used by permission.

At an operational level, it can be defined as "being of use" in the sense suggested so thoughtfully in John Irving's novel *The Cider House Rules.*

Human emotions play an important role in the ethical quandaries prevalent in health care. It is important for health care providers to recognize and acknowledge these emotional elements. Callahan[4] and Connelly[5] have written, from the point of view of those in clinical practice and of members of bioethics committees, about the ways in which clinical ethical dilemmas are intertwined with emotional factors. For optimal ethical decision making to occur, caregivers must recognize the presence of intruding psychological and emotional factors, and deal with them. This means being able to distinguish between elements of a problem that are truly ethical and those that are based on emotion.

A recent case pointed up this distinction. An ethics committee was convened to discuss the desirability of stopping aggressive treatment of a young child with multi-organ failure. As the discussion developed, it was gradually realized that the initial lack of consensus among family members had less to do with any substantive disagreement about the ethical appropriateness of stopping care and more to do with an ongoing estrangement and separation of the parents.

The concept of *collegiality* among caregivers has received little attention. In today's complex and multitiered health care system, professionals from a variety of disciplines interact with patients. I believe that many of them, especially those from such fields as nursing, social work, pharmacy, and pastoral care should have a role in ethical decision making. In the past, the resolution of ethical dilemmas (when recognized) has been deferred to the attending physician. I believe that when interested members of the health care team are excluded from the process, problems can arise, both with the patient/family (who at times have developed close personal ties with non-physician caregivers) and with those left out of the process (who see themselves as having a legitimate vested interest in the patient's welfare). I submit that better ethical decisions result if a variety of interested members of the health care team have a voice in the discussions that precede decision making. It is the feelings of collegiality among members of the team that make for consensus and proper ethical decision making.

All the above have important implications for the education of health care professionals, both their initial and their continuing education. Basic curricula need to include an overview of the ethical problems encountered in clinical practice. An important part of this perspective is gaining understanding of how to make use of the traditional ethical principles, as well as the three additional elements that I have described.

I believe that attention needs to be given to the innate disposition (character) of the caregiver — no easy matter to achieve. One approach would be to focus initial ethical discussions on the specific contextual concerns of the student. Using medical school as an example, early ethical discussions during the first two years could center around such issues as cheating, truth telling, and dealing with large educational debt. Then, in the third and fourth years when students are beginning to see patients, ethical education, as pointed out by Christakis and Feudtner,[6] can incorporate such dilemmas as those arising from student/patient encounters and from interactions between students and clinical faculty members.

Similarly, the curricula for health care professionals can include formal discussion of the emotional/psychological aspects of illness and health care, including the study of family dynamics and the concerns that arise within family groupings during times of severe illness and impending death. Especially important is the need for the caregiver to recognize and cope with the emotional conflicts and stresses that confront the professional personally.

A good way to teach collegiality is to introduce interdisciplinary education early in the training of caregivers. I have tried this on a small scale over the last five years. As part of third-year medical students' rotation on neurology, I conducted weekly seminars to discuss both the neurological and the ethical aspects of selected patients. Nursing students were invited and urged to participate actively. Evaluation of these sessions showed that both the nursing and the medical students found it helpful to interact with each other at this level.[7] I believe mutual respect and reliance can be fostered by this type of experience at the student level.

I submit that similar multidisciplinary efforts should be made part of continuing education. A seminar format helps introduce and demonstrate the importance of teamwork to health care. In addition, such continuing education endeavors can emphasize the importance of the caregiver's disposition and of the emotional factors that surround illness and health care.

I have found that one way to facilitate these objectives is to make use of the "patient's story." One example is to center the discussions around the way in which a patient describes an instance of caring behavior. Recently, a group of us interviewed a number of patients, asking them to relate examples of caring behavior on the part of their nurses or physicians. Not infrequently, a patient would recall a striking, specific instance of such behavior. These vignettes, because they are related in the patient's voice, can serve as a powerful influence to help the future caregiver develop a disposition to goodness and caring. One patient who was interviewed reported that he was a private person and that it made him uncomfortable to have his urine bag and catheter exposed to visitors. He then said, "A sure sign of a nurse caring about me happened yesterday. I had company and the nurse came in to empty the bag to measure it. She walked in, pitcher in hand, saw my company, and said she would return later to do what she needed to do. I was so impressed that she knew and cared enough about me not to draw attention to my bag and to come in later to do it."[8]

Another effective way to open a discussion of ethical issues is to use literature, particularly fiction and poetry. Literature, as a specific educational device, is receiving considerable attention today, and I find it is especially useful when used in an interdisciplinary setting. For a number of years I have taught a series of literature/ethics courses to undergraduate and graduate students, typically including nursing, premedical, and medical students, as well as occasional representatives from physical therapy, social work, hospital administration, pastoral care, and pharmacy. This multidisciplinary makeup tends to "keep the discussion honest" in terms of critical analysis and responses to the ethical problems of clinical practice, as well as setting the stage for future collaboration in patient care.

Discussion of some specific piece of literature can serve as an entry point into a discussion of ethical issues. Literary selections readily demonstrate the range of ethical problems that exists within health care and can point out the use of ethical principles to cope with the dilemmas. In addition, literature — such as the short stories of William Carlos Williams — is well suited to discussions of the disposition of caregivers, the emotional elements in ethical conflicts, and the interactions of various members of the health care team.

Ethical and value issues are inextricably interwoven throughout the fabric of patient care. Inevitably, they contribute to the complexities of caring and to the ongoing challenges encountered by caregivers. I believe that true caring is best accomplished when specific expertise and attention are devoted to resolving these unavoidable bioethical conflicts. In this essay, I have suggested ways in which health care providers can better prepare to cope with the challenges that ethical dilemmas pose.

[1] O'Neill LC, *et al.* Ethics, jurisprudence, and economics in the medical school curriculum. West J of Med 1990; 153:557-558.

[2] Silva MC, Sorrell JM. Nursing curriculums and ethics. In Research on ethics in nursing education: An integrative review and critique. New York: National League for Nursing, 1991.

[3] Pellegrino ED. The metamorphosis of medical ethics: A thirty-year retrospective. JAMA 1993; 269:1158-1162.

[4] Callahan F. Emotions' role in reaching bioethical decisions. Health Progress 1987; (June): 26-27.

[5] Connelly JE. Emotions and the process of ethical decision making. Journal South Carolina Med Assoc 1990; (December) 621-623.

[6] Christakis DA, Feudtner C. Ethics in a short white coat: The ethical dilemmas that medical students confront. Acad Med 1993;68:249-254.

[7] Freeman JW, Hohman M. Fostering humanism: Collaboration in medical ethics. South Dakota J Med 1991; 44:334.

[8] Nelson B, Meyer M, Wiltz L, Freeman JW. Caring and the health professions. (unpublished ms.)

lecture on bioethics

Jerome W. Freeman

what i mean to say while
standing podium high is
balance is everything

lament too many
judgements with too
few certainties
proclaim mencken right
for knowing that simple

answers to complex
questions are usually
wrong

believe that tumult of
suffering seeks solace
in what is done and
not done

understand the need
to keep trying

The Use of Force
William Carlos Williams

They were new patients to me, all I had was the name, Olson. Please come down as soon as you can, my daughter is very sick.

When I arrived I was met by the mother, a big startled looking woman, very clean and apologetic who merely said, Is this the doctor? and let me in. In the back, she added. You must excuse us, doctor, we have her in the kitchen where it is warm. It is very damp here sometimes.

The child was fully dressed and sitting on her father's lap near the kitchen table. He tried to get up, but I motioned for him not to bother, took off my overcoat and started to look things over. I could see that they were all very nervous, eyeing me up and down distrustfully. As often, in such cases, they weren't telling me more than they had to, it was up to me to tell them; that's why they were spending three dollars on me.

The child was fairly eating me up with her cold, steady eyes, and no expression to her face whatever. She did not move and seemed, inwardly, quiet; an unusually attractive little thing, and as strong as a heifer in appearance. But her face was flushed, she was breathing rapidly, and I realized that she had a high fever. She had magnificent blonde hair, in profusion. One of those picture children often reproduced in advertising leaflets and the photogravure sections of the Sunday papers.

She's had a fever for three days, began the father and we don't know what it comes from. My wife has given her things, you know, like people do, but it don't do no good. And there's been a lot of sickness around. So we tho't you'd better look her over and tell us what is the matter.

As doctors often do I took a trial shot at it as a point of departure. Has she had a sore throat?

Both parents answered me together, No... No, she says her throat don't hurt her.

Does your throat hurt you? added the mother to the child. But the little girl's expression didn't change nor did she move her eyes from my face.

Have you looked?

I tried to, said the mother, but I couldn't see.

As it happens we had been having a number of cases of diphtheria in the school to which this child went during that month and we were all, quite apparently, thinking of that, though no one had as yet spoken of the thing.

Well, I said, suppose we take a look at the throat first. I smiled in my best professional manner and asking for the child's first name I said, come on, Mathilda, open your mouth and let's take a look at your throat.

Nothing doing.

Aw, come on, I coaxed, just open your mouth wide and let me take a look. Look, I said opening both hands wide, I haven't anything in my hands. Just open up and let me see.

Such a nice man, put in the mother. Look how kind he is to you. Come on, do what he tells you to. He won't hurt you.

At that I ground my teeth in disgust. If only they wouldn't use the word "hurt" I might be able to get somewhere. But I did not allow myself to be hurried or disturbed but speaking quietly and slowly I approached the child again.

As I moved my chair a little nearer suddenly with one cat-like movement both her hands clawed instinctively for my eyes and she almost reached them too. In fact she knocked my glasses flying and they fell, though unbroken, several feet away from me on the kitchen floor.

Both the mother and father almost turned themselves inside out in embarrassment and apology. You bad girl, said the mother, taking her and shaking her by one arm. Look what you've done. The nice man...

For heaven's sake, I broke in. Don't call me a nice man to her. I'm here to look at her throat on the chance that she might have diphtheria and possibly die of it. But that's nothing to her. Look here, I said to the child, we're going to look at your throat. You're old enough to understand what I'm saying. Will you open it now by yourself or shall we have to open it for you?

Not a move. Even her expression hadn't changed. Her breaths however were coming faster and faster. Then the battle began. I had to have a throat culture for her own protection. But first I told the parents that it was entirely up to them. I explained the danger but said that I would not insist on a throat examination so long as they would take the responsibility.

If you don't do what the doctor says you'll have to go to the hospital, the mother admonished her severely.

Oh yeah? I had to smile to myself. After all, I had already fallen in love with the savage brat, the parents were contemptible to me. In the ensuing struggle they grew more and more abject, crushed, exhausted while she surely rose to magnificent heights of insane fury of effort bred of her terror of me.

The father tried his best, and he was a big man but the fact that she was his daughter, his shame at her behavior and his dread of hurting her made him release her just at the critical moment several times when I had almost achieved success, till I wanted to kill him. But his dread also that she might have diphtheria made him tell me to go on, go on though he himself was almost fainting, while the mother moved back and forth behind us raising and lowering her hands in an agony of apprehension.

Put her in front of you on your lap, I ordered, and hold both her wrists.

But as soon as he did the child let out a scream. Don't, you're hurting me. Let go of my hands. Let them go I tell you. Then she shrieked terrifyingly, hysterically. Stop it! Stop it! You're killing me!

Do you think she can stand it, doctor! said the mother.

You get out, said the husband to his wife. Do you want her to die of diphtheria?

Come on now, hold her, I said.

Then I grasped the child's head with my left hand and tried to get the wooden tongue depressor between her teeth. She fought, with clenched teeth, desperately! But now I also had grown furious at a child. I tried to hold myself down but I couldn't. I know how to expose a throat for inspection. And I did my best. When finally I got the wooden spatula behind the last teeth and just the point of it into the mouth cavity, she opened up for an instant but before I could see anything she came down again and gripping the wooden blade between her molars she reduced it to splinters before I could get it out again.

Aren't you ashamed, the mother yelled at her. Aren't you ashamed to act like that in front of the doctor?

Get me a smooth-handled spoon of some sort, I told the mother. We're going through with this. The child's mouth was already bleeding. Her tongue was cut and she was screaming in wild hysterical shrieks. Perhaps I should have desisted and come back in an hour or more. No doubt it would have been better. But I have seen at least two children lying dead in bed of neglect in such cases, and feeling that I must get a diagnosis now or never I went at it again. But the worst of it was that I too had got beyond reason. I could have torn the child apart in my own fury and enjoyed it. It was a pleasure to attack her. My face was burning with it.

The damned little brat must be protected against her own idiocy, one says to one's self at such times. Others must be protected against her. It is social necessity. And all these things are true. But a blind fury, a feeling of adult shame, bred of a longing for muscular release are the operatives. One goes on to the end.

In a final unreasoning assault I overpowered the child's neck and jaws. I forced the heavy silver spoon back of her teeth and down her throat till she gagged. And there it was — both tonsils covered with membrane. She had fought valiantly to keep me from knowing her secret. She had been hiding that sore throat for three days at least and lying to her parents in order to escape just such an outcome as this.

Now truly she *was* furious. She had been on the defensive before but now she attacked. Tried to get off her father's lap and fly at me while tears of defeat blinded her eyes.

Reflection on Restraints in the Nursing Home

Jerome Freeman

Of course if he fell
his hip could shatter
like a china saucer
absently nudged
over table's edge.

So Wilbur is coaxed
and cajoled to call for
help when standing.
But freedom and
spontaneity are not
easily forfeited after
83 years of custom.
And besides, he's
always been stubborn.

But now talk of righteous
restraint is in the wind
when staff gathers to
ponder his prospects.
They favor a belt to
firmly wed him to
whatever chair he is
deposited upon.

Such talk does not sit
easy with Wilbur when he
can remember it, which is
only some of the time.

The treacheries of aging
show no measure of kindness
for impulse and independence.
And he is not a fierce Ulysses
respecting temporary bonds
to safely visit some Sirens.

Ethical Dimensions
of Informed Consent

This excerpt from the statement by the American College of Obstetricians and Gynecologists is an example of how deeply medical practice has been influenced by the emergence of the ethical principle of respect for autonomy.

Informed consent is an ethical concept that has become integral to contemporary medical ethics and medical practice. In recognition of the ethical importance of informed consent, the Committee on Ethics affirms that

1. Informed consent for medical treatment and for participation in medical research is an ethical requirement (which legal doctrines and requirements can in part reflect).
2. Informed consent is an expression of respect for the patient as a person; it particularly respects a patient's moral right to bodily integrity, to self-determination regarding sexuality and reproductive capacities and to the support of the patient's freedom within caring relationships.
3. Informed consent not only ensures the protection of the patient against unwanted medical treatment, but it also makes possible the active involvement of the patient in her or his medical planning and care.
4. Freedom is maximized in relationships marked by mutuality and equality; this offers both an ethical ideal and an ethical guideline for physician-patient relationships.
5. Communication is necessary if informed consent is to be realized, and physicians can help to find ways to facilitate communication not only in individual relations with patients but also in the structured context of medical care institutions.
6. Informed consent should be looked upon as a process, a process that includes ongoing shared information and developing choices as long as one is seeking medical assistance.
7. The ethical requirement of informed consent need not conflict with physicians' overall ethical obligation to a principle of

From the American College of Obstetricians and Gynecologists. *Ethical Dimensions of Informed Consent* (ACOG Committee Opinion 108). Washington, DC: ACOG, 1992. Copyright © 1992 by the American College of Obstetricians and Gynecologists. Reprinted (with adaptation) with permission from the Jacobs Institute of Women's Health (**Women's Health Data Book,** 1993, 3 (1), pp 1-10) beneficence; that is, every effort should be made to incorporate a commitment to informed consent within a commitment to provide medical benefit to patients and thus to respect them as whole and embodied persons.

8. There are limits to the ethical obligation of informed consent, but a clear justification should be given for any abridgement or suspension of the general obligation.

9. Because ethical requirements and legal requirements cannot be equated, physicians should also acquaint themselves with the legal requirements of informed consent.

The application of informed consent to contexts of obstetric and gynecologic practice invites ongoing clarification of the meaning of these nine statements. What follows is an effort to provide this.

HISTORICAL BACKGROUND

In 1980, the Committee on Ethics of the American College of Obstetricians and Gynecologists (ACOG) developed a statement on informed consent.* This statement reflected what is now generally recognized as a paradigm shift in the ethical understanding of the physician-patient relationship. The 1970s had seen in the United States a marked change from a traditional almost singular focus on the benefit of the patient as the governing ethical principle of medical care to a new and dramatic emphasis on a requirement of informed consent. That is, a central and often sole concern for the medical well-being of the patient gave way to, or was at least modified to include, concern for the patient's autonomy in making medical decisions.

In the 1980s this national shift was both reinforced and challenged in medical ethics. Clinical experience as well as developments in ethical theory generated further questions about the practice of informed consent and the legal doctrine that promoted it. If in the 1970s informed consent was embraced as a corrective to paternalism, the 1980s exhibited a growing sense of need for shared decision-making as a corrective to the exaggerated individualism

---

*This statement, "Ethical Considerations Associated with Informed Consent," was subsequently approved and issued in 1980 as a Statement of Policy by the Executive Board of ACOG. In 1989, it was withdrawn for revision by the Committee on Ethics.

that patient autonomy had sometimes produced. At the same time, factors such as the proliferation of medical technologies, the bureaucratic and financial complexities of health care delivery systems, and the growing sophistication of the general public regarding medical limitations and possibilities continued to undergird an appreciation of the importance of patient autonomy and a demand for its safeguard in and through informed consent.

In the 1990s there are good reasons for considering once again the ethical significance and practical application of the requirement of informed consent. This is particularly true in the context of obstetric and gynecologic practice. Here medical options, public health problems, legal interventions, and political agendas have not only expanded but interconnected with one another in unprecedented ways. ACOG's concern for these matters is reflected in its more recent documents on informed consent and on particular ethical problems such as maternal-fetal conflict, sterilization, and surrogate motherhood.[1-9] While a general ethical doctrine of informed consent cannot by itself resolve problems like these, it is nonetheless necessary for understanding them.

Informed consent for medical treatment and for participation in medical research is both a legal and an ethical matter. In the short 20th-century history of informed consent, statutes and regulations as well as court decisions have played an important role in the identification and sanctioning of basic duties. Judicial decisions have sometimes provided insights regarding rights of self-determination and of privacy in the medical context. Government regulations have rendered operational some of the most general norms formulated in historic ethical codes.* Yet there is little recent development in the legal doctrine of informed consent, and the most serious current questions are ethical ones before they are ones of the law. As the President's Commission reported in 1982, "Although the informed consent doctrine has substantial foundations in law, it is essentially an ethical imperative."[10] What above all bears reviewing,

---

* The Nuremberg Code in 1948 and the World Medical Association's Declaration of Helsinki in 1964 identified ethical restrictions for medical research on human subjects. For a history of the development of such codes and a general history of the ethical and legal concept of informed consent, see Ruth R. Faden and Tom L. Beauchamp, *A History and Theory of Informed Consent* (New York: Oxford University Press, 1986). A culminating summary of federal regulations in the United States can be found in the *Federal Register* (June 26, 1991).

then, is the ethical dimension of the meaning, basis, and application of informed consent.

THE ETHICAL MEANING OF INFORMED CONSENT

The ethical concept of "informed consent" contains two major elements: *free consent* and *comprehension* (or understanding). Both of these elements together constitute an important part of a patient's "self-determination" (the taking hold of one's own life and action, determining the meaning and the possibility of what one undergoes as well as what one does).

Free consent is an intentional and voluntary act which authorizes someone else to act in certain ways. In the context of medicine, it is an act by which a person freely authorizes a medical intervention in her or his life, whether in the form of treatment or participation in research. As "consent," it implies the opposite of being coerced or unwillingly invaded by forces beyond oneself. As "free," consent implies a choice between alternatives. It includes the possibility of choosing otherwise as the result of deliberation and/or of identification with different values and preferences. Free consent, in other words, implies the possibility of choosing this or that option or the refusal of any proposed option.

Comprehension (as an ethical element in informed consent) includes awareness and some understanding of information about one's situation and possibilities. Comprehension in this sense is necessary in order for there to be freedom in consenting. Free consent, of course, admits of degrees, and its presence is not always verifiable in concrete instances; but if it is to be operative at all in the course of medical treatment, it presupposes some level of understanding of available options.

Many people who are thoughtful about these matters have different beliefs about the actual achievement of informed consent and about human freedom. Whether and what freedom itself is has often been disputed. Despite continuing differences in understanding philosophical perspectives, however, important agreement has grown in this society about the need for informed consent and about its basic ethical significance in the context of medical practice and research. It is still important to try to clarify, however, who and what informed consent serves, and how it may be protected and fostered. This clarification cannot be achieved without some continuing consideration of its basis and goals and the concrete contexts in which it must be realized.

THE ETHICAL BASIS AND PURPOSE OF INFORMED CONSENT

One of the important arguments for the ethical requirement of informed consent is an argument from *utility*, or from the *benefit* that can come to patients when they actively participate in decisions about their own medical care. That is, the involvement of patients in such decisions is good for their health-not only because it is a protection against treatment which patients might consider harmful, but because it contributes positively to their wellbeing. There are at least two presuppositions here: One is that patients know something experientially about their own medical condition that can be helpful and even necessary to the sound management of their medical care. The other is that, wherever it is possible, the active role of primary guardian of one's own health is more conducive to well-being than is a passive and submissive "sick role." The positive benefits of patient decision-making are obvious, for example, in the treatment of alcohol abuse. But the benefits of active participation in medical decisions are multifold for patients, whether they are trying to maintain their general health, or recover from illness, or conceive and deliver healthy babies, or live responsible sexual lives, or accept the limits of medical technology, or enhance whatever processes they are in that bring them to seek medical care.

Utility, however, is not the only reason for protecting and promoting patient decision-making. Indeed, the most commonly accepted foundation for informed consent is probably the principle of *respect for persons*. This principle expresses an ethical requirement to treat human persons as "ends in themselves" (that is, not to use them solely as means or instruments for someone else's purposes and goals). The logic of this requirement is based on the perception that all persons as persons have certain features or characteristics that constitute the source of an inherent dignity, a worthiness and claim to be affirmed in their own right. One of these features has come to be identified as *autonomy* — a person's capacity or at least potential for self-determination (for self-governance and freedom of choice). To be autonomous in any degree is to have the capacity to set one's own agenda and in some important way to choose one's actions and even one's attitudes, to determine the meaning of the outcome of one's life. Given this capacity in persons, it is ordinarily an ethically unacceptable violation of who and what persons are to coerce their actions or to refuse their participation in important decisions that affect their lives.

One of the important developments in ethical theory in recent years is the widespread recognition that autonomy is not the only characteristic of human persons that is a basis for the requirement of respect. Human persons, it is noted, are essentially social beings, *relational* in the structure of their personalities, their needs, and their possibilities. Given this "relationality," then, the goal of human life and the content of human well-being cannot be adequately understood only in terms of self-determination — especially if self-determination is understood individualistically and if it results in human relationships that are primarily adversarial. A sole or even central emphasis on patient autonomy in the informed consent process in the medical context risks replacing paternalism with a distanced and impersonal relationship of strangers negotiating rights and duties. If persons are to be respected and their well-being promoted, informed consent must be seen as serving a fuller notion of relationship.

Patients come to medical decisions with a history of relationships, personal and social, familial and institutional. Decisions are made in the context of these relationships, shared or not shared, as the situation allows. Above all, these decisions are made in a relationship between patient and physician (or often between patient and multiple professional caregivers).

The focus, then, for understanding both the basis and the content of informed consent must shift to include the many facets of the physician-patient relationship. Informed consent, from this point of view, is not an end, but a means. It is a means not only to the responsible participation by patients in their own medical care; it is also a means to a new form of relationship between physician (or any medical caregiver) and patient. From this perspective it is possible to see the contradictions inherent in an approach to informed consent that would, for example,

1. Lead a physician (or anyone else) to say of a patient, "I *gave* her informed consent."
2. Assume that informed consent was achieved simply by the signing of a document.
3. Consider informed consent primarily as a safeguard for physicians against medical liability.

It is also possible to see, from this perspective, that informed consent is not meant to undergird a patient's unlimited demand for treatment, arbitrary non-compliance with agreed upon treatment, or whimsical withdrawal from an agreed upon research protocol.

Freedom is maximized in relationships of trust; understanding is enhanced in the nuanced frameworks of conversation. Self-determination need not be either combative or submissive, but situated in relationships of mutuality of respect and, insofar as possible, equality of personal power. These kinds of professional relationships represent the preferred context for informed consent.

OBSTETRICS AND GYNECOLOGY: SPECIAL ETHICAL CONCERNS FOR INFORMED CONSENT

The practice of obstetrics and gynecology has always faced special ethical questions in the implementation of informed consent. How, for example, can the autonomy of patients best be respected when serious decisions must be made in the challenging situations of labor and delivery? What kinds of guidelines can physicians find for respecting the autonomy of adolescents, when society acknowledges this autonomy by and large only in the limited spheres of sexuality and reproduction? Do "recommendations" compromise patient autonomy in the context of genetic counseling? How much information should be given to patients about controversies surrounding specific treatments? How are beneficence requirements (regarding the well-being of the patient) to be balanced with rights of patient choice, especially in a field of medical practice where so many key decisions are irreversible? These and many other questions continue to be important for fulfilling the ethical requirement of informed consent.

Developments in the ethical doctrine of informed consent (regarding, for example, the significance that relationships have for decision-making) have helped to focus some of the concerns that are particular to the practice of obstetrics and gynecology. Where *women's* health care needs are addressed, and especially where these needs are related to women's sexuality and reproductive capacities, the issues of patient autonomy and relationality take on special significance. In other words, the gender of patients makes a difference where ethical questions of informed consent are concerned, because gender in our society has been a relevant factor in interpreting the meaning of autonomy and relationality. This is not to say that in some essential sense autonomy or relationality (or informed consent and relationships) ought to be different for women and men; indeed, quite the opposite. Rather, this alerts us to the possible inconsistencies in the application of the ethical requirement of informed consent.

While issues of gender are to be found in every area of medical practice and research,* they are particularly important in the area of obstetrics and gynecology. Of special relevance here, for example, are the insights now being articulated by women out of their experience — that is, their experience specifically in the medical setting, but also more generally in relation to their own bodies, in various patterns of relation with other persons, and in the larger societal and institutional contexts in which they live. These insights offer both a help and an ongoing challenge to the professional self-understanding and practice of obstetricians and gynecologists (whether they themselves are women or men).

Obstetrics and gynecology has in a special way seen new dimensions of informed consent emerge, and here new models for the active participation of health care recipients have been created. Some of these developments are the result of effective arguments that pregnancy and childbirth are not diseases, though they bring women importantly into relation with medical professionals. Even when women's medical needs are more precisely needs for diagnosis and treatment, their concerns to hold together the values of both autonomy and relationality have been influential in shaping not only ethical theory but also medical practice. Women themselves have questioned, for example, whether autonomy can really be protected if it is addressed in a vacuum, apart from an individual's concrete roles and relationships. But women as well as men have also recognized the ongoing importance of respect for autonomy as a requirement of moral justice in every relationship. Many women therefore continue to articulate fundamental concerns for bodily integrity and self-determination. At the same time they call for

---

*See, for example, a recent study of court decisions on refusal of treatment regarding dying patients (Miles SH, August A. Courts, gender, and the "right to die." *Law Med. Health Care 1990*; 18 (1-2[Spring-Summer]):85-95). The conclusion of this study is that court decisions for women patients differ from court decisions for men; that is, in general, men's previously stated wishes about "extraordinary" or "heroic" measures of treatment are taken more seriously than are women's.

attention to the complexity of the relationships that are involved when sexuality and parenting are at issue in medical care.

The difficulties that beset the full achievement of informed consent in the practice of obstetrics and gynecology are not limited to individual and interpersonal factors. Both providers and recipients of medical care within this specialty have recognized the influence of such broad social problems as the historical imbalance of power in gender relations; the constraints on individual choice posed by complex medical technology; and the intersection of gender bias with race and class bias in the attitudes and actions of individuals and institutions. None of these problems makes the achievement of informed consent impossible. But, they alert us to the need to identify the conditions and limits, as well as the central requirements, of the ethical application of this doctrine.

*   *   *

[1] American College of Obstetricians and Gynecologists, Department of Professional Liability. Informed consent. The assistant. Washington, DC: ACOG, 1988.

[2] American College of Obstetricians and Gynecologists, Department of Professional Liability. Informed consent forms. The assistant. Washington, DC: ACOG, 1988.

[3] American College of Obstetricians and Gynecologists. Ethical decision-making in obstetrics and gynecology. ACOG Techncal Bulletin 136. Washington, DC: ACOG, 1989.

[4] American College of Obstetricians and Gynecologists. Patient choice: maternal-fetal conflict. ACOG Committee Opinion 55. Washington, DC: ACOG, 1987.

[5] American College of Obstetricians and Gynecologists. Ethical issues in pregnancy counseling. ACOG Committee Opinion 61. Washington, DC: ACOG, 1988.

[6] American College of Obstetricians and Gynecologists. Sterilization of women who are mentally handicapped. ACOG Committee Opinion 63. Washington, DC: ACOG, 1988.

[7] American College of Obstetricians and Gynecologists. Ethical considerations in sterilization. ACOG Committee Opinion 73. Washington, DC: ACOG, 1989.

[8] American College of Obstetricians and Gynecologists. Human immunodeficiency virus infection: physicians' responsibilities. ACOG Committee Opinion 85. Washington, DC: ACOG, 1989.

[9] American College of Obstetricians and Gynecologists. Ethical issues in surrogate motherhood. ACOG Committee Opinion 88. Washington, DC: ACOG, 1990.

¹⁰The President's Commission for the Study of Ethical Problems in Medicine and Biomedical Research. Making health care decisions: the ethical and legal implications of informed consent in the patient-practitioner relationship. Vol 1. (Stock no. 040-000-00459-9). Washington, DC: U.S. Government Printing Office, 1982:2.

¹¹American College of Obstetricians and Gynecologists. Deception. ACOG Committee Opinion 87. Washington, DC: ACOG, 1990.

¹²he President's Commission for the Study of Ethical Problems in Medicine and Biomedical Research. Making health care decisions: the ethical and legal implications of informed consent in the patient-practitioner relationship. Vol 1. (Stock no. 040-000-00459-9). Washington, DC: U.S. Government Printing Office, 1982:Chapters 8-9.

BIBLIOGRAPHY

Beauchamp TL, Childress JF. Principles of biomedical ethics. 3rd ed. New York: Oxford University Press, 1989: Chapter 1.

Faden RR, Beauchamp TL. A history and theory of informed consent. New York: Oxford University Press, 1986.

Katz J. The silent world of doctor and patient. New York: The Free Press, 1984.

Levine RJ. Ethics and regulation of clinical research. 2nd ed. Baltimore, Maryland, and Munich, Germany: Urban and Schwarzenberg, 1986.

The President's Commission for the Study of Ethical Problems in Medicine and Biomedical Research. Making health care decisions: the ethical and legal implications of informed consent in the patient-practitioner relationship. Vol 1. (Stock no. 040-000-00459-9). Washington, DC: U.S. Government Printing Office, 1982.

The President's Commission for the Study of Ethical Problems in Medicine and Biomedical Research. Making health care decisions: the ethical and legal implications of informed consent in the patient-practitioner relationship. Vol 2. (Stock no. 040-000-00468-8). Washington, DC: U.S. Government Printing Office, 1982.

The President's Commission for the Study of Ethical Problems in Medicine and Biomedical Research. Making health care decisions: the ethical and legal implications of informed consent in the patient-practitioner relationship. Vol 3. (Stock no. 040-000-00469-6). Washington, DC: U.S. Government Printing Office, 1982.

Reflections on Informed Consent

Jerome W. Freeman, M.D.

Issues of informed consent are encountered regularly in every medical practice. Indeed, informed consent is probably an aspect of virtually every physician-patient encounter. Every time a drug is prescribed or other treatment (or non-treatment) is recommended by the physician, the stage is set for establishing the patient's informed consent. The very frequency with which opportunities for informed consent arise warrants that this process should receive major emphasis in the field of medical ethics.

The concept of informed consent is generally premised on the ethical principle of autonomy. The principle dictates that the individual has a right to freedom of choice and action. In the clinical setting, this principle is felt to warrant that the patient has a positive right to an explanation of his health problems and treatment options.

In the discussion of informed consent, two ancillary concepts deserve consideration — paternalism and fallibility in medicine. Paternalism has long been a part of medical practice. It is based on the moral principle of beneficence — *i.e.* promoting what is good for another. In medicine this has come to mean that the physician does what he or she feels is medically in the best interest of the patient, regardless of whether the patient fully comprehends the medical problem and options. In this setting the principle of beneficence may be construed as taking precedence over the principle of individual autonomy. The physician acts in an almost parental role in an effort to achieve the best medical result. In recent years, the concept of paternalism has received considerable criticism. The contention has been made that the paternalistic approach makes unwarranted infringements upon individual autonomy and disenfranchises patients' active participation in their own care. Thus issues of paternalism repeatedly arise in any analysis of informed consent.

The second concept which is necessarily relevant to an analysis of informed consent is that of medical fallibility. This issue has been effectively explored by Gorovitz and MacIntyre.[1] They argue that error in the clinical practice of medicine is unavoidable on both practical and theoretical grounds. That is, even when medicine is practiced well, some adverse outcomes will predictably result.

From *South Dakota Journal of Medicine*, April 1985. Copyright © 1988 South Dakota Journal of Medicine. Used by permission.

Clearly this concept has direct relevance to notions of informed consent — particularly in an age of heightened public expectations as to the feats modern medicine can accomplish.

A precise definition of informed consent is of great importance to clinical practice. Beauchamp and Childress[2] offer a comprehensive one, asserting that four elements must be satisfied for true informed consent to exist. These include disclosure of information, comprehension of information, voluntary consent, and competence to consent. In considering these elements, one can readily appreciate that a dialogue between physician and patient is needed for informed consent to occur. The nature of that interchange fluctuates with the degree of paternalism the physician exercises and the patient permits. The content of that communication is necessarily modified by medicine's inescapable fallibility.

Disclosure of information is primarily the responsibility of the physician. This is the portion of the consent process in which the physician details such information as treatment options and therapeutic risks. A physician in the traditional, paternalistic mold might convey little specific information in this setting, dogmatically insisting that a single treatment course is "the right one." On the other hand, an informational discussion between physician and patient can be an excellent opportunity to establish dialogue and collaboration between the two principals of the therapeutic relationship. The physician can try to learn and assuage a patient's fears, and can offer explanations for various clinical courses. Moreover, the physician can use this dialogue to communicate the concept that many decisions in medicine are ultimately the result of personal judgements by the physician, and that medicine is fallible and not always productive of an optimal outcome. A general discussion of this character may often be of more benefit to the patient than a meticulous attempt to detail all possible side effects of a treatment or drug. Such disclosure and communication is not detrimental to a therapeutic result. The patient need not lose confidence in the physician when it becomes apparent that medicine is not infallible. Indeed, the frank discussion of this concept, along with a description of common adverse outcomes or side effects, serves to forcefully demonstrate the physician's honesty and concern. Such discussion can provide the patient with a basis for trusting a physician's clinical judgment, and for enlisting a patient's confidence and support for a treatment plan. Also, this type of interchange clearly reminds the patient that he or she is an active partner in the therapeutic

process. The patient can come to view such participation and collaboration as much preferable to passive acceptance of a physician's
dictates. And finally, this dialogue enables the patient to better
understand and accept those situations in which a good clinical
result does not obtain, or when a major side effect of diagnosis or
treatment intervenes.

The latter three elements of Beauchamp and Childress' definition
of informed consent, comprehension, plus voluntary and competent consent variously describe the patient. Yet in these areas, too,
paternalism plays a major role. The physician must try to make a
judgement as to whether a patient truly comprehends the information he has provided. Moreover, it is the physician who must decide
whether the patient is capable of both voluntary and competent
consent. Often this can be very difficult. If a patient is seriously ill
— especially with a disease that might physically or emotionally
alter his thought and judgement processes — the physician may
feel obliged to make a paternalistic decision to act without the
patient's full consent. Often this decision necessitates the judgement that consent be obtained from parties deemed responsible for
the patient — *i.e.* a spouse, parent or other relative.

Despite the importance of patient autonomy, the clinical setting
is replete with situations which may limit autonomy, while fostering beneficence. Much of the interplay that develops between the
principles of autonomy and beneficence, does so as the physician
attempts to assess the patient's comprehension of his own medical
problem, and his ability to both voluntarily and competently render
consent. This very assessment presupposes and requires an element
of paternalism. As Clarke *et al.* point out: "It is the physician who
decides if the patient is rational, what options are acceptable, and
frequently, what a reasonable person would want."[3] In a similar
vein, Cross and Churchill note "the asymmetry of power and risk
in the physician-patient relationship."[4] The very nature of the clinical interaction seems to mandate that some paternalism will be
exercised by the physician.

In summary, the concept of informed consent is of major importance to the clinical practice of medicine. This concept affects how
the physician-patient dialogue evolves. Clearly, the foregoing discussion demonstrates that the goal of informed consent is a muta-
ble one, being variably affected by the four elements that constitute
consent. Most of the responsibility for assessing these elements and
insuring consent resides with a physician. In this sense, some

degree of paternalism is an integral part of the clinical process. But the paternalistic instinct, even when arising from beneficence, must be moderated by the patient's right to autonomy and to participation in his own health care decisions. The challenge to the physician is to strike the appropriate balance, in the pragmatic and fallible clinical realm, between patient consent and physician paternalism.

---

[1]Gorovitz S, MacIntyre A: Toward a theory of medical fallibility. **J Med Phil.** 1976;1:51-71.

[2]Beauchamp TL, Childress JF: Principles of Biomedical Ethics. New York, Oxford University Press, Inc. 1979, p67.

[3]Clarke JR, Sorenson JH, Hare JE: The limits of paternalism in emergency care. **Hastings Cent Rep.** 1980;10:2-22.

[4]Cross AW, Churchill LR: Ethical and cultural dimensions of informed consent. **Ann Intern Med**. 1982;96:110-113.

Informed Consent:
Another Look at Disclosure

Jerome W. Freeman, MD

Informed consent is an important element of the doctor-patient relationship. In order for informed consent to be achieved, disclosure must take place. The patient must be adequately apprised of the indications and potential risks of a proposed therapy or diagnostic evaluation. Clearly, the content and specificity of disclosure varies with the procedure in question. Nonetheless, much can be learned about appropriate disclosure and informed consent by analyzing a specific clinical instance.

Computerized tomography of the brain (CT scan) is a test which lends itself well to such analysis. Specifically, in the case of the CT scan, a determination must be made as to what a patient should be told about potential adverse reactions to the intravenous (IV) contrast agent employed. Certainly the risk of serious adverse side effects from this type of testing is low. Nausea and occasional emesis occur with some frequency. Also urticaria, usually mild, is not uncommon. Persons with compromised renal function (especially with a creatinine above 2) can have a worsening of their renal function, and occasionally severe and permanent renal impairment can ensue. A major anaphylactic reaction and associated life-threatening complications are rare.

As a consultant regularly working with a large number of physicians in various specialties, it has been my impression that the degree of disclosure provided the patient who is scheduled for a CT scan varies considerably. While some physicians routinely discuss the nature and side effects of this type of test in detail, many physicians tell their patients very little about the specifics of proposed testing. Indeed, an occasional patient has indicated to me that he or she was unaware that an intravenous injection would be given until the test was begun. Arguably, the initial and primary responsibility should lie with the attending physician who determines that a test is indicated and orders it for the patient. However, in today's medical practice the responsibility for disclosure may fall to more than one physician, *e.g.* to both the attending physician and the radiologist in the case of contrast radiography. Spring et al.[1] used a detailed questionnaire to assess the degree to which radiologists obtained informed consent prior to the administration of IV contrast agents. In this study, 66% of the respondents indicated that they obtained no specific informed consent before the procedure. Moreover, one half of those who did provide specific disclosure to the patient did not explicitly discuss the possibility of specific major adverse reactions. This lack of specific disclosure may well characterize many attending physician/patient relationships as well.

In the past, I have argued that adequate disclosure was satisfied by a description of the nature of the test (including the IV injection), the common side effects one can see (i.e. nausea and vomiting or urticaria), and by the mention that very rarely a serious allergic reaction can take place. I have frequently likened this latter possibility of a serious allergic reaction to the rare anaphylactic reaction to penicillin, on the assumption that many patients would at least generally understand the nature of such a possibility. I have not, as a rule, specifically mentioned the possibility of life-threatening complications or death, arguing that this latter possibility (about one in 50,000) is so rare as to not be a material or meaningful risk to the patient. Implicit in this stance has been the paternalistic assumption on my part that some medical risks are so remote as to not warrant explicit disclosure. In this context, I have also emphasized that total disclosure (i.e. of all conceivable risks) is not only impractical, but impossible, given the wide variety of various side effects that may have been reported and the fact that the true incidence of very rare complications can often not be accurately estimated. Also, the possibility of a unique, idiosyncratic reaction in a given patient always exists.

In making such arguments to various groups over the past five years, I have been struck by the fact that reactions to these issues of disclosure often vary depending on whether or not the individuals are medically sophisticated. Specifically, it has been my impression that groups of physicians, nurses, or medical students find the foregoing disclosure very adequate. However, my lay audiences (which have usually taken the form of undergraduate students enrolled in a biomedical ethics course) have frequently been uncomfortable with the notion that all potentially serious side effects might not be specifically disclosed by the physician. In this regard, I have discussed with these students the material significance of a 1 in 50,000 risk (i.e. of death from IV contrast). By general medical standards, this risk is an exceedingly low one. I have speculated that perhaps one has a similar or higher risk of major injury in a number of other daily activities, such as driving on an interstate highway or flying in an airplane. This type of reasoning has generally swayed some students; but a significant number have still maintained that they would like to be told specifically of any life-threatening risk, even though it might be a very rare one. They have indicated that they would prefer to make their own judgement about the significance of the possible risk. These discussions have proven personally relevant to a number of students who have previously undergone tests with IV contrast. Many of this group have acknowledged in class that they recall no specific disclosure of potentially serious morbidity or death from such testing.

Although, as physicians, we frequently do make valid paternalistic decisions, I have found these students' impressions about what should be disclosed by the physician to be somewhat unsettling. In addition, my anecdotal experiences with IV contrast testing have also influenced me. In my practice, I order such tests daily, and indeed see very little morbidity. However, I certainly have encountered individuals who have developed renal failure after this type of testing. I have consulted on an elderly woman who did have an anaphylactic reaction immediately following a CT scan and ultimately died. I have had two patients who had profound allergic reactions with marked hypotension, but who recovered uneventfully with treatment. These instances have reinforced for me the fact that the potentially serious risks of this type of testing are more than just remote, theoretical ones.

In the context of this issue of which risks the physician should disclose to the patient, I am intrigued by a new intravenous contrast consent form recently adopted by a radiology group in Sioux Falls.[2] This form, entitled "Intravascular Contrast Study Information Sheet and Consent," is somewhat lengthy and certainly detailed. The form states in part:

> "Intravascular contrast studies require that a vein or an artery be injected with a liquid. This liquid, sometimes called a 'contrast medium,' makes body parts and structure visible by x-ray photography.
>
> Occasionally there are complications and/or reactions associated with contrast studies. The most common is discoloration, bruising, pain and

swelling at the injection site. We consider this relatively minor, but it can be distressing to the patient.

During or for a few minutes after the injection of the contrast medium, you may experience a sense of warmth or flushing throughout the body and have an unusual taste in your mouth. Sometimes a patient feels nauseous or vomits during the injection. These sensations are usually brief in duration and are not considered a complication.

Occasionally patients suffer mild allergic reactions in the form of itching, sneezing, watering eyes or mild hives. Less frequently, wheezing and a stuffy nose occur. This type of reaction usually lasts only a short while. Please inform a member of the radiology team immediately if you experience these symptoms.

Serious complications occur infrequently (less than one in 10,000 examinations) and include serious allergic reactions, drop in blood pressure or convulsions. Other serious complications include severe respiratory distress or cardiovascular collapse accompanied by shock. Very rarely (in about one in 50,000 examinations), these or a combination of these complications result in death.

You will be asked to sign this form authorizing us to perform this examination. When you sign it, you acknowledge that you understand the risks associated with the procedure... "

Certainly this form is very explicit in terms of both frequent and infrequent (but significant) complications. The information is provided in a fashion which hopefully reassures the patient that most serious complications are indeed rare. A form such as this does, I believe, respond to the type of concerns for disclosure voiced by many of the students and other non-medical people with whom I have discussed these issues.

As suggested above, this type of information should optimally be provided initially by the patient's own physician. The use of a fairly detailed form for disclosure is particularly helpful in terms of providing an informational foundation which the physician can edit and interpret for the patient. The use of such a form relieves the physician of the burden of tediously elaborating a specific list of side effects to the patient every time he or she orders a test or recommends a therapy. Rather, the physician can focus his or her time on explaining what test or treatment is planned, why it is proposed, and what possible alternatives exist. The physician can give the patient a perspective on any potential side effects by contrasting whatever risks exist with the anticipated benefits of the test or therapy. Whatever questions the patient may pose can be addressed. And finally, in this role, the physician can make a paternalistic decision as to whether the patient understands the information/consent form, or whether the physician must edit or simplify the form's factual information in order for the patient to have a meaningful understanding of it. Paternalism in this sense would seem to be a complementary and necessary part of the disclosure process.[3]

SUMMARY

Many patients want explicit factual disclosure of the risks of major side effects, even when the statistical chances of such serious problems are remote. A detailed information/consent form can provide such a factual basis. Certainly, such a formal disclosure offers the physician considerable legal protection in terms of possible adverse side effects occurring to the patient.

More importantly, for the purposes of this medical-ethical discussion, this type of disclosure helps insure that the patient is able to truly make an autonomous, informed choice before proceeding with testing or treatment. Such disclosure helps establish honest and forthright communication, and can significantly enhance the quality of the doctor/patient relationship.

[1]Spring DB, Akin JR, Margulis AR: Informed consent for intravenous contrast-enhanced radiography: a national survey of practice and opinion. **Radiology** 1984;152:609-13.
[2]Intravascular contrast study information sheet and consent (Medical X-Ray Center P.C., Sioux Falls, S.D. Private communication).
[3]Freeman JW: Reflections on informed consent. South Dakota Journal of Medicine 1985;38:5-6.

Questions to Consider for Chapter Five

1. Why is "respect for the person" so important in approaching dilemmas of caring?
2. What is bioethics? What is the "principle approach" to bioethics? How have 20th century events encouraged the development of this approach? Be able to identify the principles — autonomy, non-maleficence, beneficence, and justice — and relate them to some of the dilemmas that arise in caring.
3. What are some of the limitations of the "principle approach" noted in the article, the poem, and the essay by Dr. Freeman? Why does he think that attention to the "patient's story" provides a needed corrective?
4. What issues with respect to autonomy and beneficence are raised in "The Use of Force" by William Carlos Williams?
5. "Reflections on Informed Consent" by J.W. Freeman:
   a. Why is "informed consent" crucial in respecting autonomy?
   b. What are the four elements that must be present in order for consent to be informed?
   c. What major role does paternalism play?
6. "Informed Consent: Another Look at Disclosure" by J.W. Freeman: How much disclosure is sufficient?
7. "Ethical Dimensions of Informed Consent" from the Committee on Ethics of the American College of Obstetricians and Gynecologists:
   a. What is the ethical basis and purpose of informed consent?
   b. Is the gaining of informed consent an ongoing relational process or a once-and-for-all event? Explain with reference to the relationship between a woman expecting a baby and her obstetrician/gynecologist.

Chapter Six:
Who Gets Care?

Arthur Olsen

"Brech's case pried open big concerns about
health-care costs, but fears that the county would
be flooded with high-cost requestx have proven
unwarranted... Local governments must move
with caution in funding extraordinary surgery
because medical science is advancing faster than
society's ability to pay. But commissioners made
the right call in Brech's case." — Editorial, "County
makes the right call," in the Sioux Falls *Argus
Leader,* Jan. 7, 1987.

"I think Rose was ready to go," he said, referring
to a recent talk. "I was watching TV, she said,
'Lanny it's all right.' I said, 'What's all right?' She
said, "it's all right if I die. God will take care of
everybody.'" — Lanny Brech, quoted in "Brech's
battle over; her inspiration lives," Sioux Falls *Argus
Leader,* Mar. 3, 1987.

In order to respect persons in caring decisions, it is necessary that
they, as autonomous, rational agents, be involved in medical
decisions. This is for reasons of utility and duty. A cooperating
patient will contribute to the outcome. And it is only in this way
that the patient is deeply respected. However, informed consent in
practice is not easily realized, as the readings make clear.

For you and me to make informed decisions, disclosure of information is crucial. But how much information is enough? When we
are cared for, we depend on our caregivers as teachers. Moreover,
disclosure is not a once-and-for-all event, but an ongoing process
that requires a relationship of trust between caregiver and those
cared for. Patient comprehension, which is essential, may be compromised by effects of the illness or by age. Consent-to-care decisions must be, of course, voluntary. There may be a fine line
between coercion and persuasion. And in some cases, as illustrated
by William Carlos Williams' piece "The Use of Force," it may

appear that the only way to save the life of a child who refuses to allow a physician to examine her is to use force for the child's own good. Or is force the only way? To be sure, she is a child for whom the parents may legitimately be expected to speak. Is this truly an emergency? Would another approach to the child have achieved the same result without the use of force?

Respect for persons is exhibited by enabling them to make informed decisions about their own care. It is not just a single event but a process for supporting patients in carrying out their life stories in compromised situations. For the process to be effective a relationship is required. In the words of William F. May, there needs to be a covenant between the caregiver and those cared for.[1] This covenant assumes a caregiver who respects the patient, and a patient who respects both him or herself and the caregiver.

The next readings explore a further dilemma of the call to care that arises when we endeavor to respect the personhood of all those needing care. Is there any limit to the care that can be granted because the resources are limited? If so, how shall limited goods be distributed? It is a question both of stewardship (how best to use our resources) and justice (how shall a limited good be distributed)?

One may begin with the familiar parable of the Good Samaritan in Luke's gospel, Chapter 10 : 25-37. In his book *The New Medicine and the Old Ethics* , Albert Jonsen raises the question this way: Can the Good Samaritan be a gatekeeper, that is one who decides who gets care and who doesn't, if there isn't enough to go around?[2] In the tradition of Western medicine this story has come to be the narrative that engages us with the claim of the injured neighbor who needs our care. However, what if the Good Samaritan must be concerned about many others needing care? What choices need to be made to see who gets the care if there isn't enough for all? Who decides, and by what criteria?

The philosopher Aristotle distinguished between two kinds of justice: retributive, and distributive. Retributive justice is intended to right a wrong, to restore stolen goods, to punish the offender. Distributive justice is concerned with fairness. Who gets the scarce goods when there isn't enough to go around?

With this question of justice as fair distribution in mind, we invite you to consider the case of Rose Brech, a 37-year-old woman who showed up at a meeting of the Minnehaha County Commissioners in Sioux Falls asking for $150,000 so that she could finance a heart and lung transplant operation. Are there fair limits to the care that needy people can receive?

On one level the issue is *macro-allocation* of county funds. It is a budget question. Would granting Rose Brech's request skew the county budget, taking away money needed for other county needs, such as education and police protection, or other health needs?

On another level the issue is *micro-allocation*. Assuming that there are some funds available for requests of this kind, does she qualify? There are many factors to consider besides the economic one. Is she psychologically and sociologically ready? Will she be able to deal with the trauma of surgery and have the discipline to follow rigorous medical protocols in the post-operation period?

Not to be overlooked in the discussion of fair treatment for Rose Brech is the issue of *motivation*. Are we moved to act because health care is a *right*, that to which she is entitled, or out of compassion?

Enter Rose Brech. Consider yourself either a county commissioner or a citizen in Minnehaha County.

---

[1]May, William F. *The Physician's covenant.* 1983.
[2]Jonsen, Albert R. *The New Medicine and The Old Ethics.* Harvard University Press, 1990.

The Good Samaritan
Luke 10: 25-37

[25]Just then a lawyer stood up to test Jesus. "Teacher," he said, "what must I do to inherit eternal life?" [26]He said to him, "What is written in the law? What do you read there?" [27]He answered, "You shall love the Lord your God with all your heart, and with all your soul, and with all your strength, and with all your mind; and your neighbor as yourself." [28]And he said to him, "You have given the right answer; do this, and you will live."

[29]But wanting to justify himself, he asked Jesus, "And who is my neighbor?" [30]Jesus replied, "A man was going down from Jerusalem to Jericho, and fell into the hands of robbers, who tripped him, beat him, and went away, leaving him half dead. [31]Now by chance a priest was going down that road; and when he saw him, he passed by on the other side. [32]So likewise a Levite, when he came to the place and saw him, passed by on the other side. [33]But a Samaritan while traveling came near him; and when he saw him, he was moved with pity. [34]He went to him and bandaged his wounds, having poured oil and wine on them. Then he put him on his own animal, brought him to an inn, and took care of him. [35]The next day he took out two denarii, gave them to the innkeeper, and said, 'Take care of him; and when I come back, I will repay you whatever more you spend.' [36]Which of these three, do you think, was a neighbor to the man who fell into the hands of the robbers?" [37]He said, "The one who showed him mercy." Jesus said to him, "Go and do likewise."

From *The Holy Bible*, NRSV.

Distributive Justice:
The Rose Brech Case
Ron Robinson

They used to be called "the salt of the earth," the ordinary, decent, hardworking men and women who try to claw a living out of the soil or who work as shop clerks or waiters or waitresses or who haul bricks or dig ditches or hammer nails in order to pay the rent and keep food on the table. They are proud people who don't like to accept charity, who are imbued with the American spirit of enterprise and self-determination, and who deal with hardships as they come. They pay taxes, just like everyone else, and they expect their elected officials to be frugal with public funds.

But once in a while they get into trouble and need help. And they go to the government officials they elected, and they humbly beg assistance.

That's why Rose Brech, 37, showed up at a meeting of the Minnehaha County Commission in Sioux Falls, S.D., back in the winter of 1985. Her doctor had told her that she would die very soon unless she got a new heart and new lungs. It could be done. The University of Minnesota had done the transplant operation with other patients worse off than Rose Brech, and the operation had added months and years to the lives of those patients. The catch was that the operation was terribly expensive, something over $150,000, a sum that Rose Brech could barely even comprehend, let alone come up with. She was at the courthouse to ask the commissioners to find some way to pay for her operation.

Rose Brech had become a "case," one that provides a dramatic illustration of the problems of justice that emerge when people and governments strive to do the right thing for the poor and suffering. The Good Samaritan offers a compelling paradigm for compassion, but when the model is extended from a single person to scores of people in need, the question of fairness — distributive justice, the allocation of funds — takes a paramount position. It was the problem with which the county commission was faced in the Rose Brech matter. The commission was mandated by the Constitution and by law and by human inclination to "provide for the general welfare," but there were limits to their resources. Therefore, lines had to be drawn, qualifications established, limits set in order to protect the funds under their purview from disastrous depletion. From the general principle of charity arising from the Good Samaritan's example, the application of justice came down once again to an individual in need: Rose Brech.

The commission deliberated the matter and took a vote on paying for the operation. The results: one commissioner for, four against.

The commissioners had good reasons for their decision. As far as they could see, South Dakota's welfare laws did not guarantee medical assistance for citizens who could not foot the bill. South Dakota's welfare statute was written in 1877, with only minor amendments since then. Food, clothing, and shelter were mandated for the poor in the statute, but not expensive and risky operations. In the Sioux Falls *Argus Leader* of February 5, 1986, the chairman of the Minnehaha County Commission, Ted Thoms, wrote: "Neither that original intent nor the amending legislation is thought to have intended that the county guarantee all medical assistance to all residents deemed poor." The operative word in Thom's statement is "all." He cited another statute which charged county commissions to "superintend the fiscal concerns of the county and secure their management in the best possible manner." The commission said the surgery Rose Brech needed was highly experimental, and it had established guidelines which omitted experimental procedures from consideration. The commissioners were not lacking in compassion — they had already paid her sums amounting to thousands of dollars for her hospital stays, physicians fees, and lab tests — but they felt a line had to be drawn somewhere.

When the ruling was appealed, the commissioners again said no.

Perhaps just below the surface was the fear of setting a precedent that might initiate a raid on public coffers. If the commissioners gave the money to Rose Brech, what would prevent somebody else in need from making the same claim, then another and another? Once the floodgates were opened, how could they be closed again? The commissioners would be labeled spendthrifts, careless of the taxpayer's money.

It was all very logical, and it all might have ended right there, with Rose Brech going home and waiting resolutely for the "tickle of death's feather," as Dylan Thomas called it. But besides being a very sick young woman, she was also cheerful, optimistic, and photogenic. Her smiling photograph in the Sioux Falls Argus Leader captured the attention of the public, and her story became widely circulated. With growing public support, she became determined not to give up without a fight. She got a lawyer and took the commissioners to court.

The suit was pursued in a timely manner because a life was hanging in the balance. On February 8, 1986, Circuit Judge R. D. Hurd ruled that the county must pay for Rose Brech's surgery unless the commissioners could prove it was not necessary. "In my opinion the guidelines fail," Hurd told the *Argus Leader* on February 8, 1986. While the commission could exercise discretion in apportioning funds, Hurd said, "They have to have some type of objective criteria for exercising that discretion."

"It looks like maybe I'm going to get to have a few more years," Rose Brech told reporters. It turned out that she was wrong about that.

The county commission met once more and, on a vote of 3-1, turned her down again. The reason given this time was that Brech had failed to qualify as a candidate at any major transplant center in the country. There was a subtle catch involved: qualification for transplant surgery included the ability to pay for the operation. While the implication was that Rose Brech's surgery was not seen as necessary by hospitals, the fact was that the commission itself had seen to it that she would not meet those qualifications by refusing her funding. But even if funding were found for her, Rose Brech had not attained "the psychological or sociological readiness" that hospitals required for such surgery. While her lawyer, Bill Froke, argued that such readiness was volatile and could change at any time and that physically there was no question that surgery was needed, the commission stood by its decision.

Rose Brech had attended the commission hearing this time with her husband Lanny, and an *Argus Leader* photograph showed them listening to the ruling, neither of them smiling this time. By then the public and the media were hooked. They wanted to know what happened next. A feature-length article appeared in the *Argus Leader* on March 3, 1986. The hammer head was "Faith," and the next deck of the headline read, "Disease drains Brech's energy, but not her hope."

The article, written by staff writer Julie Bolding, helped the reader identify Rose Brech as more than a name or a photograph.

Writing of Rose and Lanny, Bolding said, "She has a weak heart; he has diabetes. Neither has a job. Their home is a lower-level apartment on the 600 block of South Dakota Avenue." Her education had been sporadic, but she had one year of secretarial training and had worked as a secretary, a baby-sitter, and in home jobs before her heart condition became debilitating. Her interests were watercolor painting, crocheting, and reading the Bible. Lanny was 38. They had a 20-year-old son and a 17-year-old daughter. Her typical day was described: "Brech begins every morning with a prayer: 'Thank you, God, for a night of rest, and please let me do my best today to share a smile with someone new.'" She was described as someone who loved people, especially kids, and who had a positive view of herself.

"Right now I'm letting everything just kind of rest," she told the reporter. "And I'm just saying we're going to do what we feel we have to do. We'll know when the time is right, and God will direct us."

By that time private fund drives had collected $13,000 toward the operation. Estimates of the cost of the operation had meanwhile swollen to $175,000.

By the first of July, 1986, the private fund drive had put $25,000 into the bank for the proposed operation. Then another break came: the federal government ruled that heart transplants were normal rather than experimental. Brech did not qualify for federal government money, but it did remove the argument that the surgery she needed was too borderline to fund. Brech was still waiting to be qualified as a candidate for surgery at the University of Minnesota.

At last, just before Christmas 1986, almost exactly a year after Rose Brech had first asked the county commission for help, she was officially accepted as a patient at the University of Minnesota Hospital. She went back to the commission and asked for another vote on her case. This time she won on a unanimous vote.

The *Argus Leader* quoted her as saying, "Right now at this moment I feel like I'm the luckiest lady in the world." The echo of Lou Gehrig's famous farewell in Yankee Stadium seems in retrospect an omen.

Two months after the commission finally caved in to her appeal, Rose Brech was dead. Her death was almost on schedule. A year earlier doctors had given her 12 to 18 months to live.

Lanny Brech recalled for the *Argus Leader* one of the last conversations he had with his wife: "I was watching TV. She said, 'Lanny, it's all right.' I said, 'What's all right?'

She said, 'It's all right if I die. God will take care of everybody.'"

He added, referring to the county commission, "She had no ill feelings toward anybody. She was just thankful that in the end they came across."

Among other things demonstrated by the Rose Brech matter is that objective criteria of the kind called for by Judge Hurd are hard to come by. That Rose Brech would die without an operation was never in question. What was in question was whether an operation would save her life, whether such surgery — rare, expensive, and chancy as it was at that time — should be funded by government with tax money, and whether judgments about matters as nebulous as "psychological and sociological readiness" should deter such funding. Should the Minnehaha County Commission be held accountable for the delays leading up to Rose Brech's death any more than the psychologists and social workers who deemed that she was not prepared to undergo the only procedure that offered her hope of a longer life? Should statutes and guidelines governing the use of public funds be further amended to allow public servants to screen applicants for medical welfare more objectively, or should flexibility be built into laws and policies allowing for extenuating circumstances in specific cases? Should government or private charity alone bear the burden of health care for the indigent? Should not hospitals and doctors contribute at least some of the effort? In one form or another, government officials, medical staffs, and the general public will continue to face such choices as long as there are poor people in need of medical assistance.

Vision Quest

Jerome Freeman

In the old days
the People said
photographs
were spirit
catchers.

A faded image
of Sitting Bull
still summons
quiet dignity
but offers no
clue to secret
thoughts of why
he was standing
still and where
the world was
going.

Today another
ancestor poses
grimly for a chest
picture. Tobacco
stained fingers
fidget as the
processor issues
up a radiograph
with an angry
blemish.

While x-ray
displays tumor,
it reveals too little
of the patient.
The healer must
look beyond
frames frozen in
time and capture
the spirit with
care rather than
images.

Questions to Consider for Chapter Six

1. Know the Rose Brech story.
   a. What is her request?
   b. What are the facts of the case which are important for weighing the reaction of the county to her request?
2. Be able to distinguish between the issues of retributive and distributive justice. Which issues particularly confront the commissioners of Minnehaha County?
3. Suppose you had been one of the commissioners. How would you have voted?
4. In Luke 10: 25-37 is the parable of the Good Samaritan:
   a. What specific actions does the Samaritan take to care for the man who was beaten and left half dead on the road to Jericho?
   b. What additional questions are raised if there are many strangers at the side of the road needing help and/or if the inn in Jericho is full?

Chapter Seven:
Caring Through Death
Arthur Olsen

"People ask me all the time, 'Isn't oncology nursing sad? My answer to that is 'No.' And then they
say, 'Oh, you must distance yourself from those
patients. That's how you cope.' But to me the key is
to step in. The closer you get, the greater the relationship you have with the patient and with the
family, the easier it is to cope. You have the sense
that in essence, you are giving your all. You work
with them, you know them, they know you. You
build a relationship, and through that relationship
— if it is there and truly exists — you use your
knowledge to help them to understand that they
are not doing well with their disease." — Sue
Halbritter

"I would define a peaceful death in a public context as a death that, on the one hand, rejected a disproportionate share of resources which, through a
kind of economic violence, threatened other societal goods such as education and housing; and on
the other hand, rejected euthanasia and assisted
suicide as still other forms of violence, though
medical and social rather than economic... It is right
and proper that we bear one another's illness and
dying. We should not only be willing to care for
others; no less important, we should allow them to
care for us if there is no moral or humane way to
avoid that burden." — Daniel Callahan

Who gets care? How do we, as individuals or as a society,
prepare to care for unexpected illness? Are there any
financial limits to the care that society should provide for
those, like Rose Brech, whose financial resources are totally inadequate to pay the cost of the care that they desperately need? Without
an expensive heart-lung transplant, Rose Brech's children will be
deprived of a mother. These are the disturbing and unavoidable

questions that surround us as we consider how we might have
acted if we had been the Minnehaha County Commissioners
charged with the responsibility of responding to Rose Brech's
request to finance a heart-lung transplant operation.

These questions demand our attention and reflection as a society.
Questions of justice and fairness ought not be decided at the bedside. There the needs of the patient, not broad questions of social
justice, should come first. But at some point the questions of justice
(fairness) must be the focal point of thoughtful reflection and decision for a society. Decisions are unavoidable. Time was against Rose
Brech. Though she eventually received an endorsement from the
county commissioners, she died before an organ donor could be
found.

In the short term Minnehaha County is off the hook. There has
not been a rash of requests. But the long term issue remains.

We can always hope that advances in medical technology or
more efficient use of social resources, or a new health care plan will
help eliminate the need for the type of agonizing deliberations
made by the Minnehaha County Commissioners in the Rose Brech
case. But the evidence so far is that the hope for an easy out is illusory. The same technology that makes some procedures more
affordable often introduces other new and extensive procedures
such as MRIs, CAT scans, and organ transplants.

So the disturbing question remains. On the *macro-allocation* level,
how much can there be in the budget for such emergencies? One
strategy for suggesting limits was to say that the surgery requested
by Rose Brech was experimental. It was initially regarded as experimental by those setting the Medicaid standards. When the Medicaid ruling was changed, a rationale for saying no to Rose Brech was
eliminated. Then her case continued as a question of *micro-allocation*. Did Rose Brech herself qualify as a candidate for this treatment? Would she be able to deal with the trauma of the procedure
and have the needed discipline to benefit from the treatment?

Still with us are questions of motive or the underlying reasons
for responding to the requests of the Rose Brechs among us. In the
parable of the Good Samaritan the answer can be located theologically. The lawyer basically asks, "What does God require of me?"
Answer: "Love God with all one's heart and soul and one's neighbor as oneself." We ought to heed Rose Brech's request because she
is a child of God who needs our care. In the philosophical discussion of our communities, one hears two kinds of justification. One

view is that health care is the right of all citizens, much as education and police protection are. The other view is that health care is a privilege and the motive for special intervention is basically that of compassion, not of right. We will return to this discussion in Chapter Nine.

The subsequent readings in this section focus on the practice of caring at the end of life. Here we encounter dilemmas of a different sort: not who gets care, but when should care be stopped? What kind of care best supports those who carry out their life stories in the face of imminent death? Advances in technological medicine have made it increasingly difficult to distinguish between actions that support life and actions that get in the way of death. It is a cruel irony that there are two opposing fears with respect to treatment that are harbored in the breasts of our citizenry. One is the fear of Rose Brech, that the needed treatment will be unaffordable. The other is that unnecessary end of life treatment will be forced upon us, causing what Daniel Callahan describes as a wild, technological death.

Defining death and determining what is ethical in caring for those facing death have become equally problematic. The use of terms such as "permanent vegetative state" and "brain death" suggests that there are degrees of dying. Someone in a vegetative state is not conscious, yet there is some brain activity in the lower brain stem. A brain-dead person has a flat EKG, and is not capable of any bodily functions that are not artificially maintained. Brain death emerged as a concept to facilitate organ donation. A heart or a lung cannot be taken for a Rose Brech until the organ donor is pronounced brain dead. Someone in an apparently permanent vegetative state is not brain dead, but not consciously alive. Should they be kept alive on a ventilator? Is stopping the ventilator the moral equivalent of causing death or is it really allowing to die?

This question was faced by the parents of Karen Ann Quinlan. In 1975 their 21-year-old daughter was brought to the hospital in a comatose condition. She had stopped breathing, and by the time of resuscitation in the hospital she had suffered severe brain damage. Her breathing was sustained by a respirator. Over time she lost weight and her body contracted into a fetal position. It appeared that only a respirator was keeping her alive. The family asked that the machine be turned off, believing that their daughter would not like to live in this kind of condition. Their parish priest concurred, counselling that their Catholic faith did not require continuing extraordinary measures. But the doctor refused. When the case went before a New Jersey Superior Court the judge concurred with the doctor that terminating the respirator would be an act of homicide. Later, after appeal, the New Jersey Supreme Court granted a guarded permission to stop the ventilator. The court acknowledged Karen Quinlan's right of privacy as represented by her family, thereby acknowledging the right of a patient to refuse treatment. Turning off the machine would not be regarded as a criminal act. The court advised that, if her physicians believed that Karen would never emerge from the coma, and an ethics committee agreed with this prognosis, she could be taken off the respirator. If Karen's physicians did not agree, the family could seek a physician who would.[1]

A number of fundamental questions are raised by the case of Karen Ann Quinlan. Is there a difference between causing and allowing death? Does a patient have the right to refuse treatment? Who speaks for patients when they are unable to speak for themselves?

An elaborate vocabulary has emerged to distinguish between acts that cause death and those that allow death to occur. Hence, *passive euthanasia* means not treating and hence allowing to die. And *active euthanasia* means taking deliberate action to cause death. And there are further refinements. Is euthanasia of either type — voluntary (consciously chosen and desired) or involuntary (not consciously chosen because the patient is unconscious and unable to choose or against the will of the patient) — ever appropriate?

The language of "passive" and "active," though helpful to a point, carries with it a ring of ambiguity. Thoughtful people realize that not doing something is an action of a certain sort. Whether the action is positive or negative, there is another judgment involved, namely the state of the person's life story. In one case, acting strenuously to sustain life is appropriate because the person involved has many more possible years to live. In another case the actions taken may be said to cooperate with the person's imminent dying.

The reader will be engaged with these questions in considering the case of Nancy Cruzan whose situation parallels the dilemmas faced in the Karen Ann Quinlan case. In Cruzan's case the issue was whether or not to stop tube feeding. Debate exists whether stopping artificial feedings is comparable to stopping a ventilator or other treatment. Some argue that nutrition is a basic human need that must be provided.

Other issues abound as we consider how best to care unto death. Is there really a difference between allowing and causing death? Should a patient have the right not only to refuse life-sustaining treatment, but also to receive treatment that causes death? The essays by Daniel Callahan and Allen Verhey address this question. If I have the right to refuse treatment, how can I be sure that my wishes are known when I am not able to speak for myself? Gilbert Meilaender's piece speaks to this issue. Finally, what kind of care best supports those who seek to live out their life stories even as they are dying? The interview with Sue Halbritter will involve us in the experiences of one whose chosen vocation is to care for those dying of cancer.

---

[1] For an overview of these issues, see Donald Munson, *Intervention and Reflection: Basic Issues in Medical Ethics*, fifth edition, New York, Wadsworth Publishing, 1996, Chapter Three.

Apocalypse
Jerome Freeman

A 26-year-old mother
and wife, four months
relieved of delivery, lies
comatose in the ICU.

Her waiting husband is
cornered and frail, as he
measures my approach
with fear-filled eyes.

I despair of halfhearted
preliminaries and swallow
bile and exhale the truth
that she looks bad, the
dying soon kind.

He and I walk forever
back to her bedside.
Her quiet repose hides
the aneurysm's havoc.
All about keep mostly
thinking there's a mistake
here somewhere.

Three times in the next
hour I wash my hands.
There is not enough
time. This kind of time
is never right. All the
time, some end lies
waiting to happen.

Reflections on Special Cases:
Nancy Cruzan
Jerome W. Freeman

Over the past two decades notable patients have periodically generated national bioethical and legal conversation. The case of Karen Ann Quinlan occasioned much national attention in 1975. Other subsequent clinical cases of note have included Brother Fox, Baby John Doe, Elizabeth Bouvia, and Helen Wanglie.

The story of Nancy Cruzan can serve as a paradigm for the ethical/legal turmoil that can surround these difficult cases. Nancy was twenty-five years old in 1983 when she was involved in a serious motor vehicle accident. She was comatose at the scene and was felt to have sustained brain injury both from head trauma and lack of oxygen. As part of her initial treatment, when there was still hope of her awakening from coma, a feeding tube was placed in her stomach (gastrostomy). Despite vigorous rehabilitative efforts, Nancy showed no neurologic improvement. She remained in a type of coma called "persistent vegetative state."

Her devoted and loving family saw her daily over the next seven years and for much of that time continued to hope for improvement. However, they eventually came to the realization that her brain injury was permanent and that her condition would never substantially improve. With that understanding, the family requested that her tube feedings be discontinued. They felt that this course would be most consistent with Nancy's previously expressed wishes. Their pastor, who apparently was of much support to the family, concurred that the feedings represented extraordinary treatment and could be discontinued. However, the rehabilitation facility caring for Nancy refused to allow the feedings to be stopped. Thus developed a long saga in the court systems in which the issue was debated at length. In 1988 Nancy's case went from the lower court to the Missouri Supreme Court to the Supreme Court of the United States. After the U.S. Supreme Court sustained the Missouri Superior Court in June, 1990, the case went back to lower court systems in Missouri. While the United States Supreme Court reiterated the right of competent patients to decline treatment (including food and hydration) it was felt that a specific advance directive to this effect was lacking in Nancy's case. Ultimately, when additional friends of Nancy's came forward to indicate that she had previously discussed her wishes with regard to this type of situation, a lower Missouri court allowed her feedings to be discontinued and she died about twelve days thereafter, on December 26, 1990. Even after this court decision was rendered, there continued to be considerable disagreement about the issue. Indeed, a group of individuals particularly upset by the decision marched in protest in front of the rehabilitation hospital during the days following the cessation of tube feedings.

When appropriate action is being debated in a difficult case like Nancy Cruzan's, it is important to study the specific details of the clinical situation in search of relevant variables. This orientation is championed by an ethical approach referred to as casuistry. This process employs the use of paradigm examples or situations when faced with ethical quandaries. An important aspect of casuistry is the focusing upon the specific, intimate details of each case. The occasional notable cases mentioned at the onset of this essay, have all served as paradigms in this sense. Even in the classroom discussion of such cases, a focus on the particulars is helpful. For instance, in addition to discussing the specific medical and legal facts of Nancy Cruzan's case, it proves helpful to actually see a video depicting the condition Nancy was in at the time her fate was in the court system. Such a video also permits some insight into the type of person Nancy was, and the character and motives of her family.

The arguments made by the United States Supreme Court justices are notable. Specifically the court did not distinguish between nutrition and hydration and other forms of medical treatment. In addition, the justices carefully emphasized the principle that a competent patient can accept or decline medical treatment. Certainly these latter two considerations frequently come into play in the clinical realm as caregivers debate issues of what technically can be done and what should be done for a given patient.

Pursuing a Peaceful Death
Daniel Callahan

On the face of it, one might be forgiven for thinking that death at the hands of modern technological medicine should be a far more benign, sensitive event than it was in earlier times. Do we not have a much greater biological knowledge, thus enabling more precise prognoses of death? Do we not have more powerful analgesics, thereby enhancing the capacity to control pain?

Do we not possess more sophisticated machines, capable of better managing organs gone awry? Do we not have greater psychological knowledge, suitable to relieve the anxieties and suffering of an anticipated death? Do we not, adding all that up, have at hand exactly what we need to enhance the possibility of a peaceful death?

The answer in each case is yes and no. Yes, we do have much more knowledge than we did prior to modern medicine. But no, that knowledge has not made death a more peaceful event, either in reality or in anticipation. The enhanced biological knowledge and technological skill have served to make our dying all the more problematic: harder to predict, more difficult to manage, the source of more moral dilemmas and nasty choices, and spiritually more productive of anguish, ambivalence, and uncertainty. In part this is because, with the advent of modern medicine, the earlier superstructure of meaning and ritual was dismantled, thus setting death adrift in a world of uncertain value and import. But also in part it is because modern medicine brought with it a stance toward death that is ambivalent about its necessity and inevitability.

In response to that ambivalence, without knowing it, without using quite that language, we have come to feel only now the loss of what the late French historian Philippe Ariès called a "tame death." By that he meant a death that was tolerable and familiar, affirmative of the bonds of community and social solidarity, expected with certainty and accepted without crippling fear. That kind of human ending, common to most people throughout history until recently, Aries contrasted with the "wild" death of technological medicine. The latter death, which began to occur in the nineteenth century, is marked by undue fear and uncertainty, by the presence

From *Hastings Center Report*, July-August 1993. Taken from chapter 6 of *The Troubled Dream of Life: Living with Mortality*, Copyright © 1993 by Daniel Callahan. Reprinted by permission. © The Hastings Center.

of medical powers not quite within our mastery, by a course of decline that may leave us isolated and degraded. It is wild because it is alien from and outside of the cycle of life, because modern technologies make its course highly uncertain, and because it seems removed from a full, fitting presence in the life of the community.

The technologies of that death, ever more clever in their ability to sustain failing organs, provide a set of tools that endlessly sustain our ambivalence and allow it to be played out in tortuous detail. Precisely because they have opened up new possibilities in the ancient struggle with our mortality, those technologies have made our understanding of that mortality all the more difficult. To confound us more, they have misled us into thinking we have a greater dominance over our mortality than was earlier the case.

What can be done to gain a better way of thinking about medical technology and our human mortality? How can that technology be made to serve a peaceful death, not to be its enemy? What can be done to bring about a change? I want to try to make plausible a different way of thinking about the use of technology and then suggest some ways of implementing it. The change I propose can be put very simply, however strange and odd it may sound. We should begin backward. Death should be seen as the necessary and inevitable end point of medical care.

Death as the End Point of Medical Care

In considering its appropriate goals, medicine should, so to speak, simultaneously work backward as well as forward. Medicine now characteristically works forward only, looking to promote the good of life, both to lengthen life and improve its quality. Death is reluctantly admitted into the realm of medicine as the limit to achieving those ends, but that limit is itself uncertain at its boundary, not readily located. Thus also is the termination of treatment judged to be a lesser moral evil, because the quality of life cannot be sustained at the level at which, ideally, medicine would like to sustain it.

What if, however, we began our thinking with death? What if we asked how medicine should conduct itself to promote both a good life and a peaceful death? What if medicine once and for all accepted death as a limit that cannot be overcome and used that limit as an indispensable focal point in thinking about illness and disease? The reality of death as a part of our biological life would be seen, not as a discordant note in the search for health and well-being, but as a foreseeable endpoint of its enterprise, and its pacification as a proper goal of medicine from the outset. What if the aim of scientific medicine was not an endless struggle against death, with the fight against disease as the token of that struggle, but helping humans best live a mortal, not immortal, life?

These questions are almost naive. But I see no evidence that they are deeply and persistently asked in modern medicine. If they were, then death would have to be taken seriously, allowed an honored role in the ideals of medicine, not treated as only a necessary evil and a temporary scientific failure. The acceptance, management, and understanding of death would become as fully a part of the mainline enterprise of medicine as the pursuit of health. It would not be necessary even to conceive of a hospice movement, a separate system of caring for the dying; that would be taken for granted as central to the enterprise of medicine itself not a specially constructed sideshow, out of sight of the main tent.

If the ordinary goal of medicine is the preservation or restoration of health, death should be the understood and expected ultimate outcome of that effort, implicitly and inherently there from the start. The only question is when and how, not whether. Medicine's pursuit of health should be leavened by its need when health fails, as it must, to prepare the way for as peaceful a death as possible. If death is part of the human life cycle, then care for the dying body must be integral to the ends of medicine.

Death is, to sharpen the point, that to which medical care should be oriented from the outset in the case of all serious, potentially life-threatening illnesses, or of a serious decline of mental and physical capacities as a result of age or disease. Of each serious illness — especially with the elderly — a question should be asked and a possibility entertained: could it be that this illness is the one that either will be fatal or, since some disease must be fatal, should soon be allowed to be fatal? If so, then a different strategy toward it should come immediately into play, an effort to work toward a peaceful death rather than fight for a cure.

What am I saying that is different from the present stance of medicine? At present medicine takes as its task only the pursuit of health, or the preservation of a decent quality of life, with death as the accidental result of illnesses and diseases thought to be avoidable and contingent, even though in fact still fatal. Death is what happens when medicine fails, and is thus outside its proper scientific scope. That is why, I surmise, a great medical classic, *Cecil Textbook of Medicine*, a primary guide for physicians, refers in only twenty-five of its twenty-three hundred pages to death (and only in five to pain).[2] For a book filled with accounts of lethal diseases and ways to treat them, there is a strikingly scant discussion — three pages only — of treatment for those in the terminal phase of disease. It tells what to do to hold off death, but not what is to be done when that is not possible. That omission is a stark example of the way death is kept beyond the borders of medicine, an unwelcome, unwanted, unexpected, and ultimately accidental intruder. What if, by contrast, every section of that book dealing with potentially fatal diseases had a part dealing with the care of those dying from the disease? The care of the dying cancer patient is not identical with the care of a person dying from congestive heart disease or kidney failure. But this could never be guessed from reading standard treatment textbooks.

An incorporation of that approach in textbooks and clinical training would make clear, in the most direct way, that this disease may be, sometimes voluntarily and sometimes not, the cause of death — death, which must come to all and is thus no accident. Then the physician's task would become that of accepting a particular illness as the likely cause of death, opening the way for a peaceful death by choosing that combination of treatment and palliation of the accepted condition most likely to make it possible. The objective here would be exactly the opposite of technological brinkmanship which goes as far as possible with aggressive treatment, stopping only when it is useless to go further. In the task of allowing a peaceful death, brinkmanship would be repudiated from the outset. Active treatment to cure disease and stop death from coming would stop well short of its technical possibilities, at that point when a peaceful death could be most assured and best managed. The worry that a patient might die *sooner* than technologically necessary would be actively balanced by anxiety that a patient might die later than was compatible with a peaceful death.

Deforming Our Dying

A peaceful death can be understood both positively and negatively. I will begin with the latter, specifying some ways in which our dying can be deformed. If we can better discern some of the ways that happens, the ideal of a peaceful death can be given greater substance. Our dying can be deformed in three ways: by deforming the process of dying, by deforming the dying self, and by deforming the community of the living.

Deforming the Process of Dying. The process of dying is deformed when it is subject to the violence of technological attenuation, drawn out and unduly extended by medical interventions, directly or indirectly. Technological brinkmanship is the most common way of creating the deformity — that is, pushing aggressive treatment as far as it can go in the hope that it can be stopped at just the right moment if it turns out to be futile. That brinkmanship and the gamble it represents can both save life and ruin dying; that is the dilemma it poses. The most obvious kind of technological violence comes when a particular course of treatment — some forms of chemotherapy for cancer, or cardiopulmonary resuscitation for a dying person — itself directly imposes the violence.

Less noticed, but bound to become increasingly important, is the violence done when the cure of one disease sets the stage for the advent of another, perhaps even more cruel than the death one has just averted.

Consider, for instance. the person cured of cancer at seventy-five who is setup for the enhanced risk, by virtue of age alone, of the onset of a fatal case of Alzheimer's disease at eighty, or for an excessively long period of severe frailty. We increase the likelihood of spending our declining years helpless, demented, and incontinent if medicine saves our lives long enough to help us avert all of the lethal diseases that stand in the way of that (not so splendid) final outcome.

We may of course gain some extra good years before that happens, and for some it will not happen at all. I only want to underscore the gamble implicit here, a kind of technological Russian roulette with one's last years of life. We must reckon whether it is a good or bad gamble, and how much we are prepared to accept a deformed dying as a result. Increasing frailty and bodily decline are themselves part of the aging process, the wasting away that ordinarily precedes death in old age. There is no inherent evil in the dependency that withering can bring. My complaint is instead directed against a kind of medicine that drives us toward technological brinkmanship and thus needlessly exacerbates and attenuates the withering in destructive ways, genuinely deforming the process of dying. The process of dying is deformed when, through overconfidence in our power to manage technology and to manage our own ambivalence toward death, we fail to take account of what an overzealous medicine can do.

The process of dying is also deformed when there is an extended period of a loss of consciousness well before we are actually dead. It is deformed when there is an exceedingly and unduly long period of debility and frailty before death. It is deformed when there is a lengthy period of pain and suffering prior to death. Note the words I have used: "extended," "exceedingly," "unduly," and "lengthy." By these I mean to say that death may well and unavoidably be preceded by some pain and suffering, some loss of consciousness, some debility and frailty, but that we human beings have generated our own miseries when we allow technology to create a situation that produces exceedingly long periods of those evils. I offer no precise definition of "exceedingly." Frailty and debility can be tolerated for longer periods of time than straight pain and suffering, and a few days even of unconsciousness might be tolerable.

It is when those evils go on and on that a problem, a desperate one, arises. Left unattended, the biological process of dying would not *ordinarily* lead to such deformities, even if it will happen in some minority of cases. That is something we can know from the dying of other biological organisms, especially higher animals, and from the historical record of human death itself before our modern era, where an extended period of dying was the exception rather than the rule. Our contemporary deformities of dying, it is then fair to say, ordinarily arise only as the result of human medical intervention.

Deforming the Dying Self. The most obvious way the dying self can be deformed is by allowing the fear of death, or the fear of what dying may do to our ideal self, itself to corrupt the self. Obsessions with a loss of control, or with a diminishment of the idealized optimal self, or with the prospect of pain, are other ways this can happen. That is to turn our dying into an occasion of unrelenting self-pity and self-castigation: I can never be again what I once was, I do not want to be what I now am, and I do not want to be what I will become as my death draws even closer.

Some delicacy is in order in trying to make this point. It is understandable that we should not want to lose all control or to become less of a self than we once were, or that we should fear pain. Anxiety, even terror, is to be expected as we approach our death, both because of the physical threats of dying and because of the

challenge to our sense of self-worth and self-coherence. It is the preoccupation with those evils that introduces the potential deformity,
the feeling that we cannot be worthy human beings if they are our
fate, and an inability to think of anything but our losses, our fail-
ures, our diminution.

Deforming the Community of the Living. Just as we can harm
the self, our sense of self-worth, in responding to the threat of death,
so too can we do harm to others. If the horror of death — or, more
likely, of illness, decline, and dying together — yields social policies
designed to relieve that suffering at all costs, then the community of
the living is put at risk. A society that takes the relief of the ordinary
burdens of life (of which death is surely one) as a goal to be pursued
with singular dedication must ultimately fail, putting its members
in harm's way even as it does so.

This can happen when the pursuit of health and the avoidance of
death become an excessively high priority, gained at the cost of
ignoring other social evils. It can happen when the medical community comes to believe it must, as the price of relieving suffering,
be prepared to kill or assist in suicide, thus distorting its oldest and
most central traditions. It can happen when, as a community ideal,
a life that includes any suffering is rejected as intolerable. It can happen when a life thought "not worth living" (the Nazi expression) is
one marked by suffering, a less than ideal self, and a failure to make
adequate contributions to society.

The possibility of a peaceful death will, then, require as a minimal condition that death not be deformed, either individually or
socially. But more will be required to enhance its possibility.

Deforming a Peaceful Death

It is not difficult, just listening to the way people talk about the
kind of death they would like, to gain a decent sense of what they
would count as a peaceful death. I could try to do that, but I would
prefer to put it in my own voice, recognizing that there may be individual variations:

● I want to find some meaning in my death or, if not a full meaning, a way of reconciling myself to it. Some kind of sense must be
made of my mortality.

● I hope to be treated with respect and sympathy, and to find in my dying a physical and spiritual dignity.

● I would like my death to matter to others, to be seen in some larger sense as an evil, a rupturing of human community, even if they understand that my particular death might he preferable to an excessive and prolonged suffering, and even if they understand death to be part of the biological nature of the human species.

● If I do not necessarily want to die in the public way that marked the era of a tame death, with strangers coming in off the streets, I do not want to be abandoned, psychologically ejected from the community, because of my impending death. I want people to be with me, at hand if not in the same room.

● I do not want to be an undue burden on others in my dying, though I accept the possibility that I may be some burden. I do not want the end of my life to be the financial or emotional ruination of another life.

● I want to live in a society that does not dread death — at least an ordinary death from disease at a relatively advanced age — and that provides support in its rituals and public practices for comforting the dying and, after death, their friends and families.

● I want to be conscious very near the time of my death, and with my mental and emotional capacities intact. I would be pleased to die in my sleep, but I do not want a prolonged coma prior to my death.

● I hope that my death will be quick, not drawn out.

● I recoil at the prospect of a death marked by pain and suffering, though I would hope to bear it well if that is unavoidable.

There is a difference between this desired peaceful death and Philippe Ariè's tame death. Technological advances make it possible to manage better those conditions that could not, in the past, be made amenable to a tame death, especially the degenerative diseases of aging. We can, that is, have both the advantages of the older tame death and, with the help of technology, many improvements in contemporary death.

The most evident characteristic of a peaceful death as I have outlined it is the way it blends personal, medical, and social strands. Whatever meaning we find in our dying and death must come from within ourselves, though we may and probably will of course draw upon religious and other traditions for important help. We could also reasonably look to the larger society for public practices, rituals, and attitudes that can provide a more comforting context for the acceptance of death. A modified return to special symbols of mourning, such as black arm bands for men and dark clothes for women, as well as the enhancement of groups organized for grieving spouses, or religious services, would be examples of the possibilities here. As for the relief of pain, there we can look to medical practice and even expect from that practice some help with suffering, a more subtle condition stemming in part from an interior perception of the significance of dying and from the kind of external support we are given in the face of our anxieties.

Could a peaceful death be assured every patient? No. Medicine cannot now and probably never will be able to avert all pain and suffering or ensure a tranquil course of illness. No society could wholly overcome the fear of death or the rending of community that is death. No one can be confident that fear, anguish, or a sense of pointlessness and futility will not be one's lot, even if one has lived the kind of life most conducive to reducing that possibility. Since no one can give us, as our own, a meaning to our dying and death, we must find that for ourselves; some of us will never find it.

Since there can be no guarantee that a peaceful death will be ours, some store of courage must be available. If I am correct in my surmise that the obsessively feared loss of control of our dying is itself part of the problem — a fear that we will not be either ourselves or in command of ourselves — then one way to resist the force of this fear is to be willing to accept some loss of control. The price of obsession is undue fear. Relief can be sought in a willingness to live with, and die with, less than perfection here. Yet if we can understand that there is a middle way, then the possibility of a peaceful death can be greatly enhanced. It is at least as likely that we could create the possibility of a peaceful death for a majority of people by changing our medical attitudes and expectations as by the more violent course of euthanasia and assisted suicide, and with far less loss of other values in the process.

Medical Futility

The general orientation and resource allocation priorities of the health care system can make a considerable difference, albeit indirectly for the most part, in the care of the dying. Of more direct and immediate impact will be the aggregate effect of what clinicians at the bedside come to consider futile or marginally useful treatment. As a concept, 'futility' has both medical and moral dimensions.[3] Its medical feature is that of a probability that a particular treatment for a particular person will not be efficacious, that is, it will not return the patient to good health or sustain the patient in any medically viable way. The moral feature is a judgment that some forms of medical treatment, with either a low or no probability of success, should be morally judged to be useless. Taken together, then, a judgment of medical futility is medical insofar as it relies on judgments of probability of medical outcome, and moral in that it relies upon judgments about whether the pursuit of low-probability outcomes is morally required.

There is already considerable pressure from physicians to be allowed to make judgments of medical futility on their own, without having to ask patients or their families. Their goal is not to avoid a doctor-patient interaction, but to be spared the pressure of unrealistic patient demands. It is one thing, they say, to be asked by patients or their families to stop treatment; that is acceptable. It is still another to be asked to provide treatment of a kind physicians think futile or useless; that they take to be unacceptable, a threat to their professional integrity.

Their instinct is correct and reasonable. Physicians ought not to be required to perform procedures or provide treatment that they believe will do no good. Yet it would be arbitrary to allow physicians unilaterally to make those judgments, given the rights of patients to be informed of their situation. It would be better if the standards here were established collectively, by joint bodies of lay people and physicians.

This might best be done in individual hospitals, where joint medical-lay panels could help establish an institutional policy sensitive to local needs and values. It should not, I believe, be done with individual patients on a case-by-case basis. Judgments of futility could then be made, and treatment denied, but on the basis of consensual norms and publicly visible policies. The development of such policies would, of course, have a potentially significant impact on the options available to patients. Some general societal standards would come to replace unlimited patient choice.

What would be the pertinence of such a development for the termination of treatment? It would be valuable if in coming years some consensus were achieved about futile treatment. 'Futility' needs, however, to be understood in two senses: futile because no benefit whatever can be achieved from treatment, and futile because, given resource limitations, the treatment is economically unjustifiable. Thus we must have a general social agreement on the right of physicians to withhold medical treatment from persons in the persistent vegetative state, and an agreement on the forms of medical treatment that would be considered futile for those faced with imminent death from an acute or chronic illness or from the slow death of dementia.

A standard of futility compatible with the goal of avoiding an unnecessarily painful or extended death would be most valuable. The test of futility could be twofold: first, an inability to arrest more than momentarily (by a few days or weeks) a downward, deteriorating course; and second, the probability, should that kind of effort be made, that a peaceful death would become increasingly unlikely. At that point, curative medical treatment has indeed become futile and ought to be stopped. The standard is thus one that looks to the possibility of sustaining life in some decent fashion, but also and simultaneously to the choices necessary for enhancing the possibility of a peaceful death.

The most difficult but impending problem of futility judgments is whether to embody them in public policy. As matters now stand, it is customary for both federal and private health care plans to provide reimbursement for the care of those in a persistent vegetative state; families and medical staffs that want medical treatment to be continued for these patients can be reimbursed for its cost. Should financial support continue in the future? I believe that, in principle, it should not. Ideally speaking, it makes no sense in light of budget restraints or humane public policy to use medical technology to sustain for an extended period the life of someone who will almost certainly never return to consciousness.

The temptation here is to adopt an either-or approach. If we consider the patient alive, then we think we should provide the patient with all those forms of health care that we would provide any other live person; or if we simply consider the patient as dead, even if not legally so, we think we should stop all care. The problem, however, is that we as a society remain uncertain about the status of patients who manage to combine, in a bewildering way, elements of both life and death. An appropriate compromise, I believe, would be to provide minimal nursing care but not the extended artificial nutrition and hydration that many institutions now routinely provide — probably because of public disagreement about the moral status of someone in that condition.

My guess is that increasingly few people will for long believe that this form of "life" merits being called human. It is a moribund life sustained by technological artifact in the face of a biological condition crying out to come to an end, as in nature it ordinarily would. Yet as long as disagreement persists, it would be unwise to stop treatment precipitately or high-handedly. That could seem to bespeak an indifference to the important convictions of some people, convictions not without some merit. But every effort should slowly be made to change those convictions so that a social consensus could build to form the basis of new policy that would refuse reimbursement for patients in that condition. A softer, perhaps more tolerable alternative would be to assign a low priority to such treatment, to help assure it would not capture resources that could be better spent on more needy patients with a chance of real recovery or amelioration of their condition.

A peaceful death should have both an individual and a public face. For the individual it can bring life to a fitting close, marked by connection to the self through reason and self-consciousness, and by connection to others through dying within the circle of human companionship and caring. But death should also have a peaceful public face. The control and management of death, understood as an unavoidable part of life, should not consume an undue share of resources, as if keeping death at bay represented society's most important goal. People should have a chance to live a healthy life, avoid premature death, and then die without that technological brinkmanship that knows no boundaries in the war against mortality.

I would define a peaceful death in a public context as a death that, on the one hand, rejected a disproportionate share of resources which, through a kind of economic violence, threatened other societal goods such as education and housing; and, on the other hand, rejected euthanasia and assisted suicide as still other forms of violence, though medical and social rather than economic.

What about family burdens as a form of quasi-domestic violence? It is not improper for people to worry about being a burden on their families or to wish they could spare them undue emotional and financial hardship. We can readily recognize the possibility of taking down with us, in a parallel destruction, those family members whose devotion — economic or emotional or both — is pressed too far. It is hard to see how a death that impoverishes a family, or destroys the later years of an elderly spouse, or wrecks the family life of a dutiful child caring for an elderly parent, can be called entirely peaceful.

At the same time, however, it is right and proper that we bear one another's illness and dying. We should not only be willing to care for others; no less important, we should allow them to care for us if there is no moral or humane way to avoid that burden. We do not need a medical system and a set of moral values that will impose upon families the drain of extended illness and death, especially when that has been brought about not by natural forces but by an excessive application of life-sustaining technologies. We should be willing to bear what nature and human mortality bring to us. But there is no reason why we should have to bear artificially extended deaths. A patient should reject them for the sake of the family's welfare after he or she is gone. And when a patient is incompetent and death on the way, family members should not be forced, through guilt or a confusion about killing and allowing to die, to believe that a termination of treatment is wrongful killing. It is not killing at all.

1Philippe Ariès , *The Hour of Our Death*, trans. Helen Weaver (New York: Alfred A. Knopf, 1981), pp. 5-28; see also Philippe Ariès, *Western Attitudes Toward Death*, trans. Patricia M. Ranum (Baltimore: Johns Hopkins University Press, 1974).

2James R. Wyngaarden, Lloyd H. Smith, and J. Claude Bennett, eds. *Cecil Textbook of Medicine*, 19th ed. (Philadelphia: W. B. Saunders, 1992).

3See Lawrence J. Schneiderman, Nancy S. Jecker, and Albert R. Jonsen, "Medical Futility: Its Meaning and Ethical Implications," *Annals of Internal Medicine* 112, no. 12 (1990): 949-54: John D. Lantos et al., "The Illusion of Futility in Medical Practice," *American Journal of Medicine* 87 July 1980): 81-84: Tom Tomlinson and Howard Brody, "Futility and the Ethics of Resuscitation,"

JAMA 264, no. 10 (I990): 1276-80: Stuart J. Youngner, "Who Defines Futility?" *JAMA* 260, no.14 (1988): 2094-95.

⁴See Daniel Callahan. "Medical Futility, Medical Necessity: The Problem-Without-A-Name," *Hastings Center Report* 21, no. 4 (1991): 30-35.

Choosing Death:
The Ethics of Assisted Suicide

Allen Verhey

In March the U.S. Court of Appeals for the Ninth Circuit decided that a Washington statute which prohibited physician-assisted suicide was unconstitutional (*Compassion in Dying v. State of Washington*). Less than a month later, the U.S. Court of Appeals for the Second Circuit declared unconstitutional an 1881 New York law which prohibited assisting suicide (*Timothy E. Quill v. Dennis C. Vacco*).

Judge Stephen Reinhardt, who wrote the decision in the Washington case, started his argument with the protection of liberty in the due-process clause of the Fourteenth Amendment: "nor shall any State deprive any person of life, liberty, or property, without due process of law." Citing a passage from *Planned Parenthood v. Casey* (the 1992 Supreme Court decision regarding abortion) which said that "choices central to personal dignity and autonomy" are "central to the liberty protected by the Fourteenth Amendment," Reinhardt judged that the liberty protected in that clause must include the liberty to choose death, at least when a competent patient is terminally ill, suffering, and requesting a prescription from a physician to hasten death.

The Second Circuit was invited by plaintiffs down a similar path, but it declined "to identify a new fundamental right." Instead Judge Roger Miner turned to the equal-protection clause of the Fourteenth Amendment, deciding that the New York law which prohibited assisted suicide was a violation of that clause because it "does not treat equally all competent persons who are in the final stages of fatal illness and wish to hasten their deaths."

Those in the final stages of terminal illness who are on life-support systems are allowed to hasten their deaths by directing the removal of such systems; but those who are similarly situated except for the previous attachment to life-sustaining equipment are not allowed to hasten death by self-administered prescribed drugs.

The court held, in effect, that there is no important or legally relevant difference between refusing life-prolonging medical treatment and requesting lethal prescriptions, between withholding (or

terminating) unwanted medical treatment and prescribing drugs to
hasten death, between allowing to die and assisting in suicide.

This rejection of the traditional distinction between killing and
allowing to die also helped clear the legal ground for Judge
Reinhardt, for he found a precedent for his new liberty interest in
the 1990 opinion of the Supreme Court concerning *Cruzan v.
Director, Missouri Department of Health*. In that opinion Chief Justice
William Rehnquist wrote, "We assume that the United States
Constitution would grant a competent person a constitutionally
protected right to refuse lifesaving hydration and nutrition." That is
a precedent, of course, only if there are no important distinctions
between refusing life-prolonging medical treatment and requesting
lethal drugs, between allowing to die and killing.

These twin decisions were reached by different paths, paths
which, while breaking new ground legally, are well worn within
medical ethics. Judge Reinhardt's argument emphasizes liberty,
makes individual autonomy trump over every other moral argument, and understands self-determination to include a right to self-
destruction. Judge Miner's argument rejects the distinction between
suicide and refusing treatment, between killing and allowing to die.

The distinction between suicide and refusing medical treatment,
or between killing and allowing to die, is a "traditional" one, but I
do not hold that against it. In medicine the tradition was initiated
by those Hippocratic physicians who acknowledged the folly of
attempting to preserve the life of a patient "overmastered" by disease. In law this tradition has been a part of the common-law prohibitions of suicide and assisted suicide. This distinction was
invoked in all legislative initiatives on behalf of the patient's right
to refuse treatment. So, for example, in New York the 1990 Health
Care Agents and Proxies Act cautions, "This article is not intended
to permit or promote suicide, assisted suicide, or euthanasia."

The distinction is also a traditional one within Christianity, and
with good reason. For Christians the significance of dying — and of
suffering, too, for that matter — is determined by the scriptural stories of creation and fall and redemption, stories of a cross and of an
empty tomb.

To be sure, the significance of such events is complex; there is a
certain dialectic in the Bible's dispositions toward suffering and
dying. On the one hand, scripture underscores that life and its
flourishing belong to the creative and redemptive cause of God. The
signs of it are breath and a blessing at creation, a rainbow and a

commandment, and above all, an empty tomb. Therefore, life and its flourishing are to be recognized and celebrated as goods, and as goods against which we may not turn without turning against the cause of God. Life and its flourishing are gifts of God. They are to be received with thanksgiving and used with gratitude. Acts which aim at death and suffering do not fit this story, do not cohere with devotion to the cause of God or with gratitude for the gifts of God. Death and suffering are not to be intended, not to be chosen.

On the other hand, scripture does tell us that life and its flourishing are not the ultimate goods. They are not "second gods," to quote Karl Barth. Jesus steadily and courageously walked a path that led to his suffering and to his death. Therefore Christians may not live as though either survival or ease were the law of their being. Sometimes life must be risked. Sometimes it must be given up. And sometimes suffering must be endured or risked or shared for the sake of God's cause in the world. The refusal ever to let die and the attempt to eliminate suffering altogether are not signals of faithfulness but of idolatry. And if life and its flourishing are not the ultimate goods, neither are death and suffering the ultimate evils. They need not be feared finally, for death and suffering are not as strong as the promise of God. One need not use all of one's resources against them. One need only act with integrity in the face of them.

The moral significance of these distinctions may be difficult to defend, however, when the story within which they make sense is denied or ignored. They are hard to defend, for example, in the context of a simple utilitarian calculus. Then the only relevant consideration is outcomes, results, consequences. And if the consequences are the same, it is hard to see why — in a utilitarian calculus — the moral significance of mercifully allowing someone to die is any different from that of mercifully killing someone. Moreover, if the standard for assessing the consequences is the maximization of individual preference, and if someone (whether arbitrarily or reasonably) prefers death to life in their particular circumstances, then the utilitarian may well infer that we have a moral obligation to kill that person.

The distinction between killing and allowing to die seems more at home — at least initially — in the context of a discussion of rights and correlative duties. In this context, for example, one can distinguish between negative and positive rights, between the right not to be interfered with and the right to assistance. So, one can distinguish the right to life as a negative right — that is, the right not to be killed — from the right to life as a positive right, the right to assistance in preserving one's life. And one can also distinguish the right to die as a negative right — the right not to have one's dying interfered with — from the right to die as a positive right — that is, the right to assisted suicide. Since negative rights usually entail much more stringent correlative duties than do positive rights, and since the negative right to life imposes a duty not to kill, one could argue that, therefore, there can be no positive right to die and no correlative duty to assist in suicide. Perhaps that is why the right to life was once regarded as "unalienable."

But the notion of an "unalienable" right to life has lost something of its force in the contemporary discussion of rights. If rights are simply legitimate claims, and if I may refuse autonomously to make the legitimate claims that are mine to make, then I may refuse to claim my negative right to life. And then not only would the right to die extend to suicide, but it would also seem to extend to assistance in suicide if a contract has been freely entered. Indeed, if I refuse my negative right to life, it is hard to see why killing me would be a violation of that right. So, in this context, too, consensual killing ends up looking morally indistinguishable from allowing to die.

The distinction may not be at home in the contemporary public discourse that focuses on consequences or on rights, but it is at home in the attitudes toward suffering and dying formed by scripture. The martyrs knew the scriptural story well, and bore witness to it by choosing neither death nor suffering but by being ready to endure either for the sake of God's cause in the world and their own integrity. Their comfort was that they were not their own but belonged to God, the giver of life, from whom not even death could separate them. And their comfort was their courage.

In more mundane and commonplace ways, many patients still display the same comfort and the same courage, still "bear witness" by their readiness to die but not to kill, by refusing both offers of assisted suicide and offers of treatment which may prolong their days but only by rendering those days (or months or years) less apt for their God-given tasks of reconciliation with enemies or fellowship with friends.

Because there was breath and a blessing, because there was a rainbow and a commandment, because there was an empty tomb, Christians will not choose death, will not intend death. But because the one who was raised had suffered and died, Christians will acknowledge that there may be goods more weighty than their own survival and duties more compelling than their own ease, goods and duties which determine how they should live even while they are dying.

I do not want to suggest that the distinction between killing and allowing to die provides a formula for resolving all the hard questions. There are surely some cases where an omission of treatment can only be described as intending the death of the patient — as in the failure to treat Baby Doe's esophageal atresia, for example. And there are some cases which are hard to classify as "allowing to die" or as "killing" — the diabetic patient with painful and terminal cancer who refuses to use insulin, for example. Still, there is a theologically significant difference between intending death and foreseeing it, between choosing death and choosing how to live while one is dying, between suicide and accepting death, between killing and allowing to die.

This theological account of the distinction may not be sufficient as a public defense, even when allied with the medical and legal traditions. I hope, however, to put forward a compelling public argument for preserving this distinction. I would do so by focusing on the issue of freedom.

The courts declare that physician-assisted suicide is a way to maximize human freedom and to increase our options. Freedom is important, of course, and no Christian formed by scripture should take offense at it or at the advice to maximize it. Freedom is a gift of God and part of God's cause. "For freedom, Christ has set us free," after all.

But what do we mean by freedom? The Augustinian tradition has celebrated and cherished freedom, but its enthusiasm has been chastened by the recognition that human freedom is intimately related both to the grace of God and to the determinate features of human existence. Leaving aside the relation of human freedom to God's sovereign grace, let us consider the relation of human freedom to the determinate features of life.

Pelagius described human freedom as the capacity of a neutral agent to make choices unconstrained and uncoerced, to contemplate options without internal or external constraints. Equipoised between good and evil, undetermined even by their own previous choices, neutral selves can will what they will. The evidence for freedom on this account is human inconsistency, unpredictability, arbitrariness, the ability to will one thing one moment and a contrary thing the next.

Augustine and the tradition he founded saw nothing to cherish or respect in such an account of freedom. In Augustine's view there are no neutral selves, no agents who face choices informed by the past, and no choices which do not form the determinate features of the future and of the self. Particular human beings and their choices are formed by their natural endowments (including, we say now, their genetic endowments), their natural communities, their cultures, their past choices, and the choices of others with respect to them.

These determinate features of human existence *limit* freedom, to be sure, but they also *enable* it. There is no human freedom which does not marshal endowments, weigh the claims of particular communities, interpret their culture, assess past choices, and respond to actions upon them. Human freedom does not exist in some disinterested point which transcends all that; rather, freedom is engaged in and with the determinate features of existence. Freedom in this sense is the capacity of a self to establish a self, to form a whole out of the disparate and determinate features of life. And the evidence of freedom is not arbitrariness but consistency and predictability. The exercise of freedom determines not just a discrete action, cut off from the past and the future, but the whole of one's life.

The point is that all our choices, including our social choices, including even the presumably innocent choice to "maximize freedom," express and form the determinate features of our common life. The point can be illustrated with respect to technology. Technology is frequently introduced as a way to increase our options. But it can quickly become part of the determinate features of our existence. The technology that surrounds dying was introduced to give doctors and patients options in the face of disease and death, but such "options" have become socially enforced; at least one sometimes hears people say, "We have no choice!"

It is possible to claim, of course, that ventilators and CPR are the path of progress, but this shifts the argument from the celebration of options and the maximizing of freedom to the meaning of progress.

Even if a particular option does not become socially enforced, simply giving social legitimation to certain choices can and does effect the determinate features of our life. Our choices, even to regard certain things as choices, form selves — and our social choices, even to increase options, form our common life.

Consider, for example, the life of the clerk who works the night shift at the convenience store (the example is from David Velleman, "Against the Right to Die," *Journal of Medicine and Philosophy*, December 1992). One determinate feature of her existence is identified on the front door: "The night clerk cannot open the safe." In order to maximize her freedom and increase her options, one might decide to give her the option of opening the safe. But to increase her options in this way would change the determinate features of her life, and not happily — or innocently. Not happily — because, given the vulnerability of a night clerk, to increase her freedom in this way would minimize her security. And not innocently — because under cover of maximizing options we would be forming selves to regard the vulnerability of others as a matter of moral indifference.

The sick and suffering are vulnerable too, and maximizing their freedom may render them still more vulnerable. To the vulnerability of the sick we will return, but first notice that decisions to increase options sometimes eliminate options. For example, an acquaintance invites me to a party; it is presented as an option, of course. But by increasing my options he effectively eliminates an option I suddenly realize I had the moment before but have no longer; the option I would have preferred, namely the option of both not spending three hours with this person and not explaining to him why I would rather not (or lying). The invitation increases my options, to be sure, but it also eliminates an option.

When we provide social legitimation for the option of suicide, we may increase options, but we also effectively eliminate an option, namely, the option of staying alive without having to justify one's existence. That happens to be an option much of the Christian tradition would choose if it could, an option the Christian tradition would like to preserve and protect, for it fits the story of life as a gift, as a given.

One may choose, of course, not to be killed, but the person who makes that choice is then responsible for it, accountable for living, and can be asked to justify the choice. With this point we return to the vulnerability of the sick and suffering, for this burden of justification will be hard to bear for those who simply do not want "to be a burden." Moreover, the very giving of choice can create some pressure to make a particular choice. The vulnerable will be subject not just to malicious thugs and con artists, not just to the pressure of some relatives who would be better off financially or emotionally if they were to die, not just to the pressure of "compassionate" friends who would like to see the suffering stop, but also to their own sense of an obligation to justify their existence or to quit it. And they would respond to such pressure by drawing on resources determined in part (and undermined in part) by the social choice to provide the option of assisted suicide as a way of maximizing individual freedom.

The point is not a subtle one, but it gets lost when we overestimate our autonomy and independence. It gets lost when we lose a sense of our dependence and interdependence. Our self-concept is always confused with our interpretation of what others think and feel about us. The threat to commit suicide is sometimes, after all, an inquiry about whether anyone really cares. To reply to such a threat by giving a person the option can too easily be read as an answer to that inquiry, and it can affect the resources a person has for choosing still to live.

If such is the case with individuals, it is also true for the culture. Providing the choice of assisted suicide to the vulnerable, to the dependent, to those who are no longer in control, is recommended, doubtlessly, as a way to increase their options, to enable them to assert their autonomy and to take control. Maximizing freedom in this way expresses a culture that values autonomy, independence and control. But it also forms both attitudes toward the suffering and the attitudes of those suffering. The effect of maximizing freedom in this way may be to make it more difficult for the sick and suffering — the dependent, those whose lives seem out of control — to refuse the option of death, harder to justify their existence.

This social innovation in the name of increasing options not only eliminates the option of receiving life as a given, but also shapes the way the choice will be made. The practice of dueling offers an instructive parallel. We no longer give people the option of settling disputes by means of a duel. At least, we do not provide social legitimation for it. Cultures which provided the option of dueling were obsessed with honor. Providing the option of dueling reinforced that feature of the culture, and that very feature of the culture formed the context within which people found it difficult not to throw down — or pick up — the gauntlet.

Our culture appears to be obsessed with individual autonomy. It now wants to express (and reinforce) that feature of the common life by offering dependent people a choice, giving them an option which extends self-control. But the very reason we have for giving people the option may make it more difficult for people not to choose it.

If we go down Judge Reinhardt's path, providing the option of assisted suicide as a way to maximize freedom, we are choosing not just a discrete piece of social policy but a pattern for our life together which asks the weak and the sick to justify their existence. To refuse to provide that option, to preserve and to protect the traditional distinction between killing and allowing to die, is to choose a pattern for our life where life is received as a given even when it can no longer be celebrated as a gift, and where being dependent on others and on God is accepted as our common situation. The traditional distinction remains the path to a common life in which people need not cling desperately to life, but may not kill.

Christian Thinking
about Advance Medical Directives
Gilbert Meilaender

The past several decades have seen a strong rejection of medical paternalism and an increasing emphasis upon patient
self-determination. The presumption now is that the patient
decides what course of treatment shall be pursued. We should be
wary, however, of depicting the possibilities for treatment decisions
in this way. Even fully autonomous patients, if there are such, have
no absolute right to decide upon their course of treatment. If they
did, physicians would simply be technicians, putting their skills (for
a price) at the service of our desires. However tempted we might be
by that picture, however often medical hubris or paternalism may
push us toward it, we should not really want it.

A *patient* is something different from a *client*, and a physician is
not an automobile mechanic. When he examines, handles and even
cuts upon our body, the doctor lays hold upon our person. As
patients, therefore, we quite rightly should be involved in deliberations about the course of our treatment, for our person is involved.
But so is the doctor's person involved as he commits himself to care
for us. We should not want it any other way.

There may be times, of course. when no agreement is reached
between doctor and patient, and the best we can do is to withdraw
from the mutual bond we have forged. Lacking agreement on the
substance of the matter, we take refuge in a procedural solution that
leaves both parties free to turn elsewhere. Patients need not submit
to doctors' recommendations; doctors need not practice what they
consider bad medicine simply because patients want it. In a society
such as ours — where substantive agreement is sometimes so lacking that a commitment to "fair procedures" is almost all that we
share — Christian physicians often find themselves in difficult situations. Not wishing to abandon patients who disagree with their
judgments about the best course of treatment, they may feel drawn
or even compelled to practice what they regard as bad medicine
(which is a moral, not just a technical, category).

Moreover, there is no guarantee that the medical profession itself
will support Christian principles in the practice of medicine. That is
already the case with respect to abortion and prenatal screening.

From *Christian Century*, Sept. 11-18, 1996, excerpted from *Bioethics: A
Primer for Christians*, Eerdmans, 1996. Reprinted by permission.

and it may increasingly be true of assisted suicide and euthanasia. Christian caregiving institutions, such as hospices, will face similar difficulties if assisted suicide and euthanasia become legally permissible. To be sure, it is one thing to acquiesce in a patient's decision to pursue a course of treatment when the physician simply thinks there are better and wiser courses; it is another to do moral evil in the name of not abandoning one's patient. Christian physicians in our society will probably have to take increasing care to make clear to their patients from the outset their own understanding of good medical practice and the limits to which they adhere.

Even if patients' wishes are not entirely determinative, they may quite rightly want to be involved in deliberations about their course of treatment. (Of course, that involvement may also take the form of saying what they do *not* want to know or intentionally leaving decisions to others, and we should also respect that form of involvement. Personal involvement is not demonstrated only through a concern for mastery and control.) Sometimes, however, patients are unable to participate in deliberations about treatment. This may happen for a short time due to the trauma of injury; but more difficult are cases of patients who will be incompetent to help make decisions for the entire course of their treatment — infants and young children, the severely demented, the retarded, the permanently unconscious. In these cases we are forced to ask in earnest, who decides?

In recent years the professions of both law and medicine have recommended advance directives — either a living will or a health care power of attorney — as the best way to answer this question. In essence, these measures attempt to circumvent the question by having the patient, while still competent, determine and state how she wishes to be treated if and when she should become incompetent.

Not all patients will have executed an advance directive, however, and, in the very nature of the case, some patients will never be able to do so (because, for example, they are infants, or have been retarded from birth). In those circumstances some have turned to what is called a "substituted judgment" standard, and in fact the law sometimes forces us to turn in that direction. According to this approach, we should ask what a patient would have wanted if he were able to tell us. There are, of course, different ways to try to answer such a question. We might assume that he would want what any "reasonable person" would want in his circumstances. But then we may discover that we have no agreed-upon standard of "reasonableness." The blood transfusion that seems reasonable to me will look quite different to the faithful Jehovah's Witness. The lengthy round of chemotherapy that seems choiceworthy to you may look quite undesirable to me.

Taken seriously, therefore, the substituted judgment standard may direct our attention away from the hypothetical reasonable person to the actual person who is the patient. Sometimes we know (from family or friends, for example) a good bit about what this person might have wanted. Sometimes the evidence may be sketchier — when, for example, he once opined in a late-night conversation with friends, "I'd never want to be kept alive on any machines." And sometimes, of course, the patient will be one who has no "track record" of past opinions or decisions — for example, a newborn, or a person who has been profoundly retarded from birth. For such patients substituted judgment seems inappropriate, although courts have sometimes applied it.

Thus, for example, in the case of Joseph Saikewicz, who had been retarded from birth and at age 67 suffered from a form of leukemia for which chemotherapy was a possible treatment, the Supreme Court of Massachusetts, attempting to apply a substituted judgment standard, held that "the decision in cases such as this should be that which would be made by the incompetent person, if that person were competent, but taking into account the present and future incompetency of the individual as one of the factors which would necessarily enter into the decision-making process of the competent person." The thought of an utterly hypothetical Saikewicz — who is not the real Joseph Saikewicz at all — being given one moment of lucid rationality in which to decide whether, as the person he actually is, he would want chemotherapy is itself a *reductio ad absurdum* of the attempt to apply a substituted judgment standard in such cases.

It is only our nearly idolatrous attachment to the language of autonomy that drives us to such lengths, of course, and where the law will permit it we should not hesitate to turn from substituted judgment to an attempt simply to assess what is in the patient's *best interests*. To be sure, there is no guarantee that this language will not also lead us astray. For patients with severely diminished capacities, we may too easily be influenced by the fact that we would not desire such a life for ourselves. Instead of asking, "Is his life a benefit to him?" we need to learn to ask, "What, if anything, can we do that will benefit the life he has?" Our task is not to judge the worth of this person's life relative to other possible or actual lives. Our task is to care for the life he has as best we can. Properly applied, a best-interests standard can free us from the often futile quest to determine what he would have wanted. It can free our energies and direct them toward the right question: Given the person he is now and has become, how can we best nourish and care for the life he has?

Obviously; some of these difficulties, for some patients, can be avoided if they have expressed their treatment preferences in advance — if, that is, they have, while competent, formally stated how they wish to be treated if a day comes when they are incompetent and unable to participate in decision-making. An advance directive is an attempt to extend our autonomy into a future time when we are no longer autonomous. As such, it is a product of the emphasis upon self-determination within our society over the last several decades, and it even has about it an illusory quality that attempts to give privileged status to one moment of independence in the course of an entire life that begins in dependence and, often, ends in dependence. Therefore, if they are not used with care, advance directives give rise to a kind of metaphysical self-deception.

Two forms of advance directives have been developed. What is called a "living will" was first given legal standing by the state of California in 1976. In enacting a living will I attempt to describe in advance the possible medical conditions that might overtake me in the future, and I attempt also to stipulate how I would want to be treated (or not treated) under those conditions. Developed at a time when the chief concern was the heavy hand of medical paternalism, the living will has often been conceived as an instrument for refusing treatment, for getting rid of that heavy hand. In principle, however, there is no reason why one could not use such an instrument to express a desire *for* treatment, even for all possible treatments. And, of course, the laws of any state may set limits on the treatments one can refuse or require.

By contrast, the second kind of directive, a health care power of attorney, attempts to say less about the future. Eschewing the attempt to predict possible medical conditions or treatments, it simply designates a proxy — one who will be authorized to participate in decision-making on my behalf if I become unable to do so.

There is, I think, no single "Christian" position on advance directives, but in my judgment we would not be wise to make use of the living will. After the U.S. Supreme Court issued its decision in the Nancy Cruzan case (1989), it was reported that the Society for the Right to Die received more than 100,000 requests for information about living wills in less than a month. This testifies to an enormous sense of dis-ease within our culture. Even though the normal human biography begins and ends in dependence, we deeply desire independence. That is understandable, of course, and in itself quite appropriate. But it ceases to be appropriate when it invites and encourages us to live a lie. When we attempt so definitively to extend our autonomous choices into that period of life when we are no longer self-determining, we come very close to such self-deception. In part, we deceive ourselves into supposing that we can actually anticipate with precision future medical conditions and possible treatments — a supposition that physicians themselves regularly resisted until lingering guilt over medical paternalism and the onslaught of malpractice litigation led them to acquiesce more readily in anything that appeared to be a patient's decision. More important, however, is the deception that cuts more deeply into our sense of self and encourages us to approach even the grave in a spirit of mastery and control.

Moreover, a living will lets others off the hook too easily. Patients who are unable to make decisions for themselves because, for example, they are severely demented or permanently unconscious have, in a sense, become "strangers" to the rest of us. We see in them what we may one day be, they make us uneasy, and we react with ambivalence. No matter how devoted our care, our uneasiness with a loved one who has become a stranger to us may prompt us to do less than we ought to sustain her life. It is important, therefore, to structure the medical decision-making situation in such a way that conversation is forced among the doctor, other caregivers, the patient's family, and the pastor or priest. Advance directives, often with the force of legal recognition standing behind them, are designed to eliminate the need for such extended conversation. That is part of their problem, for they free us from the need to deal with the ambivalence we feel in caring for a loved one who has now become a burdensome stranger.

I realize, of course, that freeing loved ones from such burdens is supposed to be one of the benefits of a living will, but Christians ought to be wary of such language. For to burden one another is, in large measure, what it means to belong to a family — and to the new family into which we are brought in baptism. Families would not have the significance they do for us if they did not in fact give us a claim upon each other. We simply find ourselves thrown together and asked to share the burdens of life while learning to care for one another. Often of course, we will resent such claims on our time and energy. Indeed, learning not to resent them is likely to be the work of a lifetime. If we decline to learn the lesson, however, we cease to live in the kind of community that deserves to be called a family, and we are ill prepared to live in the community for which God has redeemed us — a community in which no one stands on the basis of her rights, and all live by that shared love Christians have called charity.

I think, therefore, that we ought to prefer the health care power of attorney to the living will. It, too, of course, reaches out into a future beyond the limits of our competence, but it does so in a way that recognizes and affirms dependence. It anticipates and accepts that others will have to bear some burdens for us as we may for them. To medical caregivers, it says simply: "Here is a person upon whom I have often been dependent for love and care in the past. Now, when I can no longer participate in decisions about my medical care, I am content to continue to be dependent upon his love and care. Talk with him about what is best for me." In the cultural circumstances in which we find ourselves, I do not think Christians can do better than this.

Another Elegy
Jerome W. Freeman

You'll know who this is for
when I say that three months
is a long time from dying.

Those intruder cells somehow
abandoned their marrow sanctuary,
seeking temporary refuge in other
hidden spaces. His blood count
soared, as a second fleeting lifetime
was composed. And the panorama
of his living and loving was focused
to a locket-sized miniature of such
brilliance that the image will always
illumine your steadfast pride that
once there was this son.

Moving In With Presence
An Interview
With Sue Halbritter

Sue Halbritter is currently Director of Oncology Services at Avera McKennan Hospital and Cancer Institute. At the time of the interview she was a certified oncology nurse at Sioux Valley Hospital, specializing in Oncology and Pain Management. Psuedonyms are used for patients and caregivers mentioned in this interview.

Art: Welcome to these conversations about caring. We are especially interested in talking to you because of your experiences in caring on the frontiers of pain, working with cancer patients. Maybe to start out you could say something about your reasons for choosing to be an oncology nurse.

Sue: A fascination with death and dying. I don't think it was morbid, but a lot of people do. I was really intrigued with the dying process that people were going through. I was in school in the 1970s, graduated in 1979. At that time this whole concept of death and dying was just developing. I was intrigued with the way people were living with dying and as a nurse wondered if we couldn't make an impact on that. The cancer population at that point also satisfied my need to delve into patho-physiology, how the body works. So I got into cancer as a way to include the psych element that I was intrigued with along with the physical element.

Jerry: Was it unusual for a nurse just beginning to...

Sue: Be involved in cancer? Yes, particularly in South Dakota because there wasn't any formal cancer program at that time. When I graduated, I moved to Minneapolis and worked there for three years in a formal cancer program. At that time nurses usually wanted to be medical, surgical, critical care, or OB nurses. To even say I wanted to work with cancer patients, that was unusual. I don't think at that time I was really prepared for what I was going to get into. I remember thinking, "I got out of school, and in school, I never took care of anybody who died. Now, why all of a sudden do I want to be with people who are dying?" I realized that I wasn't going to save the world. I think in nursing and medicine at that time the view was that you're going to go in there and make a difference, and patients are going to walk out. I got placed into an environment where they didn't do that. There were a lot of tears in the beginning until I figured out how to deal with it. Either I had to learn to cope or I wasn't going to make it myself.

Art: Would you say more about how your experiences in these situations informs a larger sense of what caring behavior really means?

Sue: People ask me all the time, "Isn't oncology nursing sad?" My answer to that is "No." And then they say, "Oh, you must distance yourself from those patients, that's how you cope." But to me, the key is to step in. The closer you get, the greater the relationship you have with the patient and with the family, the easier it is to cope. You have a sense that in essence, you have given your all. You work with them, you know them, they know you. You build a relationship, and through that relationship — if it is there and it truly exists — you use your knowledge to help them to understand that they're not doing well with their disease. But they are ultimately the ones who make the decision: "I'm not doing well with this disease, I'm going to stop therapy." Patients ask, "What is that going to mean to me?"

And the oncology nurse has the comfort level to say, "Well, you know, if you stop your chemotherapy and you stop your radiation therapy, your cancer's going to grow, and if it grows, you're probably going to die from it." And the patient admits, "Yeah, that's kind of what I thought was going to happen."

But you've got to have a comfort level or relationship there before you can have those kinds of conversations. So, caring really means just that, stepping in and building a relationship with the patients so that you can become involved with them. And the difference between a professional relationship and a personal relationship is with a professional relationship you step in, you give your all and you care for that person, but when you walk out the door, you leave it behind. And you have to trust that the professionals you leave behind in the hospital, which is my setting, will take care of that person while you're gone and that when you come back the next day you can take care of the patient again. Whereas in a personal relationship caring is ongoing, never ending. In oncology you have to separate that out a little bit, and that's the hardest part to learn, to leave it behind.

Jerry: You've been able to do that?

Sue: Yes. Every now and then, a person will impress me and I'll think about them when I get home. Usually that's because something has happened or I've been interrupted in my day's work so that I didn't have a sense of finalizing what I needed to do before I walked out the door. But I had to learn for the most part that when you walk out, you're done. In my younger days, we worked eight hour shifts, so it would not be unusual to call at 10 in the morning to see if a patient had made it through the night or to call and see how the family was doing. Now, I can't remember the last time I actually called in to work to see how a patient was doing. I just know when I come back that they may be there or they may not be there, but I have done everything that I can do in this circumstance and go from there. And, that's kind of the professional peace you've got to learn.

Mary: How long did it take you to learn that?

Sue: You learn fast. I truly believe that novice nurses who go into oncology nursing learn within a year or two, or they won't stay. They leave.

Mary: That's a question we get frequently from students... How can you possibly get this involved and still not get *too* involved?

Sue: For most people, the natural instinct is to go in and get really involved in the beginning, and then they have to learn how to back away; or they go in and remain superficial. A lot of nurses leave oncology because they can't go beyond the superficial contact and don't have any satisfaction there either because it is superficial. There's something about working with cancer patients. For you to be happy in it, you have to learn how to care. And I'm not saying nurses in other areas don't care, but the caring is different. In critical care, for example, they care about their patients, but they care more about the machines and the dynamics than they do about the essence of the person. And that's vital. If I were the ICU patient, I wouldn't want to be anywhere else but there. But, if I were dealing with death and dying, then I would not want to be with a nurse who is mostly concerned about the machines that I'm connected to. I'd want the nurse to be more concerned about ME and willing to listen to ME and what's going on with ME, because the machines probably aren't going to make a whole lot of difference in the end.

Ron: What are some of the experiences you have had that have been particularly moving for you, from which you've learned something.

Sue: From which I've learned? Well, one of them, probably the most dramatic — and it's made me fanatical about it — is lung cancer and smoking. In the beginning, in the early '80s, lung cancer patients would end up in the hospital just gasping for breath. And in those days, we certainly didn't give morphine to take away the pain of not being able to breathe. They would lie in those beds gasping for breath and then ultimately thrashing around the bed because they couldn't get their breath. All a nurse could do was try to keep them in the bed and try to calm them down with a soothing voice. And I don't doubt that it helped. But I'd often walk away saying, "How could you ever smoke?" People just need to live one hour with what I've seen and they would never smoke again.

Anyway, that's probably where my campaign has come from: that there must be a better way to treat these patients, with dignity. Not only does a pulmonary death take away the personal dignity of the person, but it takes away all the family dignity. You can't cope with watching your loved one gasping for breath. Even when they get to the point where they are so hypoxic and don't even know that they are gasping anymore, the family still sees it is very painful for the patient to go through that process. I learned that lesson early and was probably one of the very first people on my unit who would not be afraid to give morphine IV or demerol if I could get the order from the physician. And in those days, nurses didn't even give narcotics IV routinely or regularly. Usually nurses wanted a house officer to do it for them. Nurses didn't want to take the responsibility of giving those narcotic pain medicines. I think it was also at that time that I got into the ethical issue of intent. When I give the morphine for respiratory pain, I'm giving it for respiratory pain; I'm not giving it to kill the patient. I'm just trying to get them to a point where they are comfortable. But I also recognize that I may give that morphine and they may take their last breath. And I'm okay with that. I learned that really early on, because patient situations made such an impression on me.

Another area I've been intrigued with is the concept of symbolic language used by patients who are dying. As they get closer and closer to death, they will say things that make people think that they are confused. I've gotten away from assuming they are confused. I'm beginning to look for more meaning in what they are saying. Is it really confusion or are they just telling me something in another way? I've started to pay attention to that. I think that comes from experiences where patients, who've been practically comatose, sat up and reached for something. Or patients who have been comatose wake up and talk to their father who has been dead as if that father is there in the room. And the family will say, " Oh, they must be confused, Dad's been dead for years." Well, maybe

Dad's dead or maybe Dad's there and we just can't see Dad. It really doesn't matter if it's giving this person a lot of comfort to talk to this Dad, whether he is there or not. So that's the whole issue around symbolic language. One reads about it, but I don't think we're paying enough attention to it. You know, our tendency as nurses and physicians is to reorient the patients to their environment, to take away their symbolism, to take away whatever it is that they are experiencing, or to sedate them. Maybe we need to let them ramble or not sedate them.

Jerry: Do you remember any more examples?

Sue: There was one that has happened to me really recently and it left an impression on me. It was a lady who had metastatic breast cancer. She'd been comfortable and all of a sudden, for some unknown reason, she began having excruciating pain to the point where she was screaming. And we just don't see that very often. So the whole oncology unit was just in an uproar because we didn't have this patient's pain under control and she was in so much pain. One of the things that we do in a pain emergency is move in "with presence," and so nurses were taking turns sitting with her, holding her hand, talking to her, soothing her, just letting her know that if nothing else, we were with her. And then giving her pain medicine. And as we got her pain under control, she started talking. And the conversation started with me. I was having my shift with her at the bedside, and she was talking about horses. "There's a whole bunch of horses out there."

"What are the horses doing?"

"Well, they're all tied up and they want to be free."

And I said, "Why don't we start untying them? How many are there?"

She said there were nine. And she started untying these horses and releasing them.

And I asked, "What are you doing?"

"Well, I'm untying another one."

"Where did it go?"

"Well, it's wandering around in the pasture and kicking its heels."

And she was visually telling me what was going on. That's also a very powerful pain thing to do, using visualization, a non-pharmacological thing to help patients get their mind off their pain. So I encourage that. And probably at that time I hadn't thought much more about it other than to think it was a distraction.

I got a phone call and another nurse came in and sat with this lady and I said I'd be back as soon as I was done with this phone call. When I came back into the room, Pam, the other nurse, was obviously upset. She was very pale and shaken and very eager to get the heck out of that room. And I went back in and sat down with the lady and the lady had finally drifted off to sleep and was resting.

Later, I cornered Pam and I said, "What happened?"

And she said, "Well, I was sitting there with this lady and this lady opened her eyes and said to me, "He's here.""

And Pam said to the lady, "Who's here?"

And she said, "God's here."

Pam's a staunch Irish Catholic and very based in her Christianity. She said, "What is God saying to you?"

And the patient said to Pam, "He's saying that I need to give up the fight and that it's okay."

And, in the back of her mind, Pam is thinking, "This lady is full code and I don't want to do CPR on her. The doctor's not here; he's out of town. I really don't want her to die right now. She's got kids from Brookings who haven't seen her for a few days and who don't know how bad she is, and I want her kids to see her."

Pam said, "All that went through my mind in a flash, and I said to this lady, 'Well, now what's God doing?' And she said, 'God's telling me to come through this door.'"

Pam said, "You know, if you don't want to go through that door, just step aside."

And the lady just kind of sat back in bed and then just kind of sighed and Pam said, "What happened?"

And the lady said, "I got out of the way. It's okay now."

But the reason Pam was so upset came from her Christian background. She walked out of the room thinking, "I've just interfered with what God wanted for this lady. God was saying, 'It's okay, you can die now, come to me,' and I, a mere mortal, said, 'No, no you don't have to go now.'" And she was facing the idea that maybe it was this lady's time and she should have kept her mouth shut. She believed very much in the symbolic language of the discussion she was having with this lady.

As it turned out, this lady got her pain under control the next day. Her husband had been denying how sick she was, and she forced her physician to tell her husband how sick she was and that she was dying. She literally said to the physician, "Tell my husband I am dying."

And the physician said, "You know, she is really sick."

And she'd say, "No, tell my husband I am dying."

And the husband was sitting right there through this conversation. And so the physician finally said, "Yes, she is dying."

And she said, "Tell him to bring my kids so I can see them before I die."

So he brought the kids to the hospital and she died within about four hours of seeing them. So, the whole symbolic issue there was that she was very close to death and she knew it. Now, whether she saw God or not, only she will ever know. And depending on your religious background, you may think she was hallucinating because she was on high doses of morphine. Or you can believe she truly saw God there and made a decision and circumvented her death for a period of time.

I guess that's my belief — and it comes from my experience — that people have an awesome responsibility for their own lives and that they can basically decide when they are going to live and when they are going to die. Maybe not in years, but in moments and hours. There may be something that they have yet to accomplish, and despite all the odds, they will accomplish it. There have been other people who for all intents and purposes should have lived through their cancer. But they decided that their cancer was going to kill them and it did. They died at a very early stage, for whatever reason. I think a lot of it has to do with the mind. Some patients decide they are going to die and therefore they do.

Jerry: Did you get a sense of what the nine horses meant?

Sue: To me, in a lot of ways, the nine horses were release. I don't know whether it was a release of her pain, or a release of her life, or a release of both....

Jerry: Was the number nine symbolic?

Sue: I don't know if the number nine meant anything. It might have. I don't know enough about symbolic language to be able to judge. I think certain people might say that the number nine had a significance. I do know there is significance in colors. Red is usually painful, green is usually calm and soothing. The horses were being released from behind a brown rail into a green pasture. There's a lot of symbolism of peace there. I interpret colors more than I do numbers.

Jerry: I sense that over and over again you have seen people choose their moment of death.

Sue: The very first one that I ever saw, as a nurse, was a man who was sitting on the edge of the bed when I walked into the room, and I said "How are you doing? Can I do anything for you?"

And he said, "Yeah, you can call my family. I'm dying."

And I thought, "Oh, jeez!" So, I took his blood pressure and that was fine, his temperature was fine, his pulse was fine, he looked fine. He was sitting on the edge of the bed. And I thought, I better go call his family, because he wants me to.

So, I went and called the family and I said, "He wanted you to be called. His blood pressure's fine, his pulse is good, he looks good, but he wanted you to be called and he would like you to come."

I went back down to the room to tell him that I had called the family and they would be there and he had fallen back on the bed and he was dead. And, I thought "Oh, my God!" Probably at that point — you know how you have those kind of hallmarks in your life — at that point I realized that you've got to do what a patient wants you to do. Thank God I did it because at least I could tell the family, "He was alive and asking for his family and I did call you and there was nothing more I could do."

There are a lot of things like that that happen. I remember one of my most awful experiences involved a man in a real high foam bed. He had been comatose and unresponsive for days and days. His wife had maintained a bedside vigil and was just exhausted. But she had built up a relationship with the nurses and the situation had gotten to the point where she would go home at night and sleep. But she'd always say, "Please, take care of my husband. Call me if you're concerned about anything. But, I trust you to take care of him. I'll see you in the morning." And she'd always show up in the morning with donuts for the night staff for taking care of her husband.

One night it was my shift and she gave me her usual instructions: "I'm entrusting you with my husband..." and so on. Well, this man hadn't moved forever — he was comatose. I went down for coffee and as I came back the aide was walking down the hall and asked, "Where's the guy in 9?" (I even remember the room number.)

And I said, "What do you mean, where's the guy in 9?"

"Well, he's not in bed."

And I said, "What do you mean he's not in bed? He's comatose, he's got to be in bed!"

And she said, "He's not."

And I went down to the room and he had fallen out of the bed and he was on the floor between the bed and the window and was purple and dead. Purple from the waist to his head, which would make me think that he sat up and either reached for the light, or reached for his wife who always sat under the light, and then fell over dead. Both rails were up, but there's a gap in the rails, and I think he fell over and got caught and probably hung there for awhile to turn blue from the waist down. Anyway, I found him dead on the floor. I and another nurse walked into the room and both of us burst into tears. His wife entrusted us to his care and now he was on the floor, dead. We felt we hadn't done a very good job. We got him back into bed and called his wife.

So, I called his wife and I remember thinking, "What am I going to say to her?"

And she came on the phone and I said — I can't believe I said this to her, "He just slipped away.'" And I got off the phone and burst into tears. I can't believe that I said that to her.

I always wonder what happened there. How did this comatose man, who'd been comatose for days and days, get the energy to sit up? What did he see? What was he reaching for? And, hopefully, he was dead before he hit the floor. I had the pain that I was entrusted to take care of this man and in a lot of ways I feel like I failed at that moment. That was one of the those things that I took home and it's really stuck with me for a long time. You have those moments. For certain patients, I can tell you what day they died, what year they died. And it sticks with you, but that's part of the attachment.

Mary: Does the symbolic language ever come out in dreams?

Sue: Yes. Some patients talk about packing their bag to go somewhere. But often they are talking to people who aren't there. And that's always kind of eerie, because you don't know if there's someone there or not. I can't see them. Do I interfere with this conversation, or do I just let this conversation go? Or how do I acknowledge it?

Art: As you care for people in these situations, do you think of it as caring for their dying or do you think of it as caring for their living out their last days?

Sue: I believe in the hospice concept. The hospice concept is that dying patients are living, that it's about life. I truly believe that, and it's probably because I'm such a champion of pain management. I want to give them everything that they can have before they can have no more. And you begin to live your own life that way, too.

Art: Say some more about pain management and the importance of this in caring.

Sue: Pain takes away *so* much. You get to the point where you're so focused on pain, you can't do anything else. It's a vise, it's a grip. Patients use awful, awful words to describe what they're going through. And if you can get to the point where you've got their pain managed, their terminology changes. "I never realized how much I hurt. I never realized what kind of a hell I was going through until you took away the pain."

Most people don't have a sudden onset of burning or unbelievable amounts of pain. They have a little pain that they think they can deal with until they've had to deal with it for days and days on end, pain that's growing and they lose control. And, they'll say that they've lost control. I've also seen the evolution, over time, from when nurses and doctors were afraid to give pain medications, to now when for the most part pain medications are given very freely.

Then I look at my ability to care for a patient. In the past it seemed you couldn't do anything for them, and now you can help them regain control of their lives with pain medicines. It even used to be that the only thing we could offer them would be IV pain medicines. Now we've got oral ones. You can get their pain controlled and send them home and they can ramble around their house, hold their pets, watch TV, and play with their grandchildren and still be going through the acts of dying and have a life. This is different from many years ago when dying patients were confined to a hospital bed that would move them because they hurt too much to move themselves. The dying had limited visitors, because people are afraid of the hospital and because they couldn't get there because of a work schedule. So just by controlling patients' pain, we were able to change their environment, give them more life through the process and then give them dignity — put them back in control.

I always think of that movie *Terms of Endearment* where the mother is standing in the nurses' station screaming to get some pain relief for her daughter. Finally, the nurse says, "Okay." ...and then the mother kind of pulls herself together and very dignified, says, "Thank you." Why should anybody have to lose control and scream, when we've got pain relievers out there to take care of a patient? But it has not been an easy process. Sioux Falls is very modernized and physicians are very free with pain management among oncology patients here. But I can help a patient achieve pain control in Sioux Falls and she'll walk into the local pharmacy and the pharmacist can make some statement like, "That's a heck of a lot of pain medicine," and destroy all the work that's been done. Or a home town physician might say, "You know, if you take all that pain medicine, you're going to be an addict," and destroy everything that's been done.

A typical Midwestern person, being very conservative, doesn't want to be hooked on drugs and is very cautious about that kind of stuff, and would rather have pain than have the label of addict. A lot of my work now is to try to get rid of the labels. We have good narcotic medicines and physicians who'll prescribe them, but now we have to get rid of the obstacles out there in our society that precludes patients from wanting to take their medicines. And it's tough. We've got a social problem where people are taking the narcotics for reasons other than pain. But that directly impacts the people who need the pain medicines. That's why the medicines were developed in the first place. So, when patients need narcotic pain relief, I say, "Keep taking it, keep taking it, not because you're an addict, but because you want to be able to walk and talk and visit with your grandchildren."

Jerry: Can you give us some examples. If one of us broke an arm, how much morphine would we need...6 milligrams?

Sue: Probably only 2 milligrams IV.

Jerry: Yet you have seen patients who are given much more?

Sue : I have had patients on morphine drips on 1,000 milligrams an hour. I had one such lady who was sitting on the edge of the bed and telling us that she hurt. But we certainly didn't start there. She started out on a morphine drip at one milligram an hour and we titrated as needed until we ended up at 1000 milligrams an hour. You have to treat every patient as an individual. I always tell people who work with pain not to get into the numbers game, but to know the drugs, start out at the recommended daily dosage and then titrate to the desired effect.

Ron: There's an argument you hear, mostly I think from religious people, that goes, "Some people need the pain. There is a beneficial aspect. They need to suffer somehow in order to feel that they have somehow paid for..."

Sue: Their dues? Oh, yes, I have heard that, too. And if that is the patient's choice that is OK. But if that is the pastor, priest, or rabbi's choice, then I don't ascribe to it. What a person is willing to go through should be a personal choice. And when they're down and they're vulnerable, I don't think somebody else should have the right to inflict their beliefs or their thoughts on that person.

I don't think you truly know what pain is like until you've experienced it, and I would be the first to say that I probably have never experienced pain as some of my patients have. And I don't presume to understand it or interpret it for them. They have to interpret it for me. There are patients who tell me, "I'm having this pain because I was promiscuous when I was 12" or "I masturbated at the age of 9." They've been carrying that guilt around with them for years. And, to me, the appropriate response from the clergy would be to absolve them from that guilt and release them to do what they need to do.

Jerry: I think you used earlier that specific example of the fellow who had masturbated, and he was deeply distressed.

Sue: Yes, he was dying, and he was having an extraordinary amount of pain and he wouldn't take the pain medicine. And, that's another thing, we have to step in and find out. "Why won't you take the pain medicine? We can help you get more control; why won't you take it?"

"Oh, I'm paying for my sins."

"What sin are you paying for?" You have to ask and if they don't want to tell you, they won't. But you won't know if you don't ask. In this particular case, it was childhood masturbation that was troubling the patient.

And I said, "Don't you think you've paid for that already?" And, he had to think about it. He decided to take the pain medicines, but his minister came in and undid it for a while: "Pain is good, suffering is good. Christ suffered on the cross and it's okay for you to bear that cross." The patient didn't need to hear that right then and there. He was struggling with his own religion. I'm biased but one could probably think through religion and get closer to God if one was pain-free.

Art: I've heard you speak about the South Dakota Pain Initiative. What is it and how did you get involved?

Sue: The South Dakota Cancer Pain Initiative is just a copy of the original program which was started through a Robert Wood Johnson Grant in Wisconsin. The Wisconsin Pain Initiative is probably the biggest initiative in the United Sates. It was started following a research project by the World Health Organization that identified pain as a major problem for patients. I don't know the exact numbers, but around 60 percent of cancer patients were experiencing severe pain all the time; and yet we have drugs to take care of the pain. Why is that?

The research showed that it was due to patients' fears, physicians not prescribing, nurses not administering, or patients not taking appropriate medication. So, it was a multifaceted problem. The purpose of the Wisconsin Pain Initiative was to see what they could do on a local level, a grass-roots level. As a result of that, many other states have come together, recognized a need and a problem, and have developed their own state pain initiatives. I don't know how old ours is, maybe 5-6 years now.

Three nurses, one from Hospice, myself from the acute care at Sioux Valley Hospital, another clinical nurse-specialist from the acute care at McKennan Hospital were sitting around having coffee. We were very frustrated with the fact that the patient can get pain under control in Sioux Falls and then you send them home and it gets all undone. We were fighting the misconceptions of physicians and nurses as well as that of patients and families. We were very aware of the work being done in other states. What we really needed was a South Dakota Pain Initiative. We wondered how we were ever going to get one started, and we realized through that conversation that if we were ever going to get one started, we had to do it. And so the three of us explored it and in essence it started out and it has grown from there. We have tried to educate nurses, physicians, pharmacists, patients, and the public about the problems that there are in pain management, and we have tried to provide some expertise. We have said, "Let us help you. If you have questions about drugs, we can assist you."

We try to get information out to physicians and nurses about what pain medicines are available. We have triads — usually a nurse, a physician and a pharmacist — in most of the major cities in South Dakota. If a person is having problems with pain and calls in, we can refer them to either a nurse, a physician, or a pharmacist in their community who can perhaps help them. Most of what I've learned is through working with patients. And I'm no different from a lot of other nurses and a lot of physicians who have never had formal pain management education. If caregivers have a good mentor, they learn a lot; if they have a poor mentor, they may learn hardly anything. I work predominantly with pain medicines, and I don't know them all. So, you have to figure out a way to get the information out there to support the medical community.

Ron: One of the things that strikes me is that pain management involves much more than just the knowledge of pharmaceuticals. The psychology of it is fascinating, I think. You've talked about various sides involved in the whole situation: doctors, nurses, pharmacists, but you haven't said very much about family. I wonder if you could talk about how you deal with family a bit.

Sue: The family is an integral part of the whole conversation. I don't even like to have conversations with the patient without the family being there, so there is absolutely no way that what you've said can be misconstrued. Every time it's related to another person, then it gets mixed up. Any important conversation I'm going to have with a patient, particularly if they're family-based, I like to have the family there.

By 'family-based' I don't necessarily mean that they have to have a good family relationship. It's more important that the family's there if there's a bad family relationship. Trying to bring that family together in a short amount of time is just as important from the standpoint of caring for the patient as it is to take care of the patient's physical needs. It's not like a deck of cards that you can say... "this is the game"... every card is different and they're all in different places at different times. So, you might have one family member who has an "aha" today and gets it, but the other four are fighting it. Now, you've pitted one family member against the other four. You've got to provide support to the one who had the "aha" and get the other four to understand that. You never know when you walk into a room, "Am I going to deal with a family that wants everything that I can give them, or am I going to deal with a family that's concerned that I'm going to make an addict out of the patient if I give everything."

And then there's the family member who'll say to me, "Just give him a shot and make him die." Well, that's not my purpose. I'm not trying to cause a death, I'm trying to provide pain management, or symptom management. It may be diazepam for restlessness and agitation, it may be chlorpromazine for nausea and vomiting. I am trying to help them through the symptoms.

A good example was a 43-year-old woman who had been in the hospital so often that she was family to the nurses, myself included. We knew her, we knew her kids, we knew her habits, we knew her husband. Her husband had finally realized that she was dying, so he said to me, "Sue, can't you just give her a shot and make it go away? Make her suffering go away and let her die?" He said, "I'm tired, she's tired. She's fought a good fight, she shouldn't have to fight anymore."

I replied, "No, I can't give her a shot to make her die. If she's having pain, I'll most certainly give her something for pain, but I can't give her a shot to make her die."

And he said, "But you're making her suffer."

And I said, "That is your interpretation. I don't think she's suffering. I think she's having pain. We take care of the pain, not all suffering. I think you are suffering. And this is hard for you. I know it's hard for you: it's hard for me, too, because I know her and I love her. This is painful. But, an old nun (I share this story with a lot of my patients) once told me, 'When you're dying in that bed, time doesn't mean anything.' They'll slip into that other world while you wait. They'll wake up and say, 'Oh, you're still here?' or continue the conversation that they were having with you three or four hours earlier. Time means nothing to them. But, for family sitting at the bedside, time is everything and it's never ending and it's painful and it's suffering."

Towards the end, my patient did a lot of work. It was about two weeks between her husband's request to give her a shot and make her go away and when she ultimately died. I went to the funeral and he was so excited. I'd been on vacation, and he had to tell me, "You know, Sue, in those last few days we talked and I was able to tell her, 'It's okay, you can go to Jesus and it's okay. And we'll be okay. I and the boys, her sons, will be okay. We're going to miss you, but we'll be okay.' And she said to me that I needed to go out and find another wife. And I told her that I might do that and I might not do that, but thanked her for sharing that with me. And we got to talk. She'd drift in and out, so the conversation went over several days, but we got to talk. On Friday — she died on Saturday — she was looking at the window, and I said to her, "Louise, what are you looking at? and she said, 'Dad is over there.' 'You know,' I told her, 'Dad's going to be there to meet you at the pearly gates, and it's okay if you want to go with Dad now, you can. But, he'll be there for you.'"

He said, "You know, she had a lot of work she needed to do." I don't think he ever made the connection that if we had given her that shot and made her go away, she would never have been able to do that work. And also through that work, the husband did work. And he was okay. And, interestingly enough, when she died, he said, "I was in bed with her, holding her in my arms and she died.

The nurses came in and asked the questions: autopsy, funeral home, organ donation, and so on. I answered those questions and I left. My work was done."

I had come back on Monday and the nurses were all in a stew. "This guy was in denial, he couldn't deal with his wife dying, ran out of the hospital." And, yet, at the wake he said, "My work was done. It was beautiful, I didn't need to be there anymore. I left."

So when I went back after the wake to the nurses I said, "He was fine... he wasn't denying. He was right there. It was a beautiful experience for him. He just considered his work as being done."

Art: He helped her finish life.

Sue: Right. And she had work that she needed to do. Again, this is my own bias. There sometimes seems to be work that patients need to do or issues that they need to resolve, whether it be a graduation, a wedding, or a family conflict. And once that's resolved they seem to go very quickly. I think somehow we need to figure out what's important for patients and figure out how to help them more. It's a process that I don't truly understand yet.

Art: Any thoughts about what you would like students to go away with... for students for whom the threat of cancer may be far away...

Sue: Oh, yes... I don't know if they'll ever get it though. It just comes from that growth and development thing. Young people think they are infallible, that they're not going to die. Even when I deal with teenagers whose parents are dying in the bed, they seem to feel the parent is not going to die, until the day that they do. Then, "Oh, my God, they died."

Young people haven't had enough life experience to understand that life will end. As I've watched that I think maybe it's not so bad. As we get older we get more cautious. I've never skied and I don't want to ski because I might break my leg. Now, 20 years ago I might have zoomed down a mountain and never even thought twice about it. If I had broken my leg, I would have dealt with it.

It would be good for our society if we could somehow teach people to live every moment to the fullest. Time is precious. This minute you have right now, you will never ever have again. And what you do with it is your choice. And, when it comes to relationships with people, this moment with a person, you will never have again. So you can either ostracize a person who doesn't think the way you do or you can learn from that person. You learn from young people, listening to what they are saying and looking at what they're doing and learning from them.

I don't think you're ever going to teach teenagers or college students that they're going to die. I don't think that they can make that connection yet. I think that comes with time.

Mary: Time and experience.

Sue: For me, as a nurse, I truly believe I become a better nurse as I accept my own mortality. I'm a better nurse now than I was 15 or 20 years ago, because I understand that I am going to die. I've got physical signs that my body doesn't work the way it did. I don't recover from a cold as fast. I hurt myself playing volleyball and in the past I'd be bouncing around the next day. Now it's 2-3 days. So, I've got physical things that say that, "You may think you're infallible, but you're not." So, I'm a better nurse now because I've had more life experiences.

Questions to Consider for Chapter Seven:

1. Review the principles of respect for autonomy and justice as we have considered them thus far. Note how the consideration of distributive justice involves us in issues of the community. Distinguish between issues of macro- and micro-allocation.
2. Consider the case of Nancy Cruzan. Who was she? What was her medical situation? How did her situation differ from that of Karen Ann Quinlan? Why did her family ask that feeding tubes be removed? Why did the court system (in Missouri and the U.S. Supreme Court) at first deny her request? In the end why did the lower court in the State of Missouri agree?
3. How might the principles of beneficence and non-maleficence be used to argue for or against discontinuing Nancy's tube feeding? Does the effort to do good sometimes result in harm?
4. "Pursuing a Peaceful Death," by Daniel Callahan:
   a. Would you agree that our dying has been deformed by the efforts of the medical profession to extend life beyond what is natural?
   b. What would he consider to be a peaceful death?
   c. Why is he critical both of attempts to extend life beyond what is natural and to end life prematurely?
5. "Choosing death... " by Allen Verhey:

a. On what grounds has the distinction between refusing lifesaving treatment and asking for lethal prescriptions been challenged?
b. What theological and philosophical reasons does Verhey advance for supporting the distinction?
c. Would Verhey consider the case of Nancy Cruzan as one of allowing to die or assisting suicide? What is your view?
6. "Christian thinking about advanced medical directives," by Meilaender:
a. Why does Meilaender not think that patient autonomy is absolute?
b. In cases where the wishes of the patient are not available, why does Meilaender prefer the best interest standard to the substituted judgment standard?
c. Distinguish between a living will and durable power of attorney. Which does Meilaender prefer and why?
7. "Moving In With Presence," by Sue Halbritter:
a. How does an oncology nurse like Sue Halbritter step in with presence to care for a cancer patient? Is oncology nursing sad? How does oncology nursing differ from acute-care nursing?
b. Choose one of the cases that she gives. What are the caring behaviors which you find particularly striking? In Sue Halbritter's view is the situation of a cancer patient about living or dying? Explain.
c. What is the importance of "pain management" in the care of cancer patients? Why has she found it necessary to become involved in the South Dakota Cancer Pain Initiative?
d. What can healthy people learn about living from end of life care?

Chapter Eight:
Caring from the Beginning
Arthur Olsen

"...I think it's inappropriate to take a problem as complex as alcoholism and to focus on only one element of the problem, that is the pregnant woman. I think that one has to take a look at the community with whom that woman is drinking and who may be encouraging, if not demanding, that she drink with them. Even though I cringe at the thought of doing anything that would not protect future life, I'm not so sure if ultimately such an approach that isolates women is going to make a difference." — Ann Wilson, "FAS: Thinking Through Options."

"Whether we like it or not, the advancing frontier of genetics, with its impact on reproductive technology, thrusts us back into the abortion debate. Roe v. Wade (1973) did not answer the questions we will be asking in 2003. The Supreme Court decided that a woman has the right to abort during the first trimester. Genetic discrimination raises an additional question: by what criteria might a fetus be considered abortable?... A skeptic might say that as long as the woman has the right to choose, it is a moot point to talk of criteria of choice. I believe that while a woman's right to choose is a legal matter, the criteria for choosing are an ethical matter." — Ted Peters, "In Search of the Perfect Child: Genetic Testing and Selective Abortion."

The following lines from the hymn text by James Russell Lowell speak to those of us engaged in the dilemmas of caring at the end and beginning of life:

"New occasions teach new duties;
        Time makes ancient good uncouth:
They must upward still and onward
        Who would keep abreast of truth."[1]

Developments in public health and technological medicine have
shaped the new occasions for caring through death. Improved sanitation and nutrition have made it possible to live much longer
lives. New medicines and technological equipment (such as that
witnessed on the TV dramas *ER* or *Chicago Hope*) have made it possible to recover from diseases and accidents that formerly took
lives. These same developments make it possible to postpone death
by keeping comatose patients alive.

The new occasions present us with new questions and new
duties. Among the duties identified in the readings of Chapter
Seven are (1) rethinking what care means at the end of life, (2) defining death, (3) determining whether the occasions faced by Karen
Ann Quinlan or Nancy Cruzan call for support of their endangered
lives or actions that cooperate with their deaths, (4) deciding
whether there is a moral distinction between allowing and causing
death, (5) determining how we can most effectively support the life
stories of those who are dying, and (6) deciding how each of us can
best plan for our own mortality through the consideration of
advance care directives.

A constant in our discussion is the realization that caring is a
larger and more inclusive concept than curing. This is an old insight
that the astounding developments in technological medicine has
tended to obscure. Our life stories are important even after we are
beyond the power of medicine to cure. We agree with Daniel
Callahan that "if the ordinary goal of medicine is the preservation
or restoration of health, death should be the understood or expected ultimate outcome of that effort." Hence we should be attentive
both to the importance of using medical technology to support each
of our life stories and to the importance of being there with presence for those who live out their life stories in dying.

As we seek in our caring decisions to respect the autonomy of
patients at the end of life we face new legal questions and traditional moral issues in a new form. Should assisted suicide be made
legal? Is there a fundamental moral difference between causing and
allowing death?

The legal issue goes something like this: The right to accept or refuse treatment has been affirmed in the final judgments made in the cases of Karen Ann Quinlan and Nancy Cruzan. This right has been given Congressional underpinnings by the passage of the Patient's Self Determination Act in 1990. Hospitals and nursing homes are required to ask patients for their advance care directives at the time of admission. If patients have the right to refuse life sustaining treatments, do they also have the right to request treatments which would deliberately cause their deaths? Two court cases described in the article by Allen Verhey affirmed such a right. In March of 1996 the U.S. Court of Appeals declared that a Washington statute prohibiting assisted suicide was unconstitutional. Only a month later the U.S. Appeals Court for the Second Circuit declared a New York law prohibiting assisted suicide to be unconstitutional. Both of these cases were appealed to the U. S. Supreme Court which ruled against the lower courts in 1997. There is no constitutional right to die. It is legitimate for states to have laws prohibiting assisted suicide. However, the court left open the possibility that states could craft laws allowing assisted suicide in some form. Currently the Death with Dignity Act passed by the Oregon State Legislature has resisted court challenges. The Oregon law makes it legal for physicians to prescribe medication causing death (in certain carefully prescribed circumstances) if the medication is administered by the patient. Whether or not other states will follow Oregon's lead remains to be seen.

Meanwhile, debate over whether or not there is a moral difference between suicide and discontinuing medical treatment or between killing and allowing to die continues. On theoretical and practical grounds I find myself siding with those who defend the distinction. It is a matter of intent as Sue Halbritter describes it in her practice. The proper use of pain medication frees cancer-ridden patients to live out their lives. Death is not intended, though it may be inadvertently hastened. Providing the option of suicide, while appearing to increase the options available, may have the effect of putting the sick and the vulnerable in the position of justifying their continued existence.

Looking ahead, the readings in Chapter Eight consider the new occasions and duties involved in caring from the beginning. Developments in technological medicine have enhanced our ability to care for pre-natal and neo-natal life in astonishing ways. On the one hand, the many developments in reproductive technology — from in vitro fertilization to fertility drugs — have enhanced the possibilities for women to conceive and bear children in extraordinary ways. On the other hand, the new ways for caring for pre- and post-natal life that have been developed are also extraordinary. The readings in this chapter will focus on two areas of dilemmas that have emerged because of our enhanced abilities to care for pre-natal life.

One dilemma arises because of the potential of conflict between the rights and person of the mother and the rights and potential personhood of the unborn child. Technology provides access to the health of the fetus apart from the mother. Can therapy such as required caesarean delivery be forced on the mother for the sake of the fetus? Kenneth Ryan explores this new dilemma in his essay "Erosion of the Rights of Pregnant Women: In the Interest of Fetal Well-Being."

The potential of conflict between mother and unborn child is a pivotal issue in the efforts to eliminate FAS — fetal alcohol syndrome. This is explored at length in the interview with Ann Wilson. In her role in the Neonatal Intensive Care Unit at Sioux Valley Hospital, she has become deeply involved in the search for ways to prevent the birth of FAS babies. Technology has identified what folk wisdom has known for centuries, namely that the health of an unborn child is put at serious and irreversible risk when a woman consumes alcohol during pregnancy. Does it follow that the way to stop FAS is simply to stop women from drinking through education and/or intervention? Follow her narrative to see why she believes that the health of unborn babies is, at its roots, a community issue.

A second range of dilemmas is investigated in the article by Ted Peters. How shall the information now made possible by genetic testing be used? This knowledge allows us to predict with some accuracy whether or not the unborn child will be susceptible to genetic disease and/or genetic deformity. How can the information, made available through genetic testing, be ethically used? The dangers for misuse abound. Genetic privacy is an issue. Note how it could be misused by insurance companies and potential employers. However, the potential is there for genetic manipulation to help in healing.

Should genetic information ever be used as a rationale for abortion? Surely not for reasons of sex selection. Are dangers of discrimination involved as decisions are made against carrying the less than perfect child?

Of course the issue of abortion is one of the most polarizing in the U.S. religious and political landscape. The new contexts emerge with genetic information and testing. Is it possible to find common ground in this divisive debate? Are there alternatives to conflict? The article by Todd Whitmore introduces us to an actual effort of pro-life and pro-choice activists to find common ground.

As we struggle with dilemmas of caring at the beginning, it is worth noting how all of the ethical principles that we have been using can be invoked to analyze care at the beginning of life.

Autonomy is to be respected. But in case of conflict, whose autonomy is primary? That of the mother? The unborn child? What responsibility does the community have to prevent FAS? Genetic information should be private. And yet its use has public consequences — for business and for public health.

Non-maleficence. The possible harms that come about from restraining or not restraining a pregnant woman from drinking need to be considered. And the harms from using or not using genetic information must be evaluated.

Beneficence. In all of the discussion about caring from the beginning is the realization that technology is a means not an end. Because we can does not mean that we should. We must attend not only to rights but to human flourishing. Which uses of technology will best support human life?

Justice. As we consider the costs involved in caring at the beginning, we cannot avoid questions of justice. High cost technologies are expensive. Are they available also to the poor? How much of our health care budgets can be used for treating newborns with genetic defects?

---

[1] *Service Book and Hymnal of the Lutheran Church in America,* 1958. Hymn 547.

Erosion of the Rights of Pregnant Women: In the Interest of Fetal Well-Being

Kenneth J. Ryan, MD

The current interest in fetal well-being has been generated by the hope that the striking advances made in the health care of women during childbearing could be followed by similar improvements in the health of their fetuses. From the end of World War II, maternal mortality has declined dramatically in the United States and other developed countries because of medical progress in controlling the major causes of illness and death in pregnant women, i.e., blood loss, infection, and toxemia of pregnancy. Antibiotics, modern blood banking, surgical technology, and improved living conditions made these improvements in outcome possible. The better outcomes for women naturally improved the lot of their fetuses, but there have remained many fetal conditions that were not affected by this indirect approach via improvements in maternal health. With the pregnant woman's health and safety largely secure, medical attention has been more intensively focused on trying to improve the outlook for the fetus directly by making fetal evaluation and, at times, therapy a part of obstetrical care. In addition, it was hoped to improve fetal outcome by reducing unhealthy habits and lifestyles of pregnant women, such as smoking and alcohol consumption, which have an adverse effect on fetal health.

Advances in prenatal diagnosis, surveillance, and treatment in the last 25 years have made it possible to consider approaches to fetal problems in utero. Ultrasound, amniocentesis, and fetal surgery have allowed access to the fetus while it is still in the womb. This access to the fetus, however, has been at the expense of invasive procedures through the pregnant woman who must consent for the procedures not only for her unborn child but for herself as well.

It was also discovered that common practices of everyday life could have a devastating impact on pregnancy and the fetus. Thus smoking during pregnancy was noted to cause prematurity and low

Reprinted with permission from the Jacobs Institute of Women's Health
(**Women's Health Data Book,** 1990, 1 (1), pp 21-24)

birth weight. Alcohol consumption has resulted in infants with physical and mental problems, appropriately labeled fetal alcohol syndrome. Street drugs have more recently been noted to result in placental abruption, prematurity, drug dependency, and permanent physical and mental impairment after birth.

For better or worse, cesarean sections once performed largely for maternal needs are now being increasingly performed for fetal indications. Attempts have been made to evaluate the fetus by electronic monitoring and blood sampling to determine when and how delivery should be effected. Unfortunately, the predictive value of these monitoring tests has recently been discovered to be less reliable than once thought.

It has even been possible to keep pregnant brain-dead women on life support systems for a sufficient duration to allow fetal development to continue until an optimal time for delivery has been achieved. In such cases, the woman has often become merely a means to a new life.

When it is asserted that the obstetrician really has two patients to care for, the pregnant woman and her unborn child, it is generally not in the context that the interests of the two patients should be in conflict. In fact, they seldom are. Pregnant women are usually prepared to follow their obstetrician's advice, to do what is needed, and even to take great risks to their health and their lives to ensure a successful outcome to pregnancy and a healthy newborn. All of this preoccupation with fetal well-being is laudable as long as the interests of the pregnant woman are not ignored in the process; therein lies our major concern for the erosion of women's rights in the name of fetal well-being. There have been instances when procedures such as cesarean section have been forced by the courts on women if they disagree with their physicians. There have been attempts to criminalize failure of pregnant women to follow doctor's orders and to make the woman criminally liable for any adverse effects her behavior has on the newborn. In the public discussion on these issues, the two sides line up as either advocates of fetal rights or advocates of maternal rights in a stand-off reminiscent of the debate over abortion. This poses a true dilemma for the obstetrician who must try to serve the interests of both. In order to consider the issues involved, the paradigm examples of so-called "maternal-fetal conflict" are reviewed below.

PARADIGM OF MATERNAL-FETAL CONFLICT

Unwanted Cesarean Section

The classic case of maternal-fetal conflict is posed when the obstetrician recommends a cesarean section to the patient for fetal indications, and the pregnant woman declines. Although this is often designated as maternal-fetal conflict, it may more accurately be described as physician-patient conflict, especially in those cases where the pregnant woman believes she is acting in the best interests of her fetus, although contrary to a physician's advice. In one reported series of cases at major medical centers, resolution of the conflict occurred frequently via the obtaining of a court order allowing the procedure to be performed over the woman's objections. The vast majority of patients subjected to this were black, Asian, or Hispanic, almost half were unmarried, and for many, English was not their primary language. This creates an impression of discriminatory resort to the courts to force patient compliance. The reasons for the patients' refusal may be associated with misunderstanding, fear, cultural bias, or simply distrust of the system. It is not clear that the reasons for a woman's refusal are simply irrational or that she intends to harm her fetus. It is apparent from informal discussions with obstetricians that forced cesarean sections have also occurred without benefit of a court order, but one seldom sees reference to this or the outcome in such cases. The irony about forced sections is that there are several well-publicized instances when a cesarean section was deemed necessary and ordered by a court but the woman delivered with an uneventful vaginal delivery instead. This course of events occurred because the patient fled or because she simply delivered before such an order could be carried out. In some cases, the court would not order the cesarean section and an uncomplicated vaginal delivery ensued. In addition, even when some court-ordered cesarean deliveries were carried out, it was not always apparent at the birth of the infant that the suspected fetal distress did in fact exist. No one publicizes the results when court-ordered procedures are in fact truly life-saving for the fetus because that is what is expected; it is only the misadventures that make the news. When all of these misadventures are coupled with the recent perception that fetal monitoring has poor predictive value for fetal distress and that too many unnecessary cesarean sections are performed anyway, it puts a major burden on anyone who wants to force the procedure on an unwilling subject. No special justification is needed for offering a patient a cesarean delivery when it is clearly indicated for either maternal or fetal reasons, but it must be accepted that "clear indications" are sometimes in error. When one adds a degree of uncertainty to the need for the procedure, there is an undermining of the moral argument for forced compliance. On the other hand, even if all the compelled cesarean sections to save the fetus were truly indicated and not in error, it might not justify the overriding of a woman's autonomy to accomplish an operative delivery, as will be discussed in the Arguments section below.

Forced Delivery in the Terminally Ill Patient

A paradigm case that caused much discussion among ethicists involves a woman in Washington, DC with terminal cancer who was forced to endure a cesarean section at 26 weeks gestation in a vain attempt to save the fetus. Although neither the patient, her husband, nor the attending obstetricians were in favor of a preagonal cesarean section at this marginal stage of viability, hospital officials asked the court to intervene. A guardian for the fetus was appointed and the argument made that the wishes of a dying woman could be overridden in the interests of the fetus. The fetus died soon after birth, and the woman died two days later. This case is particularly poignant because of the sad and almost predictable outcome that makes the judicial order seem particularly heartless. Had the fetus been at a more reasonable stage of development, one might have had an ethical dilemma worthy of argument in court.

There is a general acceptance of performing agonal cesarean sections in emergency situations for victims of accidents or in terminal illness with either the patient's or family's consent if the fetus has reached viability. In some instances, brain-dead pregnant women have been maintained on life-support systems for sufficient time to allow fetal development to proceed to a stage when survival could be reasonably assured.

Criminalizing "Unhealthy Conduct" During Pregnancy: The Hazards of Disobeying Doctor's Orders

When her newborn infant was born with brain damage and died at 6 weeks of life, a San Diego woman was charged with criminal

neglect for not seeking medical help promptly for bleeding and the
onset of labor. She actually was jailed for 6 days before her bail was
reduced from $10,000 to $2500. The police wanted to file murder
charges against her but the prosecutor settled for a criminal misde-
meanor charge. The patient, who had two other children at home,
had been advised by her obstetrician to avoid sexual intercourse, to
stay off her feet, refrain from using illegal drugs, and to report to
the hospital promptly for any bleeding from her placenta previa.
She actually consumed amphetamines and had sexual relations
with her husband after vaginal bleeding started, and she didn't
seek help until her labor was already in progress for 6 hours. The
court ultimately threw out the charges, but new legislation to out-
law fetal abuse has been introduced in California and elsewhere.

ARGUMENTS IN THE DEBATE OVER MATERNAL VERSUS FETAL RIGHTS

The Ethics Committee of the American College of Obstetricians
and Gynecologists concluded in its review of maternal-fetal conflict
that resort to the courts is almost never justified to force therapy on
the pregnant woman. This was based on respect for her autonomy
and on the recognition of the limitations and fallibility of medical
judgment. It was noted that this could also destroy the doctor-
patient relationship. In the broader public debate on the subject,
other considerations have arisen. The Roe v. Wade decision, in
establishing some state interest in the fetus at viability, has suggested that some restriction on abortion is possible except when the
mother's health or life is in jeopardy. It, however, does not follow
that the state can or should force care or an operation on the woman
on behalf of the fetus. Furthermore, attitudes and laws about child
abuse cannot simply be transferred to the fetus while it resides in
the mother's womb. The mother cannot be forced to donate an
organ or undergo surgical procedures for the benefit of a child, no
matter how much society feels she should. The analogy from the
foregoing is that the pregnant woman should not be forced to
undergo procedures for the unborn fetus when comparable procedures are not expected for a living child after birth.

   On the other hand there is a general societal expectation that the
pregnant woman does have a duty to her unborn child. If "reasonable" diagnostic or therapeutic measures, including a cesarean section, are truly needed to protect her fetus from harm, she is expect-

ed to undergo them. On balance some feel that the interests of fetal life and well-being should offset maternal freedom, allowing society to intervene and force compliance with care if it is refused. Furthermore, the pregnant woman should not harm her fetus by behaviors such as smoking, use of drugs, or alcohol consumption. Again, some have suggested resort to the courts and even confinement to control behavior. These types of repressive measures and the laws to legitimize them would undoubtedly drive out of the health care system those who could most benefit from it. For practical purposes, exhortation, education, and counseling are the only legitimate approaches to the problem patient. We need social programs to deal with drugs and other addictive behaviors before women become pregnant.

The vast majority of women are going to do all they can for their fetuses, and rules about when to go to court should not be constructed in a free society for those women at the margin of "acceptable" behavior. We should not create an "Erewhon" in real life and criminalize failure to follow doctor's orders or unhealthful behaviors. There cannot be an "easy" solution to this dilemma of maternal-fetal conflict. Maternal and fetal interests should be interwoven rather than balanced. No matter how much society and the health care professions seek the perfect outcome for human pregnancy, it cannot be bought at the expense of the fundamental autonomy of pregnant women.

Fetal Alcohol Syndrome:
Thinking Through Options
An Interview
With Ann Wilson

Dr. Ann L. Wilson is evaluator for Native American Substance Abuse Prevention Projects, funded by the U.S. Center for Substance Abuse Prevention. She is Professor in the Departments of Pediatrics and Psychiatry, School of Medicine, U.S.D., and co-director of the Follow Up Clinic, Neonatal Intensive Care Unit, Sioux Valley Hospital. She is also coordinator of the Introduction to Clinical Medicine for first year medical school students. She wrote The History of Fetal Alcohol Syndrome in South Dakota, 1970-1992, *for the South Dakota University Affiliated Program .*

Art: Ann Wilson, how did you get involved in caring at the beginning of life — caring for children?

Ann: In considering my response to that question, I find myself thinking about my personal early experiences in life. My father directed a residential treatment center for emotionally disturbed adolescent boys. I grew up next door to this agency with fairly vivid images of these boys and the misery that many of their lives included leading to their placement at this home. I wasn't sure when I went off to college what I was going to do, although I always had a very clear sense that it would be involved in some way with human services. I also had the sense that it would be nice to prevent the struggles that I knew the boys next door had experienced. I had a belief that help offered early in life could be important in affecting lives so that future misery could be avoided.

In graduate school somehow these thoughts and dreams came together for me. During these years I developed a special interest in the prevention of child abuse. In the 1960s the Battered Child Syndrome was first introduced as a concept. When I was in graduate school in the early 1970s I can remember vividly the first lecture I heard about child abuse. I can even remember where I was sitting in the class room. What interested me so much as I listened to this lecture, more than what was being said about treating and becoming involved in the care of children who were abused, were the comments made about prevention.

While in graduate school I began taking electives with the Department of Pediatrics and one day while I was in the hospital I asked, "Where are the babies?" I was told where to go look and then the faculty person I was with said, "We'll show you where the really interesting babies are." They took me to the neonatal intensive care unit. I was in awe of what I saw through that window.

At this same time there was a growing recognition that the early hours and days of life are a sensitive time for how early parent-baby relationships are expressed in nurturant behavior. There was a big emphasis on avoiding the rigidity of some outdated delivery room practices that limited opportunities for mothers, fathers, and babies to be together during this special time of life. While the rigid practices had been established for important reasons to prevent infection, they had outlived their need. With a fervent interest in how the early hours of life can be managed to promote positive early relationships, I did my dissertation research in the delivery room making observations of mothers and infants immediately following birth.

Upon completion of my PhD, I had a wonderful opportunity to do a post doctoral fellowship in the emerging area of infant mental health. To summarize the clinical foundation for this special training are the words of Selma Fraiberg who directed the program. It was her recognition that parents "can not hear the cries of their baby until their own are heard." In other words, when parents are so overwhelmed with their own emotions related to a troubled past or current life situation their capacity to foster a warm relationship and nurture their own baby is limited. The premise of this training program was that to help parents nurture a baby, parents' needs must also be addressed so that they can have an understanding of their own behavior.

I had an experience that was such a vivid literal example of the metaphorical "cries" described by Mrs. Fraiberg. I was asked to spend some time with parents of a 3-year-old who was dying and who was in the very terminal phase of her disease. The child's mother was almost nine months pregnant and was due to deliver at any moment. The family came from a community many miles away from the hospital and they were struggling with questions about how to care for their dying child while the mother was in labor and delivery. Neither parent wanted to be separated from each other or from their child. As they were trying to decide how they were going to make this decision, I offered to be with the mother in her labor, while the husband could remain with the dying child.

As it turned out, the mother's labor and delivery went very quickly in the middle of the night and a plan never needed to be mobilized. Several days later a neighbor was coming to take the new baby home, while the mother remained in the hospital to be with her sick child. I remember that day being in the mother's hospital room on the post-partum ward. Here in the hospital room was a gorgeous nine-pound newborn baby with a beautiful head of brown hair and she was loudly crying. Her mother, seemingly indifferent to her cries, was talking about plans with the visiting neighbor. Finally, I gently said, "Would it be all right if I held your baby?" The mother seemed startled by my question saying, "Oh, I didn't notice." The reality of being able to hear cries was played out before my eyes in that little clinical vignette.

I came to South Dakota upon the invitation of Dr. Stanley Graven, who at the time was a leader in perinatal medicine. A new four-year medical school was being developed. Dr. Graven had written a grant for maternal and child health care for South Dakota, as it was among a number of states that had high rates of infant mortality. My role in all of this was to develop supportive services for babies and families and to develop curriculum around human development for the USD medical students.

In those early years I provided a great deal of direct care to families whose babies were cared for in the neonatal care unit and this continued until social workers were hired to fill this role. I often was in the hospital day and night with families as their babies were facing very serious times.

Art: Could you say just a little bit about what your role is now as your position developed?

Ann: Over the past 22 years I've been in South Dakota I have provided developmental follow-up services for babies who were ill newborns in the neonatal intensive care unit following their births. Since 1982 one of the neonatalogists and I have held a clinic in which we follow the development of babies. A clinic visit includes my doing a standardized developmental assessment with the babies and visiting with the families about how things are going and providing developmental guidance and support. The neonatologist does a physical exam and visits with the families about concerns related to their babies' physical health, growth, and nutrition.

My most significant teaching responsibility over the last ten years has included coordinating the Introduction to Clinical Medicine course for the first-year medical students. I always refer to the content of this course as covering the "people side" of medicine for the first-year medical students. It is a course that uses the biopsychosocial model as a foundation for understanding patients and it examines interpersonal and societal concerns that affect patients' lives and the care they receive. It also includes material on interpersonal dynamics that affect a patient's health. As we present that course, we do it with a lifespan perspective starting with infancy and moving onto geriatrics over the course of an academic year and talk about a variety of social issues that come to play a part in both the physicians' and patients' lives. The course includes training on interview skills as well. I also teach junior students on their pediatric rotations and psychiatry residents.

Mary: And somewhere along the line you also got involved with prevention of fetal alcohol syndrome. Could you share where that came into the story?

Ann: During my fellowship, I was involved in a case involving a little boy. I'll call him Ralph. Ralph was diagnosed with failure to thrive as his growth was not adequate for his age and he was developmentally delayed. He came from a very disorganized family. He had a teenage mom and he had been seen in every possible specialty clinic. His records described such physical features such as hypertelorism, high-arched palate, flat face, unusual facial features but no one was able to make any sense of these unusual characteristics that were also noted along with his slow growth. When none of this medical care had been successful in understanding the reason for his growth failure, he was referred to psychiatry, and specifically to the program where I was involved in my fellowship. We were to try to figure out what could help Ralph grow and to support his young mother's ability to provide him with nurturant care. My work with Ralph's mother was slow, but we did eventually develop a working relationship, but as hard as we worked together with Ralph, his growth never showed the acceleration that was needed to get him back on a growth curve.

Two years later when I was in South Dakota, I attended a conference in North Dakota and for the first time heard a lecture on fetal alcohol syndrome. A classic slide of three faces of children with FAS was shown, and I just about stood up and said, "There's Ralph!" It was finally obvious to me why that baby didn't grow. We had known that Ralph's mom had a history of binge drinking, but fetal alcohol syndrome just wasn't recognized until the early 1970s.

Another event brought fetal alcohol syndrome into bold focus for me. In 1989 at an alumni event at my college in Oregon, I was introduced to the wife of a faculty member as someone from South Dakota. She quickly remarked, "I just finished reading a marvelous book, *The Broken Cord*. It takes place somewhere out there where you live." I said, "Where's out there?" And she said, "Oh, out there," waving her hand as if to say somewhere east of Idaho.

So, I bought *The Broken Cord* and got on the airplane very early the next morning and started reading. Much to my surprise, the book describes a child from South Dakota and it was embarrassing reading because the author wrote about how little in our state was being done for fetal alcohol syndrome. As I read the book's story I kept thinking that we needed to be doing more to respond to this far-reaching problem. I had a wonderful opportunity that same year to help a Native American community write a proposal for funding for a FAS prevention project. I spent a fair amount of time over the next five years with that community working on this project, trying to find ways of preventing alcohol use during pregnancy among the patients served by this Indian Health Service hospital. Actually my involvement with this project led to ideas that I pursued in a masters thesis I completed in biomedical ethics at Augustana College.

Mary: And your FAS efforts also led to a fairly thick book.

Ann: Yes, that happened about the same time. The State asked me to write a book on the history of fetal alcohol syndrome in South Dakota.

Art: With *The Broken Cord*, did you find that your view changed about how prevention should occur?

Ann: My yes, I have experienced a great deal of personal turmoil related to concerns about the prevention of FAS. I feel as if I've almost come around full circle in my response to it. Initially, my thoughts about the prevention of FAS were very simplistic and straightforward and I thought foolproof. I figured preventing the leading cause of mental retardation would be easy — just educate women and the problem would be solved. For the woman who refused to stop drinking, I had this theory that if you decide to be pregnant, fine; if you decide to stay pregnant, fine; but you can't decide to be pregnant and inflict injury on a fetus by drinking. I reasoned that if a fetus is being harmed, society should take responsibility for its protection. As I was reading and writing on this topic, I discovered a whole body of literature that altered the way in which I perceived the notion of intruding on personal integrity and whether in the long run such an approach would be helpful. It's an issue with which I still struggle. The complexity of drinking during pregnancy became much more difficult for me to grapple with the more I became involved with trying to prevent fetal alcohol syndrome.

Jerry: When you've talked to our class in the past, you've discussed the possibility of forcing a woman to stop drinking, even by incarcerating her. As part of that discussion there have been a significant number of class members who have sided with that notion of stern intervention. How have those reactions struck you?

Ann: Well, I was there, too. That was how I first began to think about the issue. While I can understand the attractiveness of that perspective, I think it reflects an enticing, but limited, understanding of the problem. I know it is a well-accepted belief and it is being implemented in various ways. I just really do not think such an approach is going to be ultimately helpful.

Art: I remember the first time you spoke to the class you said FAS is 100 percent preventable. So the logic seemed quite clear: stop mother from drinking, and the baby will be fine. So, why not just stop the mother from drinking?

Ann: I think about 85% of the classes have indicated agreement with that approach. Why don't I agree with it? Well, for a variety of reasons. There are two ways of examining this concern. There are practical perspectives and philosophical perspectives. Practically, I believe that to fully implement an approach that would monitor substance use during pregnancy requires a very heavy-handed intrusive style of prenatal care. I think that ultimately this approach could alienate those whom care is attempting to reach. Even though it may identify a few women and incarcerate them, I think that such an approach could convert prenatal care into a kind of inspection process that would affect its unique and important role in providing preventive medical care.

Another major reason is that I think it's inappropriate to take a problem as complex as alcoholism and to focus on only one element of the problem, that is, the pregnant woman. I think that one has to take a look at the community with whom that woman is drinking and who may well be encouraging, if not demanding that she drink with them. Even though I cringe at the thought of not doing everything possible to protect future life, I'm not so sure if an approach that may isolate women will ultimately be effective.

The third reason this approach concerns me is that I am not convinced that we fully understand the complexity of all involved with alcohol-related developmental disabilities. There is no question that alcohol harms prenatal development. But we know that fetuses can be exposed to equal amounts of alcohol at the same point in their gestations and have different outcomes. There may be genetic factors that interact with alcohol exposure. Further, I think there is reason to believe that tobacco, malnutrition, or stressful and violent living circumstances may exacerbate intervention when we may not fully understand the complexity of the problem.

Finally, I think that there is the philosophical issue — and this is the point that I struggle with the most. The concern begs questions about who is in control of one's body. The argument that I find most palatable for taking intrusive steps is that the woman who is drinking in such an uncontrolled manner is so damaged herself that she does not have sufficient ability or self control to make any kind of informed decision that would positively affect her life or that of her fetus. In those situations, taking a step to protect her from her own behavior is also one that will protect her fetus.

I think what I learned the most from my community experience with preventing prenatal alcohol use, is that there are gradations of drinking and gradations of being able to help. There are some women for whom simple education is adequate. I think that in this day and age there are very few women who are uninformed regarding the harmful effects of drinking during pregnancy. Then there is another group who are drinkers who with some support and assistance are able to diminish or stop their drinking. And then, you have on the continuum a small group of women for whom nothing seems to work to support their sobriety during pregnancy. What I, however, have come to understand is that this is a group of women who tend also to have incredibly damaging life circumstances. What we have found in our demonstration project is that most of these women are also bound into relationships that inflict violence and personal injury upon them.

I wonder about all these factors when thinking about women who are drinking during pregnancy. I have a nagging feeling that we just may not know as much about the complexity of the effects of drinking on pregnancy outcome as is conveyed by those eager to take a legalistic approach to pregnancy. Also, I fail to understand why we are so eager to take such aggressive approaches to drinking during pregnancy when there are other behaviors known to have ill effects upon pregnancy outcomes.

Ron: It's interesting to me because I find some difficulty with the whole solution of saying, "All you have to do is say no." — "All you have to do is exert your will power and you will take care of these problems in your life." Especially if you're dealing with alcohol and drug addiction, isn't it beyond the will in some respects?

Ann: Few women intentionally inflict harm. There are always a few who may be psychotic and extremely disturbed that may well have malintentions, but I think it is a very rare woman who intentionally brings harm upon her pregnancy. Rather, she may be addicted to a substance that brings harm.

Art: I'm thinking of that phrase you started with, "Parents can not hear their babies' cries until their own are heard."

Ann: Precisely. I believe that statement is a profound key to a lot of what I find myself thinking about when working in this area.

Ron: What you're pretty much left with, it seems to me, is a dilemma which is tragic in its scope. Is there any way out at all, any glimmering of hope?

Ann: Compassion in society. I truly think we need to take a look at social structures that surround communities and especially the birthing of babies.

Ron: Are there any sort of measures that can be taken short of going one way or the other, any areas of grey that might be somewhat promising, aside from the remake of society into a more compassionate one?

Ann: Sure. I think that perinatal support programs can play a critical role in helping families encounter a pregnancy and enjoy its healthy outcome. The whole notion of home visitors is one that has been around for a long, long time. The notion of simply having someone involved in a caring capacity with a family whose resources might be thin is one that I think can have a profound significance for many families' lives.

However, let me tell you an interesting caveat. I've been involved with a variety of programs in the state that have provided support services to new parents and one in particular that serves teenagers in an American Indian community. The staff of this program truly hang in there with these young women, through thick and thin. They drive them to special school programs, they provide warm nutritious meals for them following their group therapy sessions, they teach them to cook, they stand by them when they get into trouble or are thrown out of their homes or school or beaten by their boyfriends, and they make a fuss about the beauty of their babies. This program truly takes care of these young women. The sad part about this program is that for many of these young women this is probably the first experience with caring relationships that they may have ever known. The staff probably provides for them their first warm, supportive, accepting, and unconditionally caring relationship. An unfortunate outcome of this project, however, is that in order for these girls to maintain their involvement in it, they need to be in the program and to remain in the program they need to become pregnant after their baby reaches the age of 18 months. There are some who find this difficult to believe, but I am convinced that some of these young women are having repeated pregnancies as a means of hanging on to their relationships with the staff of the program. I know of enough clinical vignettes that illustrate this dynamic to believe that this is an important issue. These young women, whose early lives have been impoverished in so many ways, as teenagers are discovering what we all would hope could be experienced earlier in life. I would suggest that what they are receiving from the staff of this project is contributing in positive ways to their capacity to nurture their baby as they themselves are being nurtured.

Art: You said several times that there should be a community approach to the prevention of fetal alcohol syndrome. How might that differ from advertisements directed at women: "Pregnant? Don't Drink! Pregnant? Don't Smoke!" How would a community approach differ?

Ann: The emphasis would be upon entire families and communities not drinking when a member is pregnant. I think, especially when someone who is having a struggle with drinking, others should be aware of the circumstances and modify their behavior to be supportive. That's just an example, but I think there are just lots of ways in which one can share in the excitement of a new baby and participate in that life experience.

Because I track infant mortality statistics, I was once interviewed by a reporter about preterm labor. He said, "How do you prevent preterm labor?" I replied, "With casseroles." In response he said, "You mean with hot dishes?" What I was trying to express is that it takes an incredible amount of effort when a woman needs to be on bed rest to try to delay labor. It is not easy to achieve that goal, but it can be done when others bring casseroles and help with caring for a family. Bed rest for a mother is a real feat to pull off. And yet, we know that every moment you can keep a baby inside and away from an intensive care unit thousands of dollars are saved and there is a decrease in the likelihood of morbidity for the baby. I was disappointed the reporter didn't use my quote about hot dishes in his article. I don't think he quite got my point.

Ron: Talking about community, I can't help thinking about certain adolescent communities. It seems the absolute worst kind of situation for some people is to be in communities that endorse drinking, may even endorse pregnancy as something that's accepted and expected and endorse sexual behavior. Certainly that has to be one of the patterns that has to be broken if we're to get at this problem at all, is it not?

Ann: Right. And interestingly, the data help us understand this in ways that are common sense. It's fascinating to see how long it has taken us to understand some of the dynamics. One of the very early understandings about the battered child and child abuse was how role modeling that occurs early in life becomes a pattern for the way in which one rears one's own children. That's a very basic understanding. You can pick up any newspaper and listen to any radio program and everyone seems to understand the reality of how early treatment affects adults' later interactions with children.

But what's interesting about the whole teen pregnancy issue is the data that help us understand that many of the teenagers who are becoming pregnant were sexually abused as young children. And with many of the teenagers who become pregnant, their babies are being fathered by men who are considerably older. And so, from a theoretical, analytical kind of perspective, one can say that these teens are reengaging in a previous pattern of behavior.

Art: There are some people today who think the rights of the mother are being pitted against the rights of the infant about to be born. We have all these procedures that can help us know about life before birth and we have a potential conflict between the infant and the mother. Would you comment about that? Do you feel there are dangers there?

Ann: Well, I really feel that a lot of that conflict can be negotiated if somehow we could perceive the mother and the baby as one rather than two entities. There are these famous legal cases where the mother is portrayed as opposing care that is medically viewed as in the best interests of her fetus. I always wonder when reading these cases: What's going on? What is she thinking? What's the real worry here? Who sat down and visited with her about this? Who's tried to sort it out? One law review article that I read reviewed cases of maternal/fetal conflicts that got to the court system for decision making. An analysis of these cases showed that most of the women involved didn't even speak English. I found myself thinking about who sat down and tried to understand these women's thoughts. It's like so many of the ethics cases that come up in the hospital. It seems they began as some kind of spark of an interpersonal nature between two people that doesn't get sorted out. Then an ethics case seems to brew. In fact it really was originally some kind of an interpersonal conflict that stewed and brewed without the misunderstanding getting sorted out in a way that people could compatibly continue to discuss the concerns they had. In cases with pregnant women, even though there are certain times when people seem to be behaving in totally unreasonable ways, I often wonder whether, if we truly understand what is going on in terms of a pregnant women's fears, concerns, perceptions, and tensions, we'd have a better understanding of why she seems to be making these unreasonable decisions.

Art: In class you pointed out that each of us has a history. You remember saying that? What did you mean by that?

Ann: As we look back over time we all realize that many of our perceptions, understandings, beliefs, and knowledge are based on foundations that we now see as fallacious. And that over time we can experience a fair amount of humility as we consider how with self-righteous fervor we advocated all sorts of things that now we can see as reflecting assumptions that are dangerous or counterproductive. For example, drinking during pregnancy and during the early post-partum days was considered a good thing for women to help them relax and improve their lactation. And I always think as we laugh about previous events, what are we doing today that we will be laughing about or ashamed of 30 years from now. What are we doing today that will be considered absolutely outrageous and even damaging to our health?

Art: What kinds of understanding would you like our undergraduate students to have after you have talked to them about fetal alcohol syndrome? How would you like to see them grow?

Ann: I think I would like for them to understand that these issues are exceedingly complex and that you can't examine patients' behavior outside of the context of their lives, meaning

their family, their family's history, their beliefs, their social circumstances and even the political climate that surrounds them. Ideally,
students should learn a reverence for complexity. People and their
problems are not as simple as they first appear and people's lives
are rich with meanings and complications that affect good inten-
tions.

Jerry: That type of appreciation for the complexity of these issues
is something that you grapple with in dealing with the medical students as well. Not infrequently, one encounters medical students
who feel that they have all the answers or are self-righteous in their
viewpoint.

Ann: Actually, there's a whole developmental theory of young
adulthood I discovered that helped me with this concern. Over time
one generally becomes broader in one's ability to perceive situations
and recognize when there is a greater level of gray involved. Yet,
you're right, some students clearly remain black/white thinkers:
"It's just this way and there is nothing in between and no point in
talking about it because I happen to know what's proper and the
patient obviously doesn't, so there's nothing really further to be discussed." That attitude in a student is a tremendous challenge. I
think that some students have a hard time when faced with alternative perspectives.

Jerry: Religious beliefs?

Ann: Not just religious beliefs, but political and cultural thinking
may limit students from recognizing broader perspectives on an
issue. It's hard for all of us to do this.

Jerry: Do you find both in our undergraduate classes and with
the medical students that talking about a subject like fetal alcohol
syndrome can serve to open their eyes and to broaden their horizons?

Ann: I'd like to think so. My eyes have certainly been opened and
my horizons expanded the more I have considered the issues. So I
think we all realize with some humility that we always have further
breadth to achieve in terms of how we can understand something. I
think some topics tend to be more emotionally charged than others.
When you're talking about harming an infant's future, that's a tragic concern.

Ron: Have you ever faced situations in which you had to deal
with a student who had felt that he or she had absolute scriptural
foundations for certain beliefs and was not going to waver from

those beliefs? How do you deal with somebody of that kind, who is taking, as it were, the wrong stands for the right reasons?

Ann: It's a real struggle, because I firmly believe that everyone has the right to their personal beliefs. Alternately, when I think that those beliefs are voiced in a way that could be potentially harmful to a patient, I find myself experiencing a moral dilemma in terms of how I should respond to that student. I also realize that all students need to be dealt with gently or their defensiveness won't allow them to hear anything one has to say. What I try to do is respond by saying something like, "Another way of looking at this might be..." I try to give different perspectives, but I tend to do it in a rather tentative way.

Art: One of the ideas you have expressed deals with approaching autonomy using the analogy of Odysseus to encourage the notion that somebody might voluntarily agree to some beneficial coercion. Would you comment on that example?

Ann: It's a notion that to my knowledge has not been voiced in the literature. It strikes me, in a way, that it's potentially manipulative and a little gimmicky, but I think it could be helpful, maybe even practical. One way around this whole issue of dealing with women and their pregnancies, when there are concerns about situations that impede their judgments for the best development of their fetus, is to pursue advance directives. At the onset one could say, "In the event that you are in a position that would compromise your ability to make good judgments about your health and that of the fetus, would you give us your consent to make decisions that we think would be in your best interest?" For example, you could use this approach for alcohol, but there could be other situations. If someone was comatose from an accident, would you keep them on a ventilator or wouldn't you? How do you negotiate the interests of the mother and the fetus, if the mother is incapable of making decisions at some point in time? Ideally, women at the onset of pregnancy could give their informed consent for someone to make decisions for them, if they were carefully evaluated as being unable to do so for themselves.

Art: I have one last question. We invited you to talk to us about caring at the beginning of life. When does caring for new life begin? I didn't ask you when life begins, I asked you when caring for new life begins?

Ann: From my perspective, that is an easy question to address, but I may not provide the specific answer you may be requesting. I think that caring is so much involved in the cycle of human life that one can never identify its beginning or for that matter, its ending. When one is spending time with a 6-month-old baby and trying to respond to him or her by being warm and responsive, one is essentially fostering this baby's future ability to develop intimate relationships and care for others. One is simultaneously also reflecting the kind of care one received early in life and is continuing to receive from supportive relationships. So, my only way of addressing that question is to say that there is no one point in time when caring begins. The capacity for caring is fostered throughout one's life through the relationships one experiences with others.

Common Ground, Not Middle Ground: Crossing the Pro-life, Pro-choice Divide

Todd David Whitmore
Frederica Mathewes-Green

In the wake of the murder of workers at abortion clinics, Cardinal Bernard Law of Boston called for a moratorium on clinic protests. Less noticed was his further suggestion that pro-life advocates find "common ground" with some of their opponents. "There are few persons who would claim that abortion is a moral good," he pointed out in the archdiocesan newspaper. "For most persons who champion the right to an abortion, it is seen as the only way out of a painful situation. While this is an unacceptable view for those of us who hold all human life as sacred, it does present the possibility of some common action among persons who are not agreed on the question of life."

Many Roman Catholics, and other pro-lifers, are markedly hesitant about Law's proposal. They wonder if cooperation with pro-choice advocates in some areas could lead to compromise on fundamental principles.

For Roman Catholics, the issue here is "indifferentism." In cooperating with persons who disagree sharply with core tenets of one's own tradition of faith and morals, one participates in a culture that is in many respects "indifferent" to if not outright hostile toward Christian belief. The danger is that by such cooperation one will end up affirming, however tacitly, views that are hostile to Christianity. Is day-in and day-out cooperation possible without betraying one's faith?

I believe that cooperation without betrayal is not only possible but obligatory. Creating the kind of society in which abortions are less frequent is something neither pro-life nor pro-choice advocates can do by themselves. Cardinal John O'Connor of New York declared that his archdiocese has expended more than $5 million to help 50,000 women in situations of unintended pregnancies. This is a remarkable effort unmatched by any other intermediate institution. But the cardinal is also well aware that more resources are necessary. He points out that what the Catholic community does is "only one aspect of what government and society should be doing."

The Catholic Church's financial support amounts to only $100 per woman — less than the cost of an abortion. Given the scope of the problem of aiding women in the care of children, people who disagree on the morality and legality of abortion can and ought to cooperate in providing support for women in order to reduce the incidence of abortion.

But the religious concern over indifferentism remains, and it must be met on theological grounds. The term entered official Catholic discourse with papal encyclicals in the 19th century. In the U.S. a lively debate over indifferentism occurred in the 1940s. The question then was whether Catholics could cooperate with Protestants in postwar reconstruction. Francis Connell voiced the concern of those who feared such cooperation would lend legitimacy to Protestant belief and practice. "In the United States up to comparatively recent times there was little danger of indifferentism to any great extent among Catholics," wrote Connell. "On the contrary, they were rather inclined to distrust adherents of other denominations and even to question their sincerity... In recent years a strong reaction against the spirit of mutual distrust and antagonism has taken place among both Catholics and non-Catholics... Is not the pendulum swinging from bigotry to indifferentism?"

For Connell, the answer was clear: "I am fully convinced that ordinarily the association of Catholics with non-Catholics in organizations and meetings is a grave menace to our people... and that whatever good they may be producing is far outweighed by their disastrous spiritual consequences."

Jesuit theologian John Courtney Murray countered Connell by saying that Catholics could cooperate with others and that they were morally bound to do so. Cooperation took place on the temporal plane of social interaction, and need not affect the spiritual dimension, which is the realm of doctrine, Murray wrote. If one carefully distinguished between the two planes, then indifferentism could be avoided. Whether in a particular instance one could cooperate with other Christian denominations depended on people's prudential judgment in light of two guiding principles: the need to preserve Catholic integrity and the need to advance the common good. According to Murray, it is "a problem of balance, of finding the center, and of avoiding the temptation to be drawn to one pole of the tension."

How one strikes that balance depends on one's reading of the state of Catholicism and of society. To Murray, the danger of indifferentism for Catholics was less pressing than the threat of materialism to Western society as a whole. Given the immense task of combating materialism, cooperation was not only possible but obligatory. "Confronted with this unique and colossal task, the church has appealed for allies among all men of good will, who believe in God and reverence His law. The premise of her appeal is both the nature of the task, and her own inadequacy to do it (not a doctrinal or spiritual, but a numerical and strategic inadequacy — the Church is the Body of Christ, but she is a minority group, and an 'out-group')."

The case for cooperation in reducing the number of abortions can be made on similar grounds. The common good would be furthered were the number of abortions reduced. Given the magnitude of the problem of care, cooperation across the liberal-conservative divide is necessary and therefore obligatory.

For Catholics, the possibility of sliding into indifferentism regarding the church's teaching on abortion remains a real danger. It should be made clear, however, that cooperation does not require moving toward a "middle ground" on the issues of the status of the fetus and the morality and legality of taking fetal life. Such efforts would indeed lead to theological and spiritual indifferentism. What cooperation seeks, rather, is common ground — an area of contact between pro-life and pro-choice arguments. Many Catholics know that providing alternatives to pregnant women is necessary if their pro-life stance is to have any integrity. Cardinal Joseph Bernardin's "consistent ethic of life" is the foremost attempt to link measures to protect fetal life and those that intend to promote the quality of life of women and children.

Less prevalent in the current debate is a consistent argument from the pro-choice side about the need to provide alternatives to abortion. If the aim of pro-choice advocates is to provide the widest possible array of choices so as to empower women to exercise their moral agency, then pro-choice organizations and their members are obligated to provide alternatives to women in situations of unintended pregnancy. The research of Planned Parenthood's Alan Guttmacher Institute has demonstrated that most women have abortions because they feel that they have no other choice. If the point is to embrace women's moral agency, then organizations such as the National Organization of Women and Catholics for a Free Choice have an obligation to help create a context within which that agency can be fully exercised — and not limited to the right to procure an abortion.

If this line of argument has merit, then overlapping obligations emerge which originate from quite different sources. We can have, in Murray's terms, cooperation on the "temporal plane" of social interaction rather than on the "spiritual" dimension of doctrine.

Given current public opinion, we can also locate a deeper consensus. A number of polls have identified what has mistakenly been called a "muddled middle" on abortion. Roughly 20 percent of those polled think that the crucial issue is the personhood of the fetus, and an opposing 20 percent claim that the only issue is the individual's right to choose. The middle 60 percent appear to think that both factors are relevant. For these people, the status of the fetus changes over the course of the pregnancy. They may not make any connection between the early embryo and the care of children, but they see a close link between the third trimester fetus and children. While they give considerable scope to the woman's agency at the outset, that scope narrows as the pregnancy progresses. For this broad middle of the populace, the effort to create alternatives to abortion is an attempt to reduce suffering, and there is nothing muddled about this intention. To repeat Cardinal Law: "There are few persons who claim that abortion is a moral good."

The kind of cooperation I am advocating runs some risk of fostering indifferentism with regard to Catholic teaching on abortion. Close cooperative activity on a daily basis with people who disagree with Catholic teaching on abortion may lead some Catholics to change their views. The risk of changing one's mind runs in both directions, however, and it is precisely Catholics who aid women in the care of children who offer the most compelling witness to Catholic teaching.

Can such cooperation take place? Examples of it are few, but they can be found. Perhaps the most notable is the movement guided by the Common Ground Network. The movement was begun by two people who might be least expected to search for common ground. Andrew Puzder is a lawyer who coauthored Missouri's 1986 abortion law restricting abortion in state-funded institutions. B. J. Isaacson-Jones is the president and board chair of Reproductive Health Services, which challenged the Missouri law (a challenge that led to the Supreme Court ruling in *Webster v. Reproductive Services* upholding Missouri's law). In early 1990 they entered into conversation, and were soon joined by Jean Cavender of Reproductive Health Services and Loretto Wagner, the past president of Missouri Citizens for Life and founder of Our Lady's Inn, a set of two homes for women with unintended pregnancies. The model of their conversation and, to a lesser extent, of their action, has been employed by about 20 groups nationwide.

Like Murray's thinking, their conversation began with the observation that the magnitude of the problem at hand requires cooperation between groups that are otherwise at odds. "We need to combine our resources in order to benefit women and their children," Wagner commented. Once the discussion began, Isaacson-Jones noted, "it was shockingly easy to identify issues we agree on, like the need for aid to pregnant women who are addicted to drugs, the need for better prenatal care and the need to reduce unwanted pregnancy. Neither side wants women to need abortions because they don't have the money to raise a child."

These insights have led to concrete actions. In 1990 Reproductive Health Services opened an adoption agency. In 1992 the agency placed more than 30 minority infants, more than any other agency in Missouri. The St. Louis Common Ground has produced a manual to aid foster parents and mothers of infants exposed to crack or alcohol in the womb, and has worked for legislation for a school breakfast program and for rehabilitation, housing and job training for pregnant, drug-addicted women. While Wagner comments that "we're a long way from any major joint projects," she and the others in Common Ground have done enough to demonstrate the possibility — and therefore the obligation — of expanding the range of cooperation for the common good. This is the case even though there have been and are likely to be setbacks.

In the meantime, the Common Ground effort has also demonstrated that such cooperation need not slide into indifferentism regarding Catholic teaching on abortion. Wagner is adamant on this point. "No one is ever going to convince me that it's all right to kill unborn babies, and I'm going to go on working to make abortion illegal."

In Search of the Perfect Child: Genetic Testing and Selective Abortion

Ted Peters

The triumphs of genetic research include the discovery of disease-related genes. The gene for cystic fibrosis, for example, has been found on chromosome 7. Huntington's chorea was discovered lurking on the end of chromosome 4. Inherited breast cancer was traced to chromosome 17, early-onset Alzheimer's disease to chromosome 14 and colon cancer to chromosome 2. Disposition to muscular dystrophy, sickle cell anemia and 5,000 or more other diseases is being tracked to genetic origins. The search goes on as well for the DNA switches that turn such genes on and off, and for genetic therapies that will turn the bad genes off and keep the good genes on. Such discoveries could improve medical diagnosis, prevention and therapy, thus advancing the quality of health for everyone.

Yet this apparent good news comes as bad news to those born with genetic susceptibilities to disease, because medical care is funded by private insurance companies and medical insurance is tied to employment. An identifiable genetic predisposition to disease counts as an existing condition, and insurance companies are beginning to deny coverage to people with existing conditions. As new techniques for prevention and therapy become available, the very people who could benefit may be denied access to them.

Paul Billings, a genetics researcher and ethicist at Stanford University Medical School, has collected anecdotal evidence of genetic discrimination. Testifying before Congress, Billings told of a woman who, during a routine physical, spoke to her physician about the possibility of her mother having Huntington's disease. Later, when the woman applied for life insurance, her medical records were reviewed and she lost all her insurance.

In another case, a 14-month-old girl was diagnosed with phenylketonuria through a newborn screening program. A low phenylalanine diet was prescribed, and her parents followed the diet rules. The child has grown up to be a normal and healthy person. Her health care at birth was covered by a group insurance policy associated with her father's employment, but when he changed jobs the new carrier declared her ineligible for coverage. Once a genetic predisposition for an expensive disease becomes part of one's medical record, insurance carriers and employers connected to them find it in their best financial interest to minimize or deny health coverage.

In a report by the Committee on Government Operations, U.S. Representative John Conyers (D., Mich.) responded to Billings and others: "Like discrimination based on race, genetic discrimination is wrong because it is based on hereditary characteristics we are powerless to change. The fear in the minds of many people is that genetic information will be used to identify those with 'weak' or 'inferior' genes, who will then be treated as a 'biological underclass.'"

Until recently, the federal government has been slow to respond to testimonies made on behalf of the next generation. In an effort to draw attention to the issue, researchers in the Working Group on Ethical, Legal, and Social Implications of the Human Genome Project at the National Institutes of Health and the Department of Energy created a task force that included geneticists, ethicists and representatives from the insurance industry. The central message of their 1993 report is that information about past, present or future health status — especially health status due to genetic predispositions — should not be used to deny health care coverage or services to anyone.

Some officials are listening. The Kassebaum-Kennedy health insurance reform bill passed in August prohibits categorizing a genetic predisposition as a disqualifying precondition.

Another change occurred when U.S. Marines John Mayfield and Joseph Vlacovsky refused to allow their DNA to be deposited in a Pentagon data bank. The two men were court-martialed, but later the Pentagon dropped its original plan to keep DNA information for 75 years. Fearing that genetic information could be used to discriminate, it now restricts the use of DNA to the identification of human remains on the battlefield. Donors may request destruction of their gene samples when they leave Defense Department service.

Late last year the Genetic Privacy Act was introduced in Congress as well as six state legislatures. The proposal governs collection, analysis, storage and use of DNA samples and the genetic information obtained from them. The act would require explicit authorization to collect DNA samples for genetic analysis and limit the use of information gained from them. The aim is to protect individual privacy by giving the individual the right to authorize who may have access to his or her genetic information.

This is a good start, but it is not enough. Laws to protect genetic privacy appeal to our sense of autonomy, to our desire to take control of what appears to be our own possession, our genome. But privacy protection in itself will not eliminate the threat of genetic discrimination. First of all, it probably will not work. Genetic information as well as medical records are computerized. Computers are linked. In the world of the Internet, someone who wants to penetrate the system will eventually find a way to do so. Any attempt to maintain control over genetic information is likely to fail.

Second, privacy regarding one's genome is undesirable. Knowledge of one's genome could improve preventive health care. The more our physicians know about our genetic predispositions the more they can head off difficulties before they arise. Rather than privacy, what we want is the use of genetic information that does not discriminate against people because of their genetic makeup.

A few years ago my 23-year-old godson Matthew was rushed to the hospital for emergency surgery. He was diagnosed with familial polyposis, a colon cancer in an advanced stage. In a heroic effort, the surgeon's team managed to remove all malignancy. Afterward the surgeon asked the parents if there were any cases of colon cancer in Matthew's family. "We don't know," the parents answered, explaining that Matthew had been adopted as an infant and his records were closed.

"Well," said the doctor, "this kind of cancer is genetic. Had we known that Matthew had a predisposition, we could have monitored him from age ten and removed precancerous polyps. He would never have come to this crisis situation." This case shows the value of computerized and sharable genomic information.

At some point in the future a simple blood test will reveal each of our individual genomes, and we may be able to use this knowledge to great benefit. Laws promoting genetic information, without discrimination will contribute to better health care rather than deny it.

A number of states have laws allowing genetic information to be secured from birth parents and made available to adopting parents. In this way, one can learn the frequency of a disorder in a family but not the identity of the family. As genetic testing becomes more sophisticated, DNA tests will provide the same information.

But if adopting parents view adoptable children as commodities to be consumed, such genetic testing could inadvertently lead to discrimination. If the child tests positively for a genetic defect, the adopting parents may think of the child as defective and refuse to adopt him or her. They may be caught up in the "perfect-child syndrome" and want nothing less than a perfectly healthy child. Or they may cancel the adoption because they fear that they'll lose their family health care insurance and become stuck with unpayable medical bills. The first problem is cultural or ethical, the second economic.

Can we forecast a connection between genetic discrimination and selective abortion? Yes. A couple in Louisiana had a child with cystic fibrosis, a genetic disorder leading to chronic lung infections and excruciating discomfort. When the wife became pregnant with the second child, a prenatal genetic test revealed that the fetus carried the mutant gene for cystic fibrosis. The couple's health maintenance organization demanded that they abort. If they refused to abort, the HMO would withdraw coverage from both the newborn and the first child. Only when the couple threatened to sue did the HMO back down and grant coverage for the second child.

With the advance of prenatal genetic testing, both parents and insurance carriers can find out whether a child may be prone to having a debilitating and expensive disease. It is not unrealistic to imagine the insurance industry publishing a list of disqualifying genetic predispositions. If one of the predispositions were found in a fetus, the industry would mandate an abortion under penalty of loss of coverage. This would outrage pro-life parents, and even pro-choice parents would find this financial pressure to be the equivalent of a compromise on choice.

We are moving step-by-step toward this selective abortion scenario. In addition to feeling pressure from the privately funded insurance industry, parents themselves will likely develop criteria for deciding which fetuses will be brought to term and which will be aborted. Genetic criteria will play a major role. Prenatal testing to identify disease-related genes will become routine, and tests for hundreds of deleterious genes may become part of the prenatal arsenal. Parents wanting what they believe to be a perfectly healthy child may abort repeatedly at each hint of a genetic disorder. Choice and selection will enter the enterprise of baby making at a magnitude unimaginable in previous history.

Most families will confront the issue when they find themselves in a clinic office talking with a genetic counselor. Although a genetic analysis of heritable family traits can help immensely in planning for future children, talking with a genetic counselor too often begins when a pregnancy is already in progress. The task of the genetic counselor is to provide information regarding the degree of risk that a given child might be born with a genetic disorder, and to impart this information objectively, impartially and confidentially (when possible) so that the autonomy of the parents is protected.

What is surprising and disconcerting to mothers or couples in this situation is that genetic risk is usually given statistically, in percentages. The parents find themselves with difficult-to-interpret information while facing an unknown future. Conflicting values between marital partners or even within each of them increase the difficulty — and the anxiety.

Both genetic endowment and degree of disability are relative unknowns. For a recessive defective gene such as that for cystic fibrosis, when both parents are carriers the risk is 50 percent that the child will also be a carrier and 25 percent that the child will contract the disease. With this information, parents decide to proceed toward birth or to terminate the pregnancy. Later in the pregnancy the specific genetic makeup of a fetus can be discerned via amniocentesis and other tests.

In cases of Down Syndrome, for example, which is associated with trisomy (three copies of chromosome 21), eight out of every ten negative prenatal diagnoses lead to the decision to abort. Even though the genetic predisposition can be clearly identified in this way, the degree of mental retardation that will result is unknown. Mild cases mean near-average intelligence. Yet the choice to abort has become the virtual norm. The population of Down Syndrome people in our society is dropping, making this a form of eugenics by popular choice.

In only 3 to 5 percent of cases does a positive prenatal diagnosis reveal the presence of a genetic disorder so severe that the probable level of suffering on the part of the child warrants that a parent consider abortion. In making this judgment, I am invoking a principle of compassion — what bioethicists dub the principle of non-maleficence, or reducing human suffering whenever possible. In situations where such a diagnosis is made and where prospective parents strongly desire to bring a child into the world, a number of things happen.

First, genetic counselors report that parents automatically refer to the child as a "baby," never as a "fetus." They clearly think of the life growing in the womb as a person. Second, when confronted with the bad news, they experience turmoil. The turmoil usually leads to a decision to terminate the pregnancy, but not always. It is not the job of the genetic counselor to encourage abortion; even advocates of choice on abortion defend the parents' right to decide to bring such a child to birth. Third, even when the decision to terminate is made, the grieving parents see their decision as an expression of their love, not a denial of love. It is an act of compassion.

The distinction between convenience and compassion is ethically significant here. As the practice of prenatal genetic testing expands and the principle of autonomy — the responsibility for choice — is applied to the parents and not to the unborn child, the total number of abortions will increase, perhaps dramatically. Each pregnancy will be thought of as tentative until the fetus has passed dozens or hundreds of genetic tests. A culturally reinforced image of the desirable child — the perfect-child syndrome — may lead couples to try repeated pregnancies, terminating the undesirables and giving birth only to the "best" test passers. Those born in this fashion risk being commodified by their parents. In addition, those who might be born with a disability and with the potential for leading a productive and fulfilling life might never see the light of day.

A social byproduct of selective abortion might be increased discrimination against people living with disabilities. The assumption could grow that to live with a disability is to have a life not worth living. Persons with disabilities fear that the medical establishment and its supportive social policies will seek to prevent "future people like me from ever being born." The inference is: "I am worthless to society." The imputation of dignity to handicapped persons may be quietly withdrawn as they are increasingly viewed as unnecessary and expensive appendages to an otherwise healthy society.

This would be a tragedy of the first order. Disabled persons deserve dignity and encouragement. Such people frequently gain victory in their difficult life struggles. Most disabled people report that while the disability, the pain, and the need for compensatory devices and assistance can produce considerable inconvenience, the inconveniences become minimal or even forgotten once individuals make the transition to living their everyday lives.

Whether we like it or not, the advancing frontier of genetics, with its impact on reproductive technology, thrusts us back into the abortion debate. *Roe v. Wade* (1973) did not answer the questions we will be asking in 2003. The Supreme Court decided that a woman has the right to abort during the first trimester. Genetic discrimination raises an additional question: by what criteria might a fetus be considered abortable? *Roe v. Wade* focuses on the woman's right to decide what to do with her body; now we focus on the fetuses and the criteria by which some will live and others will not. A skeptic might say that as long as the woman has the right to choose, it is a moot point to talk of criteria of choice. I believe that while a woman's right to choose is a legal matter, the criteria for choosing are an ethical matter.

Even though abortion on request is legal, not all grounds for requesting it are ethical. In the case of selective abortion, a decision based solely on the desires of the parents without regard for the child's well-being is unethical. As Martin Luther said, "Even if a child is unattractive when it is born, we nevertheless love it."

Most Christians are not ethically ready for the era of selective abortion. We are unprepared for the kind of decisions that large numbers of prospective parents will be confronting. We have thought about the issue of abortion on request and the question of when human dignity begins, but now we need middle axioms to guide the choices that will confront the next generation of parents.

First, we need to identify defective or undesirable genes prior to conception rather than after. Whether or not the conceptus has full personhood and full dignity comparable to living adults, ethicists agree that the fertilized zygote deserves a level of respect and honor that resists brute manipulation or irreverent discarding. Genetic selection in the sperm or ovum prior to fertilization, prior to the DNA blueprint of a potential person, seems more defensible.

Second, the choice for selective abortion should be the last resort. Prefertilization selection should be given priority when possible, as should prenatal gene therapy.

Third, the motive of compassion that seeks to minimize suffering on the part of children coming into the world should hold relative sway when choosing for or against selective abortion. Compassion, taken up as the principle of non-maleficence in bioethics, constitutes the way that parents show love toward children-to-be. In rare cases (3 to 5 percent of prenatal diagnoses), the genetic disorder is so severe that no approximation to a fulfilling life is possible. The decision to abort can be understood as a form of caring for the baby as well as self-care for the parents. Yet it is still a judgment call. No clear rule tells us exactly when the imputed dignity of the unborn child may be trumped by a compassionate decision to abort.

Fourth, we should distinguish between acts of eugenics and acts of compassion. The goal of eugenics is to reduce the incidence of a certain genetic trait, usually an undesirable trait. Eugenics is social in scope and derives from some social philosophy. At this point, bioethicists tend to oppose eugenic policies because, if practiced on a large scale, they could reduce biodiversity. More important, eugenics connotes the political totalitarianism of the Third Reich. The compassion or non--maleficence principle, when limited to the concrete situation of a family making a decision regarding a particular child, is much more acceptable. The line between eugenics and compassion is not a clear one, however. Some will argue that the attempt to eliminate a recessive gene for something like cystic fibrosis in future branches on a family tree is an act of compassion.

Fifth, we should distinguish between preventing suffering and enhancing genetic potential. Genetic selection to help reduce suffering is an act that, in at least a minimal sense, is directed toward the well-being of the child. In the future, when genetic selection and perhaps even genetic engineering make possible designer babies with higher-than-average intelligence, good looks or athletic prowess, then we will move closer to embracing the perfect-child syndrome. The risk of commodifying children and evaluating them according to standards of quality control increases when parents are "buying." The risk of commodification does not in itself constitute a reason to reject all genetic therapy, but it does call us to bolster a sound, biblically defensible principle: God loves people regardless of their genetic makeup, and we should do likewise.

On Cloning

Jerome Freeman

Cloning can be
Done and done and done
But not undone.
Once the line is crossed
And one becomes two
Innocence shudders
And looks away,

As we peer into the future
Of what has been wrought
And ponder our children.

Questions to Consider in Chapter Eight

1. "Erosion of the Rights of Pregnant Women" by Kenneth Ryan:
   a. How have advances in prenatal diagnosis threatened the rights of pregnant women?
   b. In your judgment is it ever right to override the autonomy of the mother on behalf of the fetus?

2. "Fetal Alcohol Syndrome..." by Ann Wilson:
   a. What combination of experience and education does Ann Wilson bring to the understanding of FAS?
   b. Why does she insist that parents cannot hear the cries of their own baby until their own are heard?
   c. Why does she believe that fighting FAS is more complicated than stopping the woman's drinking?
   d. What does Ann mean by her reference to "casseroles"? How is this related to fighting FAS?
   e. What makes for a good caregiver? Can caring be taught?

3. "Common Ground..." by Todd David Whitmore:
   a. Who are B. J. Issacson-Jones and Andrew Puzder?
   b. How were they able to find common ground on the question of abortion?
   c. What is the significance of their attempt?

4. "In Search Of The Perfect Child..." by Ted Peters:
   a. What ethical dilemmas are raised by the discovery of disease-related genes? Is it possible or desirable to protect genetic privacy?
   b. What are the dangers in the so-called selective abortion scenario? When is such a decision unethical in Peter's judgment? What guidelines or middle axioms does he suggest?

5. Are dilemmas of caring at the end fundamentally similar to or different from those at the beginning of life? Explain.

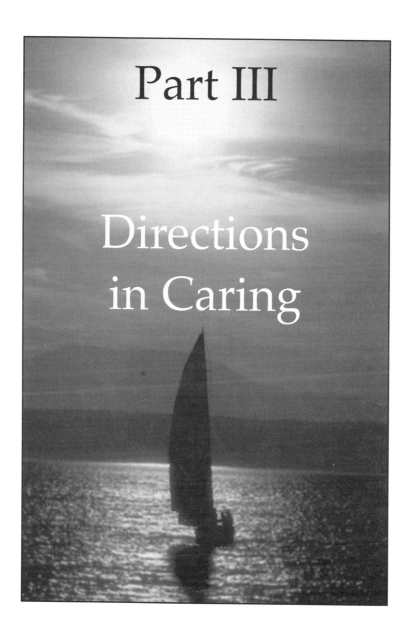

Part III

Directions
in Caring

Knowing what we do about the call to care and the dimensions of caring, and the dilemmas that we face in making caring choices, how then shall we live?

In facing this question we will need to address both economic and political issues. This is because strategies for caring must be attentive to cost and efficiency. How much caring can we afford? Are there more effective ways to deliver health care both locally or nationally? Can caring that is "managed" still be caring? What role can and should government and the private sector play in the delivery of health care? These are the topics of readings in Chapter Nine.

What can we learn from Hygeia in planning for health care? On an everyday level how can we live more caring lives? Do we do it professionally or just as individual members of the human community? Caring needs to be understood as an everyday event as we support one another in carrying out our individual life stories. These concerns are the theme of the readings in Chapter Ten.

And finally in Chapter Eleven we will see how all of the questions surrounding the call to care come together in Tolstoy 's classic *The Death of Ivan Ilyich*. How then shall we live in the face of death, whether it be our own death or the death of another? Tolstoy's honest and compassionate narrative focuses once again on the dimensions and dilemmas of caring and invites us to consider ways of choosing life in the face of death.

Chapter Nine:
How Then Shall We Live As Citizens?
Arthur Olsen

"When one person is ill, the whole of society is really ill in all its members. In the final battle against sickness the final human word cannot be isolation but only fellowship." — Karl Barth in *The Will To Be Healthy*

"We don't live in a perfect world. It's changing significantly. But young people can make a difference. Ideals are okay, but students need to work with realism too." — Jon Soderholm in "The Red Ford or the Red Porsche?"

"In the end, the kind of health care we tolerate reflects the kind of society we are or want to be. The bedside reflects back to all of us where our treasure lies. While physicians, nurses, and administrators have the immediate responsibility, they can operate only within the parameters society sets for them. If our system of "care" denies care, none of us can deny complicity. If the health care system Christians tolerate is itself a violation of Christian teaching on care of the sick, Christians cannot avoid complicity." — "Managed care: An ethical Reflection," by Edmund D. Pellegrino

In Retrospect

As we consider this final question — "How then shall we live?" — let us look back briefly over the road we have travelled. We began with the *call to care*, the claim of another person upon us like Susan. How shall we respond? How can we be of use as she struggles with issues of health and illness, life and death?

In Part I — *Dimensions of Caring* — we noted that in responding to Susan we become involved in her life story, which is not just the story of her physical problems, but her story as a whole person. We considered Susan's will to be healthy as the will to carry out her life story, including her body and her sense of self. Strategies for carrying out her life story include Hygeia(wise living) and Asclepius (medical intervention). Also included is an awareness of mortality, the limits of life, and courage to live in the face of illness and suffering.

In Part II — *Dilemmas of Caring* — we became engaged in the need for principles in the practice of biomedical ethics. Difficult dilemmas face us as we seek to make concrete decisions with respect to the call to care. Who gets care? Who decides (autonomy)? Are there limits to who gets care (justice)? As we consider the new situations that face us in caring at the beginning and end of life, how do we most effectively do good (beneficence) and avoid harm (maleficence)?

The dilemmas of caring in Part II were considered in relationship to cases. This is because caring decisions are made in the context of specific life stories: Rose Brech, Nancy Cruzan, Susan, your grandmother, your spouse.

The practice of biomedical ethics is thus three dimensional. On one plane there are two dimensions — dilemmas to consider and the deliberation about what action to take. On another plane — as in a cube — there is a third dimension: the life story. What is best for patients will depend upon where they are in living out their life stories. Knowing this will encourage each of us to approach the life-stories of our friends, and neighbors, and clients with interest and humility. At best we see only some of the pages of the other person's story. Each person's story is a kind of sacred space. Sharing the stories of others is a privilege.

Thus the purpose of the practice of biomedical ethics is to support human flourishing. What issues concern ourselves, our parents, our friends in their life stories? Is it wise living, change in life pattern, or medical intervention that is necessary? Where in the trajectory of their lives are the persons needing care? No medical interventions are forever, and recognizing mortality is a significant dimension of caring. And courage and the search for meaning are elements of caring too.

Sensing the dimensions of caring helps to establish our bearings as we struggle to make caring choices. Living healthy lives is about carrying through our life stories. Story provides the continuity of our lives.

Seeing the connection between the dimensions of caring and the dilemmas of caring is essential if we are fully to come to terms with the question of Part III — How then shall we live? How then shall we care for life as citizens (Chapter Nine), as persons (Chapter Ten), in the face of death (Chapter Eleven)?

The Politics of Caring

To care for life as citizens we must attend to the political and economic issues of health care. Our personal stories are lived out in communities. The purpose of our cities and states is to support individual citizens in living out their stories. Someone has said that the purpose of politics is to tend the garden so that all of the plants can flourish.

Although most of the cases considered have been about individuals — Jason Gaes, Susan, the girl in "Use of Force," Rose Brech, or Nancy Cruzan — the political dimension of caring has been implicit throughout our readings and narrative.

As noted earlier, the call to care, based upon the claim of another person upon us, is in the first instance a moral claim, heard individually. Moral claims are not just about individual acts but about the way we live together. Moral claims are handed on in conscience and tradition, and from time to time they are spelled out in codes and laws. And now and again they must be thought through in new contexts and spelled out in new laws. Thus, the need to respect patient autonomy is the personal, moral claim of another human being. It has also been spelled out in hospital codes and in national legislation such as the Patient's Self Determination Act passed by Congress in 1990.

It should be noted that each of the principles used in the practice of biomedical ethics has a community/political dimension.

The response to the nursing home resident who does not want restraints but is in danger of falling out of bed and breaking brittle bones, concerns not only that person's autonomy, but also the well-being of all of the other residents. Health care institutions need to develop policies to guide responses to dilemmas which may arise regarding patient autonomy.

Current debates over physician-assisted suicide are attempts to consider not only what a patient wants (autonomy) but what is best (beneficence) for the person in a broad context. Do we best serve the needs of patients by legislation allowing them to request treatment that deliberately ends their lives? Or do we best support them with legislation which prevents them from taking actions that eliminate their autonomy?

In the previous chapter, Caring from the Beginning, it became clear that considering policies to prevent harm (maleficence) to infants of mothers who consumed alcohol during pregnancy involves us in community activity. How best can the needs of the mother and her family be supported to prevent this terrible harm?

And clearly concern for justice and the fair distribution of health care must engage us as citizens in supporting a delivery system that best serves the health needs of our neighborhoods and towns. Being sure that the best of health care is available to our citizens is a political task. And a fundamental issue facing us as citizens is the cost, availability, and quality of health care that is delivered in our midst.

The Economics of Caring

A key dimension of our political deliberation is economic. Cost is important. The price of health care is increasing at an alarming rate. Access is also a critical concern. Nearly 40 million of our citizens are not covered by health care insurance. Rose Brech is a case in point. Many more are underinsured. Still another troubling consideration is that health care, though a very important community good, is not our only need. We also need schools and police protection.

We can always hope that advances in medical technology or more efficient use of social resources, or a new health care plan will reduce the need to worry about the just distribution of health care resources. The dilemma faced by the first ethics committee at Swedish Hospital in Seattle in 1961 to determine which patients with failing kidneys should get the kidney machine has been answered in two ways. Developments in technology have increased the supply of dialysis machines and made them more affordable. And by congressional action in 1972, kidney dialysis has been included as a procedure available to all under Medicare. But costs resulting from this action have made our political community wary of any new proposals to improve our health care system.

Daniel Callahan, founder and former director of the Hastings Center, writes to disabuse us of false hopes. Although we can anticipate and work for improved, cost-effective technology and better budgeting, an ultimate confrontation with the financial limits of resources for health care is unavoidable. Whereas 6 percent of our gross national product was spent on health care in 1966 and a comparable percentage was spent on education and defense, today the percentage of our GNP spent on health care is inching towards 15 percent. There is, says Callahan, a "ragged edge" in the development of new technologies in health care. Some developments do indeed reduce costs. At the same time many developments of medical technology — MRIs, organ transplants, and the like — dramatically increase health care costs at the same time that the ability of the Rose Brechs of this world to pay is tragically decreased.[1]

Are there better ways to deliver health care than the present free-enterprise system in the United States? We know that Canada, our neighbor to the north, has a single payer system that provides access to all. Patients can choose physicians and hospitals. Medical bills are sent to the government which uses tax dollars to pay. Access is thus universal in principle. There are problems, however, with delays and lack of sophisticated technological equipment. In the United States we boast of a fine medical establishment and the most advanced equipment. But there remain problems of access. How shall we support the uninsured?

In the first two years of the Clinton administration, brave attempts were made to introduce a new health care plan called managed competition. It failed to win the support of Congress and the public. Many of the president's party who supported it did not win reelection.

Though it may be premature at this point to consider a new health care plan, it is important to be aware of the ethical and economic issues that we must face as we seek to improve our health care system. The readings in this chapter have been selected to engage us in the issues and questions that we must face as we deal with questions of cost and access in health care.

The pieces by Mary Auterman and Jon Soderholm give us perspective on where we are now as we seek to pay for health care with a combination of savings, insurance, Medicare, Medicaid, and city/county aid. We need to come to terms with both spiraling health care costs and our fundamental values as a society. Is health care a right or a privilege? Can we consider cutting costs by considering that a Red Ford rather than a Red Porsche level of health care may be adequate for our needs?

Allen R. Dyer warns that patients, not costs, come first. Yet he argues that issues of cost need to be faced in the patient-physician relationship. How is that possible?

Edmund Pellegrino, physician and ethicist at Georgetown University, directs our attention to the ethical dangers in managed care. The needs of the patient, not cost-effectiveness come first. And yet he argues for the responsibility of the physician to manage costs. How is this possible? Is this enough?

The piece by William F. May goes back to the years when Clinton's new health care plan was being discussed. Though that plan was defeated, the issues are still with us. May engages us in a discussion of the necessary foundations of an adequate health care system. Are the foundations that he proposes the ones that can guide us in our efforts to make health care accessible and affordable to those who need it?

Finally, Mary Auterman, one of the pioneers in parish nursing in South Dakota, shows how the church can be a resource to community health needs.

The questions of access, cost, and quality of health care will not go away. It appears to be true that we want more services than we can afford. Can we afford all that we need? Can we insure that all who need health care receive it at least at a minimal level? It has been said that health care is already rationed in the United States. It is not available to all. Is it a rational and caring system of rationing? This is the disturbing question of justice that claims our attention as citizens.

---

[1]Daniel Callahan, *What Kind of Life: The Limits of Medical Progress*, New York, Simon and Schuster, 1990.

How Health Care Services are Paid

Mary Auterman

Health care costs are paid for in one of two ways: by the individual receiving the care and by third party payers which include public funds and insurance plans or policies.

PUBLIC FUNDS

Medicare — Instituted in 1965 and effective July 1, 1966. Covers persons 65 years of age and older (life expectancy in 1965 was 65 years of age). Individuals of any age with selected permanent disabling conditions who qualified for permanent disability under Social Security were added in 1972.

Medicare coverage is divided into two parts. Part A provides insurance toward hospitalization, rehabilitation services, home care, and hospice care and partial costs of up to 100 days in a long term care facility. Part B is voluntary and provides partial coverage of physician services for those persons covered by Part A.

Medicare clients pay an annual deductible and a coinsurance of 20 percent. The other 80 percent of the bill for covered care is paid by the government.

Medicare does not cover dental care, dentures, eyeglasses unless prescribed for certain specific medical eye disorders, routine eye exams, hearing exams, or hearing aids. Most preventative care including routine physical examination and screening tests are not included. Most prescription drugs are not included.

Medicare is funded through a Medicare tax withdrawn from the wages of every worker and deposited into a "Medicare Fund." Eligible persons must apply for Medicare coverage just prior to their 65th birthday and receive a Medicare number before using Medicare. Subscribers to Medicare Part B pay a monthly premium which is deducted from their Social Security check.

Medicare uses a prospective payment system to reimburse hospitals and physicians for care provided. The amount paid is based on diagnostic related groups (DRGs) rather than the amount of care or length of stay. The amount Medicare pays for services within each DRG is set prior to each fiscal year.

Medicaid — is a public assistance program paid by federal and state governments for people who have no insurance and meet certain income guidelines (low income). It is administered by the state government and each state government sets its own coverage guidelines; thus, it varies greatly from state to state.

Medicaid is paid for out of general tax revenues.

State and County Assistance — In addition to Medicaid, most states and county governments allot general funds for emergency indigent care not covered by Medicaid. Coverage varies with each county.

PRIVATE FUNDS — INSURANCE COVERAGE

Fee-for-Service — The traditional insurance policy. Also sometimes called the indemnity plan. The client pays a monthly or annual premium for a given amount of insurance coverage. Coverage is based on the service provided. A single policy usually includes payments for both hospital stays and for physicians, as well as any health promotion. Each company also sets its own limitations and exclusions. The percentage which the plan pays and the co-pay person pays may vary with different items. These plans usually offer the greatest freedom of choice in health care providers.

Health Maintenance Organization (HMO) — An HMO is a health care agency that coordinates health care services for individuals or groups (*e.g.*, organizations or companies, *etc.*). The HMO contracts with specific groups of physicians, hospitals, laboratories, pharmacies, *etc.* to provide services at a set cost. The member client pays a set fee for each use of service regardless of actual cost or care received.

The HMO plan stresses wellness; thus health promotion and preventative health care services are usually covered as well as illness care. Co-payment cost to the client is usually low; frequently $5.00 or $10.00 per service usage.

Disadvantages of the HMO plan include access limited to a set group of physicians and health care professionals and hospitals. The subscriber is required to use the designated health care providers except in an emergency.

Preferred Provider Organization (PPO) — A PPO consists of a group of physicians and/or a hospital that provides an insurance company or an employer with health services at discounted prices.

Contracts may be arranged with other physicians, hospitals, laboratories and pharmacies to provide services at a set maximum cost. These arrangements are known as Preferred Provider Arrangement.

The individual user of PPO services pays a deductible plus a co-pay. The co-pay is frequently a set amount for pharmacy items and percent (*e.g.,* 20 percent) co-pay for other health care services. A penalty is paid for non-emergency use of non-member physician, hospital, or pharmacy use.

Disadvantages are similar to those for HMO membership. PPOs are less likely than HMOs to include health promotion and health screening benefits.

Medigap Insurance — Medigap refers to those insurance policies available to individuals with Medicare coverage. It pays for part or all of the costs not covered by Medicare Parts A and B.

Long-term Care Insurance — Covers cost of long-term, non-acute care such as a nursing home. Most insurances do not cover long-term care. Medicare provides partial coverage for only 100 days, and only provided that the individual was hospitalized immediately prior to the admission to a long-term care facility. Long-term care insurance policies vary greatly in coverage. Some include home health care and/or adult day-care. Long-term care insurance is becoming increasingly important as the number of elderly increases. The average length of stay in a long-term care facility is 2.5 years, at an average annual cost of $47,000 in 1997.

A certain percentage of the cost of health insurance premium and of long-term care insurance are deductible as medical expenses on one's federal income tax.

The Gymnast

Jerome Freeman

I. After the Fall

Just so, life halted its orbit of joy and
plummeted toward the horizon, finding
a dark solstice.

Legs dangle like limp flags in tedious calm,
shorn of former impulse and command.

The whims of perspective leap up, baying
for attention. From uneven bars, life is a
kaleidoscope of color and movement and
joy. From bed, the night ceiling presses
downward, enforcing pallid stillness.

Mornings compose discordant hopes.
Always she thinks of movement.

II. The Vigil

Always she thinks of movement.

They say it could have been worse,
and things will get better, and just keep trying.
They seem to only half believe, or less.
The doctors float in and out to make
pronouncements from beyond the fray.

Impossible things are suggested like
poking catheters in private places and
staying on Rehab for three months.
And this, just after the week she learned
to sit up and roll over and beg
to be taken home.

Rumors are everywhere. Friends
report she moves a foot or maybe
has feeling or will walk next week.
The truth is stale. Daily morsels
of hope are hard to digest.

III. Becoming

Life begins again slowly,
as if long-held breath is exhaled.
The wheelchair fades from
prominence into surrounding hues.

Sometimes she smiles and
means it. She pieces together
meanings, taking back control
of where she'll be going from here.

The Red Ford
or the Red Porsche
An Interview with
Jon Soderholm

Jon Soderholm served in administrative positions at Sioux Valley Hospital from 1966-1997. Beginning as an assistant administrator, he served successively as senior vice-president, executive vice-president, and president of Sioux Valley Hospital.

Art: How did you get involved in health care administration at Sioux Valley Hospital?

Jon: I got into health care administration through my experience as a medic in the Army and an X-ray technician in the Air Force. After that, I looked around saying, "Where in the world do I fit? What do I want to be when I grow up?" So, I went to the University of Minnesota in a program called Hospital Administration, and did a residency at St. Luke's Hospital in St. Paul, and then came to Sioux Valley in October 1966.

Art: And in what role did you start? Did you start in the role that you ended in?

Jon: I started as an assistant administrator, chief gopher. Sioux Valley Hospital was then a 200-bed hospital.

Art: Based on your experiences, what are some of the concerns you have about the future of the health care industry?

Jon: Health care is in significant change as an industry, like all other industries. The difference in health care as opposed to banking or communications is that there are many people who think health care is a right as opposed to a privilege. And if you challenge people's rights, it causes great consternation. Hospitals have been significant institutions in this country, like schools and colleges. You expect the rest of the world to change, but you don't expect your institutions to change; you expect them to be your anchors. The difference is that it is the people's institution. It is a "right," many people think; and when you change people's rights or institutions, there is great consternation in people's minds and their lives.

Jerry: Jon, in the past, when you've talked to our class about "right" versus "privilege," you were careful never to reveal how you felt about these two different ways of viewing health care. How is it, do you think? Is health care a right or not?

Jon: First let's define "right" and "privilege." A right is something that you're born with in this country, like the ability to vote or the ability to go through public grade school and high school. A privilege is something that you earn or pay for, such as a driver's license; you earn the license by proving that you can drive. And a hunting license you earn by paying for it, and it can be taken away from you if you violate hunting regulations, whereas rights can't be taken away from you. I've believed all along that health care is neither a right nor a privilege. It's on a continuum that politically goes back and forth depending on how rich we think we are as a nation and depending on the political climate at a particular time. Under Reagan health care was more a privilege than a right. Under a more liberal administration it may become more a right. And then you mix in with that how rich are we as a nation, where are we in the economical cycle, where are we with federal or state budgets. It's going to be really interesting now that it looks as though we'll come really close to having a balanced budget next year. Perhaps we'll be more liberal and health care will become more of a right as it was in 1966 when Medicare came into being. I don't believe it's either a right or a privilege. I believe it's on a continuum that goes back and forth depending on where this country is at. Obviously, in many parts of the world health care is not a right.

Art: Would you comment on the role of Medicare contributing to our understanding that health care is a right. I can still hear the rhetoric of then-President Lyndon Johnson who said our senior citizens shouldn't have to worry about health care, so the government should provide it.

Jon: Well, my first day in health care was July 1, 1966, and that was the first day for Medicare in this country. The first several days I worked the hospital canceled vacations and put extra people on because there was the feeling there was going to be a rush to the hospital doors. But there were no more people there than came on June 30th, because people were getting their health care, by and large, across the country.

What happened later is that in the late 1960s, 1970s, and early 1980s, there were significant technological advancements in acute health care. Many things came about that most common people didn't have access to, and that technology was fueled by the Medicare dollars. There was a great burgeoning of that technology and the care that was given. Health care providers all made a lot of money because of Medicare and Medicaid. And that's not negative or wrong, but partly serendipitous that the technology came at that period of time and that the financing through Medicare was such that all the elderly could have it. There have been great technological changes between 1966 and the 1990s.

Jerry: So, how did Medicare get into such dire financial straits?

Jon: First of all, Medicare was based on a cost-plus methodology. Hospitals collected all of their receipts and put them in a cigar box, and at the end of the month they gave the box to the Feds. The Feds, at first, just accepted all those receipts and paid 2-3 percent more than that. When you're getting paid on that basis, the more people you can get through the door and the more procedures you can do, the better off you are financially. And in the process, you're taking care of more eyes, more hips, and so on. Hospitals grew, and on a cost plus basis, there was no risk...there was absolutely no risk. In the past, to buy a cardiac lab might cost a million dollars, a huge investment for a private hospital, and for Sioux Falls, South Dakota. But in reality it was not much of a risk, because two-thirds of the financing came from Medicare. And, if you were in a very small town in South Dakota and you put in a CAT scan unit, maybe you would have only 5-10 patients a year, but Medicare paid for the whole thing, on a cost-plus basis. On a cost-plus basis, hospital providers weren't taking any risk. So the federal government said, "This is craziness. We've got to somehow put those providers at some risk." The percentage of increases back in those years of medical CPI (Consumer Price Index) was just growing so fast and too fast. The federal government said, "Somehow, we got to put a stop to this." And they tried a couple different processes. They put hospitals under a freeze three times, but all that did was put up a wall, and when the freeze came off, the damn burst, and costs increased.

Jerry: When was the freeze in effect?

Jon: Back during the Johnson administration, I think. But freezes don't work, They are artificial. I'm conservative with respect to the economy: the free market works the best. In about 1983-84, the federal government said we have to do something different. And they put in the DRG based reimbursement, which basically said to providers, "You take care of people, and you get a fixed sum per disease. If you do the care for less money, you get to keep it; do it for more money, you lose it. And I believe the acute health care hospitals and physicians reacted to that in a very positive way, much better than the Feds ever expected. And what happened is that most providers who reacted to the DRGs made lots of money. They held down the increase in costs for the first time in a long time and they still made lots of money. There's a lot of profit in the system.

Art: Weren't there negative reactions? Take the small town hospital...

Jon: Sure... because what happened was that the CT Scan or the CCU that the small hospital put in had a small volume of patients. The hospital was getting paid its cost before DRGs went in. What the DRGs did was make it very difficult on the small provider, because the plan was volume-driven to a great extent. You get paid a buck for each procedure you do, but if you only do a few you can't make it. If you do a million, you make a lot of money.

Jerry: So, simplistically, the cost before DRGs of a CT Scan in a big city may have been $500, in a small town it may have been $2000.

Jon: Sure. It didn't make any difference under the old cost reimbursement what you charged. The situation was the pure opposite of what's happening now even though it doesn't make any difference what you charge now, either. In the early years you got paid your cost. If the procedure was $500, but your cost was $1000, you got $1000. Later on you got cost or charges, whatever was less. Today it doesn't make any difference what your charges are; the Feds are going to pay what they decide they are going to pay you.

Jerry: And of course, insurance companies quickly followed the government's lead, didn't they?

Jon: Not quickly. It's surprising how long it took. It took most insurance companies, at least in this part of the country, almost 15 years to follow that lead.

Art: In your judgment then, the DRGs were a successful move?

Jon: Very successful.

Art: To hold costs down?

Jon: To hold costs down and to transfer some of the risk from the Feds to the provider. But the federal government hasn't been able to stabilize volume. There are more and more people over 65. And that's the piece of the equation that the government has not been able, under the DRGs, to control. Now, with capitation, insurers can control volume to a greater extent, but not totally.

Jerry: How often, as an administrator, did you encounter families or patients angry about the DRGs? Certainly there are stories of patients being pushed out of the hospital before they thought they were ready.

Jon: Remember the Kennedys on TV prior to July of 1966, telling people that health care was their right? That's the word they used. "Your folks have a right to go to the hospital and a right to stay in the hospital." And as you remember, people went to the hospital for things that now seem pretty mundane, such as annual physicals. Or a reason like "We are going out of town and no one's home to take care of Grandma." Those reasons were very typical. Later in the 1960s the federal government tried to reduce its cost by instituting "utilization review" — that was a new term. Grandma could not come into the hospital just because you were going out of town or you could not have a physical that could be done on an outpatient basis. And patients learned they could no longer recuperate in hospitals as long as they wished. I can remember at least one time, because I had to sign a letter, telling someone, "You've got two choices: stay and pay for it yourself, or go to the nursing home and have it paid for by Medicare." In that case, Grandma died the same afternoon she transferred to the nursing home. Well, obviously, it was not a very popular or a good decision. And if we knew Grandma was going to die, we wouldn't have transferred her. But, Grandma could have lived 30 more days, too.

So, in the early years there was a lot more anger, because there was much more feeling that health care was a right, more than a privilege. And as we've moved into the DRGs, I believe there is less feeling of right and more feeling of privilege than when we started off in the Medicare Program.

Ron: The sense that I get from what you've been saying is that Medicare and Medicaid did a lot of good in some respects and not so much good in other respects.

Jon: I think they have done a lot of good. If anybody says that those programs have been bad, it's not true. They have been good programs. At times they have been administered problematically. But on the whole, since 1965-66, I'd have to give them good marks, both from the standpoint of the people that have been cared for and from standpoint of the providers. Very few providers have been hurt. Most of them made a lot of money and provided good care.

You hear—and the Feds would like to make you believe—that there's significant fraud and abuse. Yes, there is some fraud and abuse, but the regulations share some blame. When Medicare started in 1965-66 the regulations were hardly any bigger than this book. They would now fill shelves—and written in such a way that the most ethical, God-fearing person will make a mistake. There isn't a provider in this country who hasn't, under the strictest sense of the regulations, committed fraud. And that's the bad part of what we have allowed the bureaucrats and the politicians to do to us in the health care field.

Ron: It's essentially bureaucracy and bureaucratic rules and regulations that cause the problems, you think?

Jon: Well, first of all, they call medicine the practice of medicine, not the science of medicine. To the pencil-pushers of the world, the accounting guys, everything's black or white and falls either to the right or the left. In health care, it does not. People are all different. That's why they call it the practice of medicine and continue to call it the practice of medicine. It just doesn't fall so neatly into black and white in dealing with people. It's easy to second-guess and look through the retrospective scope, but when you're down on the firing line on Christmas Eve, trying to make a decision to admit or not admit, or deciding to do an invasive procedure or not, it's pretty tough. And the rules continue to change. If there's been a bad part of the Medicare Program or the Medicaid Program at present, that's it.

Ron: It seems what you're saying is that there's a tension between what the providers think should be done for patients and how the bureaucrats want to control costs with rules and regulations. Would you say that that's a fair estimation of what you're saying?

Jon: I think the rules and regulations were set up to take the heat off the politicians. Every time that the cost of health care becomes problematic for the budget—most recently, in the last 6-7 years—the politicians can point to it and say, "There's fraud, there's abuse." We've all made mistakes, but they've been, for the vast majority, really honest mistakes.

Ron: Do you think it would be possible to design a health care system that could get away from the bureaucratic aspects, the rules and regulations, and still do the good things that have been done in the past?

Jon: Sure. The world is moving in that direction right now, under a capitated system.

Art: Say more about what a capitated system is.

Jon: As an example, under a capitated system, a health care organization might have responsibility for the care of all of the inmates in the state of South Dakota. The system gets paid a given number of dollars per inmate per month. And for that, it provides outpatient

care, inpatient care, dental care, mental health care, and pharmaceuticals, both on an inpatient and an outpatient basis. The organization hires all of the employees and contracts with all of the physicians. Say there are 100 prisoners and the fee is $100 a month —
$10,000 a month. If the system spends only $5,000, it keeps $5,000.
That's a step forward in putting the risk upon the provider.

The federal government would like to use capitation for
Medicare, too. But now, as a country, we have a real problem with
65 as a retirement age. That doesn't make any sense at all. The
fastest growing group of people in this country are the centenari-
ans. While the chart used to taper off at the top, a nice Christmas
tree distribution, now it goes straight up. And the older you get, the
more health care you use. All of us come to the end at some time.

Art: You say it's a crisis?

Jon: No, we'll never let it be a crisis. Crisis would mean people
wouldn't get care and people wouldn't get paid.

Art: It seems as though there are enough signals in this country
that people aren't getting care or that the cost is going out of sight.
The percentage of the Gross National Product spent on health care
is going up.

Jon: And it can't continue to go up. But the point that you're
making is right on. The concern is that we're moving on 14.5% of
the GNP that goes for health care. We'll go bust at some point in
time. If health care was it's own country, it would be the fourth
largest country in the world. You can spend only so much before
you start taking it away from basics like education and transporta-
tion. And the other problem is there are fewer and fewer people at
the pre-65 level funding care for the elderly. When it moves to a rate
of one and one, there may be some generational wars.

Jerry: The Canadian system is frequently held up as an example.
What's wrong with a system like that in this country?

Jon: We will always struggle in this country with our ethics. If
you come to a major hospital in the U.S. on Christmas Eve or the
Fourth of July and you have a coronary, you'll be in the cath lab
within 20-30 minutes, or you'll have a whole surgical suite as soon
as you need it. It doesn't happen any place else in this world, except
for kings and princesses. And it happens for almost everybody in
this country. But that costs money, real money.

Art: What's managed care?

Jon: The term managed care means many things to many different people. To me in its strictest sense it means that you and your

physician have lost the right to make many of the decisions about the type and quantity of health care you can have. Your choice of physician will be limited to only those physicians who are in the health plans panel, unless you want to pay extra — if in fact they will give you this choice. Your physician has to ask permission to admit you to the hospital and get further permission if he wants you to stay an extra day. He has to ask permission to order certain expensive tests or treatments on either an in- or out-patient basis. He can send you only to certain specialists or use specific pharmacies for your prescription.

The insurance company is working very hard to manage, not your care, but the cost of that care.

There are those who would greatly increase this definition to include how the caregivers are organized and how care is paid for.

Art: I've heard two thrusts from you about the way forward. One has to do with the elderly, and possibly changing Medicare. The other is about the right kind of integration and efficiency.

Jon: Well, for the first part, I think everybody's going to pay more. The system is on a course toward going broke. In addition, by the year 2000 it's crazy strategically to pick age 65 as the age of eligibility for Medicare. When did Bismarck pick it, 1880? The world's become a very different place, and strategically you've got to say that using age 65 doesn't make any sense. Politically, that's going to go over like a rock.

Jon: I believe there is still significant fat in the health care system in providing care. Since 1983 we've taken out significant amounts of that. At some point — and I have seen that happen — you cross the line and people get hurt. So there's going to have to be a discussion about right and privilege. Society needs to ask hard questions. They will have to ask if Grandma at 98 gets a new hip? Because doctors can do it. It's not their fault that its $12,000 for a new hip. Society has to make the judgment. Do 98-year-olds get new hips? It's the red Ford or the red Porsche type of care.

Art: It strikes me that the line could be crossed in two ways: the health care community cutting too much, and the patients asking for more than they ought to get.

Jon: Absolutely. No doubt about it. And that's the piece that the politicians can't handle. That's one of the reasons they want to put responsibility on providers' backs.

Jerry: So partly what you're saying is that we need somehow to get more common sense in terms of what's feasible and reasonable and what isn't.

Jon: That's true. It's the issue of the red Ford and the red Porsche. I mean, if everybody could drive a red Porsche, the parking lot would be full of them out there. Most can't afford that; they drive red Fords. But, when somebody else is paying for it, then we all want the red Porsche.

Art: When you think of all we talked about today, what would be one or two points that you would most want these college students to go away with? These are kids who are nurses and biology majors and general students, and they are going out in the world. What are they most likely to carry away into the world from our conversation?

Jon: We don't live in a perfect world. It's changing significantly. But young people can make a difference. Ideals are okay, but students need to work with realism too. What you're teaching is a process that students can use to figure that out. The answers they come up with often are neither good or bad nor right or wrong.

Art: So maybe if we teach these students to be more informed, they'll be better able to be problem-solvers about health care, as providers and as consumers.

Jon: And as leaders.

Should Doctors Cut Costs at the Bedside?
Patients, Not Costs, Come First
Allen R. Dyer

Though containing medical costs has been a recurring theme for the past decade, only recently have we begun to speak directly about the possibility of rationing. Attention is now being directed to the role physicians should play at the patient's bedside. Consider the following cases:

● A physician who is caring for a young child with liver failure feels that a liver transplant, which costs $100,000, might save her life. Since her parents cannot afford that amount and their insurance will not cover the costs, should the physician even bring up the possibility of a liver transplant?

● An automobile crashes into a motorcyclist one block from a for-profit hospital. The unconscious motorcyclist is rushed to the emergency room where a neurosurgeon diagnoses an epidural hematoma that requires immediate surgery. But a hospital administrator is unable to determine whether the patient has health insurance and wants to transfer him to a public hospital on the opposite side of town. Should the physician agree to the request for a transfer?

● Dr. Brown is caring for Mr. White, a seventy-five-year-old man with terminal cancer. He is mentally alert, but depressed, and says he wants to die "with dignity." When he develops renal failure, Dr. Brown considers whether to offer renal dialysis, which Medicare will cover. She is aware that dialysis is costing the national treasury a great deal and will only temporarily benefit Mr. White. Should she provide every treatment that could benefit him? Or would she be justified in withholding a potentially beneficial but costly treatment for an elderly patient with a terminal illness?

● Mr. Smith, who has suffered two heart attacks, is in the emergency room with chest pain for the second time this month. Dr. Green is aware that Mr. Smith has become a "cardiac neurotic." With another trip to the hospital, Dr. Green feels he can reassure Mr. Smith and probably avoid admitting him. Should he arrange for Mr.

From *Hastings Center Report*, v. 16, No. 1, February 1986. Used by permission.

Smith to be admitted overnight so he can review his EKG and
enzymes in the morning?

● The same Mr. Smith has been hospitalized for eighteen days
with a third heart attack. This is the last day for which Medicaid
will pay for this diagnosis under DRGs, but Dr. Green is not comfortable sending him home at this point. Mr. Smith has hinted at
mild substernal pain. Should Dr. Green send the patient home? Or
to a psychiatrist? Or keep him for further observation?

● A psychiatrist is asked to consult with a man who suffered a
head injury a year ago in an industrial accident when a machine he
was fixing fell on his head. His neurologist says there is nothing
wrong with him physically, but he complains of headaches, says he
feels humiliated, and has become depressed. The psychiatrist
agrees to treat him for his depression, but Workman's
Compensation says it will pay only for physical treatment. The
patient's insurance company will not pay because his complaints
resulted from an industrial accident. Should the psychiatrist offer
him short-term treatment, rather than long-term therapy, which he
feels might be more beneficial?

In each of these cases cost is factored into medical decision making in a way that potentially complicates the care the physician ren-
ders. In situations like these the physician has the opportunity to
serve the common good of reducing health care costs by limiting
the care an individual patient receives. Physicians are logical agents
of rationing because they appear to have direct control over health
care dollars.

Economic and Social Distortions

However, even at the bedside the options are limited by social
and economic policies already in place which can lead to ethically
inconsistent decisions. For example, organ transplants and artificial
organ implants, still relatively few in number, may be funded by
research rather than insurance programs (as has often been the case
with live transplants), by community fund raising programs or
public appeals. Renal dialysis, on the other hand, is generally available to all who may need it under Medicare/Medicaid funding in
part because the issue of federal funding was politicized in the
1960s and there seemed to be no humane way of saying "no." The
young child might get her liver transplant only if her parents know
how to manage the system, while Mr. White might receive renal

dialysis because it would be difficult to deny it to him under the law although the benefit would be limited and temporary. Similarly, the neurosurgeon would probably render emergency care to the injured motorcyclist, but before long the town's ambulance drivers would start sorting out which hospitals will provide emergency care to their uninsured patients. In the case of Mr. Smith, although doctors have some discretion under Diagnosis Related Groups, that system provides direct incentive to limit costs to particular patients.

If physicians have limited choices at the bedside, they still wield considerable influence. In our haste to make sure health costs don't outstrip our ability to pay them, have we gone too far? Should the physician be society's agent in reducing health costs? Should rationing decisions be made by doctors at the bedside?

My answer is an emphatic "No." The physician's primary responsibility is to the patient. Since Hippocratic times a central tenet of the medical ethic has been the responsibility of the physician for the patient in a relationship of trust. To ask conscientious physicians to bear the responsibility for lowering the cost of medical care is to create a conflict of interest that threatens to alter the nature of the doctor-patient relationship and the nature of the medical profession itself.

Doctors as "Providers"

Whereas doctors were once accountable solely to their patients in a private, confidential relationship, they are now often spoken of as "providers," and patients as "consumers"of a commodity, in which third-party payers may have a legitimate interest. There are increasing pressures for doctors to answer not only to the patient but also to "society" as payer for costs incurred. The cost-consciousness movement of the past decade has rightly encouraged physicians to eliminate waste and redundancy in the expectation that costs can be brought into line without compromising the quality of care each patient receives. The possibility of rationing only becomes alarming when the possibility of compromising quality is introduced either through limiting services (by focusing on population — rather than individuals — as HMOs and DRGs do) or by introducing new technologies that may not be available to all (such as organ transplants or artificial organs).

Unlike cost, quality allows no precise calculation. Competing values are at stake, which can only be resolved in particular cases by reference to ethical principles. Those principles may be subjected to explicit analysis or they may be left implicit.

The Unacknowledged Tragic Choice

Clearly, when the choices are agonizing, there are compelling psychological reasons for not reflecting explicitly on the underlying conflicts. In a book of the same name, Guido Calabresi and Philip P. Bobbitt speak of the decisions we now face as "tragic choices." They are tragic because, in Hegel's definition of tragedy, there is no clear-cut distinction between good and evil, but rather a conflict between competing goods or values.

In this case egalitarian ideals are ultimately incompatible with any belief in a capitalist sense of freedom. If the technology for replacing body parts exists, do we make this available to everyone? If we cannot afford to, do we deny it to those who can afford to purchase it on their own? If we decide to allocate health care on the basis of wealth, can we tolerate the social inequities that allow some to live while others similarly affected must die?

It is in the nature of tragic choices, Calabresi and Bobbitt point out, that a society tries to escape them or disguise what it is doing. Is the transformation of health care from a human service into a commodity an attempt to make the tragic choices more bearable? If so, we should seek to rescue ourselves from this slippery slope by explicitly reflecting on the ethical conflicts involved.

One way of attempting to escape tragic choices is to delegate to doctors the task of rationing health care at the bedside. This assumes a passive role for the patient, which is hardly acceptable in the 1980s. Another evasion is to attempt a strictly market approach to health care: people get what they choose. This is equally unacceptable because not all people have the foresight or the economic opportunity to protect themselves against potential medical catastrophes.

Involving the Patient

Ultimately there is no way of escaping the ethical dimensions of our tragic choices. A whole spectrum of decisions must be made daily not only by physicians, patients, and families at the bedside, but by all of us as we "choose" a lifestyle that promotes or does not promote a healthy existence: Do we smoke? Get adequate exercise? Attend to health risk factors? Choose a suitable kind of health insurance and health care? At another level our political choices reflect the kind of health care we expect and will receive.

The issue of cost is now an inescapable part of medical practice. As we look for a locus of decision making where this issue can be dealt with — physician or patient/consumer or the marketplace or the political process — we should not overlook one traditionally very important location of medical decision-making, the doctor-patient relationship. Traditionally it has been the better part of discretion for the physician and patient not to discuss money matters, but such discussions may now be appropriate.

In each of my examples, the issue of cost is primarily the patient's concern, not the physician's. However, (except for the comatose motorcyclist patient) in each instance the physician may offer some counsel to the patient in what should be a joint decision-making process. For example, Dr. Green might involve Mr. Smith in an ongoing discussion about how his particular health care needs might best be met. Dr. Brown might find out whether Mr. White wants to undergo dialysis, with all its potential discomforts, and proceed accordingly. In the transplant case, the doctor could discuss with the parents whether some local funding organization might underwrite the cost of their child's transplant. Such discussions, carried out over time and in a humane and unpressured manner, are not only good economics; they are the essence of good medicine.

Managed Care:
An Ethical Reflection
Edmund D. Pellegrino

The most urgently felt ethical conflict for the conscientious physician and nurse, secular or religious, is the erosion of the primacy of commitment to the welfare of the individual patient and person in a system of managed care. This primacy is compromised by the fact that health professionals in a managed care organization are employees. As such they receive compensation from the organization; de facto they owe allegiance to the organizational goals they are paid to pursue. These goals may or may not concur with the needs of their particular patients. These obligations to the organization can conflict with the duty of acting in the patient's best interests. This puts the physician inescapably in a position of double agency, which pits the patient's needs against those of the organization, the other patients in the same plan and the physician's own self-interest.

In a managed care system, emphasis shifts from the ethics of service to a particular patient to a population-based ethic. Physicians become responsible for taking into account the effect of their clinical decisions not just on the welfare of their patients but also on that of all the other patients enrolled in the system and even of society at large. This is to say nothing of the investors whose capital is at risk or of the physician's own legitimate self-interests.

Fee-for-service medicine, of course, also involves conflicts of interests and obligations. In the past, this conflict all too frequently resulted in unnecessary treatment. This is one of the reasons why managed care has been so avidly promoted by many. The major temptation in a fee-for-service system is that physicians earn more the more they do for their patients, even if the care is unnecessary. In managed care, the opposite is true: physicians are penalized if they do "too much" — that is, provide care not "covered" by the plan. Financial penalties or bonuses for productivity, cost savings or conservation of resources are deliberate manipulations of the physician's self-interest against the patient's. In a fee-for-service system physicians are the identifiable miscreants. In managed care they share the blame. They share their acts of injustice with the organi-

Excerpted from "The Good Samaritan in the Marketplace," in *The Changing Face of Health Care*, John F. Kilner, Robert D. Orr, and Judith Allen Shelly, eds. Eerdmans, 1998. Used by permission.

zation that legitimates their actions. The other miscreants are the managed care administrators, the board of directors, and the investors, all of whom are faceless and unknown to the patient.

Managed care that makes cost-containment or profit-taking as its end, at the expense of meeting legitimate needs of sick persons, threatens the most elementary notion of Christian ethics. It makes price, availability, accessibility and the quality of medical care a function of free-market determination or negotiation. It grants the doctor or the managed care organization a presumed proprietary right over medical knowledge. The justice of the business contract requires the physician or the organization to deliver nothing more than is owed by the conditions of the contract with the plan. If a patient at a young age opts unwisely for a cheaper plan with fewer or inappropriate benefits, that's just too bad.

Nor is it a concern of the managed care organization or the physician if patients do not have the wherewithal to become "players" in the market. No provision is made for those who have no insurance or inadequate insurance. Nor is there any solicitude for the many totally or partially illiterate members of American society who cannot understand an insurance plan, to say nothing of being able to choose one over another. Yet these people too become ill. They present themselves often as emergencies. No physician in good conscience can refuse to treat them even if no plan is willing to pay for the costs of their care.

Managed care makes the physician the "gatekeeper" whose duty it is to prevent patients from too easy access to specialists, hospitals or laboratories. When these restrictions result in denial of truly unnecessary care — that is, care that does not change the natural history of the disease in some effective way — they are morally justifiable, even mandatory. This is "managed care" in its best sense. Unfortunately, managed care as it is presently organized is just as likely to result in deprivation of needed care. It is "managed" not for patient benefit but for investor interests.

A Christian ethic of care focuses first on the sick person, the one in need, now presenting herself to the physician or nurse. The sick person is Christ himself seeking help. Some significant degree of effacement of self-interest is an inescapable obligation of physicians who see health care as a vocation and a form of ministry. For Christians the practice of medicine is an obligation of the stewardship the physician exercises over medical knowledge.

As Ecclesiasticus tells us: "Healing itself comes from God the Most High like a gift received from a King. . . . He has also given some people knowledge so that they may draw credit from his mighty works." In the Christian view, medical knowledge is knowledge held in trust. It is knowledge God has built into nature which humans may exploit to help and to heal one another. To be sure, physicians are entitled and indeed obliged to provide for themselves and their families. But this cannot be the primary motivation for a Christian apostolate of healing.

As noted above, the most serious conflict of loyalties occurs in those arrangements in which the physicians or group of physicians become the insurers as well as the gatekeepers by assuming all of the financial risks but also all of the profits. In this arrangement patients lose their most important advocates in the system. Physicians are simultaneously judge and jury. They are no longer simply employees of the managed care organization. They are the organization. Patients who are unjustly treated no longer have an advocate since their physician is now identified with the system that denied their need for care in the first place.

Physicians are taking a variety of steps to respond to the shift of authority to managed care organizations and of risk away from these organizations. Physicians troubled by this power shift understandably might want to regain some of that power. But the ways this is accomplished must be scrutinized from the perspective of Christian ethics. Two of these responses deserve attention: unionization and so-called equity HMOs.

Unionization of physicians is not morally illicit per se if it is used as a device for collective bargaining. Since physicians are employees in the managed care world, they should not be denied the rights accorded other workers in any system of Christian social justice. Obviously, the strike mechanism could not be justified because this would entail compromise of patient welfare for the benefits of physicians. Even a strike to gain improvement in care violates the primary orientation of medical ethics to patient welfare. More subtle and more dangerous are the temptations to abuse of power inherent in any mechanism devised solely to gain more power. Finally, the union metaphor has connotations antithetical to the effacement of self-interest peculiar to the professional life.

Equity HMOs are equally attractive and even more susceptible to abuse and defection from the physician's obligation of advocacy. In equity HMOs, physicians own shares in the organization and assume the risks themselves in return for dividends and power over policies. In doing so, however; there is no net increment of control over individual clinical decisions. Indeed, the collective impetus to avoid or share risks and to make a profit are just as dangerous to patient welfare as they are in a non-physician-owned HMO. They operate under the same aegis of competition and survival in the marketplace.

The major source of power for physicians is moral power — the sense of communal responsibility as a profession for the welfare of those who seek their help. To compromise this power or trade it for political power is to make a Faustian compact, with its inevitable loss of soul. The same is true of "gaming" the system by deceptive representation of diagnoses or severity, even if it might serve the patient's interests. Some physicians have resorted to "paper strikes" — refusing to fill out forms as a form of protest. But if such a tempting move results in delays in patient care, refusal of claims, or patient harassment, they cannot be justified.

The fidelity of Christian physicians to a Christian ethic of healing does not excuse them from a responsibility for cost-containment. Rather, it is an obligation of that ethic to use the patient's and society's resources wisely and well. When two treatments are equally effective, the less costly may be chosen. Treatment that is not indicated by the best medical practice, overtreatment at the end of life, and treatment that is futile are infractions of medical ethics, secular and Christian. Only those treatments should be used that are effective in changing the natural history of the disease to the benefit of the patient and in which the burdens are proportionate to the benefits. Overtreatment is not in the patient's best interests. Overtreatment can be harmful since it may produce burdens, side effects, and costs without proportional benefits. Rational effective medicine is the most significant contribution physicians can make to cost-containment. Good medicine de facto eliminates unnecessary care and for the right reasons — not because it is expensive but because it is harmful to the patient.

When physicians are bonded in a covenantal trust relationship with a patient, they cannot be double agents. They must act in the interests of the patient. They cannot simultaneously be agents primarily of social good or fiscal parsimony. When these goals conflict, it is the good of the patient that must prevail. The current urging of physicians to abandon ethics of the person for ethics of the population is a violation of the covenant of healing, which requires the physician to act in the interests of the sick person. "Social ethics" practiced at the bedside places the needs of the unidentified persons whose risks are uncertain and somewhere in the future ahead of persons presenting themselves now in actual need. This is a disordered priority of obligations even in secular ethics. In Christian ethics, it is to yield the virtue of charity to the abstract demands of utilitarianism. It is as if the Good Samaritan were to pass by the stranger because there might be someone sicker at the next turn of the road.

When they are not in trust relationships with particular patients, Christian physicians can, and should, take steps to advance the health of the community using the most economical way consistent with Christian ethics. After the practice of effective, rational, evidence-based medicine, the physician can, indeed is obliged to, contribute to the optimal use of societal resources. This can be done in a variety of ways consistent with the ordering principles of Christian charity.

First, the Christian physician must encourage and support empirical studies to ascertain the relative effectiveness and benefits of treatments. These studies can legitimately focus on cost-effectiveness ratios. This is a rational way to avoid unnecessary treatment. It is the indispensable guide to scientific, evidence-based medicine to which the Christian physician, like every other conscientious physician, owes allegiance.

Christian physicians thus have a duty to act as technical experts providing reliable and objective data to their colleagues and to policy-makers who must decide which treatments to support and which not. The temptation to advance one's own specialty or treatment interest must be resisted. The antidote is research carried out objectively, rigorously and cooperatively in properly designed clinical tests.

A second obligation is to take leadership in advocating reforms to provide for the health care needs of the poor, the uninsured, the chronically ill, the aged, and the handicapped — all those whom managed care plans find unwelcome or unacceptable enrollees. These are the heavy users of medical care. They are most vulnerable in a market economy that favors young, healthy enrollees who will pay their premiums on time and not need the services of the system.

A third obligation is to educate one's own patients to the dangers — physical and fiscal — of unnecessary treatment. We must acknowledge that pressures for useless, dubious or futile measures often arise from patients and their families. In addition, education in preventive medicine is crucial to avoid catastrophic illness and the high costs of "rescue" from preventable crises. Education in advance directives, anticipating and preparing for end-of-life decisions, and accepting one's finitude are necessary correlates. Christians particularly have an obligation to identify and draw on spiritual resources to blunt the illusion of immortality that high-technology medicine can unfortunately stimulate even when the illness has become untreatable.

A fourth obligation is to avoid entering contracts with for-profit organizations, with those that offer financial rewards, bonuses or stock, or with those that require a gag rule or have other barriers to disclosure. A neglected sector of the moral life of today's physician is the sector in which one ought to say no. The idea that there are things which should never be done is becoming foreign territory to many contemporary bioethicists. If Hitler's Nazi physicians had said No!, it is highly unlikely that Auschwitz, its many counterparts, and the Holocaust itself would have been possible. There may well be times in this era of commercialized medicine when all physicians and nurses, especially those who are committed Christians, will have the responsibility of collective refusal to serve the plan.

Christian physicians must be prepared to define those ethical abuses of the relationship beyond which the erosion of the trust relationship is so clear that the individual and the profession must say no. Knowing when to refuse is essential. Physicians cannot escape moral complicity for harm to their patients resulting from their cooperation in a morally defective plan. After all, they write the orders; they can cooperate or protest. The final stewardship is theirs.

The burden of conscience placed on the individual physician who wishes to practice in conformity with Christian ethics within managed care is very great. Simple self-righteous condemnation of others is hypocrisy. Yet how far one may cooperate with a morally dubious system is a matter of conscience. We cannot expect individual physicians to bear the whole burden. They each must balance their other responsibilities to family, community and religion. The moral obligation not to cooperate with any plan that is injurious to patients is a communal and collective responsibility of the entire profession. The profession must take leadership, support its members and seek alliances with nurses and other health professionals as well as the public in advocating reform.

Helping, healing, caring and curing were so much a part of the life of Jesus that no Christians can absolve themselves of responsibility for the health care system their nation adopts. All Christians share responsibility for working toward a societal ethic of care that is imbued with the spirit of Christ's love for the sick. Without the support of the entire Christian community, it will be ever more difficult for Christian health professionals to resist the injustices of commercialization.

In the end, the kind of health care we tolerate reflects the kind of society we are or want to be. The bedside reflects back to all of us where our treasure lies. While physicians, nurses and administrators have the immediate responsibility, they can only operate within the parameters society sets for them. If our system of "care" denies care, none of us can deny complicity. If the health care system Christians tolerate is itself a violation of Christian teaching on care of the sick, Christians cannot avoid complicity.

Managed care and its commercialization are part of the larger question of a national health care system replete with ethical incongruities. On the one hand, American medicine is, for those who can afford it, the most proficient care available; the U.S. economy at the moment is better than it has been for a very long time; U.S. institutions and health care personnel are in sufficient supply. On the other hand, these resources are denied to the poor and the underinsured, and resources are increasingly more difficult for the middle class to get without harassment. In the face of plenty, U.S. medicine is frantically cutting costs and downsizing in imitation of American business and the ideology of markets and profits. How does all of this measure against the Christian ethic of concern for the sick and the poor?

Christians of all denominations must ask themselves some very serious questions — especially those Christians who have accommodated to managed care as "inevitable" or excused themselves by blaming "the system," or profiting periodically by cost-shaving. This is not the place to outline how Christians, joined to others of good will and social conscience, can mobilize to fashion a just and humane health care apparatus. Tough resource allocation decisions may be necessary, but before accepting rationing as inevitable there are questions those of us living in the U.S. must ask ourselves:

Are we practicing rational, effective medicine that reduces unnecessary care to a minimum? Have we counted the administrative costs of our complicated, multi-insurer system? What are the non-dollar costs in harassment, in delays of care, in grievance and appeal procedures, in confusion and misleading advertisements? Have we exhausted all measures short of rationing? Have we examined our enormous discretionary expenditures on amusement, spectator sports, *etc*? Have we considered the obligation of Christians to make sacrifices of some of their excess to provide for the needs of the less fortunate? Have all Christians, and especially Roman Catholics who have the largest system of health care institutions in the U.S., asked how they can cooperate and merge their resources to provide care that is not profit-oriented but, rather, based on Christian ethical principles?

Managed care per se is not inherently antithetical to Christian ethics of care. Indeed, properly organized around providing better quality and a more equitable distribution of care, it is a moral obligation. However, as it is operated today, as a commercial enterprise, market-driven and insensitive to the needs of the sick, managed care diverges daily from the gospel conception of charitable justice. For the Christian the response is not accommodation to the so-called "new" medical ethics. What is needed is a bold reassertion of the Christian meaning of healing and the vocation — not the occupation of health professionals. Accommodation to the ideology of a market-driven commercialized health care system can only end in capitulation, danger to the patient, and a repudiation of the Christian ethic of healing and caring for the sick.

The Ethical Foundations
of Health Care Reform

William F. May

Our health care system contains much of which we should be proud and much that we should conserve. It has enlisted the devotion of millions of professionals, created splendid hospitals, clinics and research institutions, and dazzled the world with its technical achievements. And it has allowed for some choice in doctors. Any reform of the system must preserve its virtues.

Yet our health care system is seriously flawed. It fails to reach many of us: at any given time, it excludes over one-seventh of the population (about 40 million people) from health care insurance; it leaves another one-seventh underinsured. The consequences for individuals and families are devastating. When we exclude people from health care they suffer a triple deprivation — the misery of illness, the desperation of little or no treatment, and the cruel proof that they do not really belong to the community. We make them strangers in their own land.

When individuals lack health care, the promise of our common life together is also diminished. In relieving private distress, the nation enables its people to contribute more fully to its public life. The nation thereby serves its own public flourishing.

Our system also does not offer enough primary, preventive, home and long-term care, and it woefully neglects mental health coverage. We tend to be acute-care gluttons and preventive-care anemics.

Reflecting this lopsided emphasis, the system oversupplies us with specialists (some 70 percent of our doctors are specialists, compared with only 30 to 50 percent in comparable industrial countries) and undersupplies us with generalists whom we need for effective preventive, rehabilitative and long-term care.

The system pays for procedures performed rather than good outcomes achieved, and it exposes those who cannot pay to dramatically lower success rates for a given procedure. It often overtreats; yet insurance sometimes disappears when most needed. It exposes to financial ruin the person who has lost his or her job. It locks others into jobs they do not want because of pre-existing medical conditions, and it often establishes lifetime limits on care.

The system burdens health care practitioners and institutions with too many regulations and forms. A financial officer at one hospital reports that her staff has to handle some 3,200 different types of accounts receivable. The head of the major city hospital in Dallas says he needs 300 people to handle what, at a comparable hospital under the Canadian system, can be dispatched by three people.

Our system also costs more to operate than any other health care system in the world; no other country exceeds 10 percent of its GNP in health care costs, yet we are above 14 percent and rising further out of control. The system now consumes one-seventh of everything that we make or do. Even this figure does not fully measure the cost. The "fringe benefit" of health care is anything but a fringe cost of producing cars, computers, refrigerators and, for that matter, education. In some of our industries, health care is the second largest cost after wages and salaries. This fact reduces the competitiveness of American businesses: Why should companies build cars in Detroit if their health care costs per worker are $500 to $750 less across the bridge in Windsor, Canada? Some commentators have argued that we have recently slowed down the increasing costs of medical care. But under three presidents we have undergone temporary slowdowns in costs only to see them speed up again. For our own sake and the sake of our children, we must be better stewards of our nation's resources.

Further, our payment system is unfair. Businesses, insurance companies, hospitals, the government and patients engage furiously in cost shifting as they fob off on others their expenses. Hospitals jack up their prices to the insured to cover their costs in caring for indigent patients. Some doctors try to skim off the well-insured patients, while avoiding others. Insurance companies pick healthy customers to avoid making payouts to the sick. Companies shift to part-time, temporary or younger employees to reduce fringe-benefit costs. The government's savings on Medicare and Medicaid patients sometimes comes at the expense of prices paid by insured patients. Some people are forced to stay on welfare because the low-paying jobs in the service industries do not provide the coverage they receive under Medicaid. All this artful dodging eventually dumps costs on workers and taxpayers, either through lower salary raises, higher taxes or higher insurance payments.

A major reform of our health care system will rank as the most comprehensive piece of social legislation since the establishment of the social security system. We cannot engage in so grand an under-

taking without being clear about its moral foundations. In my judgment, those foundations are three: 1) health care is a fundamental
good; 2) health care is not the only fundamental good; and 3) health
care is a public good.

To say that health care is a fundamental good means that health
care is one of the necessities of life. It is not an optional commodity;
like a Walkman, a tie or a scarf. Mothers instinctively affirm this
truth when they concentrate their hopes on just this: the birth of a
healthy baby — ten fingers, ten toes, a good heart, robust lungs.
Why this single, humble, anxious wish? The mother prizes her
baby's health because of the promise it holds for the child's life and
flourishing. Healthy children, and therefore health care, are part of
a nation's covenant with its future.

Because health care is a fundamental good, the American system
must honor and reflect the following five moral principles.

The system must offer universal access. Health benefits should reach
all of us without financial or other barriers. Citizens should not fear
that part-time or temporary employment, or a change or loss of a
job, will block health care coverage. No one should lose access to
health insurance due to pre-existing conditions, or to age, race or
genetic background. Barriers to access arising from linguistic and
cultural differences, geographical distance, and disability must also
come down.

Why should Americans especially insist that a basic good, such
as health care, ought to reach all citizens? Our three major religious
traditions — Protestant, Catholic, and Jewish — are communitarian. They have all insisted that no one should be left out in the cold
when it comes to the basics in life. Some individualists may counter
that our revolutionary emphasis on individual liberty made a break
with this communitarian heritage. This view of our past, however,
overlooks the first words we spoke as a nation: "We the people."
The Preamble to the Constitution does not proclaim, "We the fac-
tions of the United States" or "We the interest groups of the United
States" or "We the individuals of the United States," but "We the
people." That declaration was tested and affirmed through the bitter ordeal of the Civil War. We could not survive, half slave, half
free. Neither can we stand divided between the sick and the well,
the protected and the uninsured. Our flourishing as a people rests
upon our ability to create a health care system that binds us together as a nation. The principle of universal access goes to the soul of

reform. Currently, we are the only industrial nation, other than South Africa, that fails to offer universal access.

The system must be comprehensive. Benefits must meet the full range of health care needs. We should offer primary, preventive and some long-term care as well as acute care; home, as well as hospital care; treatment for mental as well as physical illness. An observer once saw through our lopsided allocations in the U.S. when he wrote, "Our system's philosophy might be condensed in the motto, 'Millions for [acute] care and not one cent for prevention!'" Those lines were written in 1886. When we attend too little to primary, preventive and mental health care, the cost of acute care increases: we mistarget funds, and we fail to empower people to take responsibility for their own health.

When we do not offer comprehensive coverage, we also fail to offer universal coverage. We discriminate against whole classes of the afflicted, such as the mentally ill or those in need of long term care. We would find it strange to treat renal disease but not heart attack victims. But currently many plans lavish care on the physically ill but discriminate against the mentally ill. A scheme that aspires to universal coverage must offer a comprehensive package.

The system must be fair in that it does not create a two-nation system, dividing the nation over this fundamental good, and fair in that the costs and burdens of meeting health care needs are spread across the entire community. Some might respond: don't the uninsured receive the benefit of care through the emergency room? Unfortunately, their care does not match that of the insured. Their mortality rate for a given procedure is 1.8 times higher than the rate for the insured. The astronomical costs of some acute and long-term services can impoverish the sick and the disabled and their families, and the prospect of these costs imperils the security of those of us who have not yet been stricken.

We would find it absurd to limit the protection of defense — another fundamental good — only to those who could afford a private army. We ought not limit access to medical care only to those who can hire a platoon of doctors. We also need a system that fairly shares the cost of health care. We must secure contributions from all and eliminate the widespread patterns of cost shifting and free loading. A fair sharing of benefits and burdens draws the community together and ties the generations to one another.

The system must be of high quality: Health care is too important a good not to be good. Fostering good quality requires providing health care professionals with an environment that encourages their best work, protects the integrity of professional judgment, delivers effective treatments and weeds out unethical and incompetent practitioners. It also means providing patients with sufficient information about the outcomes achieved by different plans to help them make informed, rational choices.

Ordinarily, consumers in the marketplace can enforce quality through their ability to compare products knowledgeably. But patients today do not have the information to make those judgments about doctors, hospitals and health care plans — and it is difficult to acquire this knowledge in the midst of a medical crisis.

Health care is also too important a good not to get better. Therefore, the system must also support research for improving the full range of health care services, including research on the outcomes of health care and more research directed to preventive, rehabilitative and terminal care. Without the assurance of quality in the basic health care package, the well-to-do will buy up and out, returning the country to a two-nation system.

The system must be responsive to choice. Health care is too fundamental a good, affecting each of us too intimately and fatefully, not to give us some measure of freedom to choose our doctors, the treatments we receive and the health care plans in which we receive them. Too many people lack choice altogether or enjoy choice on only one of these matters. Honoring choice in the health care system not only respects liberty; it also engages the patient in the activity of preventive, acute, rehabilitative and long-term care.

While health care is a fundamental good, it is not the only fundamental good. We must also defend the nation, provide housing and educate our children. Thus we need a system that allocates wisely and manages efficiently so as to accommodate other basic goods.

To enable us to allocate wisely, the health care system must let us compare and balance what we spend on health care against other national priorities and evaluate and choose among diverse health services. In the past, the structure and funding of the health care system has not given us enough information about costs to make clear choices among these priorities. We need this information to put ourselves in a better position to meet all our social needs and also to decide more wisely among competing health care needs. Efficient management is a moral, not just an economic, imperative. Ethics is not one sphere and economics another. The British universities had it right when they linked the study of economics, politics and philosophy. Ethics, politics and economics are interconnected.

The health care system should also be simple to use, without bureaucratic roadblocks to the delivery of care. I have two daughters who are physicians, and they find it discouraging, to say the least, to talk to a person at the other end of an 800 line, someone who has power to approve or refuse a treatment, and be asked, "How do you spell manic depressive?" Senator Robert Dole criticized the Clinton plan for its complexity by showing an organizational chart of the plan on TV — he did not mention that the current system is so complex that one could not even bring it into view on a TV camera. Nevertheless, he had a point. Whatever the reform plan, it must offer simple access for patients and ease of management for doctors and other caregivers. The Clinton administration, sensitive to this issue, would locate responsibility for individual patient care in the provider organizations rather than in the National Health Council or the statewide purchasing alliances.

The new system will also need to reduce administrative costs. Today 1,500 insurance companies compete for our health care dollars, producing huge redundancies and complexities in administration and advertising costs. Moreover, these companies largely compete not in matters of price and quality, but in the art of designing benefits packages so as to avoid claims from people when they fall sick.

Efficiency must be defined with a wise heart, not just a calculator. Providers should not be bound by medical cookbooks but should be encouraged to adopt wise treatment guidelines. Inevitably, controlling costs requires distinctions between needs and wants, effectiveness and futility, and setting priorities among health needs. Efficiency in the service of universal access is a virtue, not a limit. It can offer choices and opportunities for health care for all people, instead of denying choice to millions. We must allocate our resources wisely so that we can achieve the goals of our health care system and address our other national needs.

Health care is a public good, and a good system must help increase our sense of responsibility, both as providers and as consumers. A huge social investment has helped to educate health care professionals and sustain the good which they offer. Federal outlays for research and medical education, patients who offer their bodies to let young residents practice, community chest drives, foundation gifts, corporate grants, municipal taxes, bonds floated to build hospitals, all these aspects of health care confound the notion that health care is exclusively a private skill or a commodity up for grabs to the highest bidder. A society that carefully reckons with the social derivation of health care cannot plausibly reduce the distressed patient merely to a profit opportunity or an object of occasional charity.

The indebtedness of professionals vastly exceeds the school loans or fellowships they have received. No man or woman can go through medical school and think of himself or herself as self-made, and indeed thousands of professionals want to give back, even as they have received. The health care system must foster ways in which practitioners can make good on their profession as a calling, not just a career. The system must protect the integrity of professional judgment, weed out the incompetent or unethical practitioner, and encourage excellence.

The success of a health care system also depends upon an increased sense of responsibility on the part of the recipients of health care. We cannot solve our problems through a social mechanism alone. The success or failure of a system depends upon the "habits of the heart" of a citizenry. Patients must be active partners in their health care. Preventing a heart attack, recovering from a spinal injury, coping with a stroke — these often require changes in the patients' habits. The system cannot gratify all wants or remove the mark of mortality from our frame. We need some self-control over our wants, some composure in the midst of illness, and courage in the face of dying. No system of itself can bring these virtues to us. We need to bring them to the system so that its benefits may sustain us more fully.

The ancient Romans tended to emphasize the benefits of citizenship; the Athenians emphasized its responsibilities. For its moral and economic success, our new system of health care will require both.

These three basic convictions about the good of health care and their derivative moral principles do not lie easily together. Tensions are sure to arise between paying for the fundamental good of health care and providing for other basic goods (and relatively trivial commodities). The goals of universal and comprehensive coverage, for example, will confront the hurdle of the start-up costs which major changes in either government or business invariably entail. Differences will also develop over the best mechanism and institutions by which to reach even agreed-upon goals. Inevitably, decisions about priorities will need to be made. Clinton signaled his judgment on one of them when in the course of his February speech on health care he declared that he would not sign a bill unless it offered universal coverage. But even on this issue differences exist as to how fast the country can or will move. (The administration hopes to offer universal access within four years of the passage of legislation.)

What are the political chances of forging a new health care system that addresses our needs? Are we willing to make significant changes? My tragic law of politics goes as follows: the perception of a problem and the willingness to solve it rarely join before the solution is beyond reach. We could have reformed the health care system much more easily when Harry Truman said we needed to do it in 1948 and when health care costs were 4.5 percent of GNP. The amount was large, but relatively marginal to our total GNP. Today, however, health care costs have risen to 14 percent of GNP and 11 million people have jobs in the industry, some of them ready to attack changes that might affect their interests. The huge growth of the health care industry makes it relatively difficult to reform it. Gridlocks in government usually reflect gridlocks in society at large.

I am not unrelievedly pessimistic, however. The president has at least managed to put the problem on the national agenda. Politics, as Max Weber once put it, is at best slow boring through hard wood. I hope the Clintons have some success in sustaining the support of those 60 percent of the voters who have said they would consider some raise in taxes in order to provide universal coverage. Political solutions are possible but difficult — a good deal more difficult than my fellow Texan, just-lift-up-the-hood-and-fix-it Ross Perot, is willing to admit.

To achieve major reform we cannot treat health care simply as a partisan or an interest-group issue. We will need to return to our foundations as a people. Our founders assumed that if a nation could create a common good, it should make that good common. We can now deliver the good of health care to all our people, and this good will help secure and enhance the life, liberty and welfare that is our nation's promise to its citizens. It is time to make that promise to each other.

Is such a covenant among us realistic, coming as it does so late in the day and with well-established interests already in the field? It will surely require a broad appeal to self-interest. But it will also need to appeal to what Lincoln called "the better angels of our nature," those angels that De Tocqueville must have discerned when he wrote that a "covenant exists... between all the citizens of a democracy when they all feel themselves subject to the same weakness and the same dangers; their interests as well as their compassion makes it a rule with them to lend one another assistance when required."

Parish Nursing:
The Church as Community
Mary Auterman

The following article was previously published in the South Dakota
Nurse *and has been updated to reflect changes that have occurred in
parish nursing since that time. The concept of parish nursing is consistent
with the issues discussed in this volume. Parish nursing focuses on promoting wholistic health in an atmosphere of caring. It has a strong emphasis in health promotion and disease prevention. Addressing the economic
issues of health/illness care also includes exploring new ways to promote
the health of the community.*

Parish nursing is a relatively new speciality within nursing.
Parish nursing began in the Chicago area in 1984 and has
spread to virtually all corners of the U.S., as well as to
Canada. Interest is growing in South Dakota with about 12-15
churches who have initiated parish nursing within the past few
years. Rev. Granger Westberg is credited as the founder of parish
nursing. His ideas grew out of his experiences as a hospital chap-
lain and as a professor of health and religion at the University of
Chicago. Prior to that be had served as a Lutheran pastor in the
Chicago area. He envisioned the church as an ideal place to promote health from a wholistic approach.

The church as a place of healing has historical roots. Healing was
an integral part of the ministry of Jesus while on earth. Jesus commissioned the Apostles to teach, to preach, and to heal. The early
church ministered to those who were physically and mentally ill as
well as those with spiritual needs. Healing was common throughout the early centuries of the church. Religious orders of men and
later women were established to care for the sick and the dying.
Florence Nightingale thought the nursing role included tending to
the person's spiritual as well as physical and emotional needs
(Striepe, 1993).

The parish nurse is a registered nurse who facilitates the wholistic health needs of the congregation. The parish nurse develops a
practice in response to the unique needs and priorities of the parish
and its members across the life span. The goal is to enhance the
well-being of the members through education, assessment, and

From *South Dakota Nurse*, December 1997, pp. 25-26. Used by permission.

intervention of the individual as a whole — mind, body, and spirit. There are four basic functions which the parish nurse is called upon to perform:

(1) **Health Educator** — Parish nurses assess the health needs of the congregation and plan, organize, and implement health education programs, and provide health education materials to individuals.

(2) **Health Counselor** — The parish nurse provides private sessions to individuals to help them in modifying life styles, adjusting to transitions in health and coping with chronic illness, and other health-related concerns.

(3) **Community Liaison** — Parish nurses link persons into the community resources needed to promote, maintain, or regain health. With shortened hospital stays individuals frequently have need for other community resources but may not be aware of that need until they are discharged. The parish nurse assesses their needs and makes referral to connect them with the appropriate services. For the elderly, in particular, identifying and connecting with the various agencies can be confusing and overwhelming. The parish nurse serves as an advocate for the individual.

(4) **Coordinator and Facilitator of Volunteers** — Not all of the individual's needs require the presence of the parish nurse; nor can the nurse respond to every need. Trained volunteers serve as an extension of the church community to assist in those needs. Examples of volunteer activities include visiting those confined to their homes or nursing homes, bringing food to the ill or grieving, or supporting a new mother in infant care. The parish nurse serves as the coordinator and facilitates the use of the volunteers (Westberg, 1992).

The word healing means wholeness or harmony — within oneself, with God, and with others. The parish nurse, by her/his presence, symbolizes the connection of mind/body/spirit and assists the church in its healing mission.

The preparation for parish nursing has varied greatly in the past. Preparation components include the ethical and legal aspects of parish nursing, the theological basis of healing, documentation, standards of practice for parish nursing, community resources, assessing the spiritual needs, program development, health counseling, and working with volunteers. Programs include other content specific to the region. The International Parish Nursing Resource Center is in the process of developing a standardized core curriculum for the preparation of nurses to function in the capacity of parish nurse. The American Nurses' Association has recognized parish nursing as a specialized practice of professional nursing. In June 1998, the ANA revised and published *The Scope and Standards of Parish Nursing Practice*, which had been developed by the Health Ministries Association.

Striepe, Jan. (1993). "Reclaiming the Church's Healing Role." *Journal of Christian Nursing*. Winter, pp. 4-7.

Westberg, Granger (1992). *The Parish Nurse*. International Parish Nurse Resource Center. Park Ridge, Ill.

Questions to Consider for Chapter Nine

1. By way of review - Part I, "Dimensions of Caring":
   a. In what respects is health important for carrying out your life story?
   b. What strategy (Hygeia or Asclepius or combination) is most important for carrying out your life story?
   c. What everyday experiences of life and death have reminded you of your responsibility to care for yourself and others?
   d. At what points in your life story have you particularly felt the call to courage?
2. By way of review - Part II, "Dilemmas of Caring":
   a. Review the dilemmas considered. Which of them particularly resonate with your experience? Explain.
   b. How would you encourage yourself or others to make caring choices when dilemmas are involved?
3. "How Health Care Services are Paid," by Mary Auterman:
   a. What public funding and insurance moneys are available to pay for health care services? Be able to identify the terms: Medicare, Medicaid, state and county assistance, fee for service, HMO, PPO, Medigap, long-term care insurance.
   b. Which are available to you at the present time?
4. "The Red Ford or the Red Porsche," by Jon Soderholm:
   a. What combination of education and experience does he bring to an understanding of the economics of caring?
   b. What are some of the reasons that he believes that our health care system is facing an economic crisis? What solutions does he consider?
   c. What is Soderholm's overall assessment of Medicare?
   d. Is health care a right or a privilege? What are the issues involved in the question? His answer? Yours?
5. "Patients, Not Costs, Come First," by Allen R. Dyer:
   a. Why should rationing decisions not be made by the doctor at the bedside?
   b. How does he think that the patient/physician relationship can be used in struggling with the issues of cost in medical practice?
6. "Managed Care: An ethical reflection," by Edmund Pellegrino:
   a. What perspective does he bring to this consideration?

   b. Compare the ethical conflicts faced by health care providers in managed care and fee-for-service medicine.
   c. What are the legitimate concerns of managed care? Why is he critical of managed care as practiced?
   d. What responsibility does a physician guided by a Christian ethic of healing have for cost containment?
   e. What principles can guide the Christian physician in working to improve the health care system?
7. "The Ethical Foundations of Health Care Reform," by William F. May:
   a. In what respects does he believe that our health care system is seriously flawed? This was written in the height of the last national debate about health care. Still true?
   b. Identify and evaluate the three foundations of a health care system that he develops.
8. "Parish Nursing: The Church as Community," by Mary Auterman:
   a. How can a church serve community health needs through the service of a parish nurse?
   b. Can you think of other ways in which community organizations (other than health care institutions as such) can serve the health needs of your community?

Chapter Ten:
How Then Shall We Live As Persons?
Arthur Olsen

"A whole spectrum of decisions must be made daily not only by physicians, patients, and families at the bedside, but by all of us as we 'choose' a lifestyle that promotes or does not promote a healthy existence: Do we smoke? Get adequate exercise? Attend to health risk factors? Choose a suitable kind of health insurance and health care? At another level our political choices reflect the kind of health care we expect and will receive." — Allen R. Dyer, "Patients, Not Costs, Come First."

"In every interaction between two individuals, two human beings, there's room for a caring response. There can be a caring response, no matter what contact that you have and in what context you're communicating to that other human being. It can be the same if it's a short term relationship, as with a salesperson at Dayton's. Looking at and treating that individual as an individual, not as just a buyer or a customer, but as an individual and responding to that individual even in facial expressions... The smallest thing can demonstrate caring. When we have a problem is when we treat people as objects or classify them as customers, or as anonymous patients, or as 'a gall bladder,' rather than as a whole individual." — "Caring Behaviors," an interview with Becky Nelson.

"Where there is not vision, the people perish." — Proverbs 29:18 (KJV)

Leading caring lives is about living *practically* in the here and now but with *vision*. As Alan Dyer rightly observes, with our personal decisions we choose "a lifestyle that promotes or does not promote a healthy existence." And our "political choices reflect the kind of health care we expect and will receive." Choices follow a vision. Are the personal and political choices that we make consistent with the vision we intend?

Realism, Vision, and the Health Care System

In the consideration of the politics and economics of caring we encountered a vexing tension between realism and vision, between the concern to hold down the escalating *costs* of health care and the commitment to make health care *accessible* to those who need it.

Like it or not, cost is a factor that clashes with the goal of extending access. The Medicare Act was passed in 1965 to extend care to all persons over 65... But with a price tag. Hospitals acted as cost-plus contractors. The government was billed for the cost of the services with an allowable amount for profit. This policy enabled hospitals to equip themselves with state-of-the-art technological equipment and to increase access through the addition of hospital beds. In the judgment of many people like Jon Soderholm, Medicare has been a very important program. But the problem of runaway health care costs that Medicare has helped to generate must be confronted.

Three basic strategies have emerged for slowing down the rise in health care costs. To rein in Medicare costs, the government established caps on the amount of money available for hospital treatment of specific illnesses. These disease clusters were known as diagnostic-related-groups or DRGs. DRGs also encouraged shorter hospital stays and had the effect of penalizing the small hospital and rewarding the larger institutions serving a number of patients in the particular DRG category. The implementation of DRGs has had the effect of stimulating a second strategy, namely, the development of hospital and health care systems. The systems approach, whether in hospital care or grocery chains, exists to promote administrative efficiencies and economics of scale. The third strategy is the development of Health Maintenance Organizations. HMOs are designed to coordinate the delivery of health care services to individuals or groups. They seek to hold costs down by contracting with groups of physicians, hospitals, laboratories, and pharmacies to deliver goods and services at lower costs and to reduce the demand for health care services in two ways: by emphasizing wellness and preventive health measures; and by providing a gatekeeper mechanism to monitor both patient requests and physician recommendations for health care services.

Throughout the readings in Chapter Nine is a flag of concern that the realism of holding down the costs of health care must be joined with a renewed vision of what health care is fundamentally about. There is need for sharp focus upon the needs of ourselves and our neighbors for adequate and quality health care.

Allen Dyer does not deny that costs need to be reckoned with. But responsibility for cost cannot be located in one easy place. It cannot be left alone at the door of the physician or to the mechanisms of the market place. Dyer argues that consideration of cost should be part of the conversation between doctor and patient.

After sharply warning physicians not to abandon an "ethics of service to a particular patient to a population-based ethic," Edmund Pellegrino, a physician himself, argues that the role of the physician in keeping down costs must be rooted in the sense of what it means to be a moral physician. In the covenantal relationship with the patient, Pellegrino says, the physician is obligated neither to undertreat or overtreat. "Rational, effective medicine is the most significant contribution physicians can make to cost-containment." And the physician as citizen should work for more cost-effective treatment and take leadership in activities which insure that "the poor, the uninsured, the chronically ill, the aged and the handicapped" are included among those receiving health care. Attending to the health care system and holding costs in check are tasks not just for institutions or physicians, but for all the players in the community including the recipients of health care.

Jon Soderholm urges us to struggle with the following questions: "Is health care a right or a privilege?" And how much health care do we really need, a Red Ford or Red Porsche? And William F. May puts before us the tension between the realizations that health is a fundamental good but not the *only* fundamental good. Without a doubt the health or illness of each of us affects us all. A productive society is a healthy society. But it is not the only fundamental good. There are issues of housing, education, and police protection to consider. As citizens, we must become involved in weighing these goods as we consider ways to improve and extend health care to all who need it.

Edmund Pellegrino's charge to physicians to take leadership in activities which make sure that "the poor, the uninsured, the chronically ill, and the aged and the handicapped" receive the care that they need is sobering and inspiring. It applies not only to physicians but to all of us as citizens. And it is a charge which needs to be considered not only in relationship to national but to global health needs. It is a particularly sobering charge as we consider the enormous disparities in health care received in different parts of the world. Arguably, illness and health in one part of the world affects us all, as illustrated by the AIDS epidemic. But it is also an inspiring vision because it invites us to see the world as did the Hebrew prophets, not just from the point of illness, but from the point of view of wholeness. It is the vision of shalom that must be kept in tension with everyday, practical decisions. Living with vision is necessary for life. In the words of the writer of Proverbs, "Where there is not vision, the people perish."

Vision and Leading Caring Lives

We are called to care, not only as citizens, but also as persons leading caring lives — responsible for our own health, seeing our work as an opportunity for caring, and responding to our neighbors in a caring manner. This is the substance of the readings in Chapter Ten.

We are talking about what James Nelson identifies as "response-abilities."[1] In heeding the call to care, how do we do it? It is a matter both of knowledge and practice. The philosopher Aristotle distinguishes between the intellectual virtues and the moral virtues. Intellect is necessary to identify the ends or purposes of our actions. Moral virtue is about developing the capacity to reach our ends, to connect everyday reality with vision.

Being Responsible for Our Own Health

Four of the readings that follow deal with the call to be responsible for our own health. From her double experience as a nurse and as a frequent user of health care over the past decade, Mary Auterman suggests strategies for making health care choices as a responsible consumer. Mary Jo Kreitzer, from her vantage point as director of Complementary Care and The Center for Spirituality and Healing at the Academic Health Center at the University of Minnesota, gives us perspective on the new interest of patients in medicine that is "attentive to the spirit, mind and body." In addition to traditional medicine, the strategies of Complementary and Alternative Medicine (CAM) need to be considered. Jerome Freeman considers the use of these strategies by patients from the perspective of his practice as a physician. Physicians need to be knowledgeable about these strategies in order to assist patients in finding a suitable balance of treatment options. In the fourth reading Lawrence Hill, a professionally trained physician, shares his experience as a hypochondriac. As we seek to care for our own health, to live wisely, how do we distinguish between foolhardiness and hypochondria?

The call to care responsibly for my life follows from the will to be healthy, that is the will to carry out my life story. What this means in practice has been obscured in recent years in several ways. The comfortable habit of relying on third party payers — be it Medicare, Medicaid, or private insurance — insulates us from costs and responsibility for health care. Additionally, blind faith in technological medicine and the power of physicians to use these tools on our behalf has shielded us from the reality of our own mortality and from our personal responsibility to live wisely. William F. May, in his insightful book *The Physician's Covenant*,[2] writes to suggest a way of thinking of the relationship between physician and patient that recovers the responsible role of the patient in the healing process. The physician does not have health as a commodity to sell, but wisdom to share that will strengthen and encourage the patient in the process of healing and living. Physician and patient should think of their relationship as a covenant entered into between the doctor as teacher and the patient as learner. Healing is a cooperative venture. Part of the responsibility belongs to the patient.

Leading Caring Lives

The selection from *Kitchen Dance*, a play by Ron Robinson, directs our attention to the opportunities for caring in the occasional, casual situations in our lives. We meet Alan, a professional disc jockey and radio personality who is in Rochester at the Mayo clinic to see if the damage caused by serious alcoholism is reparable, and Jennifer, who is there with her husband who is seriously ill and facing death. Alan and Jennifer chance to stay in the same rooming house in Rochester. What insights into the meaning of caring can be gleaned from their meetings in the kitchen of the rooming house?

This play, by the way, preceded the development of this course. It was not written as a companion piece, but as a piece for the stage, and was first performed at Augustana College by a professional cast. It is included because those of us who saw it remembered it as a play that resonates deeply about leading caring lives. The play urges reflection on the dangers to a caregiver who doesn't attend to his or her own needs; and on the possibilities of growing that come about from incidental acts of kindness.

Caring in Our Vocations

The call to care addresses us not only as we seek to carry out our individual life stories but also in the work place. An important principle in health care is that of beneficence. Health care professionals seek to do the right thing in caring for patients. The virtue of the provider is exceedingly important because he or she is dealing with the lives of the vulnerable.

How can the call to care for the vulnerable, to support them in their will to carry out their life stories, be most effectively carried out?

The interview and the article by Becky Nelson, a nurse and now hospital administrator, considers this issue in the context of the hospital. Through her work and research she engages us in two fundamental and intriguing questions. What do patients perceive as caring behaviors? And how can this knowledge from the patient's point of view enable caregivers to respond more ably to the call to care?

Her approach, namely asking the receiver of care to identify caring behaviors, is allied both with respect for patient autonomy and William F. May's notion that the relationship between caregiver and patient is a covenantal one. Patients need care, but they also need to be engaged responsibly in their own healing.

To what extent are Becky Nelson's insights applicable in other fields? She believes that in every interaction between human beings there is room for a caring response. Do you agree? And if so can this insight enable us to view all of our vocations as grounded in the call to care? Her insight resonates with the view of Martin Luther that all vocations, not just the monastic orders, are calls to serve our neighbors. We hear and heed them in our particular places in the work world — whether at home, or in our jobs as cobbler, pastor, lawyer, or prince. Indeed the very word *vocation* comes from the latin word *vocare*, to call. To be in a profession is to be in a calling that serves the neighbor.

---

[1]James B. Nelson and JoAnne Rohricht in *Human Medicine*, Augsburg Publishing House, 1984, p. 215.

[2]William F. May, *The Physician's Covenant,: Im ages of the Healer in Medical Ethics*, Philadelphia, Westminster Press, 1993, chapter 4.

Making Health Care Choices

Mary Auterman

We have discussed the dimensions of caring, the ethics of caring, and the limitations of caring, with the emphasis on the responsibilities of the caregiver. In light of the papers and discussion thus far, what can be said about the responsibility of the care recipient? The debate between Hygeia and Asclepius points out the need for both healthy life habits and appropriate use of treatment or curative medicine. There are some health problems that we still do not know how to prevent even if we do "all the right things." For example, we have no control over the genes we inherit. The Biblical concepts of Shalom and of the stewardship of the "body" (*i.e.*, self as mind, body, and spirit) infer a responsibility for caring for one's being; to take effort to keep healthy. What is the responsibility of the care recipient when illness does occur?

For the most part, I have maintained a healthy, balanced diet, regular exercise, and a generally "healthy" lifestyle, yet, I have experienced a series of chronic health problems starting with atypical arthritis when I was in my early 20s. The Hygeia model of regular exercise, weight control, and a balanced diet became a way of life in order to avoid excess stress on my joints. An annual appointment with my primary physician was usually sufficient. Then at age 50, I developed an autoimmune disorder. Since then I have become a "frequent user" of health/illness care, including the services of an array of specialists. When I developed breast cancer, I did wonder at one point where Hygeia was in all this. My healthy lifestyle had failed me. I had only one of about six risk factors for breast cancer, but it occurred anyway. We could find no history in past generations indicating a genetic component. In the process, I have learned the value of being an active participant in my health/illness care management.

Three experiences stand out in my mind that reinforced the value of active participation. The first related to the arthritis. I had been experiencing increasing pain in one hip and was referred to a bone specialist. I expressed my concern about the hip pain, but he kept dwelling on the abnormal curvature in my spine which was congenital (present from birth) and was not presenting any problems at that time. I left with no answers and no treatment plan for the painful hip. I said to my primary physician that I perceived the specialist had not heard my concern. My primary physician followed up on my concern and discovered that the specialist had assumed from my history that I was referred for the back problem and had indeed not heard anything I had said.

Secondly, early in the treatment of the autoimmune disorder, I was again referred to a specialist. The specialist's philosophy of the patient's role and my philosophy differed greatly. His standard response to questions about treatment approaches was "trust me." He didn't seem to grasp that I wanted to better understand what was happening with my body and I needed information to do so. I am convinced that most chronic health problems are managed in the day-to-day living by the person experiencing the problem. To do so effectively requires that the person be knowledgeable about what is happening. After two years of frustration, I checked out other options by gathering information from colleagues, friends, and acquaintances who had contacts with other specialists in that field. I requested a "second opinion" and changed to the new physician who readily shares information and encourages active participation.

The third instance was following treatment for the breast cancer. I had worn a back support for approximately the previous 15 years. Nine months after the surgery, I was still unable to wear the support without precipitating increased swelling and discomfort in my breast, chest wall, and upper arm. Without the support, I was experiencing chronic upper and midback pain and fatigue. At a "routine" semi-annual appointment with the endocrinologist for the autoimmune disorder, the doctor asked how I was doing and feeling. I responded, that it depended on which part of my body we talked about. When she asked me to clarify, I shared my dilemma with the back pain. She suggested trying weight training to strengthen the upper back muscles. After two months in physical therapy, I not only had less back discomfort, but the exercises also helped mobilize the edema fluid, thus, increasing the comfort in the remainder of my upper body. When I finished physical therapy, I joined the wellness center and have continued the weight training as well as overall body conditioning. My energy level improved and the weight gain I was experiencing from the medication to prevent recurrence of the breast cancer stabilized. I felt as if Hygeia had returned to balance all the curative care I had received from Asclepius. I am grateful for both.

My primary physician has always respected my desire for active participation. Chronic health problems are frequently complex, resulting in the need for referrals to multiple specialists. Treatment for the complications of the autoimmune disorder resulted in appointments with physicians in five different specialties over a period of less than one year. There were three more in less than two months with the breast cancer. I had input into the selection of each of them and have never regretted the time and effort it takes for the selection process. My experience of not being heard led to another form of active participation. I type up a brief summary of my own health history, my current symptoms, medications I am currently taking (including over-the-counter products) and my perception of the current problem. Almost all of the physicians have thanked me. One told me it saved him at least an hour of time. (By this time my medical record was about an inch and a half thick.) I have the satisfaction of knowing that my concerns are communicated.

I have also learned the value of knowing how to read and interpret medical and hospital bills, insurance claim forms, and EOBs (Explanation of Benefits) forms. Treatment for the breast cancer included two surgeries, 30 radiation treatments and 26 physician appointments in a four month time span. At one time I had a three-inch stack of bills and EOBs. I identify several errors each year and report these to my employer and to the insurance company. The customer service representative with the insurance company probably groans when she hears my name. However, I have saved my insurance carrier, my employer, and myself money.

One humorous situation arose. I had a cancer insurance policy with a company which had recently moved their claims processing from Kansas to Florida and was apparently starting over with many new employees. Among the bills I submitted to that company was the one from the pathology lab. Several weeks later I received a check for "prescriptions." Nothing else was included in the services paid. I was puzzled so called the number on the voucher. After transfer to about three people, I was told that it was for the estrogen and progesterone prescription on the bill. It took several attempts before the woman seemed to grasp that the estrogen and progesterone receptor assays on the bill were laboratory tests on the tumor, not pills. On a more serious note, this incident points out the need to be a watchdog. Some employee apparently had not compared the service code number which accompanies every item on an insurance form with the payment manual.

I have also learned to be persistent as well as active in working the insurance. When the insurance carrier withheld authorization for manual lymph drainage for lymphedema following the radiation therapy, I persisted. Because manual lymph drainage (MLD) is very time consuming and thus costs between $160 and $200 per treatment, the therapist resisted scheduling appointments without insurance coverage. I talked with the surgeon, the oncologist, and the therapist's supervisor. Each sent a letter stating why the treatment was necessary and that the MLD was the current standard starting point for treatment. I followed with my own letter stating I was appealing the ruling and gave reasons why. I received coverage. My experience also contributed to a policy change in coverage with the health insurance policy at the college to cover outpatient physical therapy. It was previously covered only if started during hospitalization.

Prevention is important from an economic standpoint. Health care has become too costly to depend on treatment alone without preventive efforts. Cost of treatment during the first year following the diagnosis of my breast cancer was nearly $30,000. Dyer in his article "Patients, Not Cost, Come First" concludes that "A whole spectrum of decisions must be made daily, not only by physicians, patients, and families at the bedside, but by all of us as we 'choose' a lifestyle that promotes or does not promote a healthy existence..." He includes in those decisions the ones regarding exercise, nutrition, smoking, and attending to risk factors but also choosing a suitable kind of health care insurance and, at another level, the political choices which impact what kind of health care we expect and receive.

But how does the average person make health care decisions, particularly those relating to insurance and the political choices. There are self-help books, support groups, classes, and even Internet sites to assist with the choices relating to healthy lifestyle habits. The options are not as clear when it comes to selecting insurance coverage or making political choices. Reading insurance forms and explanations of benefits (EOBs) and navigating through the health care system are bewildering to many persons. The process begins with making the basic health care choices. Virtually everyone will need health care at some time in his or her life. Modern medicine has become highly technical and expensive and health care facilities have become complex and also costly. The increasing number of elderly will continue to add to the number with chronic health problems. That brings us back to the question, "What is the responsibility of the care receiver?"

Knowing when to see a health care provider can be vital to increasing positive outcomes regarding one's health or even survival. Chest pain or sudden weakness or loss of function of an arm, leg, or speech, diabetic emergencies, and serious trauma require immediate attention. Consider watchful waiting for less serious problems — most health care decisions are not an emergency and several days of self-care may resolve the situation. Learn the warning signs of cancer and what risk factors can be controlled to reduce the risk.

Knowing who to see and how to access the health care system can be equally important and is best done before the need. Selection of the health care provider (physician, nurse practitioner, certified nurse midwife, or other primary care practitioners) warrants as much forethought and care as selecting a new car. A few simple steps may be helpful. One way to begin is checking with people you trust and asking about their experiences and satisfaction, including those traits that are important to you in a health care provider such as their interpersonal skills, fee schedule, office hours, willingness to accept phone calls and to return phone calls, which hospital(s) he or she uses, and philosophy about alternative therapies. Checking with the Board of Medical Examiners can answer concerns of any negative reports, or investigations filed against the physician/ health care practitioner. Be leery of unlicensed practitioners and undocumented claims by health practitioners. Making the decision before you need health care (primary care provider, hospital) reduces the stress of last minute decisions and increases the chance of a satisfying experience. Use a similar process in selecting a hospital or other health care institution.

Understanding health care financing and cost, as well as how and when to select insurance (known as third party payment), can greatly reduce the fear of paying for health care/illness care and reduce stress level. Ask for an explanation of the insurance policy, what it covers and does not cover, and an Explanation of Benefits (EOB) form. Research what constitutes standard care. Being a wise health care consumer means taking responsibility for increasing one's own knowledge and understanding so that wise decisions can be made. The American Cancer Society, the American Heart Association, and the National Institute of Health all have public access web sites using language the average person can understand. There are reliable public access web sites for most chronic illnesses. Many public libraries have a section for health information and many medical libraries allow public access. The average person can understand more than they think they can.

Three Basic Principles of a Wise Consumer

● **Work in partnership with your health care provider.**
A. Communication is important; as a partner remember you have responsibilities as well as rights.
B. Consider writing your own health history and taking it with you.
C. Write down your current symptoms — onset, pattern, concerns you have.

● **Share in health care decision-making.** (Remember it's your body and your money.)
A. Let the doctor know what you want.
B. Do your own research, be informed, seek reliable sources of information.
C. Inquire about the advantages and disadvantages of the choices or why your doctor prefers a given choice.
D. Ask about alternatives — get the full range of possible effective treatments.
E. State your health care preferences, including choice of laboratory, hospital, and specialist, if needed.
F. Compare expectations.
G. Accept responsibility; let health care professionals know if you are uncomfortable with recommendations, ask for time to think about it, and return to discuss it.

● **Become skilled at obtaining health care and health care information.**
A. Ask about lab tests, their cost, benefit::cost ratio, and results.
B. Write down your questions and concerns before the appointment and take the list with you. Most physicians welcome questions and are willing to take the time to answer them. If you are not sure you will remember what was discussed, or if you are experiencing much anxiety, ask a family member or friend whom you trust to go with you. It's your right. If the

physician is uncomfortable with this strategy, that is his or her problem, not yours.

C. Ask the pharmacist for written information and precautions about your medication, if it is not provided.

Nine ways of cutting costs of health care without affecting quality

1. Stay healthy.
2. Exercise self-care and self-responsibility.
3. Get health care from a primary health care provider (family practice physician, internal medicine, Ob/Gyn, pediatrician, certified nurse practitioner); their charges are usually less than that of the specialist.
4. Reduce your medical test costs. Question why each test is being done and whether it is really necessary.
5. Reduce your drug cost. Ask about generic drugs; many generic drugs are equivalent.
6. Use specialists for special problems.
7. Use emergency service wisely. Office appointments or acute care clinics are less costly than emergency room visits. Use ER for chest pain, signs of a stroke, major trauma , *etc.*
8. Use hospitals only when you need them.
9. Get smart about your health care needs. Remember, you have lived with your body longer than anyone else has. The doctor knows what is needed for the diagnosis and the range of treatment options, but he may not be the expert in your body's response.

Understanding the insurance lingo

Policy-holder — the person who is insured.

Premium — the monthly, quarterly, annual, *etc.* amount you pay for the plan.

Deductible — the amount you pay up front for care before the plan pays anything, usually annual. Medicare requires a separate deductible for Part A and Part B.

Co-pay or co-insurance — the amount you pay for services provided, by percentage or by set dollar amount - *e.g.* $5 for each prescription or 20% of allowable charge. With managed care there may be an upper limit the health care provider may charge for a given service. The consumer/policy-holder does not have to pay the amount of the fee that was above the allowable cost in the plan.

Pre-existing condition — a health problem that existed before you enrolled in the plan; plan may exclude that condition from coverage for a set period of time; one year is common. Some policies exclude coverage for previously treated cancer for five years.

Maternity benefits — coverage for pregnancy related care including hospitalization for complications, labor, and delivery, and normal newborn care. Pregnancy is frequently treated as a pre-existing condition — i.e., plan must be in place x number of months before a pregnancy is covered. One year is common. Some insurances include maternity coverage only if specifically requested. Don't assume it is included — ask. Most policies do not extend maternity coverage to dependents.

Exclusions — what the plan will not pay (may include chiropractor, cosmetic surgery, alternative therapies, drug and alcohol treatment, or even outpatient physical or occupational therapy). Always ask about exclusions before choosing.

Limitations — restrictions on specific types of treatment; e.g., twelve sessions of physical therapy within a six month period, or limitations on the number of days of treatment for substance abuse.

EOB or Explanation of Benefits — explanation you receive from the plan/insurer stating what the plan will pay and what you pay and if what you pay is part of the deductible, the copay, or a noncovered service, etc. In a managed care plan, the EOB will also identify costs that exceed the agreed-upon cost or "above reasonable charge" and that you are not responsible for that amount.

Pre-authorization — Certain services may need separate authorization prior to each use in order to be covered by the policy including hospital admission, substance abuse treatment, inpatient rehabilitation services, organ and tissue transplants, durable medical equipment (oxygen, wheelchair, etc.), or referrals to nonparticipating physicians or providers.

Group insurance plan — college, employer, professional organization. An individual cannot be singled out for a change in coverage or cost unless all persons in the plan are treated equally.

Individual policy plan - may cover single individual or a family. Premium costs are usually considerably higher than for group insurance.

Lastly, remember that your health care providers are human. Unlike Asclepius, they have not been elevated to the realm of gods, and so experience human limitations. Most have the person's interest in mind, but need to know how the individual perceives his or her own interest. Sirach (Ecclesiasticus) 38:1-15 tells us to honor the physician. That may start by being a responsible patient.

Caring and Complementary Healing Practices

Mary Jo Kreitzer, PhD RN

Caring and healing practices vary significantly across cultures and have evolved over time. Twentieth-century Western medicine has traditionally focused narrowly on the biological mechanisms of disease and minimized the importance of the patient's experience of the disease. The separation of disease and illness from spirituality and religion has perhaps been due to both our cultural value of secularism and the emphasis on the biological origins of disease. Until the recent emergence of psychoneuroimmunology, the contribution of the mind to health and healing was largely ignored. Healthcare has also been blind to the profound difference between curing — meaning the technological correction of aberrant physiology — and healing — the restoration of wholeness. This has been true despite widespread recognition that most diseases are chronic and few people are ever truly cured.

A new consciousness is emerging that recognizes health and illness as conceptualizations deeply embedded in spiritual and cultural values. In many respects, the current interest in this topic takes us back to our roots. With the emergence of scientific medicine in the 17th Century, came dualism — separation of the mind, body and spirit and separation of health care and healing from spirituality and religion. Prior to this era, the role of priest (spiritual guide and mentor) and healer were often woven together. Hildegard of Bingen, a 12th Century mystic and healer, was well known for her expertise in healing traditions including the use of herbs, music, art and prayer. Florence Nightingale, in addition to writing extensively on the practice of modern nursing and the management of hospitals, also wrote a major treatise on spirituality. The early Greek temples were sanctuaries of healing. "The boundary between medicine and religion is shifting. It is no longer obvious that the body can be studied objectively as a mechanism that functions independently from the mind or that faith is a factor that affects only the destiny of the soul," writes Thomas Droege (1991), a theology professor at Valparaiso University. Health and spirituality, once regarded as the separate domains of medicine and religion, are increasingly seen as intertwined and complementary.

Consumer Demand

Consumer interest in care that is attentive to the spirit, mind, and body is growing, as evidenced by articles in the popular press, consumer polls and patterns of health care use. Illustrative of stories in the popular press are recent cover stories in *Time* and *Life*. *Time* Magazine (June 1996) featured a bold cover headline that read "Faith and Healing: doctors are finding some surprising evidence." *Life* magazine followed a couple of months later with a cover story entitled "The Healing Revolution."

A 1993 study by Dr. David Eisenberg (1993) at Harvard Medical School reported that one of three adults in the United States report using a complementary or alternative treatment for a health problem. Americans made more visits to alternative practitioners than they did to primary care physicians and they spent $13.7 billion for such treatments, of which more than $10.5 billion they paid out-of-pocket. Results of a followup study by Eisenberg and his colleagues (1998) estimated that visits to alternative care providers have increased 47.3% since publication of the earlier study, and expenditures related to alternative therapies now exceed $27 billion.

In two national surveys by *Time*/CNN (June, 1996) and *USA Weekend* (February, 1996), more than 70 percent of patients polled believe that spiritual faith and prayer can aid in recovery from illness. Sixty-four percent of those surveyed believe that physicians should talk to patients about spiritual issues as part of their care and pray with patients if they request it. There is some evidence that physicians are hearing this message. In a survey of physician attitudes towards complementary or alternative medicine, Berman (1995) reported that 72.4 percent of physicians expressed interest in training in the area of prayer.

Complementary/Alternative/Integrative:
What do the words mean and what does the field encompass?

There are several terms often used interchangeably to refer to this large, complex, and varied range of therapies considered outside the domain of mainstream Western medicine. Alternative was for many years the word most frequently used. Alternative, however, suggests a choice (an either-or option). To some, it implies that these therapies are used instead of conventional medicine, a presumption that does not reflect the most typical, actual patterns of use. The phrase complementary medicine was proposed to convey the notion that these approaches to healing can complement — be used together with conventional medicine. More recently, the term "integrative medicine" was coined to convey the ideal that these diverse systems of healing should be integrated with conventional medicine. Increasingly the phrase "complementary and alternative medicine" (CAM) is used.

There are actually over 1,800 modalities or therapies that this field encompasses with a wide range of philosophies and practices. Just as biomedicine is a system of care, there are complementary or alternative systems of care such as Traditional Chinese Medicine, Ayurvedic Medicine and Naturopathy. Additionally, there are culturally-based systems of healing that emanate from cultural beliefs and practices. These are often referred to as folk medical practices. There are many therapies that do not fall within either a culturally-based or alternative system of care. Examples of these complementary healing practices includes imagery, meditation, massage, herbs and healing touch.

Research Base

There is considerable variation in the quality and quantity of the research base for CAM as there is with biomedicine. There is often the erroneous assumption made that biomedicine is "scientific" while the field of CAM is "unscientific." The reality is that within both biomedicine and CAM, evidence ranges from anecdotal to empirical. The US Office of Technology Assessment has estimated that only 10-20 percent of biomedical approaches are based on controlled clinical trials. Within CAM, there are modalities such as acupuncture that have a strong research base that includes controlled clinical trials. The National Institute of Health (NIH) recently convened a research consensus conference to evaluate acupuncture research and concluded that a sufficient body of research exists to support the use of acupuncture for certain conditions. There are other modalities such as homeopathy where an abundance of anecdotal evidence exists but rigorous, empirical research has been lacking.

In 1992, the NIH created the Office of Alternative Medicine (OAM) to facilitate the evaluation of complementary or alternative modalities to determine their effectiveness and to help integrate effective treatments into the mainstream of care. The Office began with a modest appropriation of $2 million. In 1998, the budget of the OAM was close to $20 million. In addition to funding eleven OAM Research Centers, several major research projects are being initiated. Cancer clinical trials in collaboration with the National Cancer Institute will focus on the use of cartilage and nutritional intervention for the treatment of cancer. A study conducted in conjunction with the National Institute of Arthritis and Musculoskeletal Diseases will evaluate the use of glucosamine sulfate in the treatment of osteoarthritis. Duke University was recently awarded a research grant to study the use of St. John's Wort for the treatment of mild depression.

Implications for Practice

Schools of medicine and nursing throughout the country are beginning to include in the curriculum content on complementary/alternative care. It is increasingly recognized that health professionals as well as practicing MDs need to have skills that enable them to:

● Create an environment where patients feel comfortable talking about use of CAM
● Access evidence-based information on CAM modalities
● Discuss CAM treatment options with patients
● Work collaboratively with CAM practitioners

An article published in the *Annals of Internal Medicine* provides several suggestions for advising patients about the use of CAM therapies:

● Carefully explore with patients the symptoms for which they are seeking CAM modalities
● Encourage patients to maintain a symptom diary
● Discuss with patients their preferences and expectations
● Review issues of safety and efficacy
● Identify criteria of suitable practitioners
● Review treatment plans
● Follow-up to evaluate the response to treatment

Wayne Jonas MD, the director of the Office of Alternative Medicine in the NIH, notes that "The ultimate decision in medical care must rest with the patient and caregiver, but it is the role and obligation of the physician to provide information on the existing scientific evidence as well as expert opinion to assist patients in making informed decisions. It is no longer sufficient for physicians to make recommendations based solely on familiarity with the therapeutic option or to await a biological explanation or consensus panel opinion. Evidence-based choices and the skills necessary to make them should become a routine part of all medical practices." The bottom line is that good science and good patient care demands open-minded inquiry.

Mary Jo Kreitzer is director of Complementary Care and the Center for Spirituality and Healing at the Academic Health Center at the University of Minnesota.

Assessing the Efficacy and Safety of Medical Technologies. (1978) Office of Technology Assessment — Congress of the United States.

Berman, Brian (Sept. Oct 1995), "Physician Attitudes toward Complementary or Alternative Medicine: A Regional Survey." *Journal of the American Board of Family Practice*, Vol. 8, No. 5:363.

Droege, Thomas. (June 1991) *The Faith Factor in Healing.* Trinity Press International.

Eisenberg, David *et al.* (November 11, 1998) "Trends in Alternative Medicine Use in the United States: 1990-1997." JAMA (280) 18:1569-1573.

Eisenberg, D. "Advising Patients Who Seek Alternative Medical Therapies." *Annals of Internal Medicine.* 1997. 127; 1:61-69.

Eisenberg, David C. et al. (January 28, 1998) "Unconventional Medicine in the United States: Prevalence, costs and patterns of use." *New England Journal of Medicine.* 328(4):246-252.

Eisenberg, David. *The Invisible Mainstream.* Harvard Medical Bulletin. Summer 1996, 20-25.

Jonas, W. "Advising Patients Who Seek Alternative Medicine." *Annals of Internal Medicine.* 1998. 128; 4:329.

U.S. Government Printing Office. (1994). *Alternative Medicine: Expanding Medical Horizons. A Report to the National Institutes of Health on Alternative Medical Systems and Practices in the United States.* NIH Pub. No 94-066. Washington, D.C.

Practical Wisdom
Jerome W. Freeman

Recently, in the company of several colleagues, I had the opportunity to reflect upon the importance of on-the-job experience to the practice of medicine. A physician finishes medical school and residency primed with the most recent scientific data, and knows more about obscure pathways and the nuances of pharmacology than she or he ever will again. But that's only part of the story, and often not the critical theme. Rather, my fellow physicians uniformly agreed that as they gained experience and insight over time, the practical work of diagnosis and treatment was greatly facilitated. This, I believe, is what Aristotle extolled as "practical wisdom." He noted that, in addition to the importance of the theoretical sciences, one needs understanding gleaned from doing the work. I remember, as a medical student, hearing an occasional professor elaborate on the "art" and the "science" of medicine. In my judgment, much of medicine's "art" resides in the practical wisdom born of attentive experience.

In a field removed from medicine (except by analogy), my father-in-law, Francis, makes similar observations about gardening. He observes that as a young man, eager to have a prodigious garden, he "just didn't get it" in terms of ordering his priorities for success. Each spring he would enthusiastically plant a large area, envisioning the lush produce he expected to enjoy. However, his focus would invariably become distracted by other pursuits such as girls, playing baseball, or swimming. As a consequence of procrastination, he vividly recalls working his way through his midsummer gardens on his hands and knees, in search of his prized vegetables amid the weeds. And he'd vow to be more diligent the following year.

Eventually, as he grew older, Francis learned the essence of effective gardening. He stresses that timeliness is critical. Knowing when to use the hoe and cultivator makes all the difference. Young plants need to be sufficiently mature or they can be uprooted by premature cultivating. And even with judicious cultivation, stubborn weeds still appear and require timely hoeing to prevent them from flourishing. Francis notes that if the gardener ever needs to hoe an entire garden, it is likely that the cultivating was neglected for too long. He also observes that advancing age provides the

From *South Dakota Journal of Medicine*, February 1999. Used by permission.

patience and perspective needed to perform these garden tasks in their appropriate sequence. The impetuousness of youth is an impediment to orchestrating the care of the vegetable garden in optimal fashion.

Like gardening, medicine is nurtured by practical wisdom that values studied patience and perspective. These attributes assist the physician in deciding what to do and when to do it. Numerous examples from medical practice come to mind including the expanding field of complementary/alternative medicine. Clearly, the use of complementary therapies is burgeoning. In his latest study, Eisenberg (1) notes that about 40% of the population now acknowledges using some form of complementary therapy. This percentage has increased steadily over the last seven years.

The physician is confronted with the difficulties of discerning which complementary/alternative therapies a given patient is using; the safety of these regimens, especially in the context of other required medical treatment; and the efficacy of various complementary therapies. Despite the enthusiasm for complementary/alternative therapies among the public and in sections of the healthcare community, many physicians remain skeptical and disapproving of this whole field.

Prominent concerns have been recently articulated in both the *Journal of the American Medical Association* and the *New England Journal of Medicine*. Angell and Kissirer (2) contend that "What most sets alternative medicine apart, in our view, is that it has not been scientifically tested and its advocates largely deny the need for such testing. By testing, we mean the marshaling of rigorous evidence of safety and efficacy. . . " They go on to say that, "Alternative medicine also distinguishes itself by an ideology that largely ignores biologic mechanisms, often disparages modern science, and relies on what are purported to be ancient practices and natural remedies. . ." They conclude by asserting, "It is time for the scientific community to stop giving alternative medicine a free ride. There cannot be two kinds of medicine — conventional and alternative. There is only medicine that has been adequately tested and medicine that has not, medicine that works and medicine that may or may not work."

Fontanarosa and Lundberg (3), making a similar argument, note: "However, for alternative medicine therapies that are used by millions of patients every day and that generate billions of dollars in health-care expenditures each year, the lack of a convincing and compelling evidence of efficacy, safety and outcome is unacceptable and deeply troubling." Their editorial appeared in an issue of *JAMA* that was devoted to alternative therapies, including six randomized clinical trials of various alternative/complementary therapies. Some of these treatments were found helpful, others not.

I suspect that these cautionary judgments rendered in *The New England Journal of Medicine* and *JAMA* are consistent with the beliefs of a majority of physicians. However, many patients are poised to be dissatisfied with physicians who summarily reject complementary therapies.

From my perspective, this is a realm where practical wisdom can be of assistance. As physicians, we need to be understanding of the personal and societal factors that impel so many millions of patients to seek complementary/alternative therapies. Often, it is not judicious, or ultimately helpful, for us to summarily disparage these efforts. Rather, I think practical clinical wisdom demands that we try to accommodate patients' needs and desires into what we deem most appropriate medical treatment. As a part of these efforts, we should sufficiently investigate complementary therapies being used to ensure ourselves that patients are not at risk for obvious toxicities or drug interactions. For many patients, merely asking about complementary therapy is an indication that the physician is taking an holistic approach to their problem. And if no obvious harm is being done to a patient by his or her complementary remedies, I believe that the physician can be tolerant of them. Herein lies the importance of physician perspective. We don't always have to agree with what our patients do. Our mandate is to try to help people. By acknowledging some patients' wishes for complementary therapies and integrating these options with conventional medical therapy, we may well be devising the best therapeutic options for these individuals.

Certainly not all clinicians exhibit the type of practical wisdom here espoused. As with gardening, some physicians may be too focused on dramatic remedial interventions. In gardening, this type of shortsighted focus can take the form of undue enthusiasm for the year's most popular hybrids, lavish expenditure on the newest garden equipment, and premature focus upon the expected harvest. Unless the gardener does the regular work of diligently and methodically cultivating and hoeing, those expenditures and grand visions of harvest may yield disappointing results. Similarly in medicine, all of us are attracted to dramatic, decisive treatments. When we prevent a stroke with carotid endarterectomy or a heart attack with angioplasty, there is inevitably a feeling of great satisfaction for our technical and scientific prowess. However, our intimate work with patients demands more than just choosing flashy and decisive therapies. We need to know and understand our patients in order to devise the best treatments for them. In learning an individual's story, with its multi-tiered influences and motivations, it is important to focus on particulars. As Eisenberg's studies indicate, for many patients these particulars include aspects of complementary/alternative medicine.

Thus it makes sense to perceive the use of complementary/alternative therapies as opportunities to exercise practical wisdom. We need to patiently understand what our patients are doing and assist them in finding a suitable balance of treatment options. Often our small courtesies and compromises can yield gratifying results in the effort to assist our patients with their dreary burdens.

[1]Eisenberg D.M. et al. "Trends in Alternative Medicine Use in the United States, 1990-1997: Results of a Follow-up National Survey," *JAMA*, November 11, 1998, pp 1569-1579.

[2]Angell and Kissirer J.P. Alternative Medicine - "The Risks of Untested and Unregulated Remedies," *New England Journal of Medicine*, Vol 339, #12 September 7, 1998, pp 839.841.

[3]Fontanarosa P.B. and Lundberg J.D. "Alternative Medicine Meets Science." *JAMA* November 11, 1998. pp 618-619.

My Not-So-Near-Death Experience
Lawrence N. Hill, M.D.

I am a hypochondriac. My medical degree offers me no immunity to this common ailment. My case is not a bad one, but I have it nonetheless. As a practicing oncologist for nearly 20 years before taking a generalist's job with the government, I empathized with my patients and became convinced regularly that I, too, had a malignant condition. Once I went so far as to walk into the reading room of my good friend, the local radiologist, and admit that I thought I might have male breast cancer, metastatic to bone, because I had discomfort in both the breast and the anterior knee. The knee films were negative, and the symptoms immediately resolved.

This time it was different. About a year ago, the fasciculations started. At first they were mainly in my calves and occurred after tennis or similar vigorous activity. At this stage, I passed them off as insignificant. But soon they began to spread, first up my legs, then into my torso and my arms, and finally to my face. Night and day, at rest and after exercise, they were there. Thirty seconds rarely elapsed without a twitch somewhere.

Oncologists don't often see amyotrophic lateral sclerosis (ALS), but the memories gleaned in medical school of twitching, bedridden patients with tracheostomies were still vivid. *Incurable. Untreatable. Invariably fatal.* I remembered those words and phrases, but I certainly did not recall reading of any recent positive developments. I became more than a bit frightened. Previously, my thoughts of impending death had never lasted for more than a few hours, but these persisted from days to weeks to months. I was able to function; I continued to see patients and dealt with them in a professional, competent, and caring manner. Between patients, however, my thoughts turned to my own body as well as to my family and friends, who I might soon be forced to leave. I thought a lot about the physicist Steven Hawkings and figured that if I were lucky, I, too, could live a long time in a wheelchair with at least the use of a single finger. I wondered whether I could afford the special computer that allows Hawking to translate his finger movements into written and audible words.

I was living in southern Asia when the fasciculations began. I had almost no access to the recent medical literature, and the country

From *Annals of Internal Medicine*, Vol. 125, No. 10. 15 Nov. 1996.

had no highly skilled neurologists. Even if it had, I was not about to go to a neurologist. As an oncologist, I always thought it best that pancreatic cancer be diagnosed after death. In my opinion, ALS is the neurological equivalent of pancreatic cancer. I was willing to sacrifice the distinct possibility of learning that I did not have this fatal illness to avoid the equally distinct possibility of learning that I did. The anxiety of not knowing was preferable to the despair of knowing the worst.

I did have an old copy of *Brain's Neurology*. As I recall, it said something like "most fasciculations are caused by motor neuron disease," but it also said that "rarely do the fasciculations precede weakness." I had not had any real weakness that I had noticed, but that made me decide to test myself. I hadn't done a push-up since my Army days in 1959. I did 15 the first day, and 1 more every day for about a month. I was no Olympian, but I did well enough. Using the rheumatologist's simple test of grip strength, I inflated the bag of the sphygmomanometer to 20 and squeezed it; I moved 300 mm Hg without trying too hard. Every day I repeated this exercise, sometimes a few times — the result was always 300. I was certainly not grossly weak. Wasting occurs with ALS, especially in the hands. I spent an inordinate amount of time examining my hands. I once saw a fold in the hypothenar eminence of the left hand that I hadn't remembered being there before. I returned to the squeeze bag: Still 300, but who knows, maybe, in my case, the wasting would precede my paralyzed slide into oblivion. I tested my reflexes, looking for the hyperreflexia that accompanies motor neuron disease. Perhaps that knee jerk was a bit brisk, I would think, and maybe those hand cramps that I get when I use chopsticks aren't meaningless after all. My anterior horn cells began to dominate my thought processes.

Two or 3 months later, my tour of duty in southern Asia was over; several weeks of home leave in California were to precede my resettlement to southeast Asia. Obviously, California has many neurologists, including some of my old friends. I had decided not to seek an appointment with any of them. Why, I asked myself, should I have an dectromyography if my outcome will in no way be affected by the results? I had also had enough experience in my medium-sized community to remember the community's response when one of its physicians developed a life-threatening illness. I had seen medical confidentiality break down in this kind of situation as often as it was maintained. I did not want to be defined by my illness; I did not want to be known as Dr. Hill, Who Has ALS.

I did more push-ups and played lots of tennis; there was still no weakness 6 months later. I didn't have a pressure cuff, but I could still open the jelly jar when my wife couldn't. Even with these good signs, the twitching hadn't gotten any better; maybe it was a bit worse. I was pretty sure of the diagnosis. I became neither depressed nor angry. I became obsessed but, surprisingly, kept my obsession almost exclusively to myself.

Cal Ripken was about to surpass the record of Lou Gehrig. I was on a plane between Los Angeles and Washington, D.C., and the man next to me had a copy of USA Today. I saw a headline about Gehrig; the subheadline alluded to a new drug for the disease that he had made famous. The *New England Journal of Medicine* or *Annals of Internal Medicine* it wasn't, but I was prepared to read anything that might give me hope. Eventually, I mustered the courage to ask my neighbor if I could just borrow the sports section for a minute. The article disappointed me; it contained nothing of clinical significance.

My usually imperturbable wife, who is well aware of my hypochondriasis, had ignored my initial undramatic lamentations, but when she saw enough of the twitching she encouraged me, both for my benefit and her own, to talk to her brother-in-law, a neurosurgeon. We did so over a beer in his television room. There was no examination. I didn't even show him my muscles. "Probably benign," he said. I wanted to feel reassured. I did, but not very.

A week later, just before my departure for southeast Asia, my wife and I were on a golfing trip in San Diego. The game wasn't too bad; my drives, always short, weren't any shorter. At the end of a round, I was told that I had an urgent telephone call from the neurosurgeon. Thinking someone in the family had died, I nervously returned the call. He said, "I talked to a neurologist friend and he is concerned. He thinks you should come in for an exam and an EMG. And by the way, does your tongue fasciculate?" He informed me that tongue fasciculations tend to be a more specific indicator of motor neuron disease than fasciculations of the trunk or extremities.

"No thanks," I said to the examination. My reasoning had not changed. The results would in no way benefit me unless they were negative, and the consequences of a positive test result were more than I felt I could handle. I hadn't given any thought to my tongue in decades, but suddenly it was the central focus of my existence. I couldn't see any obvious fasciculations in the mirror, but maybe there was an occasional flicker. Once I saw an unmistakable twitch. I felt doomed.

Why go to Asia, I asked myself, when they will only have to send me back in a few months for custodial care? Then again, maybe I'll last longer than that. Plus, I had always wanted to see Manila, Hanoi, Phnom Penh, and the other great sights of southeast Asia. And maybe, just maybe, 1 didn't have ALS after all. That fervent hope of a benign conclusion to the entire matter was always central to my thinking. After all, all of those other illnesses I imagined had disappeared. I went to Asia. In my work during the previous 5 years, I had departed from the United States several times. The goodbyes this time were very different. I felt strongly that many of them would be ultimate farewells, but I said that to no one.

We have a better library here in Manila than we did at my last venue. It contains the 1989 edition of Adams and Victor's *Principles of Neurology*. Continuing my amateurish attempts at denial, I waited a couple of weeks before opening it. With all due respect to those fine authors, their index could be better. I read the section on ALS, which reinforced the idea that it is most unusual for the fasciculations to antedate the weakness. But unusual does not mean never. I returned to the push-up and squeeze bag ritual. I was no weaker. It wasn't until another fortnight went by that I opened the text again and looked under "fasciculations." There I found the statement, "A simple clinical rule is that fasciculations in relaxed muscle are *never* (my italics) indicative of motor system disease unless there is an associated weakness, atrophy or reflex change." My response to that simple sentence was like that of a wrongly convicted man when he hears that the governor has just reexamined the evidence and spared him the electric chair.

Since then I have learned that there is a not uncommon syndrome of widespread, continuous fasciculations that may last for months or even years. It has been described in large part in health professionals, presumably because they know about the malignant potential of muscle twitching and seek medical care accordingly. The rest of the affected population, in its ignorant bliss, thinks that they just have some twitches, not enough of a problem to warrant paying for an office call. The last line in Adams and Victor's description of the syndrome is, "eventual recovery can be expected."

I have replayed the scenario of the past year over and over in my mind. Had I sought medical attention and had I had electromyography early on, I would have spared myself months of emotional distress. I might well have come across a sage neurologist who was fully aware of the syndrome and who could have reassured me even without the invasive test. But that would have been a gamble. On the losing side of that gamble would have been the knowledge that I had a disease that would inexorably take from me my means of movement, then my means of communication with those whom I loved, and then my life. I did not like the odds. I would probably make the same choice again today.

I'm still twitching. I don't squeeze the cuff anymore, and I've ceased doing the push-ups. I don't have Lou Gehrig's disease. I am awaiting the next disorder that may cause my premature death.

From *Kitchen Dance*

Ron Robinson

The two-character play Kitchen Dance *was first presented in 1983 under the direction of veteran film actor Phillip Bruns. It has since been revived twice. Of one of the later productions,* Sioux Falls Argus Leader *critic Ann Grauvogl wrote, "With* Kitchen Dance, *Robinson offers a look at what it means to be vulnerable. His script that's often funny and insightful makes a case for opening up, for caring, for touching someone, even if it's only for a little while."*

The following is an excerpt starting about halfway through the first act, after the garrulous, irritable Alan Snyder and the gentle but firm Jennifer Bates have met and worked through their initial animosity. He is a long-time radio announcer who is in Rochester, Minnesota, to go through the Mayo Clinic in order to diagnose some problems related to a car accident caused by his excessive drinking. She is in Rochester with her ailing husband. They meet in a rooming house where they are forced to share the kitchen.

ALAN: So. Here we are in the kitchen.

JENNIFER: Kitchens are nice. I've always liked kitchens.

ALAN: Me too.

JENNIFER: On the farm, when I was little, we practically lived in the kitchen. Even when company came. Everyone would sit around the table and drink coffee and talk. It was the warmest place in the house.

ALAN: I used to like the kitchen at house parties. Close to the booze, I suppose, but something cozy about it, too. That's where the best conversations were going on.

JENNIFER: You really love to talk, don't you?

ALAN: They called me Motormouth in high school. The only thing I ever wanted to do was to be on the radio. To be anything on the radio. Cedric Adams, Bob Dehaven, they were my heroes. Studs Terkel, Ken Nordine, Alan Sheppard. I got a set of earphones. I'd stay up all night dialing around, listening to all the best stuff — New Orleans, WWL, Chicago, all those clear channel stations, all that good music, a lot of it live. Remember how they used to switch across the country on New Year's Eve, time zone to time zone, one big band remote after another? To be part of that, that was my idea of heaven.

JENNIFER: You still think it's heaven?

ALAN: I'm not sure I believe in heaven any more.

JENNIFER: What do you believe in?

ALAN: I believe there's a demon called Dead Air, a white-faced clown, with a toothy grin and black eyes you can see faint stars in. He has the stink of rotten roses on his breath, and his touch is like taking a fall on ice — knowing "this is it" and nothing to be done.

JENNIFER: Silence?

ALAN: No ordinary silence. A resonating one, like the hollow sound of a still, cold night, or the overtones of a bass drum — the part that comes after the boom.

JENNIFER: You've heard that kind of silence?

ALAN: Twice. I think it's what I'll hear when I die.

JENNIFER: Everyone dies.

ALAN: Don't they though? That's a curious comfort, Isn't it? Hallmark ought to have cards for it, like get-well cards. Die-well cards. Fancy ones with flowers, dignified ones, plain white, comic ones with cartoons, the punchline inside. Some with verses, some with quotations from Shakespeare. Special ones for relatives, others for old people, a different kind for those being cut down in their prime, cute little ones for kids with fuzzy, big-eyed animals. Cheer up, they'll all say in different ways — Cheer up, everyone dies.

JENNIFER: You don't know you're dying.

ALAN: I don't know I'm not. It feels the same.

(She goes to the refrigerator. ALAN meanwhile has seated himself)

JENNIFER: You love to talk, but you're hard to talk to, you know that?

ALAN: I know. I talk too much.

JENNIFER: *(She gets a diet soda.)* Not just that. What's hard is find-
    ing something to say to you that won't set you off. You won't
    be pitied and you won't be ignored. You remind me of my
    children, when they're hurt. They want attention, but they
    yell, "Leave me alone."

ALAN: That's twice you've accused me of being a child.

JENNIFER: There are worse things to be. I don't hate my children.

ALAN: That's reassuring.

JENNIFER: But I want to see them grow out of it — that selfish-
    ness.

ALAN: How do they do that?

JENNIFER: They make contact. A baby thinks it's the center of the
    universe. Then It starts making contact with things, people,
    other kids. It starts to learn. Trial and error.

ALAN: The slow way.

JENNIFER: Very slow. Some learn more slowly than others. Some
    never learn.

ALAN: I'll ignore that.

JENNIFER: When Viv and Tommy were younger, she had a terri-
    ble time with him. She was two years older, and I guess he
    was feeling left out. He kept breaking up Viv's games with
    other kids. She thought he was a monster. I'd try to explain
    why he was acting like that, but it did no good. They were
    forever fighting. She was turning into a monster, too. I felt
    like a referee in a wrestling match between King Kong and
    Godzilla.

ALAN: So who won?

JENNIFER: One day she cracked him on the forehead with a toy
    rake. Missed his eye by a half-inch. It took eight stitches to
    close the gash. I was going to punish her in some conven-
    tional way, but I knew that would do no good. So I sen-
    tenced her to be his nurse. She had to take care of him,
    change his bandages, read to him. She knew what a nurse

was from being in the hospital with appendicitis. Anyway, that was the turning point. Somehow she started to see what he was feeling. She smothered him with so much attention that he never bothered her and her friends again.

ALAN: Maybe he was just afraid of getting another whack with the rake.

JENNIFER: Maybe. I like to think it was the contact. Two persons get together, something rubs off on both of them. They can go their separate ways, but they've changed.

ALAN: Rub. I like that. Think of the songs they could write: "I'll be rubbing you, always."

JENNIFER: Maybe it's just imagination.

ALAN: That I've got. Too much, my parents used to say. Listening to *Inner Sanctum* or *Suspense*, I'd scare myself silly. Couldn't sleep.

JENNIFER: That's the easy kind of imagination.

ALAN: Thanks again.

JENNIFER: Anyone can imagine what's not there, bogeymen and ghosts. The trick is to imagine what's true. That's harder.

ALAN: If It's true, why do you have to imagine it?

JENNIFER: What's true isn't always obvious. They used to think the world was flat.

ALAN: *(Mock horror:)* You mean it isn't?

JENNIFER: Think of the imagination it took to get beyond that — something everybody knew — to the truth.

ALAN: You are something. You've really thought about this stuff, haven't you?

JENNIFER: A woman shouldn't think?

ALAN: I didn't say that.

(He turns on the radio.)

I'm impressed, that's all.

(Music comes up, a slow, dreamy dance tune, "You Were Meant

For Me.")

Good old Mel, always right there with a dram from the bottle of midnight memories.

JENNIFER: What are you doing?

ALAN: It's called setting a mood. Nothing does it like music.

JENNIFER: A mood for what?

ALAN: A mood to exercise imagination in. "I'm in the mood for rub."

JENNIFER: I said I don't play games.

ALAN: Wait a second. That's the way kids learn, isn't it? By playing? Like your daughter playing nurse?

JENNIFER: I've been playing nurse for a year and a half. I don't need any more of that.

ALAN: Then we can play something else. At being friends. At making contact. At make-believe ballroom.

(He takes her hand and pulls her to him, starts moving her around in a very formal, stylized dance.)

JENNIFER: That's not what I meant by contact.

ALAN: Would you rather hit me in the head with a rake?

JENNIFER: I'd rather talk.

ALAN: You can't talk anyone into anything. You said so yourself.

JENNIFER: Then stop talking.

(They dance without speaking for awhile. He tries some more elaborate steps.)

Fancy.

ALAN: You want to see fancy?

(He tries more complicated moves, but they get hopelessly entangled. She starts laughing.)

Maybe we should stick with the basics.

(They start dancing again, but now he holds her very close.)

JENNIFER: Isn't this a little too basic?

ALAN: First things first.

> (*He takes a couple more steps and the telephone rings. He tries to ignore it, but it rings again.*)

Damn.

> (*He answers it.*)

Hello? — just a second.

> (*He holds out the receiver, turns down the radio.*)

For you.

> (*She stiffens, moves to the phone with dread.*)

JENNIFER: Hello? — This is she. — Yes. — Yes, I understand. I'll be right there. Thank you.

> (*She hangs up.*)

ALAN: Your husband?

> (*She nods.*)

Anything I can—?

JENNIFER: No.

> (*She starts out.*)

ALAN: Is he — ?

JENNIFER: He's worse. I've got to go to him.

> (*She goes to her room. She quickly gathers her clothes, changes into her street boots, goes out. ALAN listens to her go. He looks around at the empty chairs.*)

ALAN: Gentlemen, there's the rub.

> (*He stands, opens the towel drawer, looks in a long time. He closes it again, looks around at the chairs.*)

We who have the imagination to know that the earth is round — We know what night this is, don't we? It's the winter solstice, the longest night. In primitive cultures, those that in their ignorance believed the world stood still at the center of the universe, the night was celebrated by a watch, a wake, and the bonfires burned until dawn. They were afraid the sun might never return.

(He finds the cards, starts to play solitaire.)

It was at such celebrations that games were invented to kill time. And when time was dead, a game was invented to bring it back again. And they called the game — Dead Air.

Curtain Act One

At the beginning of Act Two Jennifer is discovered skipping rope as penance for the guilt she feels in being attracted to Alan. He returns to the kitchen with a scrawny Christmas tree, obviously hoping that they will be able to spend Christmas Eve together, but she insists on going to the hospital to be with her husband. She is in her room, getting ready to leave, when he discovers a bottle in a towel drawer in the kitchen. Alarmed, he knocks on her door.

JENNIFER: What do you want?

ALAN: I've got to ask you something. It'll only take a second.

(She goes to the door and opens it. Her dress is unzipped down the back. He holds up the bottle.)

JENNIFER: What?

ALAN: Is this yours? If it is, I wish you'd take it with you.

JENNIFER: What is it?

ALAN: Peppermint schnapps.

(She shakes her head, befuddled.)

Booze? Sauce? Hooch? White Lightning? I found it in the towel drawer.

JENNIFER: It's not mine.

ALAN: It's not the landlady's. It doesn't have a note on it.

JENNIFER: One of the other guests must've left It. why the fuss?

ALAN: It makes me nervous.

JENNIFER: Why?

ALAN: For the same reason you'd be nervous if you found a loaded revolver in your husband's night stand.

JENNIFER: You said you'd stopped drinking, but —

ALAN: I didn't say I'd stopped drinking. I said I hadn't had a drink.

JENNIFER: What's the difference?

(She tries to get at the dress zipper but can't reach it.)

ALAN: The state of mind. You want me to get that? Turn around.

(She turns around. He zips her up) I'm an alcoholic.

JENNIFER: Oh.

(She turns back to him.)

ALAN: You don't get over it. You get lucky. If you get lucky, you get smart. You find out there are some things you can do and some things you can't do.

(He holds up the bottle.)

The first station on the line, iron rails, non-stop to hell, dead air, dead end.

JENNIFER: *(Reaching for the bottle:)* I'll take it, then.

ALAN: *(Pulling it away:)* Not so fast.

JENNIFER: No trouble. I'll stick it in a trash can somewhere.

ALAN: No. I'll take care of it. —

JENNIFER: But you said —

ALAN: I've got to take care of it. I just realized that. You can't do it for me.

JENNIFER: If you say so. I've got to be going.

(She gets her coat.)

ALAN: Don't let me stop you.

(He looks around the room)

Nice decorations. The flags of all nations, good touch.

(She starts out, turns in the doorway and gives him a look. He

looks down at his fly, then up again.)

What?

JENNIFER: You're in my room.

ALAN: Oh, yes.

(She stands aside as he goes into the hall. She closes and locks the door, goes down the hall and out. He looks after her a moment, then goes on into the kitchen. He takes the bottle to the kitchen sink, unscrews the cap, and starts to pour it out, but then turns around.)

Admitting defeat, right? I'm letting a pint of peppermint schnapps bring me to my knees. It's easy enough to stand up to temptation when there's nothing to tempt you.

(He screws the cap back onto the bottle. He sets the bottle on the table, then he gets the little tree and sets it on the other side of the table. He gets the package from his son and puts that under the tree as well. He stands back to admire his handiwork.)

Gentlemen, Merry Christmas.

(But his eyes are irresistibly drawn to the bottle.)

Blackout, end of scene.

Christmas Eve does not go well for Alan. He calls his son, Skip, and then asks to talk to his wife. When she rebuffs him, he becomes upset. She hangs up on him, he calls again, but the phone doesn't answer. Tempted to drink, he calls his AA mentor, but at last he seems ready to give in to temptation. He looks at the bottle of Peppermint Schnapps, then picks it up.

ALAN: For me?

(He unscrews the cap and sniffs it but is interrupted by a great commotion from below, glass breaking. There is the sound of footsteps on the stairs. He sets the bottle back on the table and goes to the ball door.)

Who's there?

JENNIFER: (Off:) The ghost of Christmas Present.

ALAN: Mrs. Bates?

(JENNIFER appears in the hall, obviously tipsy.)

JENNIFER: You remember that china pitcher at the bottom of the stairs?

ALAN: Yes?

JENNIFER: Good, because that's all it is, now-a memory.

(She comes into the kitchen, sits at the table. He helps her.)

ALAN: What have you done to yourself?

JENNIFER: *(A bit indignant:)* What do you mean?

ALAN: I mean you're drunk.

JENNIFER: I am? Am I really? I thought I was just slightly whacked out of shape. *(She sees the bottle)* For me?

(She reaches for it, but he grabs it away from her, screws on the cap and sets it on the counter.)

ALAN: Maybe you'd better give it a rest.

(He sits down with her.)

What happened?

JENNIFER: Is it warm in here?

ALAN: You've got your coat on.

(JENNIFER opens the window.)

Steady.

(He helps her with her coat, shuts the window.)

JENNIFER: Santa Claus tried to pick me up.

ALAN: What?

JENNIFER: I said, Santa Claus tried to put the make on me. At the bar. *(She sits at the table.)*

ALAN: What were you doing at a bar?

JENNIFER: I went to the hospital first. Gary was having pain. They gave him a sedative. He dozed off. He looked so peaceful. I sat there a long time, watching him sleep. I started to envy him. Then I left. It was still early.

ALAN: Why didn't you come back here? I could have used the company.

JENNIFER: I was afraid.

ALAN: What of?

JENNIFER: I don't know. Of what could happen.

ALAN: What did you think was going to happen?

JENNIFER: I don't know.

ALAN: Nothing you wouldn't want to happen.

JENNIFER: That's what I was afraid of — So I had the time and there was this bar. You wouldn't believe the people at a bar on Christmas Eve.

ALAN: Yes I would.

JENNIFER: So I started talking to Santa Claus. Very sad. He's got this seasonal job. Tomorrow he joins the ranks of the unemployed. I felt sorry for him. That's my weakness, feeling sorry for people.

ALAN: And he bought you a couple of drinks —

JENNIFER: A couple drinks. And then he started getting fresh — putting his mittens where they didn't belong —

ALAN: And then, like a good little girl —

JENNIFER: I kneed him in the nuts and came home.

ALAN: You what?

JENNIFER: *(Singing:)* "Jingle balls, jingle balls — "

ALAN: Santa Claus?

JENNIFER: It was sad. A bar on Christmas Eve has to be the saddest place.

ALAN: I know.

JENNIFER: *(Opens window.)* Is it warm in here?

ALAN: Maybe you'd better get to bed.

JENNIFER: Don't start that again.

ALAN: *(Closes window.)* I mean sleep.

JENNIFER: I'm not sleepy. I'm hungry. I didn't have anything to eat. That's the trouble. Never get drunk on an empty stomach.

ALAN: Why did you want to get drunk?

JENNIFER: Do I need an excuse? *(Opens oven and peers in.)* I'm hungry. I need an olive.

ALAN: Sit down. I'll get it for you.

(He gets a jar of olives from the refrigerator. She gets one out with her fingers and eats it.)

You want a fork?

(She gives him a nasty look.)

For your olives?

JENNIFER: *(Eating another:)* Finger food.

ALAN: Don't eat too many. You'll get sick.

JENNIFER: You can't eat too many olives.

ALAN: You can get too much of anything.

JENNIFER: Except T-L-C.

ALAN: Except what?

JENNIFER: Tender loving care. You can't get too much of that. Or olives.

(She tries to fan herself with her skirt.)

Why is it so warm in here?

ALAN: It's the booze.

JENNIFER: It's like a steam bath. Can't we open a window?

ALAN: It's freezing outside. You'd get pneumonia.

JENNIFER: I never get sick.

(She kicks off her shoes.)

ALAN: There's always a first time.

JENNIFER: Not for me. Everyone else in the family gets sick. Not me. There's got to be someone left to play nursemaid. Nurses don't get sick. *(Frantically fanning herself with her skirt:)* I am being boiled in oil. I'll get the window.

(She starts to the window, staggers into him. He catches her and holds her up)

Want to dance?

ALAN: Why don't we waltz to your room?

JENNIFER: You've got a one-track mind, don't you?

ALAN: I think you could use some sleep. Come on.

(He tries to steer her to the hallway. She tries to make a dance out of it, humming "You Were Meant For Me. ")

JENNIFER: You're a good dancer, you know that?

ALAN: I know. Be careful, now.

(He gets her into the hallway.)

JENNIFER: I could never get Gary to dance.

(He gets her to the door, but it is locked.)

ALAN: Where's your key?

JENNIFER: In my purse.

(He props her up against his door.)

ALAN: You stay right here. I'll get it.

(He lets her go. Her knees start to buckle. He holds her up against the door until she's balanced. He goes to the kitchen to get the key.)

JENNIFER: It's hot in here.

(She pulls her dress up over her head, but she can't get it the rest of the way off. ALAN returns.)

ALAN: What are you doing?

JENNIFER: I'm suffocating. Get me out of here.

(He pulls the dress off her head. He drapes the dress on a hall stand and tries to get the door opened while she leans on him)

You're a nice man. You know who you remind me of?

ALAN: Your husband?

JENNIFER: My father.

ALAN: Wonderful. Arthur Godfrey, Franklin McCormick and your father.

(He gets the door open, helps her in and seats her on the edge of the bed.)

JENNIFER: My father didn't want me to get married. He wanted me to be a teacher.

ALAN: *(Turning down the covers:)* A teacher is a good thing to be.

JENNIFER: That's what my father thought. He thought teachers had all the answers.

ALAN: Don't teachers have all the answers?

JENNIFER: Not the teachers I had. They had nothing but questions. And my father died. And I'm not a teacher. So what's it all about?

ALAN: Who knows?

JENNIFER: That's what I want to know. what's it all about?

(She stands up, hoists her slip and hooks her panty hose down, tries to pull them off while standing up.)

What difference does it make? Being a teacher or being a nurse or being a wife or being a mother. It's all the same isn't it? You're so busy being something, you don't do anything. You don't get anything done.

(She gets the panty hose off except for the toes, jerking at them all the time. Finally they slip free.)

ALAN: You want to do something?

JENNIFER: I want to do something.

ALAN: Get in bed.

(She looks at the bed, lies down, suddenly docile. He starts out.)

JENNIFER: Don't I get a bedtime story?

ALAN: You want a bedtime story?

(She nods, closes her eyes.)

"Once upon a time — " Let's see — "Once upon a time, there was a princess. A beautiful princess, much more beautiful than her ugly stepsisters. One day, while she was playing in the garden beside the castle, a frog came along — " Mrs. Bates?

(He pulls the covers over her, starts out.)

JENNIFER: Go on.

ALAN: "So the frog said, 'Lovely Princess, will you give me a kiss? One little kiss?'"

(He stops, looks at her. She is dozing off. He bends over her and kisses her.)

Don't you want to know how the story ends? Mrs. Bates? Princess?

(She's asleep. ALAN looks at her a long moment. All the tension has gone out of her face now. He shakes his head in wonder.)

Amazing. Absolutely amazing.

Black Out, End of Scene

ACT II, SCENE III

(Christmas Morning. JENNIFER is in her room, asleep. ALAN is sitting at the kitchen table, staring at a glass of liquid on the table in front of him. A half empty coke bottle is on the table as welL The schnapps bottle is not to be seen. ALAN lifts the glass, sniffs at it, sets it back down.)

ALAN: It doesn't look so bad. It doesn't smell so bad.

(He lifts the glass as though to drink, but he can't go through with it. He puts it back.)

Ice. That's what it needs. A little ice.

(He gets a tray of ice-cubes from the refrigerator, the old -fashioned kind. He tries to get the cubes out but can't.)

Damn!

(He knocks the tray against the edge of the sink. That awakens JENNIFER, who sits up.)

JENNIFER: What?

(She blinks, trying to focus her eyes.)

What?

(Then it hits her. A gigantic headache.)

Oh no.

(She holds her head. Meanwhile, ALAN has turned on the water in the sink and is running it over the tray of ice. JENNIFER puts down her hand and listens.)

How did I — ?

(She peeks under her sheet, sees she is wearing a slip.)

Oh no.

(She sits up, moaning with the pain.)

Who — ?

(And then a thought more horrible than her hangover comes to her. She covers herself with her hands.)

Oh God, no. Not — Santa Claus?

(In the kitchen, ALAN finally manages to get a couple of cubes out, takes them over to the glass, dumps them in, stirs them with his finger. He sniffs his finger and makes a face. JENNIFER squints at the clock on the dresser.)

Oh no.

(She tries to stand up but rises too quickly and gets hammered between the eyes for her effort. She sits down again. Then she spies the soft pretzel of her pantihose on the floor. She picks it up and looks at it.)

Oh no.

(She looks around the room, trying to see the rest of her clothing.)

My dress. My shoes. My purse, for God's sake.

(She gets up, paws around in her bed clothes, finds her robe and

pulls it on. She goes to the door, opens it. The first thing she spots is her dress draped on the hall stand.)

Oh no.

(ALAN has seated himself at the table again, and is looking at the glass, trying to brace his resolve. JENNIFER staggers to the bathroom and slams the door after her. ALAN hears it, turns to call into the hallway.)

ALAN: Mrs. Bates? Are you up?

(He gets no answer. He goes back to staring at the brown liquid in the glass.)

Don't think I'm afraid of you. I've beaten worse than you. Get that straight, at least.

(JENNIFER comes out of the bathroom, appears at the door of the kitchen. She sees him looking at the glass. As she watches, he picks up the glass and brings it to his mouth. She is aghast.)

JENNIFER: Oh no!

(She bursts in, grabs the glass away from him.)

What are you doing?

ALAN: Mrs. Bates, I —

JENNIFER: What are you doing with this?

ALAN: Look, it's all right, I was just —

JENNIFER: It is not all right. It's been almost a year. That's what you said. And — *(She looks at him, then at the glass.)* It's me, isn't it. It was me coming in last night — How did I come in?

ALAN: Very unsteady.

JENNIFER: Very — And — Was I — Can you tell me something? Was I with anybody?

ALAN: Anybody? Besides me?

JENNIFER: Heavy-set guy? With a beard?

ALAN: You were alone.

JENNIFER: *(Relieved:)* I was alone.

ALAN: But unsteady.

JENNIFER: Unsteady. I may have had one or two drinks. I should have been more thoughtful. Seeing me like that, you must've —

ALAN: It didn't bother me, really.

(He tries to get closer to her.)

Now give me the —

JENNIFER: *(Pulling the glass away:)* I can't let you. It would be my fault.

ALAN: It's not what you —

JENNIFER: Stay away!

ALAN: Don't!

(She drinks the liquid from the glass, chug-a-lug. He watches astounded. She finishes, gasping.)

JENNIFER: Hair of the dog. — Isn't that what they call it?

(She licks her lips, makes a face.)

Tastes like the whole dog. what was it?

ALAN: I was trying to tell you —

(JENNIFER suddenly feels very uncomfortable.)

JENNIFER: My God, what was that?

ALAN: Castor oil and Coke.

(She starts gagging, runs to the bathroom. He calls after her.)

It was supposed to make it go down easier.

(The bathroom door slams shut. He shrugs, fills the ice tray and puts it back in the refrigerator. JENNIFER appears in the door again, gives a little groan. ALAN turns to her.)

How do you feel?

JENNIFER: Like I've been hit with a rake.

(She wobbles to the table, sits.)

I need aspirin.

ALAN: Can I get it for you?

> (JENNIFER points to cupboard. He goes to the cupboard, gets the aspirin bottle, puts it on the table.)

ALAN: Listen, maybe you'd like to take my enema for me too.

> (She looks at him wanly. He gets her a glass of water as she struggles with the cap on the bottle.)

Having trouble with that? Let me.

JENNIFER: It's got a secret lock. It can't be opened by kids or sick people.

> (He opens the bottle. She takes the pills as she did before, putting them on the back of her tongue one at a time. ALAN watches, fascinated.)

ALAN: It's like watching a circus act. The pill-swallower.

JENNIFER: I'm so embarrassed.

ALAN: That can be worse than the hangover sometimes.

JENNIFER: I don't drink much usually. I don't know what got into me.

> (She leans back in her chair, accidentally kicks her shoes. She looks down and sees them.)

What are my shoes doing out here?

ALAN: You took them off out here.

JENNIFER: (Suspecting the worst:) What else did I do?

ALAN: You were warm. I think you wanted to take everything off.

JENNIFER: Oh no.

ALAN: Have you ever done that before? Blacked out after drinking?

JENNIFER: Never. why?

ALAN: It's one of the first signs of a drinking problem.

JENNIFER: I'm not a — (But suddenly she is not so sure.) Am I?

ALAN: Probably not.

JENNIFER: Why did I do that?

ALAN: You had your reasons. Everyone does.

JENNIFER: *(Apprehensive:)* You — You put me to bed?

ALAN: Tucked you in and told you a fairy tale.

JENNIFER: Oh no.

> *(She holds her head)*

> I could just die.

ALAN: I didn't take advantage of you. — If that's what you're thinking.

JENNIFER: Was I — falling down?

ALAN: You were funny.

JENNIFER: I'll bet.

ALAN: It's one of the choices you have as a drunk. Funny, abusive, violent, self-pitying — I usually opted for maudlin, with a dash of abuse.

JENNIFER: It must have been terrible for you. To have to deal with me, I mean.

ALAN: It wasn't that bad. You were very talkative.

JENNIFER: What did I say?

ALAN: You mentioned your father. How he wanted you to be a teacher.

JENNIFER: I can't remember any of that. *(She holds her head.)* I think my headache is getting worse instead of better.

ALAN: *(Holding up his hands:)* Want to try the magic hands cure?

> *(JENNIFER shrugs. ALAN gets behind her, starts massaging her neck.)*

> The only real cure is time. But this might help a little.

JENNIFER: Feels good — Thanks for taking care of me last night.

ALAN: Actually, I ought to be thanking you. You saved me from the demon of dead air last night.

JENNIFER: I did? How?

ALAN: Perfect timing. I was about to start sucking at that bottle of schnapps. You came in just in time.

JENNIFER: I remember the bottle. I should've taken it with me.

ALAN: I should've let you. It's always a mistake to turn down help when it's offered. Somewhere in the back of my mind, I think I intended to give in all along. I called my wife and made a fool of myself and that was all I needed. I'd like to blame it on someone else, but it's really me. I dig a hole and jump into it and then I look around to see who shoved me.

JENNIFER: So I interrupted you. Then what?

ALAN: There's nothing quite as sobering as seeing someone else drunk. Someone like you especially.

JENNIFER: I thought you said I was funny.

ALAN: Funny and sad at the same time. When you went to sleep, I couldn't stop looking at you. A sleeping beauty. You looked so — vulnerable. I gave you a kiss.

JENNIFER: *(Stiffening:)* You what?

ALAN: Watch it. You're stringing your violin again. It was a fatherly kiss. All of a sudden I wanted to protect you.

(*JENNIFER pulls away from him.*)

What's the matter?

JENNIFER: I don't want you protecting me. I don't want you thinking about it. There's nothing to protect me from.

ALAN: I don't think you understand. All my life I've felt trapped — like I was inside a bottle. I could see out, I could yell out, but I couldn't get out. The only thing I knew or felt was my own hurt. But as I watched you sleeping, it came to me that for that little time I hadn't been thinking about myself. I hadn't been pitying myself or hating myself or trying to kill myself in fast or slow motion. I'd broken out. All I'd been thinking about was you.

JENNIFER: Feeling sorry for me?

ALAN: Worrying about you. Because I'd been there.

JENNIFER: How did you know where I was?

ALAN: I could guess. Sixth sense, remember?

JENNIFER: You know why I went to the bar?

ALAN: You felt guilty.

JENNIFER: I was guilty. Tried and convicted. It was no fairy tale.

ALAN: On what charge?

JENNIFER: Adultery. Giving in to passion. And while my husband was deathly ill.

ALAN: Did I miss something? I don't remember you giving in.

JENNIFER: I gave in all right. It was just a fluke I didn't carry through. A technicality.

ALAN: Some technicality.

JENNIFER: I know what I was feeling.

ALAN: You're being pretty hard on yourself, aren't you?

JENNIFER: No more than I deserve.

ALAN: That's the kind of thinking that can land you in the jug for good. Shouldn't you be sure you've done something wrong before you sentence yourself to life?

JENNIFER: I would have gone to bed with you that first night. I would have done it last night. Maybe that's why I was drinking, getting ready, drowning my conscience. — If you asked me right now —

ALAN: Don't say It.

JENNIFER: It's true. I'll tell you something your sixth sense didn't tell you. — Before Gary got sick, I was thinking about divorce. It hadn't been good with us for a long time. He'd been sleeping around. But when I found out he was sick — that he was dying — I couldn't go through with it. How could I? So I settled into my martyrdom. I pulled it in around me for a year and a half. Don't tell me about prisons — I live in one.

ALAN: I guess I was too wrapped up in myself to see before this.

JENNIFER: Those courses I took at the "U," there were all these
young people in them. Kids. And always laughing. You
notice how kids are always laughing? — They reminded me
of all I'd given up. Of course I'd given it up gladly, but that
didn't seem to make any difference just then. I couldn't stand
myself for what I found myself thinking. I'd started out
thinking — "If Gary dies — " And somehow that turned into
— "When Gary dies — "

ALAN: When he dies — what?

JENNIFER: I'd be free. Free!

*(She starts sobbing. He moves to her and holds her. Finally she can
go on.)*

One more thing to lash myself with. And that's why I can't
let him go, no matter how easy it would be. Because I'd have
to live with that forever.

ALAN: I think I understand. I do.

JENNIFER: And if that's not enough, you come along with your
romantic ideas —

ALAN: Romantic? Me?

JENNIFER: All hearts and flowers inside. And you got to me. If
you'd been half as tough as you pretend to be — But you
turned out to be the one thing I had no defense for — a gentle man.

(She kisses him, a sad and hopeless kiss.)

ALAN: We are in a hell of a fix, aren't we?

JENNIFER: It's impossible.

(She pushes away from him.)

Just impossible!

*(She runs to her room. She gets out a suitcase and starts packing
rapidly, carelessly. ALAN sits at the table, tries to think things
through. JENNIFER starts to talk to herself, almost inaudibly at
first, and in fragments, then more loudly and coherently.)*

— a long time ago — plenty of other places — just cut it off — before it gets started —

(ALAN hears her, goes to the hall door to listen. She goes on.)

A year and a half, and I'm not going to ruin it all now. — I'll get away, that's all, just get it out of my head.

(ALAN goes to her door and listens.)

I can be alone. — I'm perfectly happy alone, — And I don't need crutches. — I'm not afraid of silence. — I'm not afraid of dead air.

(ALAN shoves the door. It swings open.)

ALAN: Then why are you talking to yourself?

JENNIFER: What?

ALAN: If you're not afraid of dead air why are you talking to yourself?

JENNIFER: Was I?

(She sits on the bed.)

Oh no. I was. I've caught your craziness.

ALAN: It's not so crazy. It's as old as the second generation of Adam whistling your way past the graveyard.

(He looks at the suitcase.)

You think this is the only way out of the fix? Pack and run?

JENNIFER: *(Unhesitating:)* Yes.

ALAN: You can't cure misery with more misery. I've tried it.

JENNIFER: *(Out of her room to the kitchen:)* You can't cure it at all.

ALAN: *(Following her:)* You can treat the symptoms.

JENNIFER: But we can't —

ALAN: We can't do a lot of things. But some we can do. We can come back here at night. We can have chili. We can talk. I can teach you gin rummy and double solitaire —

JENNIFER: And cheating?

ALAN: No cheating. We'll play by the rules. We'll obey all the
   red-letter notes to the last dot. If we lose, we lose.

JENNIFER: You think so? You think we can do all that? Without
   driving each other crazy?

ALAN: There are worse things to be than crazy. You can be alone.
   You can be dead.

JENNIFER: That still frightens you, doesn't it?

ALAN: Sure. But there's not a damned thing I can do about it.
   Death always gets the last dance. But there are more dances
   on the card before that.

   *(He holds his arms out, a formal invitation to dance. She takes his
   hand.)*

   What, a week at least?

JENNIFER: A week. One week.

ALAN: And we know exactly where we stand, which is a hell of a
   lot more than most people do.

JENNIFER: And maybe I can teach you something, too.

ALAN: You already have.

JENNIFER: Something different. Something better than talking
   together. Being quiet together.

   (There is a pause, just to the breaking point.)

ALAN: *(Unable to contain himself:)* I'd flunk.

JENNIFER: *(Hugging him:)* Shh. You can always talk when you're
   alone.

   *(There is another, longer pause. ALAN looks as though he might
   burst at first, then he looks at her, shakes his head in wonder. She
   smiles. They settle into a comfortable togetherness. She starts humming: "You Were Meant For Me." Slowly they start to dance. It is
   as it was in the beginning, very formal, very prim, and they are
   hardly touching. Finally, she speaks.)*

JENNIFER: Merry Christmas, Mr. Snyder.

ALAN: Merry Christmas, Mrs. Bates.

Blackout, End of Scene

That, of course, is not the end of the story. In the play, as in real life, things are more complicated. The cancer that had been threatening the life of Jennifer's husband goes into remission. At the end of their week, Alan and Jennifer go their separate ways. And we learn that for Alan, as well, things have changed. He calls his son and reveals that doctors have found a tumor in his brain. After he hangs up, the phone rings. He answers, but there is nobody there, only dead air. After he leaves, the phone rings again and again.

Caring Behaviors
An Interview
With Becky Nelson

Becky Nelson is currently President of Sioux Valley Hospital. She has served previously as Vice President of Patient Services and as Nursing Director of Critical Care Services.

Art: Becky Nelson, could you give us some background about how you got involved in nursing and when you started thinking about caring as a concept?

Becky: I had always been somewhat exposed to the medical profession. At 17 I graduated from high school and planned to go to SDSU Pharmacy School. My little brother, eight years younger than I am, had shot himself accidentally when he went to put his gun away. The bullet went in right above his lip and out right before his ear and shattered his teeth, but didn't go into the brain. It was really a rather bad wound. He was admitted to pediatrics at St. Luke's.

It was my first exposure to nursing. I sat up there constantly because I had been the one who had taken him out hunting and didn't get his gun put away, so I was feeling pretty responsible. I did the vigil with everybody else, but I think I was pretty much the constant one, and I was fascinated by nursing.

Even back then I could sense the difference between nurses. The difference was more than technical skills. I would connect with some, and others I had less of a connection with, and sometimes even a problem with. As I have reflected in later years back on that experience, I think that was the beginning of my wondering what that difference was between nurses. The hospitalization of my brother and my experiences with the nurses is what caused me to go into nursing.

I graduated from Presentation College and started at Dakota Midland and started in critical care right away. It was a combined ICU-CCU Unit, so we had some patients who were awake and interacting, and, obviously, patients who were not. But even back then, there was a sense within myself that I had a connection with some patients that was warmer than with other patients. I would feel guilty about not liking some or not doing everything I could, and I would wonder why I acted differently towards some patients. I also noted the difference between my colleagues who were working. I think the differences are what intrigued me the most. Why would I feel more caring — and probably patients and families experienced me more caring with certain patients while others experienced me differently?

Two years later, when I became a head nurse, I really started experiencing the differences in family and patient interaction. Families and patients would come to me as head nurse, back in those days, and talk to me about a nurse or other caregiver who just didn't care. That started me wondering again why there was that difference. And often it would be highly technically skilled nurses who just didn't "have it" with patients and just didn't connect.

When I talk about connectivity, that is a far more mature concept than I had back then. I was looking at the difference, and I began to wonder why some nurses seemed more caring than others. Coming from a management perspective, I wondered if you could teach someone to be caring.

When a nurse would say to me, "You know, I don't exactly understand what I am doing wrong... what the concern is." I would wonder myself, "Can I give her explicit examples that would help her know maybe how to do it differently or better the next time that she was with a patient?"

Art: Would you say that your interest in caring came out of your practice and not from your classes in nursing?

Becky: Absolutely. In fact, I have to say that as a result of my observations on pediatrics at St. Luke's with my younger brother, I really did believe that nursing was absolutely the most caring profession. I even remember thinking, "Would I have IT? Would I be caring enough?" It was one thing to go into pharmacy and count pills. I had worked with my dad in the pharmacy for years. It would be another thing to go into this caring profession of nursing and really stick by a patient.

Ron: I think that for a lot of people there still is a feeling that caring is instinctive. When you talk about somebody being a caring person, you think the person was born that way. It's not something that has to be learned. What are the aspects of caring that have to be learned and that are not necessarily instinctive?

Becky: What I learned in my research and in some of my discussions is the concept of primacy. The patient's interest and the patient's well-being is important, as well as relating to that individual as a whole person: spiritual, psychological, and emotional, and not reducing the patient to a leg, an arm, or a gall bladder. I think that can be learned and can be continually reinforced throughout an individual's experience and education. I think the other part of caring is the support, the taking of time. When I say "taking of time," I am in dangerous waters because time is such an important variable for everybody and the response often is, "If I had more time, I would do that, but since I don't have time I can't be more caring." I don't believe that. I don't believe it is a matter of dedicating ten minutes with nothing else to do. You can be caring and responding to a patient while you are doing other tasks for that patient.

Caring is the recognition that this individual is another human being and that I am caring for that individual as a privilege, not as my right or as my employment contract. I've been granted that privilege to care for that patient and I am treating my relationship with that patient as a privileged relationship; not making decisions for that patient unilaterally, but rather involving the patient in those decisions and discussions. And those can be the very smallest discussions. I'm not talking about highly ethical or life-threatening or life-and-death decisions, I'm talking about even the smallest of decisions: "How would you like your bath today?" or "Would you like to walk today?" and giving the alternatives and treating that person as human. Not all of that is instinctive. I think the manner in which you communicate with a patient often may be instinctive, but I think you can still show a caring attitude by developing an awareness and a skill in treating a patient as an individual, treating a patient as the primary concern.

Mary: Can you give some of the examples, things that you have found in your research?

Becky: When I did my research for my Masters in Nursing, my focus was to determine what behaviors a nurse exhibited or demonstrated, whether verbally or non-verbally, to a patient that gave the patient the impression that the nurse cared about them. That is, the nurse didn't just take care of the patient, but really cared about the person. With the help of my advisers, I designed a chronological qualitative study that involved extensive interviews with patients. I really used just two open-ended questions. Interestingly, I didn't have to offer a lot of feedback in order to get a response. I was cautious about leading the patient and leading the discussion more than I had to.

The first question was if the patient had felt that a nurse cared about him or her and what she did or said to the patient that caused him or her to think that the nurse cared about them. The second question was, "How did it make you feel?"

The most profound and most descriptive experience was that of a 68-year-old man. He was a very prominent individual in the city, educated, intelligent, and successful. I cite those attributes, if you will, just to demonstrate the position he was put in and the stark difference between the world that he left and the world that he was living in the hospital. He was in the hospital and very dependent on other people. He was a very private individual; he had a wife and three daughters, so he'd lived in a household of women. He joked that you had to be extra careful when you lived in a houseful of women because of the things that you'd see with all the women running around the house. He was a very private individual.

His condition required a foley catheter being inserted through the penis and up the urethra and into the bladder. The catheter tubing emptied into a bag. We had an elderly nun in nursing school who taught us when we emptied a bedpan to cover it with a white cloth and to carry it down the hall. That was to protect the dignity of the individual. And I remember thinking that that was kind of an old fashioned idea, but I have to tell you in the interview with this man, that memory was there.

He had a real problem, and he verbalized it, with his urine bag. His first discussion was about the bag being on the side of the bed and that people could walk down the hallway and look in and see the bag of urine hanging from the bed. He said to me that the most uncomfortable part of that is that people know where that tube is going. I don't think that he even said the word "penis," that's how private he was. He said, "It's so humiliating to have people see a part of me hanging in that bag and then knowing where that tube is going." And he would move that bag. He would adjust it, pick it up and carry it over and hang it on the other side of the bed. He demonstrated how he would put it on the other side of the bed so people couldn't see it from the doorway.

One day he was having company. His sister from out of town was having a birthday and family members decided to come and visit him. He had rested in the morning, gotten ready for this visit and he said right before the visit he had arranged the urine bag so it was as covered up as much as possible. He even adjusted the sheets so that they hung down over the bag. I could tell he had even looked at how the chairs would be positioned around the bed.

As the family was visiting, the nurse walked in with a pitcher to empty and measure the urine. He was on a water pill, a diuretic, and his urine needed to be measured every hour. He said "She walked in and stopped and looked at me and I looked at her and I'm sure my face was full of horror. I just about died because I knew exactly what she was going to do. I just pleaded with her through my eyes not to do that. She stopped and kind of caught herself and said, 'Oh, oh, I forgot something. I'll be back,' and turned around and walked out. I knew that she knew what I had communicated to her with my eyes, and I knew she wouldn't be back."

The rest of the visit he didn't worry about the nurse coming back in. He figured the nurse had gotten the message and wouldn't be back. She came in later after the company had left to empty the urine and said to him, "I just couldn't do it then. I came back to empty this urine now." And he thanked her for doing that and said, "I know that you did that for me. I know that you knew what that meant to me and that you quickly changed your mind and didn't empty the urine."

What is so evident is that this story demonstrates a caring individual. The nurse knew enough about him to understand how private he was and how much that meant to him. And the other notable thing about the nurses's action is that she was willing to go against protocol, against policy and procedure, to individualize the plan of care, and not empty that urine on schedule. She reassured him that it was okay that she had gone against protocol. "I knew that you had plenty of urine, so it wasn't going to be an issue. I didn't have to measure it then. I knew it was going to be okay to wait to measure it."

And that in itself gave the man the message that he was being cared for by a very competent individual who wasn't going to risk his clinical condition just to protect his emotions. And I think there was a certain comfort in his knowing that the nurse would have measured the urine on schedule if it had been important. She might have changed the way she did it, but would have still gotten it done. So that gave him some sense of confidence as well. It was a story that he has repeated to others, so I know this meant a lot to him.

There were many other patient stories. One of the others that I was quite impressed with was an older woman who had a chest tube. It was a pretty much chronic situation. She too was a very independent woman, having always taken care of herself. She was very intelligent, educated, and had worked a good share of her adult life. What she was so impressed with was a nurse making the effort to teach her how to disconnect the chest tube in order for her to walk to the bathroom. This situation arose because of the humiliation that this individual experienced when she soiled her bed. She would turn the light on and there might not be a fast enough response to help her to the bathroom. It was terribly difficult for her. So, a nurse taught her the mechanics of suction and also educated her to the risks of disconnecting that suction improperly, and made her promise that she wouldn't unhook it unless it was absolutely necessary. But if it was, the woman would know how to do it and she would know how to get to the bathroom on her own. This woman observed, "The nurse thought enough about me and thought I could understand... thought I was smart enough to understand." The nurse recognized enough about the patient to know that she would be able to grasp this technique. She again took account of the patient's interests and made a decision that could have possibly ended up to be a complication. But this meant a lot to this woman.

Another narrative dealt with a college professor who had a fractured leg and was placed in traction. This individual was looking at a long period of convalescence in the hospital. In the interview he talked about the traction. "I know that I was a real bother for the nurses, I was constantly putting on my light, having them come in. I wasn't sleeping and I was bothering them all of the time." He told me about a nurse who he thought was absolutely the most caring individual. She recognized that he was concerned about his traction and that he was terribly afraid that something might happen with the traction. He knew enough to make him nervous, and he was scared to death that this traction wouldn't stay intact and that he would then not heal or would end up needing surgery.

He said, "The nurse and I had a long talk, because I was asking questions about the traction." I think she was kind of busy that day, but she had called for the orderly, the person who has the mechanical expertise for traction and sets it up. The nurse came into the room with the orderly and said to the patient, "What I've asked Tom to do is to go over the construction of the traction with you. He has pictures and he's going to walk you through the mechanics of the traction."

And the orderly looked at the patient and said, "Okay. I've never done this before." But he sat down with the book and they spent a half hour going through it. And the patient said, "I was thrilled, because I understood exactly how the traction was set up. But what meant so much to me, was that the nurse then said, 'Now listen. I had the orderly explain to you because I wanted you to have a full understanding of how this traction works, but what's really important for you to know is that it's not your job to monitor this traction; that's our job, and I check it all of the time.' And she explained that the weights were at the end of the bed and she could see when they were not in proper position, even from the hallway. 'I check it anytime I'm in here and I check it anytime I'm doing anything with your IV. Anytime I'm doing anything, I am checking that traction. But that doesn't mean that if you have a question or you think something doesn't look right that you can't put your light on and call me, because then I'll come in and check it. So we're both checking it, but you're not responsible for it.'"

And that meant so much to him because he even said, "After I learned about it, I even got a little more scared. But when she reassured me, I knew that she and I together were going to make this work."

That also came in other stories: the sense that the nurse was always there and that the caring nurses were the ones who gave patients the impression of being there. So presence was the other concept. Caring nurses gave the impression that they were always present to the patient. Patients would even say something like, "In the middle of the night, I knew she was there. In the middle of the night she'd be there with her flashlight. I just knew she was there. I knew everything was going to be okay because Becky was on."

Jerry: What do you think about using stories to try to teach caregivers? Do you think stories work well?

Becky: I absolutely think stories work well. The first time that I gave a presentation, I didn't understand the concept of stories. I tried to give it with overheads and it was a failure. It just didn't go well. So what I've learned is that you can talk conceptually and theoretically, but when people really learn is through these stories, these explicit examples of what they can do.

What I have found interesting is that after my lectures people often share their own stories. So the audience not only learns from my stories, but from other people's as well. Then, at the conclusion of a talk, people may come up and talk to me about stories that they were a little cautious about sharing publically, but really important stories. I think teaching by stories and example causes people to reflect back on their own world.

Art: I remember the first time you presented to our class. I can still see the young woman in the classroom who had just had an experience in hospitals. "Do you know what it's like to be on a bed-pan?" The stories just bubbled out of her.

Ron: It's been my experience, and I think the experience of a lot of people who have been in hospitals, that nurses sometimes have to do things that are not very pleasant for the patients. "You must walk." Or, "Come on now, cough!" And it's almost like punishment. And they give shots and draw blood. You name it, there are all sorts of unpleasant things that nurses have to do. Is there some conflict between the sense of showing care and the necessity of doing the proper thing? Have you run into any instances of that and are there any ways of getting around it?

Becky: That's an excellent question. Some of the stories about caring behaviors of a nurse revolved around causing that pain. One example that I remember distinctly is a man who recalled his first experience of getting up after a major surgery. He talked about how much the nurse cared about him. When she first came in, he declared, "'You gotta be kidding. I'm not going anyplace,'" And he said that the nurse responded to him patiently and without getting angry. She sat down at the edge of the bed next to him and explained to him why he had to get up and walk and even explained a little about lung physiology. He recalled, "I learned that it's not just that I have to breathe deeply, but movement causes the cells in my lungs to move, so I won't get pneumonia." Then, they got him sitting on the edge of the bed and he started crying and said, "I just can't do this," and she said, "Yes you can, and we're going to be here helping you. All kinds of patients do this. Every surgical patient thinks they can't do it and they CAN do it. I've helped a million times."

Art: So a good order overrides somebody's autonomy.

Becky: That's right. Exactly.

Ron: So much of the caring behavior that you describe involves informing the patient about things in some detail. Are there any cases where it's necessary to keep things from the patient? Is it possible for a patient to know too much?

Becky: I think that's an excellent question, too. The essence of caring is knowing the individual well enough and trying to make the best estimate of what is important for the patient to know and what would be harmful for the patient to know. Sometimes trying to understand "How would I feel by knowing these things?" helps. I think an uncaring behavior would be to indiscriminately and generically disclose every detail to all patients.

Ron: Isn't there some importance to the extent to which a patient can understand what you are saying? I know that I've seen situations where a nurse or a doctor will explain something, then leave and the patient will say, "What was that all about? I have no idea what they were talking about." In a way, it may have become a little more frightening because they didn't understand the terminology that was being used.

Becky: That is very common. Often when nurses were cited as being caring, it was when they came back and reexplained what the doctor had said. And a caring physician was often one who took the time to "draw pictures, so I could look at it, see it." Little extra touches help. So it's not always time spent; sometimes it's just the manner.

Jerry: I know with respect to nursing there is pressure to do more and more with fewer staff. It is certainly more of a challenge than ever to be successful in demonstrating caring, I would think.

Becky: If I was four years into this profession, I would say, "Absolutely. Absolutely, you're right." But I'm 23 years in this profession and 21 of those years being in a management, administrative type of role, I've lived through these same environments. There has always been a cyclical pressure to lower costs and there's always the particular pressure to lower labor costs, because labor is the greatest cost. Nursing has lived through a number of attempts to redesign and give some nursing responsibility to assisted personnel, because RN's are paid too much: "Let nurses do the thinking part and let somebody else do the touching part." This to me is no different than it was 20 years ago — just taking in new terminology. Now, it's "managed care." The difference, I hope, this time is that we have a much more sophisticated public than we have ever had before, so the public's tolerance of these changes and the impact that they have on the caring responsive nurses at the service level, may be challenged.

Jerry: But it can be done? You're not pessimistic that the nurse can continue to evidence caring?

Becky: No. I am optimistic. It can still happen.

Art: As you think of the students in our class...some are going into nursing, some are going into medicine, but many aren't. Thinking particularly of those that aren't, what kind of thing would you especially like people to remember who aren't going into the helping professions...but who are teachers, patients, whatever.

Becky: What would I like them to remember about caring? That in every interaction between two individuals, two human beings, there's room for a caring response. There can be a caring response, no matter what contact that you have and in what context you're communicating. When we have a problem is when we treat people as objects or classify them as customers, or as anonymous patients, or as "a gall bladder," rather than as a whole individual.

Art: I've thought often of interviewing students and asking them, "what would be an example of a caring behavior exemplified by a teacher?" I'd love to do that. In the past, I've heard you cite an example of a caring teacher.

Becky: My example was my professor in Brookings who called on a Tuesday afternoon at 3:30 and said that he had heard that the weather forecast was bad. He didn't want me to even try to come the next day to class or agonize the whole night wondering if I should try to go to class. And I thought that he knew me well enough to know that I would have tried to go. Just as the patients I've questioned had that sense of caring, this professor knew enough about me in order to look out for me. That is exactly how I felt when he made that call. I thought "He knows enough about me to know that I would probably try to go to school, to drive when I shouldn't, and so he took the time to call and tell me not to come the next day."

And just now I'm thinking back to when I was sitting with my brother. I hadn't really thought of it before as caring, but the nurse said, "Becky you can go home. You don't need to stay here. It wasn't your fault. Go home." She took the time to do that. It wasn't, "We don't want you here,." It was more caring about me than anything. Opportunities to care are everywhere.

Questions to Consider for Chapter Ten:

1. "Making Health Care Choices," by Mary Auterman:
   a. Why, from her point of view, are each of us responsible for making health care choices?
   b. What knowledge about the health care system is most important for making wise choices?
2. "Caring and Complementary Healing Practices," by Mary Jo Kreitzer:
   a. What is involved in CAM. (Complementary and Alternative Medicine)? Why are patients interested in these healing modalities?
   b. What implications are there for the practice of traditional medicine?
3. "Practical Wisdom," by Jerome Freeman:
   a. Why are many physicians concerned about patient use of complementary/alternative therapies?
   b. What is the approach of practical wisdom that Freeman recommends?
4. "My Not-So-Near Death Experience," by Lawrence N. Hill:
   a. Drawing on the essay, how would you define a "hypochondriac?"
   b. What experience led him to think that he might have ALS, known as Lou Gehrig's disease?
   c. Why didn't he check it out? Are his reasons rational? Explain.
5. Excerpts from *Kitchen Dance*, by Ron Robinson:
   a. How do Alan's personality and behavior change in the course of the play? What motivates the changes?
   b. Jennifer's punishment for her daughter's hitting her son is to sentence the daughter to be the boy's nurse. This action might be called an exercise in caring. How did the lesson work out? How is the action reflected in the relationship between Alan and Jennifer?
   c. How exactly does the care that Alan comes to have for Jennifer affect him? What is the irony here? Does this case reflect a larger generality concerning the benefits bestowed upon the caregiver?
   d. What evidence is there that Jennifer's role as a caregiver to her husband and her children has affected her adversely? Does

this case reflect a larger generality concerning the ill effects that may be visited on the caregiver? Do nurses get sick?

6. "Caring Behaviors," an interview with Becky Nelson:

   a. What combination of education and experience does she bring to an understanding of caring behaviors? How does she find out what patients regard as caring behavior?

   b. Drawing on the stories she tells, identify three or four behaviors of health care workers that patients describe as caring.

   c. Can caring behaviors be taught or are they only instinctive? Her view? Yours?

   d. Do caring behaviors sometimes cause pain? Explain.

   e. Are the insights about caring applicable outside the field of health care? Her view? Yours?

On Catheters and Caring

Jerome Freeman

for Becky

Afloat in the
hospital sea
of hostile
procedures and
alien reasons,

he lies anchored
by his catheter
and bag to new-
found vulnerability.

Little premium
is given to privacy
as bustling staff
cruise past the urine
bag, hanging in full
view at bed's stern.

Visitors cluster about
like jolly islands and
pretend not to think
about the drainage
eel winding down from
the unseen penis. But
talk ceases uneasily
as the nurse enters
with collecting vial
to record the hour's
accumulated flow.

Arresting protocol, she
ignores the waiting urine
and burdens herself with
excuses of being needed
elsewhere. And only
the patient feels the caring
of that moment, when she
bends the rules to salvage
remains of his tattered
dignity, until he can
sail away.

Chapter Eleven:
How Then Shall We Care
in the Face of Death?

Ron Robinson

"Sometimes people who are together are, if not hostile to one another, at least estranged in mood and feeling, till perchance a story, a performance, a picture, or even a building, but oftenest of all music, unites them all as by an electric flash, and, in place of their former isolation or even enmity, they are all conscious of union and mutual love. Each is glad that another feels what he feels; glad of the communion established, not only between him and all present, but also with all now living who will yet share the same impression; and more than that, he feels the mysterious gladness of a communion which, reaching beyond the grave, unites us with all men of the past who have been moved by the same feelings, and with all men of the future who will yet be touched by them. And this effect is produced by the religious art which transmits feeling of love to God and one's neighbour, and by universal art transmitting the very simplest feeling common to all men." — Leo Tolstoy, *What is Art?*, 163-164.

"What I am about to say of communication will take it for granted that men cannot communicate by means of sound over either wire or air. They have got to communicate through love. Communication that is not also communion is incomplete. We *use* communication; we *participate* in communion. . . . It is the duty of the man of letters to supervise the culture of language, to which the rest of culture is subordinate, and to warn us when our language is ceasing to forward the ends proper to man. The end of social man is communion in time through love, which is beyond time." — Alan Tate, *The Man of Letters in the Modern World*, 16, 22.

L eo Tolstoy's belief in art as communion helps to explain much of his writing, including his classic, *The Death of Ivan Ilyich.* Both Tolstoy and Alan Tate, cited above, were professed Christians for whom terms like *communion* and *love* were not the least embarrassing. Both believed in the kinship of mankind under the parenthood of God. We are asked to see all human beings as brothers and sisters, to get inside them imaginatively and to feel with them. That is what the golden rule asks of us. How can you do unto others unless you somehow learn to imagine what others are feeling? This question goes to the very heart of caring. Having felt what others feel we are then moved by conscience to do what others would have us do. Conscience is simply a preference for goodness. Tolstoy and many others believed that this preference was something that all people hold in their hearts.

Tolstoy wrote *The Death of Ivan Ilyich* after having gone through a profound period of self-examination and the formulation of a doctrine which urged renunciation of riches, the sanctity of work, nonresistance to wickedness, and non-participation in society's cruel machinery, including war and jurisprudence. This teaching touched many, including Mahatma Gandhi, and was the standard by which Tolstoy lived out his remaining days. His way of life strained his marriage, and he died after having fled his home estate. He left behind not only a body of work that takes its place today at the forefront of world literature, but also a legacy of what it means to live a principled life.

A reader who has waded through the epic *War and Peace* will be surprised to discover *The Death of Ivan Ilyich* to be among the world's most pithy works. The story, part parable and part tragedy (often cited as a model for works such as *Death of a Salesman),* is not much longer than many short stories, and it examines a vacuous life with amazing restraint and indirection. In the first chapter, the mode is lightly satirical. The story opens with Ivan already dead, mourned formally and hypocritically by friends and family, but cared about chiefly to the extent that his death will alter their lives. The reader is introduced to the brutal honesty of this work when it is revealed that the feeling prevalent among Ivan's mourners is a sense of relief that he died rather than they. Anyone who has attended a funeral will recognize the truth of the description of the participants bewildered about how they are to behave, awkwardly bestowing unfelt condolences. Pyotr Ivanovich, nominally one of Ivan's best friends, is summoned by the widow to discuss Ivan's pension. Seated on an ottoman with unruly springs, Pyotr clumsily attempts to maintain his dignity, but is shaken when the widow tells him that Ivan died an agonizing death over a three-day period. Pyotr is reminded that the same thing could happen to him at any time. The scene is frankly comic, both illustrating and reproving the selfishness and hypocrisy abundant in such situations. Only Ivan's son seems truly moved to tears by Ivan's death. And only the peasant servant Gerasim seems to penetrate the general morass with his casual observation, "It's God's will, sir. We all have to die someday."

In chapters two and three, the reader is taken back to see how Ivan's life unfolded. It is a life "simple — commonplace — horrifying." Ivan was a judge, a detail which should send up a warning flag for those aware of Tolstoy's attitude toward the court system. Moreover, Ivan was infected with all the faddish French phrases, fleeting fashions, and petty ambitions of the *bourgeoisie* (what today we might label as *boomer* or *yuppie*). Tolstoy was amused by the prevailing sense of the inferiority of Russian culture and the corresponding idolatry of all things French. Ivan's world is peppered with French *bon mots*, most particularly *comme il faut*, which may be translated "as it should be," that is, according to the genteel fashions of the day. Ivan aggressively pursues what today is called a "lifestyle," forgetting entirely the admonition engraved on the medallion on his watch chain, *respice finem*, "consider the end." He marries for convenience, has children, and carries on a life both "pleasant and proper," and — we are asked to understand without being told — chillingly devoid of meaning. In his professional life, he easily falls into the abuse of power, "the chance to ruin whomever he chose." And having climbed the ladder of professional success, Ivan devotes himself to establishing a fine house, pleasant surroundings, the appearance of tranquility, despite nagging thoughts about something being missing. "So they lived," we are told. "Everything went along without change and everything was fine." Except, of course, that nothing was fine.

In chapters four, five, and six, Ivan's slide into illness is chronicled with terrifying subtlety. He finds himself being diagnosed and treated by doctors whose professional indifference mirrors his own callousness as a judge. Slowly he comes to realize that he is dying, although nobody else will acknowledge the possibility.

In chapters seven through eleven Ivan starts to question his way of life in light of the death sentence hanging over him. He starts to see the emptiness in his life for the first time, along with the shallowness and self-centeredness of most of his friends and family. Only the peasant servant Gerasim shows any candor, patience, and true fellow-feeling. Gerasim is a remarkable creation, deriving from Tolstoy's belief in the essential simplicity and goodness of common people. Gerasim embodies all that anyone could ask in a caregiver. "Why shouldn't I help you. You're a sick man," he says, demonstrating that his compassion is gratuitous, his only payment the hope that someone would treat him in the same way. This attitude, a manifestation of the golden rule, is so simple as to be staggering. Gerasim is merely "doing the right thing," according to his lights. He doesn't ask or expect to receive any special recognition for behavior he sees as self-evident, and yet he is unique in this work as being the only person capable of behaving in that way. Simple as the principle may be, it is not facile. Indeed, we are asked to believe that all the characters are trying to do the right thing, with the only disagreement being what the right thing is. One way is *comme il faut*, and the other way is the "real thing."

Finally, in the last chapter, Ivan finds a kind of resolution. In one lucid moment before his final death-struggle, he invites the gift of grace. Having worked through the anguish of his own mortality and his regret for a wasted life, he faces the torture of physical destruction. It is a mark of Tolstoy's adherence to truth that he does not allow what amounts to a confession and a plea for absolution to keep Ivan from the pain of death. What is lifted is the horror of death. The difference is between the suffering of the body and the suffering of the soul.

Ivan is hardly the traditional hero. He is as unsympathetic a protagonist as one might imagine. And yet readers recognize in Ivan something of themselves, perhaps because Leo Tolstoy put so much of himself into the character. What starts out as a caricature seems intended to engage readers by the end as a fully realized human being, one very much like them, and they are invited to examine their own lives in the light of their mortality and to exhibit a compassion of superhuman proportions. It is not enough to pity Ivan. We are urged to love this unlovable person unconditionally, to empathize with him.

How then shall we live? Tolstoy might answer, *"Respice finem,"* *"Look to the end."* Only by remembering our inevitable death can we hew to a course that avoids the shoals of "lifestyles," selfishness, and greed. The way is simple, but not easy. Indeed, the sacrifices and the compassion required of such a course may be beyond any but the saints. Yet we are compelled by Tolstoy's art to enter into communion. In this communion readers may even discover "love to God and one's neighbor."

The Death of Ivan Ilyich
Leo Tolstoy

Chapter 1

In the large building housing the Law Courts, during a recess in the Melvinsky proceedings, members of the court and the public prosecutor met in the office of Ivan Egorovich Shebek, where the conversation turned on the celebrated Krasov case. Fyodor Vasilyevich vehemently denied that it was subject to their jurisdiction, Ivan Egorovich clung to his own view, while Pyotr Ivanovich, who had taken no part in the dispute from the outset, glanced through a copy of the News that had just been delivered.

"Gentlemen!" he said. "Ivan Ilyich is dead."

"Really?"

"Here, read this," he said to Fyodor Vasilyevich, handing him the fresh issue, still smelling of printer's ink.

Framed in black was the following announcement: "With profound sorrow Praskovya Fyodorovna Golovina informs relatives and acquaintances that her beloved husband, Ivan Ilyich Golovin, Member of the Court of Justice, passed away on the 4th of February, 1882. The funeral will be held on Friday at one o'clock."

Ivan Ilyich had been a colleague of the gentlemen assembled here and they had all been fond of him. He had been ill for some weeks and his disease was said to be incurable. His post had been kept open for him, but it had been speculated that in the event of his death Alekseev might be appointed to his place and either Vinnikov or Shtabel succeed Alekseev. And so the first thought that occurred to each of the gentlemen in this office, learning of Ivan Ilyich's death, was what effect it would have on their own transfers and promotions or those of their acquaintances.

"Now I'm sure to get Shtabel's post or Vinnikov's," thought Fyodor Vasilyevich. "It was promised to me long ago, and the promotion will mean an increase of eight hundred rubles in salary plus an allowance for office expenses.

"I must put in a request to have my brother-in-law transferred from Kaluga," thought Pyotr Ivanovich. "My wife will be very happy. Now she won't be able to say I never do anything for her family."

"I had a feeling he'd never get over it," said Pyotr Ivanovich. "Sad."

"What, exactly, was the matter with him?"

"The doctors couldn't decide. That is, they decided, but in different ways. When I last saw him, I thought he would recover."

"And I haven't been there since the holidays. I kept meaning to go."

"Was he a man of any means?"

"His wife has a little something, I think, but nothing much."

"Well, there's no question but that we'll have to go and see her. They live so terribly far away."

"From you, that is. From your place, everything's far away."

"You see, he just can't forgive me for living on the other side of the river," said Pyotr Ivanovich, smiling at Shebek. And with that they began talking about relative distances in town and went back to the courtroom.

In addition to the speculations aroused in each man's mind about the transfers and likely job changes this death might occasion, the very fact of the death of a close acquaintance evoked in them all the usual feeling of relief that it was someone else, not they, who had died.

"Well, isn't that something — he's dead, but I'm not," was what each of them thought or felt. The closer acquaintances, the so-called friends of Ivan Ilyich, involuntarily added to themselves that now they had to fulfill the tedious demands of propriety by attending the funeral service and paying the widow a condolence call.

Fyodor Vasilyevich and Pyotr Ivanovich had been closest to him. Pyotr Ivanovich had studied law with Ivan Ilyich and considered himself indebted to him. At dinner that evening he told his wife the news of Ivan Ilyich's death, conjectured about the possibility of having her brother transferred to their district, and then, dispensing with his usual nap, he put on a dress coat and drove to Ivan Ilyich's home.

A carriage and two cabs were parked before the entrance. Downstairs in the hallway, next to the coat stand, a coffin lid decorated with silk brocade, tassels, and highly polished gilt braid was propped against the wall. Two women in black were taking off their fur coats. One of them he recognized as Ivan Ilyich's sister; the other was a stranger. Schwartz, his colleague, was just starting down the stairs, but on seeing Pyotr Ivanovich enter, he paused at the top step and winked at him as if to say: "Ivan Ilyich has really bungled — not the sort of thing you and I would do."

There was, as usual, an air of elegant solemnity about Schwartz, with his English sidewhiskers and his lean figure in a dress coat, and this solemnity, always such a marked contrast to his playful personality, had a special piquancy here. So, at least, Pyotr Ivanovich thought.

Pyotr Ivanovich stepped aside to let the ladies pass and slowly followed them up the stairs. Schwartz did not proceed downward but remained on the landing. Pyotr Ivanovich understood why; obviously, he wanted to arrange where they should play whist that evening. The ladies went upstairs to the widow's quarters, while Schwartz, his lips compressed into a serious expression and his eyes gleaming playfully, jerked his brows to the right to indicate the room where the dead man lay.

Pyotr Ivanovich went in bewildered, as people invariably are, about what he was expected to do there. The one thing he knew was that on such occasions it never did any harm to cross oneself. He was not quite certain whether he ought also to bow and so he adopted a middle course: on entering the room he began to cross himself and make a slight movement resembling a bow. At the same time, to the extent that the motions of his hands and head permitted, he glanced about the room. Two young people, apparently nephews, one of them a gymnasium student, were crossing themselves as they left the room. An old woman was standing motionless. And a lady with peculiarly arched brows was whispering something to her. A church reader in a frock coat — a vigorous, resolute fellow — was reading something in a loud voice and in a tone that brooked no contradiction. The pantry boy, Gerasim, stepped lightly in front of Pyotr Ivanovich, sprinkling something about the floor. Seeing this, Pyotr Ivanovich immediately became aware of a faint odor of decomposition. On his last visit Pyotr Ivanovich had seen this peasant boy in Ivan Ilyich's study; he had acted as a sick nurse to the dying man and Ivan Ilyich had been particularly fond of him.

Pyotr Ivanovich went on crossing himself and bowing slightly in a direction midway between the coffin, the church reader, and the icons on a table in the corner. Then, when he felt he had overdone the crossing, he paused and began to examine the dead man.

The body lay, as the dead invariably do, in a peculiarly heavy manner, with its rigid limbs sunk into the bedding of the coffin and its head eternally bowed on the pillow, exhibiting, as do all dead bodies, a yellow waxen forehead (with bald patches gleaming on the sunken temples), the protruding nose beneath seeming to press down against the upper lip. Ivan Ilyich had changed a great deal, grown even thinner since Pyotr Ivanovich had last seen him, and yet, as with all dead men, his face had acquired an expression of greater beauty — above all, of greater significance — than it had in life. Its expression implied that what needed to be done had been done and done properly. Moreover, there was in this expression a reproach or a reminder to the living. This reminder seemed out of place to Pyotr Ivanovich, or at least inapplicable to him. He began to feel somewhat uncomfortable and so he crossed himself hurriedly (all too hurriedly, he felt, from the standpoint of propriety), turned, and headed for the door.

In the adjoining room Schwartz was waiting for him, his feet planted solidly apart, his hands toying with the top hat he held behind his back. One glance at his playful, well-groomed, elegant figure was enough to revive Pyotr Ivanovich. He felt that Schwartz was above all this and would not succumb to mournful impressions. His very appearance seemed to say: "In no way can the incident of this funeral service for Ivan Ilyich be considered sufficient grounds for canceling the regular session; that is, nothing can prevent us from meeting tonight and flipping through a new deck of cards while a footman places four fresh candles around the table. There is, in fact, no reason to assume this incident can keep us from spending a pleasant evening." And he said as much to Pyotr Ivanovich in a whisper, proposing they meet for a game at Fyodor Vasilyevich's.

But Pyotr Ivanovich was not destined to play cards that evening. Praskovya Fyodorovna, a short, stocky woman (far broader at the hips than at the shoulders, despite all her efforts to the contrary), dressed all in black, with a lace shawl on her head and with the same peculiarly arched brows as the woman facing the coffin, emerged from her chambers with some other ladies whom she showed to the door of the room where the dead man lay, and said:

"The service is about to begin, do go in." Schwartz made a vague sort of bow, then stopped, neither accepting nor rejecting the invitation. Recognizing Pyotr Ivanovich, Praskovya Fyodorovna sighed, went right up to him, took his hand, and said: "I know you were a true friend of Ivan Ilyich's. . ." and looked at him, awaiting a fitting response. Pyotr Ivanovich knew that just as he had to cross himself in there, here he had to press her hand, sigh, and say:

"I assure you!" And so he did. And having done so felt he had achieved the desired effect: he was touched and so was she.

"Come, before it begins, I must have a talk with you," said the widow. "Give me your arm."

He gave her his arm and they proceeded toward the inner rooms, past Schwartz, who threw Pyotr Ivanovich a wink of regret that said:

"So much for your card game. Don't be offended if we find another player. Perhaps you can make a fifth when you get away."

Pyotr Ivanovich sighed even more deeply and plaintively, and Praskovya Fyodorovna squeezed his hand gratefully. On entering her drawing room, decorated in pink cretonne and lit with a dim lamp, they sat down beside a table: she on a sofa, Pyotr Ivanovich on a low ottoman with broken springs that shifted under his weight. Praskovya Fyodorovna wanted to warn him against sitting there but felt such a warning was not in keeping with her situation and decided against it. As he sat down on the ottoman Pyotr Ivanovich recalled how, in decorating the room, Ivan Ilyich had consulted him about this pink cretonne with the green leaves. The whole room was crammed with furniture and knickknacks, and as the widow stepped past the table to seat herself on the sofa, she entangled the lace of her black shawl in a bit of carving. Pyotr Ivanovich rose slightly to untangle it, and as he did the springs of the ottoman, freed of pressure, surged and gave him a little shove. The widow started to disentangle the lace herself and Pyotr Ivanovich sat down again, suppressing the rebellious springs beneath him. But the widow had not fully disentangled herself and Pyotr Ivanovich rose once again, and again the ottoman rebelled and even creaked. When all this was over, the widow took out a clean cambric handkerchief and began to weep. The episode with the lace and the battle with the ottoman had chilled Pyotr Ivanovich's emotions and he sat there scowling. The strain of the situation was broken when Sokolov, Ivan Ilyich's footman, came to report that the plot Praskovya Fyodorovna had selected in the cemetery would cost two hundred rubles. She stopped weeping and, glancing at Pyotr Ivanovich with a victimized air, told him in French how hard this was for her. He responded with a silent gesture indicating he had no doubt this was so.

"Please feel free to smoke," she said in a magnanimous yet crushed tone of voice and turned to Sokolov to discuss the price of the grave. As he lit his cigarette Pyotr Ivanovich heard her make detailed inquiries about the prices of various plots and arrive at a very sound decision. Moreover, when she had settled that matter, she made arrangements about the choristers. Then Sokolov left.

"I attend to everything myself," she said to Pyotr Ivanovich, moving aside some albums on the table. And noticing that the ashes of his cigarette were in danger of falling on the table, she quickly passed him an ashtray and said: "I believe it would be sheer pretense for me to say that I am unable, because of grief, to attend to practical matters. On the contrary, if anything can. . . I won't say console but. . . distract me, it is seeing to all these things about him." Again she took out a handkerchief as if about to weep but suddenly seemed to have mastered her emotion, and with a little toss of her head she began to speak calmly.

"But there is a matter I wish to discuss with you."

Pyotr Ivanovich bowed his head in response, taking care not to allow the springs of the ottoman, which immediately grew restive, to have their way.

"He suffered terribly the last few days."

"Did he?" asked Pyotr Ivanovich.

"Oh, frightfully! He screamed incessantly, not for minutes but for hours on end. He screamed for three straight days without pausing for breath. It was unbearable. I don't know how I bore up through it all. You could hear him three rooms away. Oh, what I've been through!"

"And was he really conscious through it all?" asked Pyotr Ivanovich.

"Yes," she whispered, "to the very last. He took leave of us a quarter of an hour before he died and even asked us to take Volodya away."

Despite a distasteful awareness of his own hypocrisy as well as hers, Pyotr Ivanovich was overcome with horror as he thought of the suffering of someone he had known so well, first as a carefree boy, then as a schoolmate, later as a grown man, his colleague. Once again he saw that forehead, that nose pressing down on the upper lip, and fear for himself took possession of him.

"Three days of terrible suffering and death. Why, the same thing could happen to me at anytime now," he thought and for a moment felt panic-stricken. But at once, he himself did not know how, he was rescued by the customary reflection that all this had happened to Ivan Ilyich, not to him, that it could not and should not happen to him; and that if he were to grant such a possibility, he would succumb to depression which, as Schwartz's expression had made abundantly clear, he ought not to do. With this line of reasoning Pyotr Ivanovich set his mind at rest and began to press for details about Ivan Ilyich's death, as though death were a chance experience that could happen only to Ivan Ilyich, never to himself.

After giving him various details about the truly horrible physical suffering Ivan Ilyich had endured (details which Pyotr Ivanovich learned strictly in terms of their unnerving effect upon Praskovya Fyodorovna), the widow evidently felt it necessary to get down to business.

"Ah, Pyotr Ivanovich, how hard it is, how terribly, terribly hard," she said and again began weeping.

Pyotr Ivanovich sighed and waited for her to blow her nose. When she had, he said: "I assure you!..." and again she began to talk freely and got down to what was obviously her chief business with him: to ask how, in connection with her husband's death, she could obtain a grant of money from the government. She made it appear that she was asking Pyotr Ivanovich's advice about a pension, but he saw that she already knew more about this than he did, knew exactly, down to the finest detail, how much could be had from the government, but wanted to know if there was any possibility of extracting a bit more. Pyotr Ivanovich tried to think of some means of doing so, but after giving the matter a little thought and, for the sake of propriety, condemning the government for its stinginess, said he thought no more could be had. Whereupon she sighed and evidently tried to find some pretext for getting rid of her visitor. He surmised as much, put out his cigarette, stood up, shook her hand, and went out into the hall.

In the dining room with the clock which Ivan Ilyich had been so happy to have purchased at an antique shop, Pyotr Ivanovich met a priest and a few acquaintances who had come for the service, and he caught sight of a handsome young woman, Ivan Ilyich's daughter. She was dressed all in black, which made her slender waist appear even more so. She had a gloomy, determined, almost angry expression and bowed to Pyotr Ivanovich as if he were to blame for something. Behind her, with the same offended look, stood a rich young man Pyotr Ivanovich knew — an examining magistrate who, he had heard, was her fiancé. Pyotr Ivanovich gave them a mourn-

ful bow and was about to enter the dead man's room when Ivan
Ilyich's son, a schoolboy who had an uncanny resemblance to his
father, appeared from behind the stairwell. He was a small replica
of the Ivan Ilyich whom Pyotr Ivanovich remembered from law
school. His eyes were red from crying and had the look common to
boys of thirteen or fourteen whose thoughts are no longer innocent.
Seeing Pyotr Ivanovich, he frowned in a shamefaced way. Pyotr
Ivanovich nodded to him and entered the room where the body lay.
The service began: candles, groans, incense, tears, sobs. Pyotr
Ivanovich stood with his brows knitted, staring at the feet of people
in front of him. Never once did he look at the dead man or succumb
to depression, and he was one of the first to leave. There was no one
in the hallway, but Gerasim, the pantry boy, darted out of the dead
man's room, rummaged with his strong hands through the mound
of fur coats to find Pyotr Ivanovich's and helped him on with it.

"Well, Gerasim, my boy," said Pyotr Ivanovich in order to say
something. "It's sad, isn't it?"

"It's God's will, sir. We all have to die someday," said Gerasim,
displaying an even row of healthy white peasant teeth. And then,
like a man in the thick of work, he briskly opened the door, shouted to the coachman, seated Pyotr Ivanovich in the carriage, and
sprang back up the porch steps as though wondering what to do
next.

After the smell of incense, the corpse, and the carbolic acid, Pyotr
Ivanovich found it particularly pleasant to breathe in the fresh air.

"Where to, sir?" asked the coachman.

"It's not that late, I'll drop in at Fyodor Vasilyevich's."

And so he went. And when he arrived, he found they were just
finishing the first rubber, so that it was convenient for him to make
a fifth for the next.

Chapter 2

Ivan Ilyich's life had been most simple and commonplace — and
most horrifying.

He died at the age of forty-five, a member of the Court of Justice.
He was the son of an official who, in various Petersburg ministries
and departments, had established the sort of career whereby men
reach a stage at which, owing to their rank and years of service,
they cannot be dismissed, even though they are clearly unfit for any
responsible work; and therefore they receive fictitious appoint-

ments, especially designed for them, and by no means fictitious salaries of from six to ten thousand on which they live to a ripe old age.

Such was the Privy Councillor Ilya Efimovich Golovin, superfluous member of various superfluous institutions.

He had three sons, of whom Ivan Ilyich was the second. The eldest had established the same type of career as his father, except in a different ministry, and was rapidly approaching the stage where men obtain sinecures. The third son was a failure. He had ruined his prospects in a number of positions and was now serving in the Railway Division. His father and brothers, and especially their wives, not only hated meeting him but, unless compelled to do otherwise, managed to forget his existence. The sister had married Baron Greff, the same sort of Petersburg official as his father-in-law. Ivan Ilyich, as they said, was *le phenix de la famille*. He was neither as cold and punctilious as his elder brother nor as reckless as his younger. He was a happy mean between the two — a clever, lively, pleasant, and respectable man. He and his younger brother had both attended the school of jurisprudence. The younger brother never graduated, for he was expelled when he reached the fifth course. On the other hand, Ivan Ilyich completed the program creditably. As a law student he had become exactly what he was to remain the rest of his life: a capable, cheerful, good-natured, and sociable man but one strict to carry out whatever he considered his duty, and he considered his duty all things that were so designated by people in authority. Neither as a boy nor as an adult had he been a toady, but from his earliest youth he had been drawn to people of high standing in society as a moth is to light; he had adopted their manners and their views on life and had established friendly relations with them. All the enthusiasms of childhood and youth passed, leaving no appreciable impact on him; he had succumbed to sensuality and vanity and, in his last years at school, to liberalism, but strictly within the limits his instinct unerringly prescribed.

As a student he had done things which, at the time, seemed to him extremely vile and made him feel disgusted with himself; but later, seeing that people of high standing had no qualms about doing these things, he was not quite able to consider them good but managed to dismiss them and not feel the least perturbed when he recalled them.

When he graduated from law school with a degree qualifying him for the tenth rank of the civil service, and had obtained money from his father for his outfit, he ordered some suits at Sharmer's, the fashionable tailor, hung a medallion inscribed *respice finem* on his watch chain, took leave of his mentor and prince, who was patron of the school, dined in state with his friends at Donon's, and then, with fashionable new luggage, linen, clothes, shaving and other toilet articles, and a traveling rug (all ordered and purchased at the finest shops), he set off for one of the provinces to assume a post his father had secured for him there as assistant on special commissions to the governor.

Ivan Ilyich immediately made his life in the provinces as easy and pleasant as it had been at law school. He worked, saw to his career, and, at the same time, engaged in proper and pleasant forms of diversion. When from time to time he traveled to country districts on official business, he maintained his dignity with both his superiors and inferiors and fulfilled the duties entrusted to him (primarily cases involving a group of religious sectarians) with an exactitude and incorruptibility in which he could only take pride.

In his official duties, despite his youth and love of light forms of amusement, he was exceedingly reserved, punctilious, and even severe; but in society he was often playful and witty, always good-humored and polite — *a bon enfant*, as the governor and his wife, with whom he was like one of the family, used to say of him.

In the provinces he had an affair with one of the ladies who threw themselves at the chic young lawyer; there was also a milliner: there were drinking bouts with visiting aides-de-camp and after-supper trips to a certain street on the outskirts of town; there were also attempts to curry favor with his chief and even with his chief's wife. But all this had such a heightened air of respectability that nothing bad could be said about it. It could all be summed up by the French saying: "*Il faut que jeunesse se passe.*" It was all done with clean hands, in clean shirts, and with French phrases, and, most importantly, among people of the best society, consequently, with the approval of those in high rank.

Ivan Ilyich spent five years of his service career in this manner, and at the end of that time there was a change in his official life. New judicial institutions had been formed and new men were needed.

Ivan Ilyich became such a new man.

He was offered a post as examining magistrate and he accepted it, even though it meant moving to another province, giving up the connections he had formed, and establishing new ones. His friends met to bid him farewell: they had a group photograph taken and presented him with a silver cigarette case, and he set off to assume his new position.

As an examining magistrate, Ivan Ilyich was just as *comme il faut* and respectable, just as capable of separating his official duties from his private life and of inspiring general respect as he had been while acting as assistant on special commissions. He found the work of a magistrate far more interesting and appealing than his former duties. In his previous position he had enjoyed the opportunity to stride freely and easily in his Sharmer uniform past the crowd of anxious, envious petitioners and officials waiting to be heard by the governor, to go straight into his chief's office and sit with him over a cup of tea and a cigarette. But few people had been directly under his control then — only the district police officers and religious sectarians he encountered when sent out on special commissions. And he loved to treat these people courteously, almost as comrades, loved to make them feel that he who had the power to crush them was dealing with them in such a friendly, unpretentious manner. But there had been few such people. Now, as an examining magistrate, Ivan Ilyich felt that all, without exception — including the most important and self-satisfied people — all were in his power, and that he had only to write certain words on a sheet of paper with an official heading and this or that important, self-satisfied person would be brought to him as a defendant or a witness, and if Ivan Ilyich did not choose to have him sit, he would be forced to stand and answer his questions. Ivan Ilyich never abused his power; on the contrary, he tried to exercise it leniently; but the awareness of that power and the opportunity to be lenient constituted the chief interest and appeal of his new post. In the work itself — that is, in conducting investigations — Ivan Ilyich soon mastered the technique of dispensing with all considerations that did not pertain to his job as examining magistrate, and of writing up even the most complicated cases in a style that reduced them to their externals, bore no trace of his personal opinion, and, most importantly, adhered to all the prescribed formalities. This type of work was new, and he was one of the first men to give practical application to the judicial reforms instituted by the Code of 1864.

On taking up the post of examining magistrate in the new town, Ivan Ilyich made new acquaintances and connections, adopted a new stance, and assumed a somewhat different tone. He put a suitable amount of distance between himself and the provincial authorities, chose his friends from among the best circle of lawyers and wealthy gentry in the town, and assumed an air of mild dissatisfaction with the government, of moderate liberalism, of enlightened civic responsibility. And though he remained as fastidious as ever about his attire, he stopped shaving his chin and allowed his beard to grow freely.

In the new town, too, life turned out to be very pleasant for Ivan Ilyich. The people opposed to the governor were friendly and congenial, his salary was higher, and he began to play whist, which added considerably to the pleasure of his life, for he had an ability to maintain his good spirits while playing and to reason quickly and subtly, so that he usually came out ahead.

After he had been working in the town for two years, Ivan Ilyich met his future wife. Praskovya Fyodorovna Mikhel was the most attractive, intelligent, and outstanding young lady of the set in which Ivan Ilyich moved. In addition to the other amusements and relaxations that provided relief from his work as an examining magistrate, Ivan Ilyich began a light flirtation with Praskovya Fyodorovna.

As an assistant on special commissions Ivan Ilyich had, as a rule, danced; as an examining magistrate he danced as an exception. He danced to show that although he was a representative of the reformed legal institutions and an official of the fifth rank, when it came to dancing, he could also excel at that. So he occasionally danced with Praskovya Fyodorovna at the end of an evening, and it was mainly during the time they danced together that he conquered her. She fell in love with him. Ivan Ilyich had no clear and definite intention of marrying, but when the girl fell in love with him, he asked himself: "Really, why shouldn't I get married?"

Praskovya Fyodorovna came from a good family and was quite attractive; she also had a little money. Ivan Ilyich could have counted on a more illustrious match, but even this one was quite good. He had his salary, and her income, he hoped, would bring in an equal amount. It would be a good alliance: she was a sweet, pretty, and extremely well-bred young woman. To say that Ivan Ilyich married because he fell in love with his fiancée and found her sympathetic to his views on life would be as mistaken as to say that he married because the people in his circle approved of the match. Ivan Ilyich married for both reasons: in acquiring such a wife he did something that gave him pleasure and, at the same time, did what people of the highest standing considered correct.

And so Ivan Ilyich got married.

The preparations for marriage and the first period of married life, with its conjugal caresses, new furniture, new dishes, new linen — the period up to his wife's pregnancy — went very well, so that Ivan Ilyich began to think that marriage would not disrupt the easy, pleasant, cheerful, and respectable life approved of by society (a pattern he believed to be universal); that it would even enhance such a life. But during the first months of his wife's pregnancy, something new, unexpected, and disagreeable manifested itself, something painful and unseemly, which he had no way of anticipating and could do nothing to avoid.

For no reason at all, so it seemed to Ivan Ilyich — *de gaité de coeur*, as he told himself — his wife began to undermine the pleasure and propriety of their life: she became jealous without cause, demanded he be more attentive to her, found fault with everything, and created distasteful and ill-mannered scenes.

At first Ivan Ilyich hoped to escape from this unpleasant state of affairs by preserving the same carefree and proper approach to life that had served him in the past. He tried to ignore his wife's bad moods, went on living in a pleasant and easygoing fashion, invited friends over for cards, and made an effort to get away to his club or his friends' homes. But on one occasion his wife lashed out at him with such fury and such foul language, and persisted in attacking him every time he failed to satisfy her demands (apparently having resolved not to let up until he submitted — that is, until he stayed home and moped as she did) that Ivan Ilyich was horrified. He realized that married life — at least with his wife — was not always conducive to the pleasures and proprieties of life but, on the contrary, frequently disrupted them, and for that reason he must guard against such disruptions. Ivan Ilyich tried to find some means of doing this. His work was the one thing that made any impression on Praskovya Fyodorovna, and so he began to use his work and the obligations it entailed as a way of combating his wife and safeguarding his independence.

With the birth of the baby, the attempts to feed it and the various difficulties, the real and imaginary illnesses of mother and child, which Ivan Ilyich was supposed to sympathize with but failed to understand, his need to fence off a world for himself outside the family became even more imperative.

To the degree that his wife became more irritable and demanding, Ivan Ilyich increasingly made work the center of gravity in his life. He grew more attached to his job and more ambitious than before.

Very soon, within a year after his wedding, Ivan Ilyich realized that married life, though it offered certain conveniences, was in fact a very complex and difficult business, and that to do one's duty to it — that is, to lead a proper, socially acceptable life — he had to develop a clearly defined attitude to it, just as one did with respect to work.

And Ivan Ilyich developed such an attitude. Of married life he demanded only the conveniences it could provide — dinners at home, a well-run household, a partner in bed, and, above all, a veneer of respectability which public opinion required. As for the rest, he tried to find enjoyment in family life, and, if he succeeded, was very grateful; but if he met with resistance and querulousness, he immediately withdrew into his separate, entrenched world of work and found pleasure there.

Ivan Ilyich was esteemed for his diligent service, and after three years he was made assistant public prosecutor. His new duties, the importance of them, the possibility of indicting and imprisoning anyone he chose, the publicity his speeches received and the success they brought him — all this further enhanced the appeal of his work.

Other children were born. His wife became more and more petulant and irascible, but the attitude Ivan Ilyich had adopted toward domestic life made him almost impervious to her carping.

After serving for seven years in this town, Ivan Ilyich was transferred to another province as public prosecutor. They moved, they were short of money, and his wife disliked the new town. Although his salary was higher, the cost of living was greater; moreover, two of their children had died, and so family life became even more unpleasant for Ivan Ilyich.

Praskovya Fyodorovna blamed her husband for every setback they experienced in the new town. Most of the topics of conversation between husband and wife, especially the children's education, brought up issues on which they remembered having quarreled, and these quarrels were apt to flare up again at any moment. All they had left were the rare periods of amorousness that came over them, but these did not last long. They were merely little islands at which the couple anchored for a while before setting out again on a sea of veiled hostility, which took the form of estrangement from one another. This estrangement might have distressed Ivan Ilyich had he felt it should not exist, but by now he not only regarded it as a normal state of affairs, but as a goal he sought to achieve in family life. That goal was to free himself more and more from these disturbances, to make them appear innocuous and respectable. He managed to do this by spending less and less time with his family and, when obliged to be at home, tried to safeguard his position through the presence of outsiders. But what mattered most was that Ivan Ilyich had his work. His entire interest in life was centered in the world of official duties and that interest totally absorbed him. The awareness of his power, the chance to ruin whomever he chose, the importance attached even to his entry into the courtroom and manner of conferring with his subordinates, the success he enjoyed both with them and his superiors, and, above all, his own recognition of the skill with which he handled cases — all this gave him cause for rejoicing and, together with chats with his colleagues, dinner invitations, and whist, made his life full. So that on the whole Ivan Ilyich's life proceeded as he felt it should — pleasantly and properly.

He went on living this way for another seven years. His daughter was then sixteen years old, another child had died, and one son remained, a schoolboy, the subject of dissension. Ivan Ilyich wanted to send him to the school of jurisprudence, but out of spite Praskovya Fyodorovna enrolled him in the gymnasium. The daughter had studied at home and made good progress; the boy, too, was a rather good student.

Chapter 3

Ivan Ilyich spent seventeen years of his married life this way. He was already an experienced public prosecutor who had declined several positions in the hope of obtaining a more desirable one, when an unforeseen and unpleasant circumstance virtually disrupted the peaceful course of his life. He expected to be appointed presiding judge in a university town, but Hoppe managed to move in ahead and get the appointment. Ivan Ilyich was infuriated, made accusations, and quarreled with Hoppe and his immediate superiors. They began to treat him with disdain and during the next round of appointments again passed him by.

This happened in 1880, the most difficult year in Ivan Ilyich's life. For one thing, it turned out that he could not make ends meet on his salary; for another, that he had been neglected, and that what he considered the most outrageous, heartless injustice appeared to others as quite commonplace. Even his father did not consider it his duty to help him. Ivan Ilyich felt that everyone had abandoned him, convinced that the position of a man earning three thousand five hundred rubles was entirely normal and even fortunate. He alone knew that what with the injustices he had suffered, his wife's incessant nagging, and the debts he had incurred by living above his means, his position was far from normal.

That summer, in order to save money, he took a leave of absence and went to the country with his wife to live at her brother's place. In the country, with no work to do, Ivan Ilyich for the first time in his life experienced not only boredom but intolerable anguish; he decided that he simply could not go on living this way, that he had to take some decisive measures.

After a sleepless night spent pacing the terrace, he made up his mind to go to Petersburg and punish those people — those who had failed to appreciate him — by trying to get himself transferred to another ministry.

The next day, despite all the efforts of his wife and his brother-in-law to dissuade him, he set off for Petersburg. He had only one purpose in going: to obtain a post with a salary of five thousand rubles. He was no longer bent on any particular ministry, field, or type of work. He only wanted a post that would pay him five thousand; it could be a post with the administration, the banks, the railways, the Dowager Empress Maria's charitable institutions, or even the customs office, but it had to pay five thousand and allow him to stop working for a ministry that failed to appreciate him.

And his trip was crowned with amazing and unexpected success. At Kursk an acquaintance of his, F. S. Ilyin, boarded the train, sat down in the first-class carriage, and told Ivan Ilyich that the governor of Kursk had just received a telegram announcing an important change of staff that was about to take place in the ministry: Ivan Semyonovich was to replace Pyotr Ivanovich.

The proposed change, in addition to the significance it had for Russia, was of particular significance for Ivan Ilyich, since it brought to power a new man, Pyotr Petrovich, and, it appeared, his friend Zakhar Ivanovich-a circumstance that was highly favorable for Ivan Ilyich. Zakhar Ivanovich was a colleague and friend of his.

In Moscow the news was confirmed, and on reaching Petersburg, Ivan Ilyich looked up Zakhar Ivanovich, who guaranteed him an appointment in the Ministry of Justice where he had served before.

A week later he telegraphed his wife: "Zakhar in Miller's place. With first report I receive appointment."

Thanks to this change of staff, Ivan Ilyich unexpectedly received an appointment in his former ministry that placed him two ranks above his colleagues, paid him a salary of five thousand rubles, and provided an additional three thousand five hundred for the expenses of relocation. His resentment against his former enemies and the whole ministry vanished completely and he was perfectly happy.

Ivan Ilyich returned to the country more cheerful and contented than he had been in some time. Praskovya Fyodorovna's spirits also picked up, and they concluded a truce. Ivan Ilyich told her how he had been honored in Petersburg, how all his enemies had been disgraced and fawned on him now and envied his position; and he made a point of telling her how much everyone in Petersburg had liked him.

Praskovya Fyodorovna listened, pretended to believe all of this, never once contradicted him, and devoted herself exclusively to making plans for their life in the city to which they were moving. And Ivan Ilyich was delighted to see that her plans were his, that he and his wife were in agreement, and that after a little stumble his life was resuming its genuine and natural quality of carefree pleasure and propriety.

Ivan Ilyich had come back for only a brief stay. On the tenth of September he had to assume his new position; moreover, he needed time to get settled in the new place, to move all their belongings from the provinces, to buy and order a great many more things. In short, to arrange their life in the style he had set his mind to (which corresponded almost exactly to the style Praskovya Fyodorovna had set her heart on).

Now that everything had worked out so well and he and his wife were at one in their aims and, in addition, saw very little of each other, they were closer than they had been since the first years of their married life. Ivan Ilyich had intended to take his family with him at once, but at the urging of his sister-in-law and brother-in-law, who suddenly became unusually amiable and warm to Ivan Ilyich and his family, he set off alone.

He set off, and the happy frame of mind induced by his success and the understanding with his wife, the one intensifying the other, never once deserted him. He found a charming apartment, exactly what he and his wife had dreamed of. Spacious reception rooms with high ceilings in the old style, a magnificent and comfortable study, rooms for his wife and daughter, a study room for his son — all as though it had been designed especially for them. Ivan Ilyich himself undertook the decorating, selecting the wallpaper and the upholstery, purchasing more furniture, mostly antiques, which he thought particularly *comme il faut*, and everything progressed until it began to approach the ideal he had set himself. When only half the decorating had been completed, the result exceeded his expectations. He sensed how elegant and refined an atmosphere, free of vulgarity, the whole place would acquire when it was finished. As he fell asleep he pictured to himself how the reception room would look. When he glanced at the unfinished drawing room he conjured up an image of the fireplace, the screen, the what-not, the little chairs scattered here and there, the plates and china on the walls, and the bronzes, as they would appear when everything was in place. He was thrilled to think how he would surprise Pasha and Lizanka, who also had good taste in these matters. They had no idea what was in store for them. He had been particularly successful at finding and making inexpensive purchases of old furniture, which added a decidedly aristocratic tone to the whole place. In his letters to his family he deliberately understated everything in order to surprise them. All this was so engrossing that even his new post, work he loved, absorbed him less than he had expected.

During court sessions he sometimes became distracted, wondering whether he should have straight or curved cornices for the draperies. He was so preoccupied with these matters that he often did some of the work himself — rearranged the furniture, rehung the draperies. Once, when he mounted a stepladder to show a perplexed upholsterer how he wanted the draperies hung, he missed a step and fell, but being a strong and agile man, he held on to the ladder and merely banged his side against the knob of the window frame. The bruise hurt for a while, but the pain soon disappeared. All through this period Ivan Ilyich felt particularly well and cheerful. "I feel fifteen years younger," he wrote his family. He expected to finish in September, but the work dragged on until mid-October. Yet the result was stunning — an opinion voiced not only by him but by everyone else who saw the place.

In actuality, it was like the homes of all people who are not really rich but who want to look rich, and therefore end up looking like one another: it had damasks, ebony, plants, carpets, and bronzes, everything dark and gleaming — all the effects a certain class of people produce so as to look like people of a certain class. And his place looked so much like the others that it would never have been noticed, though it all seemed quite exceptional to him. When he met his family at the station and brought them back to their brightly lit furnished apartment, and a footman in a white tie opened the door to a flower-bedecked entrance hall, from which they proceeded to the drawing room and the study, gasping with delight, he was very happy, showed them everywhere, drank in their praises and beamed with satisfaction. At tea that evening when, among other things, Praskovya Fyodorovna asked him about his fall, he laughed and gave them a comic demonstration of how he had gone flying off the stepladder and frightened the upholsterer.

"It's a good thing I'm so agile. Another man would have killed himself, but I got off with just a little bump here; it hurts when I touch it, but it's already beginning to clear up — it's just a bruise."

And so they began to live in their new quarters which, as always happens when people get settled, was just one room too small, and on their new income which, as is always the case, was just a bit less — about five hundred rubles — than they needed. But it was all very nice. It was particularly nice in the beginning, before the apartment was fully arranged and some work still had to be done: this thing bought, that thing ordered, another thing moved, still another adjusted. And while there were some disagreements between husband and wife, both were so pleased and had so much to do that it all passed off without any major quarrels. When there was no work left to be done, it became a bit dull and something seemed to be lacking, but by then they were making acquaintances, forming new habits, and life was full.

Ivan Ilyich spent his mornings in court and came home for dinner, and at first he was in fine spirits, — though it was precisely the apartment that caused him some distress. (Every spot on the tablecloth or the upholstery, every loose cord on the draperies irritated him; he had gone to such pains with the decorating that any damage to it upset him.) But on the whole Ivan Ilyich's life moved along as he believed life should: easily, pleasantly, and properly. He got up at nine, had his coffee, read the newspapers, then put on his uniform and went to court. There the harness in which he worked had already been worn into shape and he slipped right into it: petitioners, inquiries sent to the office, the office itself, the court session — preliminary and public. In all this one had to know how to exclude whatever was fresh and vital, which always disrupted the course of official business: one could have only official relations with people, and only on official grounds, and the relations themselves had to be kept purely official. For instance, a man would come and request some information. As an official who was charged with other duties, Ivan Ilyich could not have any dealings with such a man; but if the man approached him about a matter that related to his function as a court member, then within the limits of this relationship Ivan Ilyich would do everything, absolutely everything he could for him and, at the same time, maintain a semblance of friendly, human relation — that is, treat him with civility. As soon as the official relations ended, so did all the rest. Ivan Ilyich had a superb ability to detach the official aspect of things from his real life, and thanks to his talent and years of experience, he had cultivated it to such a degree that occasionally, like a virtuoso, he allowed himself to mix human and official relations, as if for fun. He allowed himself this liberty because he felt he had the strength to isolate the purely official part of the relationship again, if need be, and discard the human. And he did so not only in an easy, pleasant, and proper manner, but with style. In between times he smoked, had tea, talked a little about politics, a little about general matters, but most of all about appointments. And then tired, but with the feeling of a virtuoso — one of the first violinists in an orchestra who had played his part superbly — he would return home. There he would find that his wife and daughter had been out paying calls or had a visitor; that his son had been to the gymnasium, had gone over his lessons with a tutor, and was diligently learning all that students are taught in the gymnasium. Everything was just fine. After dinner, if there were no guests, Ivan Ilyich sometimes read a book that was the talk of the day and in the evening settled down to work — that is, read official papers, checked laws, compared depositions, and classified them according to the legal statutes. He found such work neither boring nor engaging. It was a bore if it meant foregoing a card game, but if there was no game on, it was better than sitting home alone or with his wife. Ivan Ilyich derived pleasure from giving small dinner parties to which he invited men and women of good social standing; and the dinners he gave resembled the ones they usually gave as much as his drawing room looked like all the other drawing rooms.

Once they even had an evening party with dancing. Ivan Ilyich was in fine spirits and everything went off well except that he had an enormous fight with his wife over the pastries and bonbons. Praskovya Fyodorovna had her own plans about these, but Ivan Ilyich insisted on ordering everything from an expensive confectioner; he ordered a great many pastries, and the quarrel broke out because some of the pastries were left over and the bill came to forty-five rubles. It was such an enormous, nasty fight that Praskovya Fyodorovna called him an "imbecile" and a "spoiler," while he clutched his head and inwardly muttered something about a divorce. But the party itself was gay. The best people came and Ivan Ilyich danced with Princess Trufonova, sister of the Trufonova who had founded the charitable society called "Take My Grief Upon Thee."

The pleasures Ivan Ilyich derived from his work were those of pride; the pleasures he derived from society those of vanity; but it was genuine pleasure that he derived from playing whist. He confessed that no matter what happened, regardless of all the unhappiness he might experience, there was one pleasure which, like a bright candle, outshone all the others in his life: that was to sit down with some good players, quiet partners, to a game of whist, definitely a four-handed game (with five players it was painful to sit out, even though one pretended not to mind), to play a clever, serious game (when the cards permitted), then have supper and drink a glass of wine. After a game of whist, especially if he had won a little (winning a lot was distasteful), Ivan Ilyich went to bed in a particularly good mood.

So they lived. They moved in the best circles and their home was frequented by people of importance and by the young. There was complete accord between husband, wife, and daughter about their set of acquaintances and, without discussing the matter, they were equally adept at brushing off and escaping from various shabby friends and relations who, with a great show of affection, descended on them in their drawing room with the Japanese plates on the walls. Soon these shabby friends stopped intruding and the Golovins' set included only the best. Young men courted Lizanka, and the examining magistrate Petrishchev, the son and sole heir of Dmitry Ivanovich Petrishchev, was so attentive that Ivan Ilyich talked to Praskovya Fyodorovna about having a sleighing party for them or arranging some private theatricals.

So they lived. Everything went along without change and everything was fine.

Chapter 4

They were all in good health. Ivan Ilyich, sometimes complained of a strange taste in his mouth and some discomfort in his left side, but this could hardly be called ill health.

Yet the discomfort increased, and although it had not developed into real pain, the sense of a constant pressure in his side made Ivan Ilyich ill-tempered. His irritability became progressively more marked and began to spoil the pleasure of the easy and proper life that had only recently been established in the Golovin family. Husband and wife began to quarrel more often, and soon the ease and pleasure disappeared and even the propriety was barely maintained. Scenes became more frequent. Once again there were only little islands, very few at that, on which husband and wife could meet without an explosion.

Praskovya Fyodorovna had good reason now for saying that her husband had a trying disposition. With her characteristic tendency to exaggerate, she said he had always had such a horrid disposition and that only someone with her goodness of heart could have put up with it for twenty years. It was true that he was the one now who started the arguments. He invariably began caviling when he sat down to dinner — often just as he was starting on his soup. Either he noticed that a dish was chipped, or the food was not good, or his son had put his elbow on the table, or his daughter had not combed her hair properly. And for all this he blamed Praskovya Fyodorovna. At first she fought back and said nasty things to him, but once or twice at the start of dinner he flew into such a rage that she realized it was due to some physical discomfort provoked by eating, and so she restrained herself and did not answer back but merely tried to get dinner over with as quickly as possible. Praskovya Fyodorovna regarded her self-restraint as a great virtue. Having concluded that her husband had a horrid disposition and had made her life miserable, she began to pity herself. And the more she pitied herself, the more she hated her husband. She began to wish he would die, yet she could not really wish that, for then there would be no income. This made her even more incensed with him. She considered herself supremely unhappy because even his death could not save her. She was exasperated yet concealed it, and her suppressed exasperation only heightened his exasperation.

After a scene in which Ivan Ilyich had been particularly unjust and, by way of explanation, admitted being irritable but attributed this to illness, she told him that if he was ill he must be treated, and she insisted he go and consult a celebrated physician.

He did. The whole procedure was just what he expected, just what one always encounters. There was the waiting, the doctor's exaggerated air of importance (so familiar to him since it was the very air he assumed in court), the tapping, the listening, the questions requiring answers that were clearly superfluous since they were foregone conclusions, and the significant look that implied: "Just put yourself in our hands and we'll take care of everything; we know exactly what has to be done — we always use one and the same method for every patient, no matter who." Everything was just as it was in court. The celebrated doctor dealt with him in precisely the manner he dealt with men on trial.

The doctor said: such and such indicates that you have such and such, but if an analysis of such and such does not confirm this, then we have to assume you have such and such. On the other hand, if we assume such and such is the case, then... and so on. To Ivan Ilyich only one question mattered: was his condition serious or not? But the doctor ignored this inappropriate question. From his point of view it was an idle question and not worth considering. One simply had to weigh the alternatives: a floating kidney, chronic catarrh, or a disease of the caecum. It was not a matter of Ivan Ilyich's life but a conflict between a floating kidney and a disease of the caecum. And in Ivan Ilyich's presence the doctor resolved that conflict brilliantly in favor of the caecum, with the reservation that if an analysis of the urine yielded new evidence, the case would be reconsidered. This was exactly what Ivan Ilyich had done a thousand times, and in the same brilliant manner, with prisoners in the dock. The doctor summed up just as brilliantly, glancing triumphantly, even jovially, over his glasses at the prisoner. From the doctor's summary Ivan Ilyich concluded that things were bad, but that to the doctor and perhaps everyone else, it was of no consequence, even though for him it was bad. And this conclusion, which came as a painful shock to Ivan Ilyich, aroused in him a feeling of great self-pity and equally great resentment toward the doctor for being so indifferent to a matter of such importance.

But he made no comment, he simply got up, put his fee on the table, heaved a sigh, and said: "No doubt we sick people often ask inappropriate questions. But, in general, would you say my illness is serious or not?"

The doctor cocked one eye sternly at him over his glasses as if to say: "Prisoner, if you do not confine yourself to the questions allowed, I shall be obliged to have you expelled from the courtroom."

"I have already told you what I consider necessary and suitable," said the doctor. "Anything further will be revealed by the analysis." And with a bow the doctor brought the visit to a close.

Ivan Ilyich went out slowly, seated himself despondently in his sledge and drove home. All the way home he kept going over in his mind what the doctor had said, trying to translate all those vague, confusing scientific terms into simple language and find an answer to his question: "Is my condition serious? Very serious? Or nothing much to worry about?" And it seemed to him that the essence of what the doctor had said was that it was very serious. Everything in the streets seemed dismal to Ivan Ilyich. The cab drivers looked dismal, the houses looked dismal, the passersby, the shop — everything looked dismal. And in light of the doctor's obscure remarks, that pain — that dull, nagging pain which never let up for a second — acquired a different, a more serious implication. Ivan Ilyich focused on it now with a new sense of distress.

He reached home and began telling his wife about the visit. She listened, but in the middle of his account his daughter came in with her hat on — she and her mother were preparing to go out. She forced herself to sit and listen to this tedious stuff but could not stand it for long, and his wife, too, did not hear him out.

"Well, I'm very glad," she said. "Now see to it you take your medicine regularly. Give me the prescription, I'll send Gerasim to the apothecary's." And she went off to dress.

While she was in the room Ivan Ilyich had scarcely paused for breath, but he heaved a deep sigh when she left.

"Well," he said, "maybe there's nothing much to worry about."

He began to take the medicine and follow the doctor's instructions, which were changed after the analysis of his urine. But then it appeared that there was some confusion between the results of the analysis and what should have followed from it. It was impossible to get any information out of the doctor, but somehow things were not working out as he had said they should. Either the doctor had overlooked something, or lied, or concealed something from him.

Nonetheless, Ivan Ilyich followed his instructions explicitly and at first derived some comfort from this.

After his visit to the doctor, Ivan Ilyich was preoccupied mainly with attempts to carry out the doctor's orders about hygiene, medicine, observation of the course of his pain, and all his bodily functions. His main interests in life became human ailments and human health. Whenever there was any talk in his presence of people who were sick, or who had died or recuperated, particularly from an illness resembling his own, he would listen intently, trying to conceal his agitation, ask questions, and apply what he learned to his own case.

The pain did not subside, but Ivan Ilyich forced himself to think he was getting better. And he managed to deceive himself as long as nothing upset him. But no sooner did he have a nasty episode with his wife, a setback at work, or a bad hand at cards, than he immediately became acutely aware of his illness. In the past he had been able to cope with such adversities, confident that in no time at all he would set things right, get the upper hand, succeed, have a grand slam. Now every setback knocked the ground out from under him and reduced him to despair. He would say to himself: "There, just as I was beginning to get better and the medicine was taking effect, this accursed misfortune or trouble had to happen." And he raged against misfortune or against the people who were causing him trouble and killing him, for he felt his rage was killing him but could do nothing to control it. One would have expected him to understand that the anger he vented on people and circumstances only aggravated his illness and that, consequently, the thing to do was to disregard unpleasant occurrences. But his reasoning took just the opposite turn: he said he needed peace, was on the lookout for anything that might disturb it, and at the slightest disturbance became exasperated. What made matters worse was that he read medical books and consulted doctors. His condition deteriorated so gradually that he could easily deceive himself when comparing one day with the next — the difference was that slight. But when he consulted doctors, he felt he was not only deteriorating but at a very rapid rate. And in spite of this he kept on consulting them.

That month he went to see another celebrated physician. This celebrity told him practically the same thing as the first but posed the problem somewhat differently. And the consultation with this celebrity only reinforced Ivan Ilyich's doubts and fears. A friend of a friend — a very fine doctor — diagnosed the case quite differently, and though he assured Ivan Ilyich that he would recover, his questions and suppositions only made him more confused and heightened his suspicions. A homeopath offered still another diagnosis and prescribed certain medicine, and for about a week Ivan Ilyich took it without telling anyone. But when a week passed with no sign of relief, he lost faith in both this and the previous types of treatment and became even more despondent.

Once a lady he knew told him about a cure effected with wonder-working icons. Ivan Ilyich caught himself listening intently and believing in the possibility. This incident alarmed him. "Have I really become so gullible?" he asked himself. "Nonsense! It's all rubbish. Instead of giving in to these nervous fears, I've got to choose one doctor and stick to his method of treatment. That's just what I'll do. Enough! I'll stop thinking about it and follow the doctor's orders strictly until summer and then see what happens. No more wavering!"

It was an easy thing to say but impossible to do. The pain in his side exhausted him, never let up, seemed to get worse all the time; the taste in his mouth became more and more peculiar; he felt his breath had a foul odor; his appetite diminished and he kept losing strength. There was no deceiving himself: something new and dreadful was happening to him, something of such vast importance that nothing in his life could compare with it. And he alone was aware of this. Those about him either did not understand or did not wish to understand and thought that nothing in the world had changed. It was precisely this which tormented Ivan Ilyich most of all. He saw that the people in his household particularly his wife and daughter, who were caught up in a whirl of social activity — had no understanding of what was happening and were vexed with him for being so disconsolate and demanding, as though he were to blame. Although they tried to conceal this, he saw that he was an obstacle to them, and that his wife had adopted a certain attitude toward his illness and clung to it regardless of what he said or did. Her attitude amounted to this: "You know," she would say to her acquaintants, "Ivan Ilyich, like most people, simply cannot adhere to the course of treatment prescribed for him. One day he takes his drops, sticks to his diet, and goes to bed on time. But if I don't keep an eye on him, the next day he'll forget to take his medicine, eat sturgeon — which is forbidden — and sit up until one o'clock in the morning playing cards."

"Oh, when was that?" Ivan Ilyich retorted peevishly. "Only once at Pyotr Ivanovich's."

"And last night with Shebek."

"What difference did it make? I couldn't sleep anyway because of the pain."

"Well, it really doesn't matter why you did it, but if you go on like this, you'll never get well and just keep on torturing us."

From the remarks she made to both him and others, Praskovya Fyodorovna's attitude toward her husband's illness was that he himself was to blame for it, and that the whole thing was simply another way of making her life unpleasant. Ivan Ilyich felt that these remarks escaped her involuntarily, but this did not make things any easier for him.

In court, too, Ivan Ilyich noticed, or thought he noticed, a strange attitude toward himself. At times he felt people were eyeing him closely as a man whose post would soon be vacant; at other times his friends suddenly began teasing him, in a friendly way, about his nervous fears, as though that horrid, appalling, unheard-of something that had been set in motion within him and was gnawing away at him day and night, ineluctably dragging him off somewhere, was a most agreeable subject for a joke. He was particularly irritated by Schwartz, whose playfulness, vivacity, and *comme il faut* manner reminded him of himself ten years earlier.

Friends came over to make up a set and sat down to a game of cards with him. They dealt, bending the new cards to soften them; Ivan Ilyich sorted the diamonds in his hand and found he had seven. His partner said: "No trumps," and supported him with two diamonds. What more could he have wished for? He ought to have felt cheered, invigorated — they would make a grand slam. But suddenly Ivan Ilyich became aware of that gnawing pain in his side, that taste in his mouth, and under the circumstances it seemed preposterous to him to rejoice in a grand slam.

He saw his partner, Mikhail Mikhailovich, rapping the table with a vigorous hand, courteously and indulgently refraining from snatching up the tricks, pushing them over to him, so that he could have the pleasure of picking them up without having to exert himself. "Does he think I'm so weak I can't stretch my hand out?" Ivan Ilyich thought, and forgetting what he was doing, he overtrumped his partner, missing the grand slam by three tricks. And worst of all, he saw how upset Mikhail Mikhailovich was while he himself did not care. And it was dreadful to think why he did not care.

They could see that he was in pain and said: "We can stop if you're tired. Rest for a while." Rest? Why, he wasn't the least bit tired, they'd finish the rubber. They were all gloomy and silent. Ivan Ilyich knew he was responsible for the gloom that had descended but could do nothing to dispel it. After supper his friends went home, leaving Ivan Ilyich alone with the knowledge that his life had been poisoned and was poisoning the lives of others, and that far from diminishing, that poison was penetrating deeper and deeper into his entire being.

And with this knowledge and the physical pain and the horror as well, he had to go to bed, often to be kept awake by pain the greater part of the night. And the next morning he had to get up again, dress, go to court, talk and write, or if he did not go, put in those twenty-four hours at home, every one of them a torture. And he had to go on living like this, on the brink of disaster, without a single person to understand and pity him.

Chapter 5

One month went by this way, then another. Just before the New Year his brother-in-law came to town and stayed with them. Ivan Ilyich was at court when he arrived. Praskovya Fyodorovna was out shopping. On his return home Ivan Ilyich found his brother-in-law — a robust, ebullient fellow — in the study unpacking his suitcase. The latter raised his head on hearing Ivan Ilyich's step and looked at him for a moment in silence. That look told Ivan Ilyich everything. His brother-in-law opened his mouth to gasp but checked himself. That movement confirmed it all.

"What is it — have I changed?"

"Y-yes... you have."

After that, try as he might to steer the conversation back to his appearance, Ivan Ilyich could not get a word out of his brother-in-law. When Praskovya Fyodorovna came back, her brother went in to see her. Ivan Ilyich locked the door of his room and began to examine himself in the mirror — first full face, then in profile. He picked up a photograph he had taken with his wife and compared it to what he saw in the mirror. The change was enormous. Then he bared his arms to the elbow, examined them, pulled down his sleeves, sat down on an ottoman, and fell into a mood blacker than night.

"I mustn't! I mustn't!" he said to himself. He jumped up, went to his desk, opened a case file, started to read but could not go on. He unlocked his door and went into the hall. The door to the drawing room was shut. He tiptoed over and began listening.

"No, you're exaggerating," said Praskovya Fyodorovna.

"Exaggerating? Can't you see for yourself? He's a dead man. Just look at his eyes. Not a spark of life in them. What's wrong with him?"

"No one knows. Nikolaev (another doctor) said something, but I don't understand. Leshchetitsky (the celebrated doctor) said just the opposite."

Ivan Ilyich walked away, went to his room, lay down and began thinking. "A kidney, a floating kidney." He remembered everything the doctors had told him about how the kidney had come loose and was floating about. And by force of imagination he tried to catch that kidney and stop it, to hold it in place. It took so little effort, it seemed. "I'll go and see Pyotr Ivanovich again" (the friend with the doctor friend). He rang, ordered the carriage, and got ready to leave.

"Where are you going, Jean?" asked his wife in a particularly sad and unusually kind tone of voice.

This unusual kindness on her part infuriated him. He gave her a somber look.

"I've got to go and see Pyotr Ivanovich."

He went to his friend with the doctor friend and together they went to the doctor. They found him in, and Ivan Ilyich had a long talk with him.

As he went over the anatomical and physiological details of what, in the doctor's view, was going on in him, Ivan Ilyich understood everything.

There was just one thing, a tiny little thing in the caecum. It could be remedied entirely. Just stimulate the energy of one organ, depress the activity of another, then absorption would take place and everything would be fine.

Ivan Ilyich was somewhat late getting home to dinner. He conversed cheerfully after dinner but for some time could not bring himself to go to his room and work. At last he went to his study and immediately set to work. He read through some cases, concentrated, but was constantly aware that he had put off an important, private matter which he would attend to once he was through. When he finished his work he remembered that this private matter involved some thoughts about his caecum. But instead of devoting himself to them he went into the drawing room to have tea. Guests were there talking, playing the piano, and singing; among them was the examining magistrate, a desirable fiancé for their daughter. Ivan Ilyich, as Praskovya Fyodorovna observed, was more cheerful that evening than usual, but never for a moment did he forget that he had put off that important business about his caecum. At eleven o'clock he took leave of everyone and went to his room. Ever since his illness he had slept alone in a little room adjoining his study. He went in, undressed, and picked up a novel by Zola, but instead of reading he lapsed into thought. And in his imagination that longed-for cure of his caecum took place: absorption, evacuation, and a restoration of normal functioning. "Yes, that's the way it works," he told himself. "One need only give nature a hand." He remembered his medicine, raised himself, took it, then lay on his back observing what a beneficial effect the medicine was having, how it was killing the pain. "Only I must take it regularly and avoid anything that could have a bad effect on me. I feel somewhat better already, much better." He began probing his side — it was not painful to the touch. "I really can't feel anything there, it's much better already." He put out the candle and lay on his side — his caecum was improving, absorbing. Suddenly he felt the old, familiar, dull, gnawing pain — quiet, serious, insistent. The same familiar bad taste in his mouth. His heart sank, he felt dazed. "My God, my God!" he muttered. "Again and again, and it will never end." And suddenly he saw things in an entirely different light. "A caecum! A kidney!" he exclaimed inwardly. "It's not a question of a caecum or a kidney, but of life and. . . death. Yes, life was there and now it's going, going, and I can't hold on to it. Yes. Why deceive myself? Isn't it clear to everyone but me that I'm dying, that it's only a question of weeks, days — perhaps minutes? Before there was light, now there is darkness. Before I was here, now I am going there. Where?" He broke out in a cold sweat, his breathing died down. All he could hear was the beating of his heart.

"I'll be gone. What will there be then? Nothing. So where will I be when I'm gone? Can this really be death? No! I don't want this!" He jumped up, wanted to light the candle, groped for it with trembling hands, dropped the candle and candlestick on the floor and sank back on the pillow again. "Why bother? It's all the same," he thought, staring into the darkness with wide-open eyes. "Death. Yes... death. And they don't know and don't want to know and have no pity for me. They're playing." (Through the door of his room he caught the distant, intermittent sound of a voice and its accompaniment.) "It's all the same to them, but they'll die too. Fools! I'll go first, then they, but it will be just the same for them. Now they're enjoying themselves, the beasts!" His resentment was choking him. He felt agonizingly, unspeakably miserable. It seemed inconceivable to him that all men invariably had been condemned to suffer this awful horror. He raised himself.

"Something must be wrong. I must calm down, think it all through from the beginning." And he began thinking. "Yes. The beginning of my illness. I banged my side, but I was perfectly all right that day and the next; it hurt a little, then got worse; then came the doctors, then the despondency, the anguish, then more doctors; and all the while I was moving closer and closer to the abyss. Had less and less strength. Kept moving closer and closer. And now I've wasted away, haven't a spark of life in my eyes. It's death, yet I go on thinking about my caecum. I think about how to mend my caecum, whereas this is death. But can it really be death?" Once again he was seized with terror; he gasped for breath, leaned over, began groping for the matches, pressing his elbow for support on the bedside table. It was in his way and it hurt him; he became furious with it, pressed even harder, and knocked it over. And then breathless, in despair, he slumped down on his back, expecting death to strike him that very moment.

Just then the guests were leaving, Praskovya Fyodorovna was seeing them off. Hearing something fall, she came in.

"What is it?"

"Nothing. I accidentally knocked it over."

She went out and came back with a candle. He lay there, breathing heavily and rapidly like a man who has just run a mile, and stared at her with a glazed look.

"What is it, Jean?"

"N-nothing. I kn-nocked it over." (What's the point of telling her? She won't understand, he thought.)

And she really did not understand. She picked up the stand, lit the candle for him, and hurried away — she had to see another guest off.

When she returned he was still lying on his back, staring upward.

"What is it? Do you feel worse?"

"Yes."

She shook her head and sat down.

"I wonder, Jean, if we shouldn't send for Leshchetitsky."

That meant calling in the celebrated doctor, regardless of the expense. He smiled vindictively and said: "No." She sat there a while longer, then went up and kissed him on the forehead.

As she was kissing him, he hated her with every inch of his being, and he had to restrain himself from pushing her away.

"Good night. God willing, you'll fall asleep."

"Yes."

Chapter 6

Ivan Ilyich saw that he was dying, and he was in a constant state of despair.

In the depth of his heart he knew he was dying, but not only was he unaccustomed to such an idea, he simply could not grasp it, could not grasp it at all.

The syllogism he had learned from Kiesewetter's logic — "Caius is a man, men are mortal, therefore Caius is mortal" — had always seemed to him correct as applied to Caius, but by no means to himself. That man Caius represented man in the abstract, and so the reasoning was perfectly sound; but he was not Caius, not an abstract man; he had always been a creature quite, quite distinct from all the others. He had been little Vanya with a mama and a papa, with Mitya and Volodya, with toys, a coachman, and a nurse, and later with Katenk — Vanya, with all the joys, sorrows, and enthusiasms of his childhood, boyhood, and youth. Had Caius ever known the smell of that little striped leather ball Vanya had loved so much? Had Caius ever kissed his mother's hand so dearly, and had the silk folds of her dress ever rustled so for him? Had Caius ever rioted at school when the pastries were bad? Had he ever been so much in love? Or presided so well over a court session?

Caius really was mortal, and it was only right that he should die, but for him, Vanya, Ivan Ilyich, with all his thoughts and feelings, it was something else again. And it simply was not possible that he should have to die. That would be too terrible.

So his feelings went.

"If I were destined to die like Caius, I would have known it; an inner voice would have told me. But I was never aware of any such thing; and I and all my friends — we knew our situation was quite different from Caius's. Yet now look what's happened! It can't be. It just can't be, and yet it is. How is it possible? How is one to understand it?"

He could not understand it and tried to dismiss the thought as false, unsound, and morbid, to force it out of his mind with other thoughts that were sound and healthy. But the thought — not just the thought but, it seemed, the reality itself — kept coming back and confronting him.

And one after another, in place of that thought, he called up others, hoping to find support in them. He tried to revert to a way of thinking that had obscured the thought of death from him in the past. But, strangely, everything that had once obscured, hidden, obliterated the awareness of death no longer had that effect. Ivan Ilyich spent most of this latter period trying to recapture habits of feeling that had screened death from him. He would say to himself: "I'll plunge into my work; after all, it was my whole life." And driving his doubts away, he would go to court, enter into conversation with his colleagues and, in his habitually distracted way, take his seat, eyeing the crowd with a pensive look, resting both his emaciated arms on those of his oaken chair, bending over as usual to a colleague, moving the papers over to him, exchanging remarks in a whisper, and then suddenly raising his eyes, holding himself erect, would utter the well-known words that began the proceedings. But suddenly, in the middle of the session, the pain in his side, disregarding the stage the proceedings had reached, would begin its gnawing proceedings. Ivan Ilyich would focus on it, then try to drive the thought of it away, but the pain went right on with its work. And then *It* would come back and stand there and stare at him, and he would be petrified, the light would go out of his eyes, and again he would begin asking himself: "Can *It* alone be true?" And his colleagues and subordinates, amazed and distressed, saw that he who was such a brilliant, subtle judge had become confused, was making mistakes. He would rouse himself, try to regain his composure, somehow bring the session to a close, and return home sadly aware that his judicial work could no longer hide what he wanted it to hide; that his judicial work could not rescue him from *It*. And the worst thing was that *It* drew his attention not so that he would do anything, but merely so that he would look at *It*, look *It* straight in the face and, doing nothing, suffer unspeakable agony.

And to escape from this situation Ivan Ilyich sought relief — other screens — and other screens turned up and for a while seemed to offer some escape; but then they immediately collapsed or rather became transparent, as though *It* penetrated everything and nothing could obscure *It*.

Sometimes during this latter period he went into the drawing room he had furnished — the very drawing room where he had fallen, for the sake of which, he would think with bitter humor, he had sacrificed his life, for he was certain that his illness had begun with that injury. He went in and saw that a deep scratch had cut through the varnished surface of a table. He tried to find the cause of the damage and discovered that the bronze ornament on an album had become bent. He picked up the album, a costly one that he had put together with loving care, and became indignant with his daughter and her friends for being so careless: in some places the album was torn, in others the photographs were upside down. Painstakingly he put everything in order and bent the ornament back into place.

Later on it would occur to him to transfer the whole *établissement* with the albums to another corner of the room, next to the plants. He would call the footman. Either his wife or daughter would come in to help; they would disagree, contradict one another; he would argue, get angry. But that was all to the good, because it kept him from thinking about *It*. *It* was nowhere in sight.

But when he began moving the table himself, his wife said: "Let the servants do it, you'll only hurt yourself again." And suddenly *It* flashed through the screen and he saw *It*. *It* had only appeared as a flash, so he hoped *It* would disappear, but involuntarily he became aware of his side: the pain was still there gnawing away at him and he could no longer forget — *It* was staring at him distinctly from behind the plants. What was the point of it all?

"Can it be true that here, on this drapery, as at the storming of a bastion, I lost my life? How awful and how stupid! It just can't be! It can't be, yet it is."

He went to his study, lay down, and once again was left alone with *It*. Face to face with *It*, unable to do anything with *It*. Simply look at *It* and grow numb with horror.

Chapter 7

It is impossible to say how it happened, for it came about gradually, imperceptibly, but in the third month of Ivan Ilyich's illness his wife, his daughter, his son, his acquaintances, the servants, the doctors, and — above all — he himself knew that the only interest he had for others was whether he would soon vacate his place, free the living at last from the constraint of his presence and himself from his sufferings.

He slept less and less. They gave him opium and began morphine injections. But this brought no relief. At first the muffled sense of anguish he experienced in this semiconscious state came as a relief in that it was a new sensation, but then it became as agonizing, if not more so, than the raw pain.

Special foods were prepared for him on the doctors' orders, but these became more and more unpalatable, more and more revolting.

Special arrangements, too, were made for his bowel movements. And this was a regular torture — a torture because of the filth, the unseemliness, the stench, and the knowledge that another person had to assist in this.

Yet it was precisely through this unseemly business that Ivan Ilyich derived some comfort. The pantry boy, Gerasim, always came to carry out the chamber pot. Gerasim was a clean, ruddy-faced young peasant who was thriving on town food. He was always bright and cheerful. At first it embarrassed Ivan Ilyich to see this young fellow in his clean Russian peasant clothes performing such a revolting task.

Once, when he got up from the pot too weak to draw up his trousers, he collapsed into an armchair and, horrified, gazed at his naked thighs with the muscles clearly etched on his wasted flesh. Just then Gerasim entered the room with a light, vigorous step, exuding a pleasant smell of tar from his heavy boots and of fresh winter air. He was wearing a clean hemp apron and a clean cotton shirt with the sleeves rolled up over his strong arms; obviously trying to suppress the joy of life that his face radiated, and thereby not offend the sick man, he avoided looking at Ivan Ilyich and went over to get the pot.

"Gerasim," said Ivan Ilyich in a feeble voice.

Gerasim started, fearing he had done something wrong, and quickly turned his fresh, good-natured, simple, young face, which was showing the first signs of a beard, to the sick man.

"Yes, sir?"

"This must be very unpleasant for you. You must forgive me. I can't help it."

"Oh no, sir!" said Gerasim as he broke into a smile, his eyes and strong white teeth gleaming. "Why shouldn't I help you? You're a sick man."

And with strong, deft hands he performed his usual task, walking out of the room with a light step. Five minutes later, with just as light a step, he returned.

Ivan Ilyich was still sitting in the armchair in the same position.

"Gerasim," he said when the latter had replaced the freshly washed pot. "Please come and help me." Gerasim went over to him. "Lift me up. It's hard for me to get up, and I've sent Dmitry away."

Gerasim took hold of him with his strong arms and with a touch as light as his step, deftly, gently lifted and supported him with one hand, while with the other he pulled up his trousers. He was about to set him down again, but Ivan Ilyich asked that he help him over to the sofa. With no effort and no apparent pressure, Gerasim led — almost carried — him to the sofa and seated him there.

"Thank you. How skillfully... how well you do everything."

Gerasim smiled again and turned to leave, but Ivan Ilyich felt so good with him there that he was reluctant to have him go.

"Oh, one thing more. Please move that chair over here. No, the other one, to put under my feet. I feel better with my legs raised."

Gerasim carried the chair over and in one smooth motion set it down gently in place and lifted Ivan Ilyich's legs onto it. It seemed to Ivan Ilyich that he felt better when Gerasim lifted his legs up.

"I feel better with my legs raised," said Ivan Ilyich. "Bring that pillow over and put it under them."

Gerasim did so. He lifted his legs up again and placed the pillow under them. Again Ivan Ilyich felt better while Gerasim raised his legs. When he let them down he seemed to feel worse.

"Gerasim," he said. "Are you busy now?"

"Not at all, sir," said Gerasim, who had learned from the working people in town how to speak to the masters.

"What else do you have to do?"

"What else? I've done everything except chop wood for tomorrow."

"Then could you hold my legs up a bit higher?"

"Why of course I can." Gerasim lifted his legs higher, and it seemed to Ivan Ilyich that in this position he felt no pain at all.

"But what about the firewood?"

"Don't worry yourself about it, sir. I'll get it done."

Ivan Ilyich had Gerasim sit down and hold his legs up, and he began talking to him. And, strangely enough, he thought he felt better while Gerasim was holding his legs.

After that, Ivan Ilyich would send for Gerasim from time to time and have him hold his feet on his shoulders. And he loved to talk to him. Gerasim did everything easily, willingly, simply, and with a goodness of heart that moved Ivan Ilyich. Health, strength, and vitality in other people offended Ivan Ilyich, whereas Gerasim's strength and vitality had a soothing effect on him.

Ivan Ilyich suffered most of all from the lie, the lie which, for some reason, everyone accepted: that he was not dying but was simply ill, and that if he stayed calm and underwent treatment he could expect good results. Yet he knew that regardless of what was done, all he could expect was more agonizing suffering and death. And he was tortured by this lie, tortured by the fact that they refused to acknowledge what he and everyone else knew, that they wanted to lie about his horrible condition and to force him to become a party to that lie. This lie, a lie perpetrated on the eve of his death, a lie that was bound to degrade the awesome, solemn act of his dying to the level of their social calls, their draperies, and the sturgeon they ate for dinner, was an excruciating torture for Ivan Ilyich. And, oddly enough, many times when they were going through their acts with him he came within a hairbreadth of shouting: "Stop your lying! You and I know that I'm dying, so at least stop lying!" But he never had the courage to do it. He saw that the awesome, terrifying act of his dying had been degraded by those about him to the level of a chance unpleasantness, a bit of unseemly behavior (they reacted to him as they would to a man who emitted a foul odor on entering a drawing room); that it had been degraded by that very "propriety" to which he had devoted his entire life. He saw that no one pitied him because no one even cared to understand his situation. Gerasim was the only one who understood and pitied him. And for that reason Ivan Ilyich felt comfortable only with Gerasim. It was a comfort to him when Gerasim sat with him sometimes the whole night through, holding his legs, refusing to go to bed, saying: "Don't worry, Ivan Ilyich, I'll get a good sleep later on"; or when he suddenly addressed him in the familiar form and said: "It would be a different thing if you weren't sick, but as it is, why shouldn't I do a little extra work?" Gerasim was the only one who did not lie; everything he did showed that he alone understood what was happening, saw no need to conceal it, and simply pitied his feeble, wasted master. Once, as Ivan Ilyich was sending him away, he came right out and said: "We all have to die someday, so why shouldn't I help you?" By this he meant that he did not find his work a burden because he was doing it for a dying man, and he hoped that someone would do the same for him when his time came.

In addition to the lie, or owing to it, what tormented Ivan Ilyich most was that no one gave him the kind of compassion he craved. There were moments after long suffering when what he wanted most of all (shameful as it might be for him to admit) was to be pitied like a sick child. He wanted to be caressed, kissed, cried over, as sick children are caressed and comforted. He knew that he was an important functionary with a graying beard, and so this was impossible; yet all the same he longed for it. There was something approaching this in his relationship with Gerasim, and so the relationship was a comfort to him. Ivan Ilyich wanted to cry, wanted to be caressed and cried over, yet his colleague Shebek, a member of the court, would come, and instead of crying and getting some affection, Ivan Ilyich would assume a serious, stern, profound expression and, by force of habit, offer his opinion about a decision by the Court of Appeals and stubbornly defend it. Nothing did so much to poison the last days of Ivan Ilyich's life as this falseness in himself and in those around him.

Chapter 8

It was morning. He knew it was morning simply because Gerasim had gone and Pyotr, the footman, had come, snuffed out the candles, drawn back one of the curtains, and quietly begun to tidy up the room. Morning or night, Friday or Sunday, made no difference, everything was the same: that gnawing, excruciating, incessant pain; that awareness of life irrevocably passing but not yet gone; that dreadful, loathsome death, the only reality, relentlessly closing in on him; and that same endless lie. What did days, weeks, or hours matter?

"Will you have tea, sir?"

"He wants order, so the masters should drink tea in the morning," thought Ivan Ilyich. But he merely replied: "No."

"Would you care to move to the sofa, sir?"

"He wants to tidy up the room and I'm in the way. I represent filth and disorder," thought Ivan Ilyich. But he merely replied: "No, leave me alone."

The footman busied himself a while longer. Ivan Ilyich stretched out his hand. Pyotr went up to him obligingly.

"What would you like, sir?"

"My watch."

Pyotr picked up the watch, which was lying within Ivan Ilyich's reach, and gave it to him.

"Half-past eight. Are they up?"

"No, sir. Vasily Ivanovich (the son) went to school and Praskovya Fyodorovna left orders to awaken her if you asked. Shall I sir?"

"No, don't bother," he said. "Perhaps I should have some tea," he thought, and said:

"Yes, tea... bring me some."

Pyotr headed for the door. Ivan Ilyich was terrified at the thought of being left alone. "What can I do to keep him here?" he thought. "Oh, of course, the medicine."

"Pyotr, give me my medicine," he said. "Why not?" he thought. "Maybe the medicine will still do some good." He took a spoonful and swallowed it "No, it won't help. It's just nonsense, a hoax," he decided as soon as he felt that familiar, sickly, hopeless taste in his mouth. "No, I can't believe in it anymore. But why this pain, this pain? If only it would let up for a minute!" He began to moan. Pyotr came back.

"No, go. Bring me some tea."

Pyotr went out. Left alone Ivan Ilyich moaned less from the pain, agonizing as it was, than from anguish. "The same thing, on and on, the same endless days and nights. If only it would come quicker! If only what would come quicker? Death, darkness. No! No! Anything is better than death!"

When Pyotr returned with the tea, Ivan Ilyich looked at him in bewilderment for some time, unable to grasp who and what he was. Pyotr was disconcerted by that look. Seeing his confusion, Ivan Ilyich came to his senses.

"Yes," he said. "Tea... good. Put it down. Only help me wash up and put on a clean shirt." And Ivan Ilyich began to wash himself.

Pausing now and then to rest, he washed his hands and face, brushed his teeth, combed his hair, and looked in the mirror. He was horrified, particularly horrified to see the limp way his hair clung to his pale brow. He knew he would be even more horrified by the sight of his body, and so while his shirt was being changed he avoided looking at it. Finally it was all over. He put on a dressing gown, wrapped himself in a plaid, and sat down in an armchair to have his tea. For a brief moment he felt refreshed, but as soon as he began to drink his tea he sensed that same taste again, that same pain. He forced himself to finish the tea and then lay down, stretched out his legs, and sent Pyotr away.

The same thing again and again. One moment a spark of hope gleams, the next a sea of despair rages; and always the pain, the pain, always the anguish, the same thing on and on. Left alone he feels horribly depressed, wants to call someone, but knows before-hand that with others present it will be even worse. "Oh, for some morphine again — to sink into oblivion. I'll tell the doctor he must think of something to give me."

One hour then another pass this way. Then there is a ring in the entranceway. The doctor perhaps? The doctor indeed — fresh, hearty, stocky, cheerful, and with a look on his face that seems to say: "Now, now, you've had yourself a bad scare, but we're going to fix everything right away." The doctor knows this expression is inappropriate here, but he has put it on once and for all and can't take it off — like a man who has donned a frock coat in the morning to make a round of social calls.

The doctor rubs his hands briskly, reassuringly. "I'm chilled. Freezing cold outside. Just give me a minute to warm up," he says in a tone implying that one need only wait a moment until he warmed up and he would set everything right.

"Well, now, how are you?"

Ivan Ilyich feels the doctor wants to say: "How goes it?" but that even he knows this won't do, and so he says: "What sort of night did you have?"

Ivan Ilyich looks at the doctor inquisitively as if to say: "Won't you ever be ashamed of your lying?" But the doctor does not wish to understand such a question.

"Terrible. Just like all the others," Ivan Ilyich said. "The pain never leaves, never subsides. If only you'd give me something!"

"Yes, you sick people are always carrying on like this. Well, now, I seem to have warmed up. Even Praskovya Fyodorovna, who's so exacting, couldn't find fault with my temperature. Well, now I can say good morning." And the doctor shakes his hand.

Then, dispensing with all the banter, the doctor assumes a serious air and begins to examine the patient, taking his pulse, his temperature, sounding his chest, listening to his heart and lungs.

Ivan Ilyich knows for certain, beyond any doubt, that this is all nonsense, sheer deception, but when the doctor gets down on his knees, bends over him, placing his ear higher, then lower, and with the gravest expression on his face goes through all sorts of contortions, Ivan Ilyich is taken in by it, just as he used to be taken in by the speeches of lawyers, even though he knew perfectly well they were lying and why they were lying.

The doctor is still kneeling on the sofa, tapping away at him, when there is a rustle of silk at the doorway and Praskovya Fyodorovna can be heard reproaching Pyotr for not informing her of the doctor's arrival.

She comes in, kisses her husband, and at once tries to demonstrate that she has been up for some time, and owing simply to a misunderstanding failed to be in the room when the doctor arrived.

Ivan Ilyich looks her over from head to toe and resents her for the whiteness, plumpness, and cleanliness of her arms and neck, the luster of her hair, and the spark of vitality that gleams in her eyes. He hates her with every inch of his being. And her touch causes an agonizing well of hatred to surge up in him.

Her attitude toward him and his illness is the same as ever. Just as the doctor had adopted a certain attitude toward his patients, which he could not change, so she had adopted one toward him: that he was not doing what he should and was himself to blame, and she could only reproach him tenderly for this. And she could no longer change this attitude.

"He just doesn't listen, you know. He doesn't take his medicine on time. And worst of all, he lies in a position that is surely bad for him — with his legs up."

And she told him how he made Gerasim hold his legs up.

The doctor smiled disdainfully, indulgently, as if to say: "What can you do? Patients sometimes get absurd ideas into their heads, but we have to forgive them."

When he had finished his examination the doctor glanced at his watch, and then Praskovya Fyodorovna announced to Ivan Ilyich that whether he liked it or not, she had called in a celebrated physician, and that he and Mikhail Danilovich (the regular doctor) would examine him together that day and discuss his case.

"So no arguments, please. I'm doing this for my sake," she said ironically, letting him know that she was doing it all for his sake and had said this merely to deny him the right to protest. He scowled and said nothing. He felt that he was trapped in such a mesh of lies that it was difficult to make sense out of anything.

Everything she did for him was done strictly for her sake; and she told him she was doing for her sake what she actually was, making this seem so incredible that he was bound to take it to mean just the reverse.

At half-past eleven the celebrated doctor did indeed arrive. Again there were soundings and impressive talk in his presence and in the next room about the kidney and the caecum, and questions and answers exchanged with such an air of importance that once again, instead of the real question of life and death, the only one confronting Ivan Ilyich, the question that had arisen concerned a kidney or a caecum that was not behaving properly, and that would soon get a good trouncing from Mikhail Danilovich and the celebrity and be forced to mend its ways.

The celebrated doctor took leave of him with a grave but not hopeless air. And when Ivan Ilyich looked up at him, his eyes glistening with hope and fear, and timidly asked whether there was any chance of recovery, he replied that he could not vouch for it but there was a chance. The look of hope Ivan Ilyich gave the doctor as he watched him leave was so pathetic that, seeing it, Praskovya Fyodorovna actually burst into tears as she left the study to give the celebrated doctor his fee.

The improvement in his morale prompted by the doctor's encouraging remarks did not last long. Once again the same room, the same pictures, draperies, wallpaper, medicine bottles, and the same aching, suffering body. Ivan Ilyich began to moan. They gave him an injection and he lost consciousness.

When he came to, it was twilight; his dinner was brought in. He struggled to get down some broth. Then everything was the same again, and again night was coming on.

After dinner, at seven o'clock, Praskovya Fyodorovna came into his room in evening dress, her full bosom drawn up tightly by her corset, and traces of powder showing on her face. She had reminded him in the morning that they were going to the theater. Sarah Bernhardt had come to town, and at his insistence they had reserved a box. He had forgotten about this and was hurt by the sight of her elaborate attire. But he concealed his indignation when he remembered that he himself had urged them to reserve a box and go, because the aesthetic enjoyment would be edifying for the children.

Praskovya Fyodorovna had come in looking self-satisfied but guilty. She sat down and asked how he was feeling — merely for the sake of asking, as he could see, not because she wanted to find out anything, for she knew there was nothing to find out; and she went on to say what she felt was necessary: that under no circumstances would she have gone except that the box was reserved, and that Helene and their daughter and Petrishchev (the examining magistrate, their daughter's fiancé) were going, and it was unthinkable to let them go alone, but that she would much prefer to sit home with him, and would he promise to follow the doctor's orders while she was away.

"Oh, and Fyodor Petrovich (the fiancé) would like to come in. May he? And Liza?"

"All right."

His daughter came in all decked out in a gown that left much of her young flesh exposed; she was making a show of that very flesh which, for him, was the cause of so much agony. Strong, healthy, and obviously in love, she was impatient with illness, suffering, and death, which interfered with her happiness.

Fyodor Petrovich came in, too, in evening dress, his hair curled *á la Capoul*, a stiff white collar encircling his long, sinewy neck, an enormous white shirtfront over his chest, narrow black trousers hugging his strong thighs, a white glove drawn tightly over one hand, an opera hat clasped in the other.

Behind him the schoolboy son crept in unnoticed, all decked out in a new uniform, poor fellow, with gloves on and those awful dark circles under his eyes, whose meaning Ivan Ilyich understood only too well. He had always felt sorry for his son. And he found the boy's frightened, pitying look terrifying to behold. It seemed to Ivan Ilyich that, except for Gerasim, Vasya was the only one who understood and pitied him.

They all sat down and again asked how he was feeling. Then silence. Liza asked her mother about the opera glasses. This led to an argument between mother and daughter about who had mislaid them. It occasioned some unpleasantness.

Fyodor Petrovich asked Ivan Ilyich if he had ever seen Sarah Bernhardt. Ivan Ilyich did not understand the question at first, but then he said: "No, have you?"

"Yes, in *Adrienne Lecouvreur.*"

Praskovya Fyodorovna said she had been particularly good in something or other. The daughter disagreed. They started a conversation about the charm and naturalness of her acting — precisely the kind of conversation people always have on the subject.

In the middle of the conversation Fyodor Petrovich glanced at Ivan Ilyich and stopped talking. The others also looked at him and stopped talking. Ivan Ilyich was staring straight ahead with glittering eyes, obviously infuriated with them. The situation had to be rectified, but there was no way to rectify it. The silence had to be broken. No one ventured to break it, and they began to fear that the lie dictated by propriety suddenly would be exposed and the truth become clear to all. Liza was the first who ventured to break the silence. She wanted to conceal what they were feeling but, in going too far, she divulged it.

"Well, if we're going, it's time we left," she said, glancing at her watch, a gift from her father. And smiling at her young man in a significant but barely perceptible way about something only they understood, she stood up, rustling her dress.

They all got up, said goodbye, and left.

When they had gone, Ivan Ilyich thought he felt better: the lie was gone — it had left with them. But the pain remained. That same pain, that same fear that made nothing harder, nothing easier. Everything was getting worse.

Again time dragged on, minute by minute, hour by hour, on and on without end, with the inevitable end becoming more and more horrifying.

"Yes, send Gerasim," he said in reply to a question Pyotr asked him.

Chapter 9

His wife returned late that night. She tiptoed into the room, but he heard her; he opened his eyes and quickly closed them again. She wanted to send Gerasim away and sit with him herself, but he opened his eyes and said:

"No, go away."

"Are you in very great pain?"

"It doesn't matter."

"Take some opium."

He consented and drank some. She went away.

Until about three in the morning he was in an agonizing delirium. It seemed to him that he and his pain were being thrust into a narrow black sack — a deep one — were thrust farther and farther in but could not be pushed to the bottom. And this dreadful business was causing him suffering. He was afraid of that sack, yet wanted to fall through; struggled, yet cooperated. And then suddenly he lost his grip and fell — and regained consciousness. Gerasim was still sitting at the foot of the bed, dozing quietly, patiently, while Ivan Ilyich lay with his emaciated, stockinged feet on his shoulders. The same shaded candle was there and the same incessant pain.

"Go, Gerasim," he whispered.

"It's all right, sir. I'll stay awhile."

"No, go."

He lowered his legs, turned sideways with his arm nestled under his cheek, and began to feel terribly sorry for himself. He waited until Gerasim had gone into the next room, and then, no longer able to restrain himself, cried like a baby. He cried about his helplessness, about his terrible loneliness, about the cruelty of people, about the cruelty of God, about the absence of God.

"Why hast Thou done all this? Why hast Thou brought me to this? Why dost Thou torture me so? For what?"

He did not expect an answer, and he cried because there was no answer and there could be none. The pain started up again, but he did not stir, did not call out. He said to himself: "Go on then! Hit me again! But what for? What for? What have I done to Thee?"

Then he quieted down and not only stopped crying but held his breath and became all attention: he seemed to be listening — not to an audible voice, but to the voice of his soul, to the flow of thoughts surging within him.

"What do you want?" was the first thought sufficiently intelligible to be expressed in words. "What do you want? What do you want?" he repeated inwardly. "What? Not to suffer. To live," he replied.

And once again he listened with such rapt attention that even the pain did not distract him.

"To live? How?" asked the voice of his soul.

"Why, to live as I did before — happily and pleasantly."

"As you lived before, happily and pleasantly?" asked the voice.

And in his imagination he called to mind the best moments of his pleasant life. Yet, strangely enough, all the best moments of his pleasant life now seemed entirely different than they had in the past — all except the earliest memories of childhood. Way back in his childhood there had been something really pleasant, something he could live with were it ever to recur. But the person who had experienced that happiness no longer existed. It was as though he were recalling the memories of another man.

As soon as he got to the period that had produced the present Ivan Ilyich, all the seeming joys of his life vanished before his sight and turned into something trivial and often nasty.

And the farther he moved from childhood, the closer he came to the present, the more trivial and questionable these joyful experiences appeared. Beginning with the years he had spent in law school. A little of what was genuinely good had still existed then: there had been playfulness and friendship and hope. But by the time he reached the upper classes, the good moments in his life had become rarer. After that, during the period he worked for the governor, there had also been some good moments — memories of his love for a woman. But then everything became more and more mixed, and less of what was good remained. Later on there was even less, and the farther he went, the less there was.

His marriage — a mere accident — and his disillusionment with it, and his wife's bad breath, and the sensuality, and the pretense! And that deadly service, and those worries about money; and so it had gone — a year, two years, ten years, twenty years — on and on in the same way. And the longer it lasted, the more deadly it became. "It's as though I had been going steadily downhill while I imagined I was going up. That's exactly what happened. In public opinion I was moving uphill, but to the same extent life was slipping away from me. And now it's gone and all I can do is die!

"What does it all mean? Why has it happened? It's inconceivable, inconceivable that life was so senseless and disgusting. And if it really was so disgusting and senseless, why should I have to die, and die in agony? Something must be wrong. Perhaps I did not live as I should have," it suddenly occurred to him. "But how could that be when I did everything one is supposed to?" he replied and immediately dismissed the one solution to the whole enigma of life and death, considering it utterly impossible.

"Then what do you want now? To live? Live how? Live as you did in court when the usher proclaimed: 'The court is open!' The court is open, open," he repeated inwardly. "Now comes the judgment! But I'm not guilty!" he cried out indignantly. "What is this for?" And he stopped crying and, turning his face to the wall, began to dwell on one and the same question: "Why all this horror? What is it for?"

But think as he might, he could find no answer. And when it occurred to him, as it often did, that he had not lived as he should have, he immediately recalled how correct his whole life had been and dismissed this bizarre idea.

Chapter 10

Another two weeks passed. Ivan Ilyich no longer got off the sofa. He did not want to lie in bed and so he lay on the sofa. And as he lay there, facing the wall most of the time, he suffered, all alone, the same inexplicable suffering and, all alone, brooded on the same inexplicable question: "What is this? Is it true that this is death?" And an inner voice answered: "Yes, it is true." "Then why these torments?" And the voice answered: "For no reason — they just are." Above and beyond this there was nothing.

From the start of his illness, from the time he first went to a doctor, Ivan Ilyich's life had been divided into two contradictory and fluctuating moods: one a mood of despair and expectation of an incomprehensible and terrible death; the other a mood of hope filled with intent observation of the course of his bodily functions. At times he was confronted with nothing but a kidney or an intestine that was temporarily evading its duty; at others nothing but an unfathomable, horrifying death from which there was no escape.

These two moods had fluctuated since the onset of his illness, but the farther that illness progressed, the more unlikely and preposterous considerations about his kidney became and the more real his sense of impending death.

He had merely to recall what he had been like three months earlier and what he was now, to remember how steadily he had gone downhill, for all possibility of hope to be shattered.

During the last days of the isolation in which he lived, lying on the sofa with his face to the wall, isolation in the midst of a populous city among numerous friends and relatives, an isolation that could not have been greater anywhere, either in the depths of the sea or the bowels of the earth — during the last days of that terrible isolation, Ivan Ilyich lived only with memories of the past. One after another images of his past came to mind. His recollections always began with what was closest in time and shifted back to what was most remote, to his childhood, and lingered there. If he thought of the stewed prunes he had been served that day, he remembered the raw, shrivelled French prunes he had eaten as a child, the special taste they had, the way his mouth watered when he got down to the pit; and along with the memory of that taste came a whole series of memories of those days: of his nurse, his brother, his toys. "I mustn't think about them — it's too painful," he would tell himself and shift back to the present. He would look at the button on the back of the sofa and the crease in the morocco. "Morocco is expensive, doesn't wear well; we had a quarrel over it. But there had been another morocco and another quarrel — the time we tore papa's briefcase and got punished, but mama brought us some tarts." And again his memories centered on his childhood, and again he found them painful and tried to drive them away by thinking about something else.

And together with this train of recollections, another flashed through his mind — recollections of how his illness had progressed and become more acute. Here, too, the farther back in time he went, the more life he found. There had been more goodness in his life earlier and more of life itself. And the one fused with the other. "Just as my torments are getting worse and worse, so my whole life got worse and worse," he thought. There was only one bright spot back at the beginning of life; after that things grew blacker and blacker, moved faster and faster. "In inverse ratio to the square of the distance from death," thought Ivan Ilyich. And the image of a stone hurtling downward with increasing velocity became fixed in his mind. Life, a series of increasing sufferings, falls faster and faster toward its end — the most frightful suffering. "I am falling..." He shuddered, shifted back and forth, wanted to resist, but by then knew there was no resisting. And again, weary of contemplating but unable to tear his eyes away from what was right there before him, he stared at the back of the sofa and waited — waited for that dreadful fall, shock, destruction. "Resistance is impossible," he said to himself. "But if only I could understand the reason for this agony. Yet even that is impossible. It would make sense if one could say I had not lived as I should have. But such an admission is impossible," he uttered inwardly, remembering how his life had conformed to all the laws, rules, and proprieties. "That is a point I cannot grant," he told himself, smiling ironically, as though someone could see that smile of his and be taken in by it. "There is no explanation. Agony. Death. Why?"

Chapter 11

Two more weeks went by this way. During that time the event Ivan Ilyich and his wife had hoped for occurred: Petrishchev made a formal proposal. It happened in the evening. The next day Praskovya Fyodorovna went into her husband's room thinking over how she would announce the proposal, but during the night Ivan Ilyich had undergone a change for the worse. Praskovya Fyodorovna found him on the same sofa but in a different position. He was lying flat on his back, moaning, and staring straight ahead with a fixed look in his eyes.

She started to say something about his medicine. He shifted his gaze to her. So great was the animosity in that look — animosity toward her — that she broke off without finishing what she had to say.

"For Christ's sake, let me die in peace!" he said.

She wanted to leave, but at that moment their daughter came in and went over to say good morning to him. He looked at her as he had at his wife, and when she asked how he was feeling coldly replied that they would soon be rid of him. Both of them were silent, sat there for a while, and then went away.

"Is it our fault?" Liza asked her mother.

"You'd think we were to blame. I'm sorry for papa, but why should he torture us like this?"

The doctor came at his usual time. Ivan Ilyich merely answered Yes or No to his questions, glowered at him throughout the visit, and toward the end said:

"You know perfectly well you can do nothing to help me, so leave me alone."

"We can ease your suffering," said the doctor.

"You can't even do that; leave me alone."

The doctor went into the drawing room and told Praskovya Fyodorovna that his condition was very bad and that only one remedy, opium, could relieve his pain, which must be excruciating.

The doctor said his physical agony was dreadful, and that was true; but even more dreadful was his moral agony, and it was this that tormented him most.

What had induced his moral agony was that during the night, as he gazed at Gerasim's broadboned, sleepy, good-natured face, he suddenly asked himself: "What if my entire life, my entire conscious life, simply was not *the real thing*?"

It occurred to him that what had seemed utterly inconceivable before — that he had not lived the kind of life he should have — might in fact be true. It occurred to him that those scarcely perceptible impulses of his to protest what people of high rank considered good, vague impulses which he had always suppressed, might have been precisely what mattered, and all the rest not been the real thing. His official duties, his manner of life, his family, the values adhered to by people in society and in his profession — all these might not have been the real thing. He tried to come up with a defense of these things and suddenly became aware of the insubstantiality of them all. And there was nothing left to defend.

"But if that is the case," he asked himself, "and I am taking leave of life with the awareness that I squandered all I was given and have no possibility of rectifying matters — what then?" He lay on his back and began to review his whole life in an entirely different light.

When, in the morning, he saw first the footman, then his wife, then his daughter, and then the doctor, their every gesture, their every word, confirmed the horrible truth revealed to him during the night. In them he saw himself, all he had lived by, saw clearly that all this was not the real thing but a dreadful, enormous deception that shut out both life and death. This awareness intensified his physical sufferings, magnified them tenfold. He moaned and tossed and clutched at his bedclothes. He felt they were choking and suffocating him, and he hated them on that account.

He was given a large dose of opium and lost consciousness, but at dinnertime it all started again. He drove everyone away and tossed from side to side.

His wife came to him and said:

"*Jean*, dear, do this for me." (For me?)

"It can't do you any harm, and it often helps. Really, it's such a small thing. And even healthy people often..."

He opened his eyes wide.

"What? Take the sacrament? Why? I don't want to! And yet..."

She began to cry.

"Then you will, dear? I'll send for our priest, he's such a nice man."

"Fine, very good," he said.

When the priest came and heard his confession, he relented, seemed to feel relieved of his doubts and therefore of his agony, and experienced a brief moment of hope. Again he began to think about his caecum and the possibility of curing it. As he took the sacrament, there were tears in his eyes.

When they laid him down afterward, he felt better for a second and again held out hope of living. He began to think of the operation the doctors had proposed doing. "I want to live, to live!" he said to himself. His wife came in to congratulate him on taking the sacrament; she said the things people usually do, and then added:

"You really do feel better, don't you?"

"Yes," he said without looking at her.

Her clothes, her figure, the expression of her face, the sound of her voice — all these said to him: "*Not the real thing.* Everything you lived by and still live by is a lie, a deception that blinds you from the reality of life and death." And no sooner had he thought this than hatred welled up in him, and with the hatred, excruciating physical pain, and with the pain, an awareness of inevitable, imminent destruction. The pain took a new turn: it began to grind and shoot and constrict his breathing.

The expression on his face when he uttered that "Yes" was dreadful. Having uttered it, he looked his wife straight in the eye, and with a rapidity extraordinary for one so weak, flung himself face downward and shouted:

"Go away! Go away! Leave me alone!"

Chapter 12

That moment started three days of incessant screaming, screaming so terrible that even two rooms away one could not hear it without trembling. The moment he had answered his wife, he realized that he was lost, that there was no return, that the end had come, the very end, and that his doubts, still unresolved, remained with him.

"Oh! Oh! No!" he screamed in varying tones. He had begun by shouting: "I don't want it! I don't!" and went on uttering screams with that "O" sound.

For three straight days, during which time ceased to exist for him he struggled desperately in that black sack into which an unseen, invincible force was thrusting him. He struggled as a man condemned to death struggles in the hands of an executioner, knowing there is no escape. And he felt that with every minute, despite his efforts to resist, he was coming closer and closer to what terrified him. He felt he was in agony because he was being shoved into that black hole, but even more because he was unable to get right into it. What prevented him from getting into it was the belief that his life had been a good one. This justification of his life held him fast, kept him from moving forward, and caused him more agony than anything else.

Suddenly some force struck him in the chest and the side and made his breathing even more constricted: he plunged into the hole and there at the bottom, something was shining. What had happened to him was what one frequently experiences in a railway car when one thinks one is going forward but is actually moving backward, and suddenly becomes aware of the actual direction.

"Yes, all of it was simply *not the real thing*. But no matter. I can still make it *the real thing* — I can. But what is the real thing?" Ivan Ilyich asked himself and suddenly grew quiet.

This took place at the end of the third day, an hour before his death. Just then his son crept quietly into the room and went up to his bed. The dying man was still screaming desperately and flailing his arms. One hand fell on the boy's head. The boy grasped it, pressed it to his lips, and began to cry. At that very moment Ivan Ilyich fell through and saw a light, and it was revealed to him that his life had not been what it should have but that he could still rectify the situation. "But what is the real thing?" he asked himself and grew quiet, listening. Just then he felt someone kissing his hand. He opened his eyes and looked at his son. He grieved for him. His wife came in and went up to him. He looked at her. She gazed at him with an open mouth, with unwiped tears on her nose and cheeks, with a look of despair on her face. He grieved for her.

"Yes, I'm torturing them," he thought. "They feel sorry for me, but it will be better for them when I die." He wanted to tell them this but lacked the strength to speak. "But why speak — I must do something," he thought. He looked at his wife and, indicating his son with a glance, said:

"Take him away... sorry for him... and you." He wanted to add: "Forgive" but instead said "Forget," and too feeble to correct himself, dismissed it, knowing that He who needed to understand would understand.

And suddenly it became clear to him that what had been oppressing him and would not leave him suddenly was vanishing all at once — from two sides, ten sides, all sides. He felt sorry for them, he had to do something to keep from hurting them. To deliver them and himself from this suffering. "How good and how simple!" he thought. "And the pain?" he asked himself. "Where has it gone? Now, then, pain, where are you?"

He waited for it attentively.

"Ah, there it is. Well, what of it? Let it be."

"And death? Where is it?"

He searched for his accustomed fear of death and could not find it. Where was death? What death? There was no fear because there was no death.

Instead of death there was light.

"So that's it!" he exclaimed. "What bliss!"

All this happened in a single moment, but the significance of that moment was lasting. For those present, his agony continued for another two hours. Something rattled in his chest; his emaciated body twitched. Then the rattling and wheezing gradually diminished.

"It is all over," said someone standing beside him.

He heard these words and repeated them in his soul.

"Death is over," he said to himself. "There is no more death."

He drew in a breath, broke off in the middle of it, stretched himself out, and died.

Questions to Consider for Ivan Ilyich:

Our consideration of the Call to Care began with the story of Susan, our friend who faces serious illness, and who comes to us for support. We conclude, as we began, with a story. This time Leo Tolstoy's master story, *The Death of Ivan Ilyich*. It is appropriate that we end as we began, with story. Story keeps our vision of caring whole. The will to be healthy is the will to carry out one's life story. This includes both the story of our physical well being and our will to meaning. We invite you now to consider the final question of our course — How then shall we care for life in the face of death? — in the context of Tolstoy's narrative about Ivan, a story about how he and his family, friends, co-workers, and doctors dealt with the reality of his illness and death.

1. Ivan's Life at Home and at Work:
   a. How did Ivan go about choosing a career?
   b. What is Tolstoy's purpose in describing why Ivan got married?
   c. With what strategy does Ivan fend off the responsibilities of family life?
   d. Ivan obviously loves his work, but what in particular does he love about it and what does that tell us about him?
   e. In the description of Ivan's daily duties, the word "official" is repeated several times, at least once in contrast to "fresh and vital." What is Tolstoy telling us about the nature of the job and the nature of the man?
   f. Ivan recognizes the doctor's manner with him as comparable to his own manner in court. What is that manner? Aside from the irony, what is its significance?

2. Dimensions of Caring in Ivan's World:
   a. How do Ivan's colleagues respond to hearing about Ivan's death? What does this tell us about Ivan, his friends, and human nature?
   b. How do the reactions of Ivan's son and of Gerasim, the peasant pantry boy, differ from those of the other mourners and from each other?
   c. What does the attitude of Ivan's wife tell us about the way people often view illness?

     d. What is it that Gerasim represents that brings comfort to Ivan in his dying? What is it that Gerasim has that others seem to lack?

     e. What does his son Vasya offer to Ivan that the rest of his family do not?

3. Ivan's Search for Meaning:

     a. Tolstoy says Ivan Ilyich's life was simple, commonplace, and horrifying. Identify the commonplace elements. What is so horrifying about his life story?

     b. The description of Ivan's earlier life is sprinkled with French phrases. What do they tell us about Ivan?

     c. "So they lived," Tolstoy reiterates at the end of Chapter Three. How, in brief did they live? Of what significance was their way of life?

     d. In the later chapters Ivan is plagued with the suspicion that he had not lived the life that he ought to have lived. What is the lie that so torments Ivan?

     e. What better model of living is offered, if any? What is "the real thing"?

     f. Tolstoy is recognized as one of the most religious writers of his time. How, in the novel is Tolstoy's religiosity revealed?

4. And finally:

     a. Looking back at the uses of literature noted in the introduction to this chapter, in what sense is this story literature as communion?

     b. How in your judgment has Tolstoy answered the question of our course? How then shall we live in the face of death?

Hospital Reverie

Jerome Freeman

Beyond the window,
crickets and whippoorwills
perform evening song
while the day rewinds itself
around a spool of memory.

From sick bed vantage,
she is mindful of where
she's been and imagines

staying the watch when
there's nothing left to do
but care, and

making a difference in
people's lives most of
the time, and

being given another
chance to get things
right, and

leaving hospital ward
again, restored.

Appendix

The goal of our course and the accompanying material is to engage the student in the practice of biomedical ethics. The generic syllabus will indicate how the materials were used to engage the student in conversations with us, each other, and our guests about the *dimensions* and *dilemmas* of caring. The description of the project — on the "frontiers of caring" — and the guidelines for carrying it out will indicate how we engaged the students in issues related to *directions* of caring. Serious response to the call to care means addressing the questions of direction. How then shall we live as citizens and as persons leading caring lives as we care for life in the face of death? The course concludes with the presentation of the group projects.

AN INVITATION TO CARE:
ISSUES OF LIFE, HEALTH, DEATH

Goals of Capstone Courses:

1. Capstone courses complete the "Augustana Plan" for general education. The New Student Seminar is designed to introduce students to the purposes of an Augustana education. Capstone courses are designed to encourage students to integrate their college experiences in relationship to fundamental questions and issues.

2. Capstone courses encourage integration by drawing on the resources of faculty from different disciplines and students from a variety of majors in facing fundamental questions.

3. Capstone courses encourage participants to understand the meaning of living a moral life as it relates to the claims of church and society. How then shall we live in relationship to fundamental questions and issues?

Course Description:
Participants in this course will explore the meaning of life, health, and death in the light of human experience, recent developments in health and illness care, and the moral and public policy dilemmas that have attended these developments. Selections from works of literature, philosophy, theology, and public policy will be used. The capacity of caring for the human life of self and others will be

addressed. The fundamental question to be considered is, "How then shall we care for life in the face of death?"

Goals of this Capstone Course:

1. To consider the fundamental questions about the meaning of life that grow out of a study of the experience of death, illness, and health. How does dying provide insights into life? How does illness provide insights into health? How is health perceived? What is health? How then shall we live in the face of illness and death?

2. To encourage an integrated approach to these questions through the selection of readings from literature, philosophy, theology, and public policy and by drawing on the resources of faculty and students from different disciplines and majors.

3. To encourage participants through discussion and group projects to consider the fundamental questions and issues raised in relationship to the claims of church and society. How then shall I care for life (my own and that of others)? How can I most effectively work with others in caring for life?

Topical Outline, Generic Syllabus:
(75 minute class periods; twice weekly)

Class 1   Introduction: The Call
                   Distribute syllabus
                   Overview of course & project
                   Susan's Case
                   Definitions of terms: Life, Health, Death,
                   Sanctity of Life

Part I Dimensions of Caring
Class 2   Chapter 1
                   Olsen, "Health as the Will to Carry Out Our
                   Life Story"
                   Freeman, "On Hearing the Story: A Parable"
                   Weinberg, "The Laying on of Hands"
                   Freeman, "On Nursing"
                   Nouwen, "Care of the Elderly"

Class 3	Barth, "The Will to Be Healthy" Tillich, "The Meaning of Health"
Class 4	Chapter 2 Olsen, "Health, Wholeness, and Intervention" Auterman, Robinson - "Hygeia & Asclepius" Sirach 38:1-15 "Honor the Physician" Articles with comments due. Project groups assigned
Class 5	Chapter 3 Olsen, "Health, Life, and Mortality" Robinson, "On Joining the Majority" Resonance: personal experiences, shared feelings Meeting of groups - choose topics
Class 6	Chapter 4 Olsen, "Caring, Meaning and Courage" Gaes, From *My Book for Kids with Cansur*
Class 7	Frankl, *Man's Search for Meaning,*
Class 8	Finish discussion of Frankl Freeman, "Witness and Legacy" and "Holocaust Exhibit and the Dance"
Class 9	*Test 1*

Part II Dilemmas of Caring

Class 10	Introduction of Ethical Principles Justice, Autonomy, Paternalism, Beneficence, Nonmaleficence Progress report on group project
Class 11	Chapter 5 Olsen, "Respecting the Person" Freeman, "Reflections on the Teaching of Bioethics"

Freeman, "Lecture on bioethics"
Williams, "Use of Force"

Class 12   American College of Obstetricians and Gynecologists.
"Ethical Dimensions of Informed Consent"
Freeman, "Reflections on Informed Consent"
Freeman, "Informed Consent: Another Look at
Disclosure"
Justice (and courage) —6 mm segment from
"Code Gray"
Freeman, "Informed Consent" (poem).

Class 12   Chapter 6
Olsen, "Who Gets Care?"
Robinson - "Rose Brech"

Class 13   Video - U.S. and Canadian health care
systems
Project Progress Reports

Class 14   Chapter 7
Olsen, "Caring Through Death"
Freeman "Vision Quest"
Freeman, "Nancy Cruzan

Class 15   Callahan, "Pursuing a Peaceful Death
Verhey "Choosing Death: The Ethics of
Assisted Suicide"
Meilaender, "Christian thinking about advance
medical directives"
Freeman, "Another Elegy"

Class 16   Interview: Sue Halbritter - "Moving In With
Presence"
Project progress report

Class 17   Chapter 8
Olsen, "Caring from the Beginning"
Ryan, "Erosion of the Rights of Women: In the
Interest of Fetal Well-Being"

Class 26   Chapter 11
                Robinson, "How Then Shall We Care for Life in the
                Face of Death"
                Tolstoy: From *The Death of Ivan Ilyich*

Class 27   *Test 3*
                Project Plans for reporting; papers due

Class 28   Project Rounds

Class 29   Project Rounds

Class 30   Project Rounds

Class 31   Evaluation. Recommendations to the community
                on Directions for Caring based on the group projects.

Guidelines for Capstone Projects and Reports

1. Each group will focus on one topic. Care is to be taken to limit the
   focus so that groups can get into case histories relating to each
   topic. Each member of the group is to be assigned research tasks
   to help identify major issues associated with the topic and possible cases that may be investigated on a primary level (that is, not
   just by reading and regurgitating information from other
   sources, but by interviewing those who have actually participated in some aspect of the topic.)

2. Once the major issues have been identified and possible cases
   listed, the group will choose two or three cases which best illustrate the most important issues. It is important that in choosing
   cases and issues associated with them, that as little overlapping
   as possible be achieved. A "case" may be liberally interpreted to
   include any one of the following: an incident or a narrative that
   illustrates issues of the topic, organizations or groups that have a
   vested interest in the topic, or officials who are charged with
   making or administrating laws associated with the topic. In dealing with Native American Health Care, for example, a case might
   be a doctor or nurse who has worked or is working on a reservation, a representative of a local or area organization dealing
   with health care for Native Americans, a spokesman for the

Aberdeen Area IHS, an individual Native American who has a representative story concerning health care for Native Americans, or a South Dakota senator or representative who has influence on national policies related to health care of Native Americans.

3. Once two or three cases have been selected, assign two to four members of the group to deal with each case, so that every member of the group will be responsible for treating some aspect of at least one case.

4. After case assignments are made, those assigned to a case need to subdivide aspects of the case so that the issues can be treated most efficiently and with as little overlapping as possible. All members of the case group may wish to participate in meetings or interviews with subjects associated with the case, or in some instances, each member of the case group may be assigned to conduct meetings or interviews with a subject who represents only one aspect of the case.

5. After fact-finding interviews have been conducted, assemble each case group to discuss what the information they have gathered about the case demonstrates concerning the topic. The case group will then report to the main group.

6. The main group will meet to hear case reports, to decide what the cases "go to show" about the topic, and to decide how the cases and the information can best be presented in the class presentation at the end of the course.

7. The class presentations are to be engaging and as effective as the creativity of each group allows. The presentation may involve visual aids, dramatic recreations, role-playing, or any other format that is deemed effective in getting across the lessons to be learned from the cases and the more general research involved.

8. A project plan will be due from each group the period before the presentation of that group is scheduled. This plan is to consist of a bibliography listing sources for the information to be used in the presentation, a summary of the cases involved in the presentation, identification of the issues to be presented, a statement

pulling the aspects of the topic together and suggesting community action that might be taken related to the topic.

9. A report from each member of the group, no more than two or three pages, narrating the member's contribution to the presentation and to the secondary and primary research involved in that presentation.

BIBLIOGRAPHY

American College of Obstetricians and Gynecologists. "Ethical Dimensions of Informed Consent." *Women's Health Issues*, vol. 3, No. 1, Spring 1993: 1-10.

Angell, M. and J.P. Kissirer. "Alternative Medicine: The Risks of Untested and Unregulated Remedies." *New England Journal of Medicine*, vol. 339, No. 12, 7 September 1998: 839-841.

Auterman, Mary. "Parish Nursing: the Church as Community." *South Dakota Nurse*, vol. 39 (4), 1, 26 December 1997.

Barth, Karl. "The Will to Be Healthy." *Church Dogmatics* III/4, trans. A. T. Mackay *et al.*, Edinburgh: T &T Clark, 1961: 357-363.

Beauchamp, T.L. & James F. Childress. *Principles of Biomedical Ethics*. New York: Oxford U. P., 1994.

Bradt, K.M. *Story of a Way of Knowing*. Sheed and Waid, l997.

Buber, Martin. *I and Thou*. Trans. Ronald Gregor Smith. New York: Charles Scribner's Sons, 1958.

Callahan, Daniel. "Pursuing a Peaceful Death," taken from Ch. 6, *The Troubled Dream of Life: Living with Mortality*. New York: Simon & Schuster, 1993: 209- 219.

————. *What Kind of Life*. New York: Simon & Schuster, 1990.

Dubos, Rene. "Hygeia & Asclepius." *Mirage of Health: Utopias, Progress, and Biological Change*, Ch. 5. New Brunswick: Rutgers U. P., 1987.

DuBose, Edwin R., Ron Hamel, and Lawrence J. O'Connell, eds. *A Matter of Principles: Ferment in the U.S. Bioethics*. Valley Forge, Pennsylvania: Trinity P. International, 1994.

Dyer, Allen R. "Should Doctors Cut Costs at the Bedside? Patients, Not Costs, Come First." *Hastings Center Report*, vol. 16, No. 1, February 1986: 5-7.

Eisenberg, D. M. *et al.* "Trends in Alternative Medicine Use in the United States, 1990-1997: Results of a Follow-up National Survey." *JAMA*, 11 November 1998: 1569-1579.

Frank, Arthur. *At the Will of the Body: Reflections on Illness.* New York: Houghton Mifflin, 1991.

Frankl, Viktor E. *Man's Search for Meaning.* New York: Washington Square P., 1963.

Freeman, Jerome W. *Starting from Here: Dakota Poetry, Pottery, and Caring.* Sioux Falls: Ex Machina, 1996.

―――. *Come and See: Reflections on Values and Caring in Medicine.* Sioux Falls: The Center for Ethics and Caring, Sioux Valley Hospital, 1995.

―――. "Reflections on the Teaching of Bioethics." *The Journal of Continuing Education in the Health Professions*, vol. 14, 1994: 56-60.

―――. & Charles M. Lewis. *Easing the Edges: Dakota Poetry and Images.* Sioux Falls: Penstemon, 1994.

―――. & Jean Bailey. *Something at Last: Dakota Poetry and Sketches.* Sioux Falls: Penstemon, 1993.

―――. "Informed Consent: Another Look at Disclosure." *South Dakota Journal of Medicine.* March 1988:19-21.

―――. "Reflections on Informed Consent." *South Dakota Journal of Medicine.* April 1985: 5-6.

Gaes, Jason. *My Book for Kids with Cansur.* Aberdeen: Melius Publishing Inc., 1987.

Hill, Lawrence N. "On Being a Patient: My Not-So-Near-Death Experience." *Annals of Internal Medicine*, vol. 125, No.10, 15 November 1996: 855-857.

Interpreter's Bible Dictionary. New York: Abingdon P., 1962. Vol. II, "Healing, Health," by R. V. Harrison: 541-548. Vol. III, "Peace In the Old Testament," by E. M. Good: 704-706.

Jonsen, Albert R. *The New Medicine & the Old Ethics.* Cambridge: Harvard U. P., 1990.

————. and Stephen Toulman. *The Abuse of Casuistry: A History of Moral Reasoning.* Berkeley: U. of California P., 1988.

Kant, Immanuel. *Moral law: Groundwork of the Metaphysics of Morals.* Routledge Chapman and Hall, 1992.

King, Imogene. *A Theory for Nursing: Systems, Concepts, Process.* New York: Wiley, 1981.

Lal, P. *Introduction to The Bhagavad-Gita.* Calcutta: Writer's Workshop Books, 1978.

Lammers, Stephen B. and Allen Verhey, eds. *On Moral Medicine: Theological Perspectives in Medical Ethics.* Grand Rapids: Eerdmans, 1989.

Luke 10: 25-37. "The Good Samaritan." *The Holy Bible,* Newly Revised Standard Version.

MacIntyre, Austair. *After Virtue.* Notre Dame, Indiana: U. of Notre Dame P., 1981.

May, William F. "The Ethical Foundations of Health Care Reform." *Christian Century,* June 18, 1-8, 1994: 572-576.

————. *The Patient's Ordeal.* Bloomington: Indiana U. P., 1994.

————. *The Physician's Covenant.* Philadelphia: Westminster P., 1983.

Meilaender, Gilbert. "Christian Thinking about Advance Medical Directives." *Christian Century,* 11-18 September 1996: 854-857. Excerpted from *Bioethics; A Primer for Christians.* Grand Rapids: Eerdmans, 1996.

Mill, John Stuart. *Utilitarianism*. Hackett, 1979.

Munson, Ronald. *Intervention and Reflection: Basic issues in Medical Ethics*, 4th ed. Belmont: Wadsworth, 1992.

Nelson, Becky, Mark Meyers, Laurie Wiltz, & Jerome Freeman. "Caring and the Health Professions." *South Dakota Journal of Medicine*, vol. 48, (1), January 1995: 17-20.

Nelson, James B., and JoAnne Rohricht. *Human Medicine: Ethical Perspectives on Today's Medical Issues*, rev. ed. Minneapolis: Augsburg, 1984.

Nightingale, Florence. *Notes on Nursing: What it is and What it is Not*. London: Hartison and Sons (1857), reproduced by offset, Philadelphia: Edward Stern and Co., 1946.

Nouwen, Henri J.M., "Care and the Elderly," in Carol LeFevre & Peggy LeFevre, eds., *Aging and the Human Spirit: a Reader in Religion and Gerontology*, 2nd ed. New York: Exploration P., 1985.

Parse, Rosemarie Rizzo. *The Human Becoming School of Thought*. Thousand Oaks, California: Sage Publications, 1998.

Pellegrino, Edmund D. "Managed Care: an Ethical Reflection,"excerpted from "The Good Samaritan in the Marketplace," in *The Changing Face of Health Care*, John F. Kilner, Robert D. Orr, and Judith Allen Shelly, eds. Grand Rapids: William B. Eerdmans Publishing Co., 1998.

Peters, Ted. "In search of the perfect child: Genetic testing and selective abortion." *Christian Century*, 30 October 1996: 1034-1037.

Robinson, Ronald. *Kitchen Dance*. Vermillion: U. of South Dakota P., 1991.

Ryan, Kenneth J. "Erosion of the Rights of Pregnant Women: In the Interest of Fetal Well Being." *Women's Health Issues*, vol. 1, No.1, Fall 1990: 21-24.

Sirach 38: 1-15. "Honor the Physician." *The Holy Bible*, NRSV.

Tate, Alan. *The Man of Letters in the Modern World.* New York: Meridian Books, 1958: 16, 22.

Tillich, Paul. "The Meaning of Health." *Perspectives in Biology and Medicine* 5, Autumn 1961.

————. *The Courage To Be.* New Haven: Yale U. P., 1952.

Tolstoy, Leo. *The Death of Ivan Ilyich.* New York: Bantam Books, 1981.

————. *What is Art?* Aylmer Maude, trans. New York: T.Y. Crowell, 1899: 63-165.

Verhey, Allen. "Choosing death: The ethics of assisted suicide." *Christian Century*, 17-24 July1996: 716-719.

Watson, Jean. *Nursing: The Philosophy and Science of Caring.* Boulder: Colorado Associated U. P.

Weinberg, Richard B. "Laying on of Hands." *Annals of Internal Medicine*, 117, 1992: 83-84.

Whitmore, Todd David. "Common ground not middle ground: Crossing the pro-life, pro-choice divide." *Christian Century*, 3-10 January 1996: 10-15.

Williams, William Carlos. *The Farmer's Daughters: The Collected Short Stories of William Carlos Williams.* Norfolk, Connecticut: New Directions Publishing, 1961.